# RIDING IN THE SHADOW OF DEATH

**Chris Keltie**

***'It was a wild and reckless life there on the Squadron, young lives were cheap, but whenever we had any time we were never still, but dashed off to one of the towns for a few hours of fun. Some of the lads had trouble sleeping at night and had to force themselves to carry on, most of us were keen and loved the life of reckless adventure; but the strain was rather heavy and leave was necessary pretty often, because we rode always in the shadow of death.'***

**Warrant Officer, Norman E Jarvis, 410413 RAAF. (F/Lt Bill North's Bomb Aimer)**

Cover designed by Kelvin Blyth at Kelvin Blyth Studios

12 Station Road
Over
Cambridge
Cambridgeshire
CB24 5NJ

First published June 2013 (Second edition published January 2014)

By Chris Keltie Publishing
75 Dunstan Road, Golders Green,
London, NW11 8AE



www.chriskeltie.co.uk



British Library Cataloguing in Publication Data.

A catalogue record for this book is available from the British Library.

ISBN 978 0 9571189 0 4 Hardback. 978 0 9571189 1 1 Paperback.

Typesetting and origination by Chris Keltie Publishing

Printed in Great Britain by Copy Write, 758 Finchley Road, Golders Green, NW11 7TH

**To Bill and Margaret North, thank you for your true kindness throughout our family's good and bad times...**

Bill and Margaret North

*'If one person goes away with a better knowledge of Bomber Command, their losses and what they gave for our country, we are one step closer to repaying our debt to them.'*

**Lincolnshire Aviation Heritage Centre.**

*'Riding in the Shadow of Death, captures the apocalyptic nature of the task Bomber Command was charged with carrying out.'*

**Noeline Arnott.**

# Contents

# Abbreviations

(6/7) Six out of seven crew killed

(7/7) Seven out of seven crew killed

a/c Aircraft

AFU Advanced Flying Unit

AG Air Gunner

AGS Air Gunnery School

AVM Air Vice Marshall

CinC Commander in Chief

EFTS Elementary Flight Training School

ETA Estimated Time of Arrival

FTR Fail To Return

Flt/Eng Flight Engineer

F/Lt Flight Lieutenant

F/S Flight Sergeant

F/O Flight Officer

ITW Initial Training Wing

LAC Leading Aircraftman

LFS Lancaster Finishing School

MUG Mid-Upper Gunner

NF Night Fighter

NUR National Union of Railwaymen

| | |
|---|---|
| ORB | Operational Record Book |
| OTU | Operational Training Unit |
| PRC | Personnel Reception Centre |
| PRO | Public Records Office |
| POW | Prisoner of War |
| P/O | Pilot Officer |
| RAF | Royal Air Force |
| RAAF | Royal Australian Air Force |
| RCAF | Royal Canadian Air Force |
| RNZAF | Royal New Zealand Air Force |
| Sgt | Sergeant |
| SFTS | Service Flight Training School |
| Squ | Squadron |
| S/L | Squadron Leader |
| USAAF | United States Army Air Force |
| W/O | Warrant Officer |
| W/C | Wing Commander |
| WOP | Wireless Operator |
| WRNS | Womens Royal Naval Service |

# Foreword

## Marshal of the Royal Air Force Sir Michael Beetham, President of the Bomber Command and 50 and 61 Squadron Associations. 27 Oct 2008, Letter to the Daily Telegraph.

In paying tribute to 'the Few' Churchill stated: 'The fighters are our salvation but the bombers alone provide the means of victory.'

In other words, to defeat Nazi Germany, defending our island would not be enough: Britain had to attack. And between the Dunkirk evacuation of 1940 and the D-Day landings of June 1944, there was no way of directly attacking Germany itself – other than by bombing.

Night bombing in those early days was in its infancy. Navigation aids were rudimentary – aircrews still used sextants. Yet they were expected to pinpoint military and industrial targets, often a single factory, deep inside Germany at night.

Frequent bad weather and poor visibility made this a near impossible challenge. Eventually the War Cabinet ordered that, unless weather conditions allowed otherwise, attacks had to be directed mainly on the area-bombing of industrial cities – to increase the likelihood of damaging something – even if it was only the morale of German industrial workers.

Although many of the aircrews would have preferred otherwise, there was little choice and of course, the Germans had already pioneered the practice of area-bombing cities during the Blitz, killing 43,000 British civilians.

By 1943/44 Bomber Command was sending hundreds of bombers a night over Europe – forcing the Germans on to the defensive. This had a vital strategic effect: one million men, tens of thousands of weapons and aircraft and a mass of resources had to be diverted from the Germans' struggle with the Russians on the Eastern Front to defend the homeland against the bomber attacks from the West.

Albert Speer, Hitler's armaments minister, later described the bomber offensive from the Nazis' perspective as 'the greatest lost battle of the war'.

But the cost was painfully heavy. All RAF aircrews were volunteers, with an average age of 22. Of 125,000 bomber aircrew involved, more than 55,000 were killed, over 8,000 were wounded and nearly 10,000 were prisoners of war. This was on a scale proportionate to British casualties in the trenches during the worst period of World War One.

Bomber Command's contribution to victory (and loss of aircrew lives) was widely recognised at the time. But no specific campaign medal was awarded at the end of the war. Churchill, sensing potential political squeamishness when the devastation of Germany by bombing would become clear, distanced himself from the bombing campaign he had personally initiated and encouraged.

In July 1945 he was also out of office and the new Labour Government under Clement Attlee steadfastly refused requests for a medal. This shows how quickly the circumstances under which the War Cabinet had ordered the policy, in the darkest days of the conflict, were forgotten!

Bomber Command was originally set up to bomb purely military targets and indeed did so in attacking every aspect of Germany's war machine: armaments factories, ports, U-boat pens, shipping, oil refineries, transport links, troop concentrations, air bases, rail links, communications, military headquarters and even dams. But much of the effort, in darkness and impossible conditions, had to be in the form of area bombing. It was crude but effective: Germany's war making capacity was held back and eventually crippled. When the Allied armies finally did invade Europe in 1944 they fought their way to liberate Europe with massive direct bomber support.

It is the recognition of what was achieved in the wide range of our sustained operations over the whole five years of the war that we now seek. A Memorial in Central London to the many young men who died and to the vital contribution made by Bomber Command to victory would provide that recognition.*

F/Lt Michael Beetham, May 1944, 50 Squadron.

**Sir Michael Beetham GCB, CBE, DFC, AFC, DL was a Lancaster Bomber Pilot with 50 Squadron in WW2, flying his first raid over Berlin at the age of 20. After his Operational Tour he became a Flying Instructor at No 5 LFS Syerston and then a Flight Commander at 57 Squadron, East Kirkby. Postwar he became the Commander of 214 Squadron at Marham, the first air to air refuelling Squadron. After a variety of senior postings including at NATO HQ, he went on to become Chief of the Air Staff, the professional head of the Royal Air Force, masterminding Operation Black Buck, the long range Vulcan Bomber raid on Port Stanley Airport during the Falklands Campaign.**

*At the original time of book writing there was no Memorial and Bill North sadly did not live to see this moving day. Sir Michael Beetham campaigned tirelessly for permanent recognition of Bomber Command crewmen, attending the long awaited Bomber Command Memorial Ceremony Day on the 28 June 2012. The Memorial was unveiled in Green Park by HM the Queen.

# Introduction

**There it was, sitting on the side cabinet next to the TV in the front room; the thing, the image that would fascinate me for the next 43 years...**

In March 1970 my Dad David, my Mum Anne, and I moved into a suburban semi at 103 Regal Way in Kenton, Harrow, London. Our new next-door neighbours, Bill and Margaret North, welcomed us with open arms and invited us into their house for tea and a chat. I was 7 years old and can remember it as if it were yesterday. I was standing in the North's front downstairs living room looking out onto the green suburban street. I had a striking first impression of Bill North. His face was open, kind and had a mature, engaging quality. Bill's eyes also had a cheeky twinkle in them, making it easy to maintain contact. Although he seemed older than my parents, he had a calm strong presence that made me feel very comfortable.

Shifting my gaze to the right away from Bill's face I caught sight of their TV, which sent a thrill through me. Our family didn't have the pleasure of owning such a thing yet. My eyes then locked onto something else, an image that drew me in. On the side cabinet next to the TV was a framed black and white photograph of a WW2 Bomber with crew members standing next to it. It was a picture taken in 1944 at 1661 Heavy Conversion Unit (HCU) RAF Winthorpe, of Bill North and his crew standing next to a Short Stirling Bomber. This picture instantly fascinated me and has done ever since. I couldn't take my eyes off it. As everybody chattered, their voices slowly faded away as I stepped closer to the photograph.

I looked into the faces and eyes of all the crew members and scrutinised the huge airframe of the Stirling Bomber and was awestruck. The overwhelming impression it made on me then I have always carried with me. I was sure I could see Bill North standing in the line of men in the photograph, although he was much younger and wearing a uniform. His face was equally as striking as my short first impression from a few seconds before.

Bill's voice broke through my intense moment. 'What are you looking at?'

I answered, 'What is that?' pointing at the picture.

'That is me there on the left and the other men are my crew members. That is a Short Stirling Bomber, I was a pilot in the RAF during World War Two and I flew this aeroplane.' The Stirling looked huge, I was amazed that something so big could lift off the ground and fly.

Thus began my passion for aeroplanes from the Second World War, and the history from that period. We were lucky enough at 103 and 105 Regal Way to be directly underneath the flight path to RAF Northolt and would often get the treat of Vulcans and Hercules going over the houses. Most wonderful of all would be when we heard the unmistakable throaty roar of Merlin engines in the distance, giving us a couple of minutes warning that a Lancaster Bomber and sometimes fighter escort of Spitfires and Hurricane from the Battle of Britain Memorial Flight would soon be passing overhead. We would rush out into the garden and stare up in awe as the beautiful beast and its little friends would pass directly overhead.

My Mum and Dad had an extremely stormy relationship that was quite apparent to those who lived around us; my Mum could shout with such force that not only did Bill and Margaret hear the goings on through the thin party wall, but I am sure the people at the end of Regal Way could hear her too. Bill would often give my Dad quite knowing looks as they left for work in the mornings. My life at home growing up in the 1970's was pretty turbulent. As well as the stress at home, the world I was growing up in was full of political, social and industrial turbulence. There seemed to be terrorist organisations killing people all over the place, the TV was full of grim and dramatic images. The controversial school I attended in South Kensington was full of apprehension and fear (St Vedast Independent School was notorious for corporal punishment and extreme discipline, eventually being closed down by the Government).

The one steady grounding influence amongst the chaos was Bill and his family. Bill and Margaret's house was like a calm port in the wild storm that was my life. When you entered their peaceful living room it was like stepping out of time. You could hear the steady constant ticking of their clock and Bill would be sitting there ready with his dry sense of humour. Bill and Margaret North were the kindest people in the world and took me under their wing; I ended up nipping around to see them all the time to escape from the turmoil. There were hours of the card game Canasta that my brothers and I used to play with them and the endless games of Monopoly with Bill's youngest son Rhys that went on for days and days.

Their TV also seemed to be a focus of attention on my visits. Bill and I used to sit and watch the news in all its graphic detail. We also watched The World at War series and a program called Pathfinders, a fictitious drama about the RAF Pathfinder Squadrons. Alongside this Bill would tell me stories about his life during WW2 while serving with Bomber Command. Bill never volunteered to talk about his war experiences, but if you asked him he would tell you. His story was revealed bit by bit over the years. As time passed and I grew older Bill would frequently get a briefcase out that contained a unique collection of documents relating to his RAF service. There were pictures, letters, diaries and a Flying Log Book that detailed all Bill's training flights and Operations. These documents fascinated and inspired me and were like holding history in my hands.

It was only 25 years after the end of WW2 when I first met Bill. Children's comics were full of war stories, war films were regularly shown on TV and the vast majority of boys' toys in those days were war-themed (toy soldiers, tanks, planes, guns etc). The 1970s was a turbulent time for me, with family dramas and the stresses of growing up to contend with, as well as the excitement of discovering rock music - but throughout all this Bill was a constant, stable and reassuring presence in my life. The more I found out about him the more I realised what an extraordinary man my unassuming next-door neighbour and good friend was. With his cheeky sense of humour and his laid back, calm, gentle and kind manner, he always impressed the hell out of me. Nothing seemed to faze him. To the end of his long life in 2011, I felt as comfortable talking with him as that first day we met when I was a little boy of seven in March 1970.

1977 was a year to remember for our two families and the residents of Regal Way. It was a year that is literally burned into my memory. A fine example of Bill and his family's coolness 'under fire' came about when the country was on 'Green Alert.' I was 13 years old and that year we had witnessed the Queen's Silver Jubilee street party celebrations. On the14th November 1977 the Fire Brigade began a strike that lasted 9 weeks. Print workers and BBC network engineers were on strike too. The whole country was plunged into a national emergency with the armed forces covering 'shouts' in outdated military Green Goddess fire appliances. They attended a hospital fire in London's East end and two children were killed in a London house fire putting pressure on home secretary Merlyn Rees to end the deadlock. Our turn at Regal Way came next and made my younger twin brothers Richard and John infamous to this day.

I was at Saturday morning lessons at St Vedast Independent School in Kensington and my Mum was in the bath. My Dad was looking at a house boat that was for sale on the River Thames in Richmond because we were thinking of moving. My four-year-old twin brothers, Richard and John, were downstairs at 103 Regal Way playing with a box of matches that they had got hold of by climbing up a bookcase. They struck one and set fire to bits of paper in a tin by the foam sofa in the front window bay. A fine thread hanging out of the sofa acted like a fuse as it burned away and disappeared; suddenly the foam sofa exploded in a fire ball taking the curtains with it.

Richard ran upstairs to get my mum and John hid downstairs. My mum came downstairs naked to be confronted by a raging inferno. The postman was trying to kick the front door in when mum opened it and handed Richard over to him. She then crawled back into the smoke and flames looking for John. She couldn't find him anywhere and was forced back in despair to the kitchen and then out into the side extension as the fire exploded and blew the rear windows out. In the meantime Alun, one of Bill's three sons tried to get in through the back of the house after climbing over the fence only to be beaten back by the flames too. In the extension Mum luckily saw a little foot poking out from underneath some furniture; she grabbed John and ran out to the back garden. Alun had by then come back with a wet towel to find Mum coming out with John in her arms. He took them both to the far end of the garden where he sat her down and gave her a blanket.

Bill had organised the neighbours with hosepipes and buckets of water and kept the fire at bay until the Green Goddesses turned up 40 minutes later. After the fire had been put out the wall between the two houses was red hot and Bill and Alun had to take all their books off the bookshelf in their living room as another safety precaution. I came home from school not knowing a thing was wrong and after the short walk from Preston Road Station was confronted with the awful scene. As I turned to face our house from Regal Way I stopped dead for two minutes eyes fixed wide open and my brain not quite registering what it was seeing. My Dad had tried to ring home and got no answer which was unusual. Worried he rang Bill and Margaret and has never forgotten Bill's cool, but thoughtful answer. 'There's been a bit of a fire David, but everyone's ok!'

The Keltie boys, Xmas 1973. Left to right, Chris, John, David and Richard and Angus our cat on the sofa that caught fire (Anne Keltie).

Bill, Margaret, David, Alun and Rhys were fantastic. They took us in and looked after us until we booked into a local hotel for a few days. Everybody in the street helped us clear up and sort the house out. From the start to the finish of the whole dramatic episode Bill had stayed cool as a cucumber and I was to find out from my later research that this was the same cool and level headed Bill who had survived all those crazy, near death situations in WW2. Even afterwards, and bearing in mind my brothers had nearly burnt their house down as well, there was no blame or criticism of our family, just pure kindness and love.

Bill also saved me on more than one occasion from the school bullies that chased me down Regal Way from Uxendon Manor Primary School. As I reached our houses seriously out of breath from the chase with the bullies right behind me, Bill magically appeared and saved me. One firm look from him and a vocal warning scared them off, slinking away with their tails between their legs.

Bill and Margaret's TV was a pleasure zone to another world for me; I used to constantly nip around after school for tea and cakes and, come to think of it, to escape there as many times as I could. Once I went round and Margaret was sitting there excitedly saying 'Bill's going to be on the news tonight!' Bill was a Trade Union official with the National Union of Railwaymen, who were in dispute with the government. Margaret and I watched the 6 o'clock news together, 'Look, here he comes walking down the steps!' she shouted, and there was 2 or 3 seconds worth of Bill on the TV screen, coming out of 10 Downing Street.

A short time later we saw him walking down Regal Way from Preston Road Station with his distinctive limp from his war wounds (although he said it was from playing rugby; my Mum who was a physiotherapist would treat Bill on and off for problems with his knee). We rushed up to him and said, 'We just saw you on TV'. Bill of course in his usual way was not fazed by the attention and with a warm smile made light of it, just like he did with his RAF service.

The Pathfinders TV series was a 1972-3 drama about the fictitious 192 Squadron, based on the legendary 156 Pathfinder Squadron with 8 Group that used to mark targets for Bomber Command. Bill would sit and watch with me and guide me through the drama of bombing missions. Then there was the 1973-4 Jeremy Isaacs, Thames Television's *World at War* series which I was absolutely addicted too; it was one of the most expensive TV series made at the time. It was later mentioned that the only ingredient missing from the production was the knowledge about 'Enigma' code breaking at Bletchley Park; this information was still Top Secret in the 1970's. I was to find out later that Margaret North worked at Bletchley Park with Alan Turing.

The opening titles and flaming images over composer Carl Davis' haunting soundtrack made the hairs on the back of my neck stand up on end. The series, narrated by Laurence Olivier, was raw, unglamorous, intense but informative and its impact everlasting. There were gritty eyewitness accounts from people who were close to recognised figures and from civilians and military personnel. These interviews fascinated me as the people revealed their personal experiences before the cameras. (I eventually got to conduct my own interviews with war veterans in the course of researching Bill's war record). We saw real dead bodies and service men, women and civilians from all nations in their moments of death, it was awful and awe-inspiring. These two series especially had a profound effect on me as I was growing up. They inspired and stimulated my interest in World War Two and Bomber Command and its many missions, of which Bill was an eye-witness. My family eventually got our own TV, a rental model with a coin slot that took ages to warm up. Watching it didn't have quite the same excitement as going round to visit Bill and Margaret, so I continued to go round there to watch television with them regularly.

My dramatic home life at 103 Regal Way, set against the chaos in the world around us, was influenced by a mixture of television, music, news and WW2, all neatly held together by the steady calming presence of Bill North. Bill was a constant right the way through my hectic life even after I left home at 20 years old. I worked my way through a number of jobs which included contract cleaning, gardening, trainee Trade Mark Agent, carpenter in the building trade, taxi driving and in and out of the music business. Stability finally came my way when I got married to Wendy Portinari in 1990 and had two beautiful babies Jess and Izzy.

I saw Bill whenever I visited my Mum at 103 Regal Way, which was pretty much once a week, and Izzy, my younger daughter, grew very close to him on our many visits. He always called her Lizzy even though we corrected him many times. Until the day he died, Bill's memories of his RAF service, wartime experiences and lost friends still felt like yesterday to him, even after over 60 years had passed. The mind is a curious thing; some things fade away and others stay fresh for a lifetime.

103 and 105 Regal Way, 28 July 2006 (CK).

At Regal Way Bill had a bird feeder attached to a branch that came from a firethorn bush in our garden. The branch grew right in front of the back room where Bill used to sit. It gave him a perfect view of the birds flying to and fro in the garden, he was fascinated by them. This was the sacred branch and whenever we did gardening at 103 Regal Way we always made sure that it wasn't accidently cut when we were pruning. My mum sold our house at 103 Regal Way in May 2006 and moved to a new flat in Harrow. My brother John and I went to see Bill one day and were shocked to find the new owners had cut the whole bush down. The bird feeder had no place to hang anymore! We were devastated, but Bill in his usual way took this all in his stride. After Bill left Regal Way and moved to Basingstoke, his three sons, David, Alun and Rhys fixed up a feeding stand outside the window in his new room, so he could continue to watch these beautiful creatures in flight.

In March 2009, nearly 39 years to the day after I had first met him, I popped in to see Bill with my brother John. (Very sadly, Margaret North had passed away in 1998 from Raynaud's disease.) At 45 years old, I found myself standing in Bill's back living-room, staring at the same photo of Bill and his crew which had so fascinated me when I was 7. It felt as if someone had hit the fast forward button on my life. I was now nearly as old as Bill had been when I first met him; and Bill was 87. Just to confirm how fast time had passed by there was a picture of a beautiful young woman sitting on the side cabinet. I asked Bill who it was in the picture and he said it was his granddaughter Lisa. I was amazed. My outstanding memory of her was when she was about 7 years old and charging around like a lunatic in the back garden with her brother David.

We were looking at the contents of Bill's briefcase again and there were papers spread out all over the living room floor. It was like a treasure chest with its unique collection of documents relating to his RAF service; it always felt like it transported us back through time. As we were talking and asking Bill questions (Bill was always at perfect ease with any question relating to his experiences even the sad and gruesome ones - 'If you ask me I will tell you'), that the thought occurred to me that someone should write a book about his incredible life. So as we were again looking at the contents of that magical briefcase, I said to Bill, 'You know there is a story here that needs to be told, somebody should write this.'

Bill replied, 'Well why don't you write it then.'

I was gobsmacked. I instantly replied yes and I felt honoured and privileged to have his permission to do so.

Bill North with his RAF Log Book, 23 July 2009 (CK).

When I first agreed to write this book with Bill I had no idea what I was getting myself into and what a time consuming thing it would become. It took on a life of its own and became something that I had no control over. All I knew was that I really wanted to do it no matter what. It pushed and pulled me around as I followed its path, looking for clues and unravelling the puzzle and mystery that dragged me towards its conclusion.

In the beginning it was just Bill and I. Then Bill wanted David, Alun and Rhys on board, but only them. Bill in his usual unassuming way didn't want me to tell people apart from close family that I was writing this book, but from day one I shouted about it from the rooftops in an effort to publicise and promote it. I have worked closely with Bill, Alun and his family over the last 5 years to try to complete this story. The first document I worked with was Bill's RAF Flying Logbook. It was something I had looked at many times, but never studied in detail. The first thing I had to do was visualise and record where Bill's service sat historically in WW2. As time progressed and the jigsaw puzzle came together this, alongside the other Veterans Log books, proved to be the most important documents I had to do research with. The other key document that was the glue that joined everything together was the War Diary of Bill's Bomb Aimer, Norman Jarvis.

The amount of information I began to collect and process was phenomenal and at times I felt lost and out of my depth. There was virtually no space left in my head and my wife Wendy had whole conversations with me which I didn't hear a word of. (I have to thank her for putting up with me when I was like this.) I would take and follow research as it came up, charging off to the Public Records Office, making phone calls, copying, scanning, saving files, e-mailing, editing, re-reading, watching documentaries and making journeys all over the country, especially to Lincolnshire to interview other War Veterans. There were books, notes, papers and chapters lying all over the house, which to an outsider looking in would seem like total chaos.

Bill's 'history in your hands' briefcase, 20 April 2011 (CK).

My main frustration was always the limited amount of time I had to commit to it as I shared my day and night between my family and financial commitments. What little spare time I had over the last 5 years I dedicated to trying to get the book finished. It has been written and researched a bit here and a bit there and whenever I could stretch time to suit my needs. There were people and crew members' families in Australia, New Zealand, Canada, Ireland and the UK all eagerly awaiting its arrival. I feel like a seasoned time traveller as I have travelled back and forth through the years on my journey with this book. In 2010 I nearly lost my father David to bowel cancer and we were on tenterhooks regarding his well-being whilst he recovered at home with my family. The book got put on semi-hold during this difficult time, but it refused to lie still and in a strange sort of way came back stronger after its forced break. We then had a second scare in 2012 when the cancer returned and he had another operation to remove his stomach, from which he made a remarkable recovery whilst living with us again. He was in the wars again in November 2012 when he was knocked off his bike and broke his right leg and elbow, also again making a remarkable recovery. The book seemed to slow down again, but my love of the subject matter and respect for Bill North always overrode these frustrations life seemed to present to us.

My journeys to see Bill over this time became longer and longer. I didn't know it at the time, but I was spoilt when we lived next-door to each other. I only had to jump over the garden fence or go out of the front door to see him. When I left home and moved to Golders Green it was a twenty minute journey back to Regal Way to see my Mum and to nip next-door to see Bill. When my Mum sold 103 and moved away it felt really strange visiting

Bill and standing outside looking, but not being able to enter our old home where there were so many memories imprinted in the bricks and mortar.

From the start of writing the book, once a week on a Thursday was the day Bill and I would get together. I met Lisa North many times at Regal Way, when by coincidence we would arrive at the same time or Bill would ring me and say 'get here at so and so time Lisa will be here.' Alun was also present a few times and it always felt really good to be there at the same time and share memories. Bill was always a phone call or a car journey away. He was always there to tirelessly answer my endless questions and I never ever took for granted the fact that my good friend was an important witness to modern history. I always felt honoured to be in his presence and to be able to immortalise his contribution to the fight against Hitler's tyranny.

When Bill finally became less mobile and had a fall at home he went into Willesden General Hospital for a while in late 2010. My Dad who was still on chemotherapy had just left us to go and live back at home in Primrose Hill by himself and we were worried sick about him. I had a big scare when I turned up at Regal Way and there was no answer at 105. I eventually tracked down Alun whose telephone number I had lost and went to see Bill at Willesden General; it was here that I met the charismatic Rob Greenwood for the first time. From there Bill was transferred to Basingfield Court care home in Basingstoke and then to Basingstoke Hospital. The journey was now 53 miles and roughly an hour and a half; it now became once every two weeks and would become a real test on the limited amount of time I had to dedicate to the story. During December 2011 Bill started to fade fast while in Basingstoke Hospital. We were nearly completed with the book when he sadly passed away. As I struggled and fought a battle with time itself to share this story, I sadly watched one of 'the many' slip away right before my eyes. After Bill's funeral I returned to the book with much sadness, but also with a new sense of purpose.

There have been many miles travelled and untold hours of research and writing that often would happen at 3 to 4 in the morning when the house was quiet and there were none of life's distractions. Many times I would be sitting by myself in the kitchen, my faithful Acer laptop in front of me, when completely unexpectedly the hairs on the back of my neck would stand up on end. A little shiver would pass through me as I looked around the kitchen and out into the darkness of the garden searching for a reason. I could not venture an explanation for this, but can only say it was not something that made me afraid but rather gave me inspiration to carry on. I have laughed and cried many, many times on this journey, sometimes unexpectedly, but generally always at the same moments in the story. It has truly been an emotional and physical rollercoaster, but at the same time spiritually and emotionally rewarding. I feel honoured and privileged to have had Bill's permission to share with the rest of the world a story that needs to be told.

Along the way many stories within stories have revealed themselves to us. The desire to ensure that no twist or turn (nothing) is lost to time has been irresistible and presented us with the danger of becoming carried away. It has been a huge discipline to keep these stories related to Bill's, and his comrade's journey through the shadow of death. Some of these many stories have been shared at Bill's request to give examples of and demonstrate how lucky he was to survive at all. I have discovered on this journey the strong emotional connection felt by family members of the second and third generation to the past and present members of Bomber Command, the experiences they went through and how it still affects them today. The remarkable bond with the Commonwealth countries like Australia, New Zealand and Canada that was forged in adversity is something I feel strongly, especially after becoming friends with family members of Bill's crew and other Veterans.

Throughout Bill's story much attention has been paid to the iconic vessel that carried our crewmen, the Lancaster Bomber. This is the aircraft that Bill loved and revered and 60 years later still moved him to tears. Alongside Bill, the Avro Lancaster is one of our main characters and again at his request it is recorded as an integral and emotional component of the fabric of his story. As each crew finished their Tour of Ops with their chosen thoroughbred, so the a/c went on steadfastly flying missions, each one like its crews potentially being its last. The relationship of all who served this historic machine is touched upon. The men and women who built it, those who serviced and repaired it and the chosen few that flew and died in it.

In the course of researching and writing this book I feel I have got to really know, not just Bill, but also his crew and got a real sense of what those young men went through during those dark and trying times of the Second World War. They disappeared every night into the shroud of darkness that saved their lives a thousand times. I began to feel I understood the strange fascination of night bombing, from the long intense journeys fraught with danger and the intense Technicolor chaos over the target, to flying home through the gold and reds of dawn above the silver sheen of the sea to the peace and tranquillity of the Lincolnshire countryside.

A generation of thoughts, sensations, experiences, hopes, fears and personal silences are now revealed as a 19 year old Cardiff boy is catapulted into the turmoil of war from his desk at Unity House in Euston and

Wallingford in Oxfordshire. Bill North returned home seemingly the same cool and steady character; the only difference being he was now a man with eternal memories, bonds and friendships that spread ever outward and onward like everlasting ripples from a pebble thrown into an endless pond.

I hope that the reader feels the same as I do and can gain insight into the lives lived and lost of those courageous young men who, against perilous odds, served with Bomber Command. Of the 125,000 that volunteered, 55,573 were killed (20,000 with no resting place), 5,327 were killed during training, 8,403 were wounded, 9,838 became POWs and approximately 8,000 ended up in RAF psychiatric hospitals suffering from post traumatic stress. USAAF (United States Army Air Force) bomber crews would on average last just 14 out of 25 missions before joining their 26,000 lost comrades. These figures, alongside an in depth study of the loss statistics, will starkly reveal how lucky Bill North and his crew were to survive their traumatic ride through death's dark shadow.

This book is dedicated to the selfless courage and dedication of Flight Lieutenant Bill North and his crew and all the lost and surviving RAF, RAAF, RNZAF, RCAF, Polish and USAAF aircrews, as well as all the other nationalities that served in the combined forces under Bomber Command, to whom we all owe so much.

So here it is, a wartime adventure and life story that is anything but ordinary; let's start at the very beginning...

# Chapter One

## Growing up in Cardiff

William North was born on the 11th May 1922 in digs at 25 Manor Street, Cardiff, Wales where his parents, William and Rachel, were living. The family later moved on to 177 Mynachdy Road, Gabalfa, Cardiff where he grew up with his sisters Nancy and Iris.

Left William and Rachel North and right Nancy North and William (Bill) North (*North family*).

I think it's important to have a quick look at the series of social, political and technological events that were influencing the world that Bill was growing up in, this will help to set the scene for the dramatic future events that would unfold. Bill's father William witnessed the horrors of WW1, he had joined the Machine Gun Corps because they paid an extra 12/6 (twelve shillings and sixpence – 63p in modern coins). When he saw a friend in Cardiff City Centre, the friend asked with astonishment 'Why did you join the MGC and not the Infantry?'

Bill's dad replied, 'Because I wanted the extra 12/6 to buy a push bike with.'

His concerned friend's reply was a grim warning: 'You know the Machine Gunners only last two minutes before they are killed on the front line and if the Germans catch them they are shot instantly.'

His friend was right. Bill's Dad William witnessed slaughter and carnage beyond belief, but he made it through the war sustaining only a slight injury. Bill's Grandfather and Father were strong Union men and, as

I will explain later, also became involved in the General Strikes throughout the 1920's.

A quick aside; the name William has been passed down from Grandfather to Father and Father to son and to Bill's son David in true Welsh tradition. Margaret North refused to call their first born William saying, 'It would be too confusing, because if she called their name they wouldn't know which one was being called.' He was called David William instead!

Even after the horrific bloodshed and destruction of WW1, the 1920's and 30's were a time of change, turmoil and revolution, there was still an underlying uneasiness that permeated society. Bill North was born a little less than 3 years after the Treaty of Versailles was signed on 28 June 1919 and the horrors of WW1 were still fresh in people's minds.

**South Wales News, Wed 1 October 1919:**

**1.** Members of the Cardiff Strike Committee. Left to Right—Mr Moorhouse, Mr S.W.John, Mr Prance, Mr R.Hughes and Mr T Gear.

**2.** Arrival of the 'South Wales News' by motor-car at Swansea in the early hours of the morning.

**3.** Milk-churns, unfortunately empty, accumulating at the railway stations.

**4.** A veteran among the strikers; Mr. W North, one of the oldest employees of the Cardiff Railway company.—(Photos by *Chapman and 'South Wales News.'*) The veteran striker Mr W. North was Bill's grandfather William North who worked for the Cardiff Railway Company. The Cardiff Railway Company Emblem and motto. Wrth Ddwr a Than: By Fire and Water. The Cardiff Railway company merged with GWR (Great Western Railways) in 1924. (source: *Cardiff railway history, Urban75 blog*)

Bill came from a proud Trade Union family associated with the Railways. His Grandfather William and his father William were both in the NUR, (National Union of Railwaymen). His father was a Railway Checker at Cardiff Docks inspecting the rolling stock and both men were involved in the General Strikes of 1919 and 1926. Bill's grandfather and father had a short trip on the train into work at the docks from Llandaf Rail Station. Mynachdy Road sits in-between Llandaf and Cathays Rail Stations and the line ran directly to Cardiff Docks Station. The rail track ran from north to south and passed directly by the end of Mynachdy Road.

In 1919 the NUR and ASLEF (the train drivers union) jointly organized a national railway strike which Bill's Grandfather is pictured above taking part in; this prevented a proposed wage reduction and won an eight-hour maximum working day. During the great depression in the 1920's South Wales and Cardiff were one of the worst affected areas of the country and many people lost their jobs. Fortunately for Bill's family his father William kept his job at Cardiff Docks so they didn't suffer the same degree of poverty experienced by many families. His job allowed the family free rail travel and Bill remembers some fantastic family holidays to Ilfracombe and the Devon coastline.

Bill from early days was pretty much was left to his own devices whilst growing up. He used to play out in the streets with his friends and used to walk through the tunnel at the end of Mynachdy Road to get to the fields where he used to spend hours playing. From these fields you could see Llandaf Cathedral and the River Taff meandering its way down into 'Tiger Bay.' His mother and father grew their own vegetables at home and this took up most of the space in the garden. This is something Bill and Margaret continued to do at 105 Regal Way; I can remember the back half of their garden was always filled with vegetables too.

Bill was a member of the Boys' Brigade of which he had many fond memories. The Boys' Brigade (BB) was a Christian youth organization, formed by William Alexander Smith in Glasgow in 1883 to combine drill and fun activities with Christian values. Its object was *'The advancement of Christ's kingdom among Boys and the promotion of habits of Obedience, Reverence, Discipline, Self-respect and all that tends towards a true Christian manliness.'* Bill certainly possessed all of these qualities. He also attended Heath Sunday School at East Glamorgan Presbyterian Church and passed an exam in British International Lessons on 7 March 1934 - Mr Rees from Abenaron was the examiner. Bill passed an exam for the 'Special Places' award at Cathays High School, Crown way, Gabalfa, Cardiff in July 1934. His first day at Cathays High School was in September 1934 and Bill was 12 years old. The school was about a 20 minute walk down Llantarnam Road from 177 Mynachdy Road.

While Bill was growing up in the sleepy back streets of Cardiff he was blissfully unaware of the Nazi's measured rise to power and the technological, social and political developments that influenced the 1920's and 30's. There were many advances in technology that affected everyday life including radio, TV and the motor car. Europe witnessed a rise in political extremism with swings to the far left (Communist) and far right (Nationalist) wings. Germany's far right wing was the National Socialist German Workers Party, NSDAP or Nazi Party and was led by Adolf Hitler. It was fuelled by Germany's bitter political and economic discontent – largely a consequence of the Versailles Treaty that brought WW1 to an end.

Bill at Cathays High School 1934, top row 5th from the right (*Bill North*).

Bill left school in April 1937 when he was 15 and his first job was as a Junior Clerk at the metal works of John Williams and Sons, East Moors Road, down near Cardiff Docks. He was to remain there until 7 January 1939. The company manufactured windows, staircases, steel and alloy products. While Bill was working here Austria was annexed into the German Third Reich on 12 March 1938. Hitler received a hero's welcome in Germany and addressed a crowd of one million people in Berlin.

While working at John Williams and Sons, Bill attended evening classes at nearby Allensbank Junior Evening Institute and Mr Wainwright, the Head Teacher at the Institute, wrote a glowing reference for Bill on 14 November 1938. *'William North has attended the above Institute during the whole of last winter and also during the present session and has been one of our best students. He has passed the examinations for English,*

*Bookkeeping, taking Mathematics and Shorthand successfully, at the close of last winter's work he was particularly good in Mathematics. He has also taken leading parts in class debates and has spoken well on those occasions. His character is everything that can be desired and he has proved a most exemplary student, and I am sure he would acquit himself well in any job he undertook.'*

In January 1939 Bill was offered a job as a Junior Clerk with the NUR following in his Grandfather and Father's Union footsteps; understandably John Williams and Sons were very sorry to lose him. In his reference letter dated 7 January 1939 from John Williams and Sons, G.R. Faulks the director of the company says, *'Mr William North has given complete satisfaction, we understand he is leaving us to take a better post and we shall be sorry to lose him.'* This was the same day the German Battleship Scharnhorst was commissioned and the German war machine was preparing itself to conquer Europe. Bill's childhood spanned the Depression, with its industrial turmoil, poverty and the world witnessing extremes in politics with the rise of fascism, communism and civil unrest on the European continent. Despite this, Bill had a happy childhood with wonderful memories and his family remained as close as ever through those troubled times. As the dark cloud of war loomed again over Europe, the family would be tested again and again. By this time Bill had acquired all the leadership qualities and steady personality that would carry him through his war service and his life.

While Europe was reaching political boiling point, Bill moved down to London and took up his post with the NUR at Unity House in Euston in 1939 (now the site of University College Hospital). He was living in digs in Harrow at this time and travelled into Euston on the Metropolitan line. Whilst working at the NUR, during the run up to the outbreak of war, he had time to reflect on the future. Bill said, *'We all began to feel uncomfortable with the tension that was building up in Europe. The feeling that war was coming began to grow stronger by the day and was a constant worry and topic of conversation. There was also, at the same time, though a real sense of excitement amongst the young men at the time that we would be serving our country in some form or other.'*

The Munich Agreement of September 1938 allowed Hitler to move into the Sudetenland, which was the German speaking part of Czechoslovakia. When German troops took over the rest of Czechoslovakia on the 16 March 1939; there was no cheering from the population as there had been in the Sudetenland, just silence. This was the first move on a non German speaking country and confirmed Hitler's imperialist intentions. Next Hitler demanded the return of the city of Danzig in the Polish Corridor between East Prussia and Germany; so far Hitler had got his own way without serious opposition. British Prime Minister Neville Chamberlain now pledged Britain's support, alongside that of France, to assist Poland if Hitler were to make any more aggressive moves.

Hitler invaded Poland on the 1 September 1939 and the British Government declared war on Germany on 3 September 1939; Bill was now 17 years old. After a few months of relative quiet, called the 'Phoney War', Germany invaded France on the 10 May 1941; it was the day before Bill's 18th birthday. In exactly 4 years time he would fly on his first Bomber Command Operation with his crew, joining in the fight back against German aggression. A swift charge through Belgium and into France saw the swastika flying over Paris on the 14 June 1941. The BEF (British Expeditionary Force) had been pushed back to Dunkirk and many French and British soldiers were saved in the famous evacuation. Hitler was now making plans to conquer Britain. Herman Goring planned to achieve superiority over British airspace and the Battle of Britain ensued (Margaret North's boyfriend at the time, Harry Cyril Groves, was an RAF pilot who was killed during the Battle of Britain).

Unlike other European countries, Britain had always relied on volunteers to fight in times of war. Conscription (compulsory military service) had been introduced in 1916 when more men were needed to fight in the trenches, but it was discarded when the war ended. During the 1930's some men still chose to enter the Armed Forces after leaving school and in 1937 there were 200,000 soldiers in the British Army. Generally, the Armed Forces were seriously lacking in manpower. On 26 May 1939 the Government introduced the Military Training Act 1939; all men between the ages of 20 and 21 had to register for six months military training. Bill was only just 17 at this point so this did not apply to him.

Most European countries except Britain had kept conscription running between the wars and were able to raise quite substantial Armies. The National Service (Armed Forces) Act 1939 was immediately enforced on the day of Britain's declaration of war. It replaced the Military Training Act 1939 and imposed full conscription on all men between 18 and 41 who were not working in 'reserved occupations'. At the same time a list of 'reserved occupations' was published. This listed occupations that were essential to the war effort and stated that those employed in listed jobs were exempt from conscription. Listed occupations were Dock Workers, Miners, Farmers, Scientists, Merchant Seamen, Railway Workers, Utility Workers :- Water, Gas and Electricity. Although Bill worked for the railways as a junior clerk, this did not count as a 'reserved occupation' and from 11 May 1940 when he was 18, he was eligible to be called up. In 1941 single women aged between 20 and 30 were also conscripted, this included Margaret Watkins (Bill's eventual wife) who joined the WRNS (Women's Royal Naval Reserve or Wrens).*

After the Dunkirk evacuation, Germany began the bombing campaign against British Airfields and then cities, including Bill's home city of Cardiff. Back home at 177 Mylanchy Road, Bill and his family had to take cover in their Anderson shelter in the back garden a few times during Luftwaffe attacks.

Bill's sister Iris explains the attacks on Cardiff: *'Our Father used to be an air raid warden and was always on watch duty, we had an Anderson shelter at the rear of the garden in Mynachrdy Road that we sheltered in. Bill was home on leave in 1943 and had woken up unexpectedly; he was having a shave as we were all going for a day out to Porthcawl. Dad was home and Mum said, 'Bill's woken up unexpectedly early, I don't think he realises he could have a few more hours sleep, do you want go to and tell him.' Dad who had a very dry sense of humour said, 'No, let him carry on shaving.'*

*The air raid sirens suddenly went off and Bill came out and said, 'Right then is everybody ready to go to Porthcawl.' Dad was rushing round like a lunatic and said 'Everybody down to the shelter now!' We all went down to the Anderson shelter and the whole way down Bill was still moaning 'I don't know what all the fuss is about I thought we were going to Porthcawl.' As we all sat there Dad was out in the street rounding up all the residents as the bombs began to fall around us. We were counting the explosions as they got closer and closer. The ground was shaking and the noise was deafening, there was a gap in the explosions and we all thought the next bomb was for us. There was a huge explosion right next to us and we all looked at each other thinking that our house had been hit. When it was over and we went outside, there had been a direct hit on the house at the end of our garden right near our shelter. My friend from my class at Cathay's School, Dorothy Patterson and two of her family had died in the blast, we were all really shocked at how close it was and that it was people we knew. We all had to go into school the next day and everybody was crying, there was no counselling or help for the children or family's, we all just had to bear it and carry on as normal!'* Bill and his family too, had had that dark shadow pass right over them in their home at Mynachdy Road in the peaceful backstreets of Cardiff.

The NUR decided that they would evacuate all their staff out of London during 'The Blitz' and Bill and his workmates were evacuated to Wallingford in Oxfordshire. Bill was living in digs in Wallingford and travelled the short distance to NUR HQ at Castle Friary. It was while Bill was living in Wallingford that he came to the decision to volunteer for the RAF. He was still only 18 years old though and waited until his 19th birthday on 11 May 1941 before he could put his plan into action. His thought process was a simple one. He was going to get his call up papers soon (Conscription Law) so he thought he would get in there first and do something he wanted to do and would volunteer to become a pilot. Bill said, *'I knew at some point soon we would all be getting our call up papers for conscription, so I decided to try and jump the gun. I knew that the RAF was all voluntary and that at least I could have a choice as to what service I would serve in. I had no particular interest in flying or aircraft when I was growing up, but was inspired by the Battle of Britain pilots; so I knew I wanted to fly and would do whatever it took to become a pilot in the RAF.'* Bill can't remember exactly which recruiting office he walked into, but it was either in or near Wallingford. The first step on the journey was to pass the medical exam for fitness to become aircrew.

A 19 year old boy from Cardiff, and 6 of his comrades, were about to play a significant part in a World War, thus helping to bring to an end evil beyond words. Bill's training and service came at the most intense period of WW2 - from its lowest point where the Axis and Japanese forces seemed like they were going to rule the world, to the turning points at Stalingrad in early 1943 and the slow United States recovery of its Pacific Islands. The culmination was the 'North Crew's' contribution to the long awaited D-Day landings, enabling Allied Forces to gain a foothold on the European Continent. Bomber Command played a significant part in wearing down the German war effort, resources and morale. The entry of America into the War gave the Allies vital advantages in contributing to the downfall of the Reich and the eventual apocalyptic conclusion of the war.

* (Conscription facts from BBC History website).

# Chapter Two

## Volunteering for RAF Service

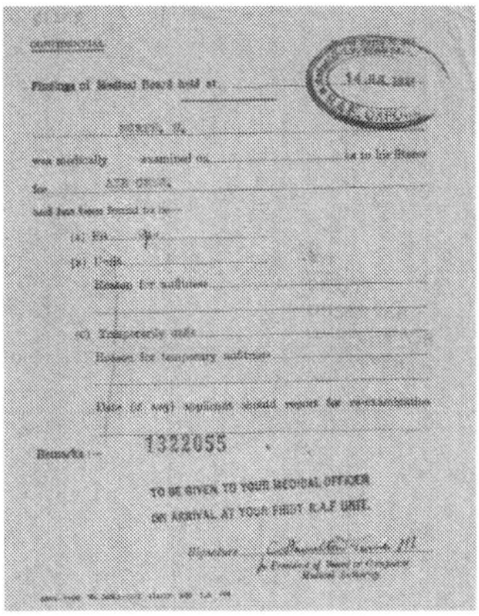
1322055

TO BE GIVEN TO YOUR MEDICAL OFFICER
ON ARRIVAL AT YOUR FIRST R.A.F. UNIT.

RAF recruiting poster, 1941. (*Imperial War Museum*) and Bill's RAF Medical certificate. (*Bill North*)

Bill went for his RAF medical on the 14 July 1941 at RAF Oxford and passed with no problems. The medical certificate would be required to be presented to staff at his first posting. While Bill was just at the beginning of his RAF journey, Bomber Command was still relentlessly flying missions. Having spent a spring offensive prioritised on German shipping, ports, U-boat bases and shipyards, Bomber Command now resumed its operations to mainland Germany; the targets for 14 July were Bremen and Hanover.

Handley Page Hampden, May 1942, 455 Squ (RAAF), (source, *COL 182 IWM*).

The a/c used by Bomber Command at this point in the War were the twin engine Hampdens, Blenheims, Wellingtons, the US Douglas Bostons and Whitleys (the oldest of the five types). In early 1941 Bomber Command received its first four engined bombers, the Halifax and the Stirling. Bill was to later fly in the Short Stirling which came into Operational service in January 1941; its first mission was on 10/11 February 1941 to Vlaardingen near Rotterdam. The Halifax entered service with 35 Squadron at Linton-on-Ouse in November 1940 and its first Operational raid was to Le Havre on the 11/12 March 1941.

The medical exam was an intense and rigid affair and many candidates would fail on a variety of things like colour blindness, fitness etc - those who passed moved on to the next stages. These men were given the rank of Sergeant and classed as fit to train as Pilots, Navigators and Bomb Aimers (Observers), Wireless Operators, Air Gunners and Flight Engineers. The potential crewmen were also required to pass a Maths and English exam; this was no problem for Bill. RAF crew were all volunteers, one in four of them were from overseas, mostly Commonwealth countries. There was a real mixture of men from completely different backgrounds, from Public School Boys to the Working Classes. Part of the attraction for some was that the money was slightly higher than other services (8 shillings a day for a Sgt) and they received a pair of shoes, boots and sheets with their blankets. After passing their medicals, RAF Reception Centres were the first stop, usually for about 4 weeks. Here aircrew received their uniforms and injections (Lords Cricket Ground in St. Johns Wood, London was a major reception centre).

Initial Training Wings (ITW) was generally the next port of call for prospective RAF aircrews after Reception Centres. At ITW the crews would be assigned to the aircrew duties they would train for, attending hours and hours of lectures and endless parades. There was great emphasis on physical fitness, which was a part of everyday life with Physical Education instructors pushing the recruits through their paces. Bill can't remember which Reception Centre he went to, but after this he was transferred in August/September 1941 to an ITW in Blackpool to do his Wireless Operator and Air Gunner Training (WAG) at Winter Gardens. This wasn't quite what he had in mind!

During the War many coastal towns were used by the RAF as Initial Training Wing centres, due to the good availability of accommodation for the recruits and the large sea front areas where they could parade and do PE. The RAF selected Blackpool as one of its largest Training Wing centres, because as a popular holiday town there were a large number of guest houses available to house new recruits, and it had a long open seafront which was used for 'square bashing' (daily parades/marching). It was also home to No 9 Recruitment Centre and No. 5 School of Technical Training where recruits trained to become air mechanics; there were training camps at Weeton and Kirkham (where Blackpool Airport is now located). Wellington bombers were also constructed locally at the Vickers-Armstrong factory at Squires Gate, later used for the manufacture of prefabricated houses. Blackpool became an 'RAF town', it was crammed full with service personnel, evacuees and Government employees. In total some 769, 673 airmen did their Initial Training in Blackpool.

This photograph of Bill North was taken by Burton & Garland Ltd, 86 Talbot Road, Blackpool and is dated Xmas 1941. The white stripe on the RAF Forage cap and the white wings on the left shoulder indicated that he was aircrew in training (*Bill North*).

Bill and I were discussing this period of his training in Blackpool. The general details of the Air Gunnery School and the training he was given there will be explained a bit later, when I run through Dennis Bartlett's Gunnery training. I was reading sections of Derek Brammer's excellent book on 61 Squadron '*Thundering Through The Clear Air*' with Bill and came across a part on Wireless Operators training (p57). The recruits had to listen to a tape for a full hour with two lots of Morse code coming over their earphones. They had to learn how to identify the different sounds marking a tick if they were the same, or a cross if one got shorter or it was different. After intensive Morse code training recruits would be expected to reach the required sending speed of 12 words minimum per minute, eventually reaching 18 words per minute.

Bill explained he had forgotten these details, but it was probably because he was seriously restless with this part of aircrew training and desperately wanted to be transferred to Pilot training. He vocalised this frustration to his superiors and was made to sit another educational exam, which he passed. He was then finally accepted for Pilot Training starting in Torquay on the south Devon coast.

Bill began his pilot's training at Torquay in April 1942. The war had gone fully global by this time but the outcome was still in the balance. Just as Bill was about to undergo Pilot Training, Bomber Command's new, four engined 'Heavy' Bomber, the Avro Lancaster, came into full Operational service. The RAF had also gained a new charismatic Commander in Chief, AVM (Air Vice Marshall) Arthur Harris; this was a turning point in the war for Bomber Command and for its dedicated aircrews.

29 Sept 1942, three Lancaster BIs of 44 Squ, **Left to right:** W4125, KM-W, being flown by Sergeant Colin Watt, Royal Australian Air Force; W4162, KM-Y, flown by Pilot Officer T.G. Hackney (later killed while serving with No. 83 Squadron) and W4187, KM-S, flown by Pilot Officer J.D.V.S. Stephens DFM, who was killed with his crew two nights later during a raid on Wismar (source, *COL TR 197 IWM*).

The original prototype Lancaster BT308 was the first of the new type delivered to 5 Groups Squ's for familiarisation training. Nearly one year after BT308's maiden flight, from the first batch of L7 production Lancasters L7537, coded KM-L was delivered to 44 (Rhodesia) Squ at Waddington on 24 December 1941. On the 3 March 1944, four Lancs took off from Waddington for the aircraft's first Ops to lay mines (Gardening) in the Heligoland Bight (*Lancaster at War 2*, Mike Garbett and Brian Goulding).

The following are some of the war news stories that Bill would have heard or read as he was beginning his training:

**Chronology of World WarII (www.onwar.com/chrono/index.htm) News Report, 9 April 1942.**

In the Philippines, American General King surrenders 75,000 men (12,000 Americans) to the Japanese. The Bataan Death March begins for the prisoners and they are taken to San Fernado, 100 miles away. Many thousands of them die on the march. Resistance continues in isolated areas of Luzon and other islands. General Wainwright and his troops continue to hold out on Corregidor Island.

In the India Ocean, the Japanese fleet continues its attacks. It is hunting the main British fleet. Trincomalee is attacked by Japanese aircraft and the British carrier HMS Hermes is attacked and sunk.

In Burma, in the Irrawaddy Valley, both the Japanese and British forces prepare offensives. The Japanese however have the advantage of earlier reinforcement and are in a position to attack first.

On the Eastern Front, German forces in the north advance to begin the relief of the encircled 16th Army forces at Demyansk. Meanwhile, in the Crimea, Soviet attacks are renewed with little success in the area.

**Torquay. No. 13, ITW. April 1942.**

(During April/May 1942 Bomber Command attacked the Naval base at Kiel and the big German cities of Cologne, Essen, Rostock, Hamburg, Dortmund Mannheim and Stuttgart.)

Torquay was another of the seaside towns which played a major part in the war effort by providing accommodation and Hotels for the RAF to train aircrews, with some 49,000 aircrew passing through ITW here (incidentally, Torquay also played a vital role in the preparations for Operation Overlord, with US Forces locating in the area). Torquay was swamped with training Aircrews and the other wings located here were 1, 3 and 5, all of whom were located in Hotels and buildings around the town. The RAF requisitioned many of the hotels in Torquay for use in Initial Training Wings. The Palace Hotel was also 'borrowed' and opened as a convalescent hospital and training facility for RAF officers, it was later renamed the RAF Hospital Torquay and many aircrew were sent to recover here. No 13 ITW was formed in Torquay in June 1941 to train Pilots, Observers and Navigators from the Commonwealth and Allied Air Forces. The intakes were smaller and the courses longer, so only about 3,000 men passed through the Wing. The Headquarters were in the Belgrave Hotel at first and later at Torre Abbey.

Bill was on a 13 week training course and studied various subjects including theory of flight, meteorology, cloud formation, navigation, aircraft recognition and silhouettes (he kept his pack of silhouette cards to the end of his days). This was a pack of some twenty white cards with black silhouettes of German and Allied planes on them. Bill had to learn the difference between aircraft types, essential for staying alive in dangerous skies. I flicked through these cards on a number of occasions and they were still like new. Holding something that was made and used in 1942 was fascinating. Bill said this part of the training was a bit boring again and he still couldn't wait to get on with the real deal, which was flying. A great deal of importance was put on Physical Education which he didn't mind so much. One drill Sergeant was very vocal and would shout obscenities at them all if no civilians were nearby. Arms drill was daily and the men would get some cheeky comments from the local girls who would watch them all. The nickname for Aircrew in training was 'Erks'.

D Flight, No 2 Squ, 13 ITW, 1942. Bill North, first on the left bottom row. This was probably taken either in the grounds of the Belgrave Hotel or Torre Abbey. These photos were generally taken at the end of the course before the lads parted company (*Bill North*).

While Bill was training to become a pilot, he was himself in danger from German bomber pilots, as Torquay was hit a number of times by Luftwaffe raids during 1942. On the 7th June 1942, Torquay was attacked, just two months after Bill had started his training. Without any warning four aircraft flew in low from the sea over the crowded beaches and seafront and dropped their bombs. One exploded behind the amusement arcades near the Torbay Hotel, but fortunately nobody was injured. Bill was lucky not to get the worst of it. After he left Torquay, Luftwaffe attacks intensified the following year, with damage to the RAF Hospital and a Parish Church causing large fatalities.

There was a good deal of general frustration at Torquay with many aircrew wanting to move on and get their postings. There were a lot of high jinks in Torquay, including one incident where two recruits climbed up a high telegraph pole in the road just outside their hotel and tied a cracked lavatory pan on top of it. As their wing paraded outside the hotel in the morning the whole squadron had a good laugh at it. Another example of aircrew of the frustration was one Squadron downing their rifles whilst on drill and just walking off. As the training periods came near to ending the aircrew were assured that they would receive their postings soon.

Postings were made from ITW to the many Elementary Flying Training Schools located in the Commonwealth where they became Pilots, Navigators, Air Bombers and Wireless Operators/Air Gunners. This was the moment Bill had been waiting for; he was finally going to get a chance to fly, although it wouldn't be definite until he had passed his Initial Flying Test to see if he was competent enough to be sent for full Pilot Training.

## No18 EFTS, FAIROAKS, (Elementary Flying Training School).

(From the 30/31 May to 17 August 1942 was the beginning of the infamous '1000' Bomber raids on Germany.)

The RAF's primary aircraft used for training during WW2 were the Tiger Moth and the Avro Tutor, which were used mainly by Elementary Flying Training Schools. These training schools had been established after the decision during the 1930's that civilian-run flying schools would have responsibility for basic training and the RAF Flying Training Schools would concentrate on Advanced Flying Training. There were EFTS schools located all over the Commonwealth in South Africa, New Zealand, Kenya, India, Canada, Australia and Rhodesia (now called Zimbabwe).

The next port of call for Bill was Fairoaks civilian airport (18 EFTS) which was run by Universal Flying Services. Fairoaks was a large flying school located on the edge of Chobham near Woking in Surrey. Bill was put onto a 12 hour flying course to see if he was suitable for Pilot Training. He would fly, for the first time, in a Tiger Moth.

Here's how Bill himself described the experience: *'I can remember taking off on my first solo flight and thinking, well that was easy, then looking back down at the air strip and thinking, oh dear, how am I going to land again, it looks really hard.'*

Bill however completed his 12 hour grading course at Fairoaks, flying solo in under 10 hours. I asked Bill what this meant. He said that it was quite an achievement and still got great satisfaction from explaining this.

They had flight theory and then pilot instructors flew with them initially; when they felt the student was ready they would then be allowed to fly the Tiger Moth by themselves. As Bill mentioned he thought taking off was easy, but landing was a bit daunting. The fact Bill flew by himself after only 10 hours instruction (under the allotted 12 hours) proved that he was a natural pilot and had suitability for Advance Pilot Training. It is most likely that Bill trained with Wing Commander CEF (Cyril) Arthur, who was the top instructor at Fairoaks.

(Cyril Arthur was still teaching up until the 1970's and totalled an astounding number of flying hours (13,900), having taught people to fly in Tiger Moths since 1914. He had been an instructor at 18 EFTS Fairoaks since 1937, training some 6,000 pilots. 'That aeroplane won the war, me boy', he was quoted as saying, referring to the phenomenal significance of the Tiger Moth to the RAF's pilots proficiency. The airfield is still open today and operating light aircraft and the Metropolitan and Surrey Police helicopters are based there. It is apparently haunted by the ghost of a Spitfire pilot who crashed there).

Fairoaks Airport: **Left**, 'Diamond Lil' with Ronald Cobbett and Wing Commander Cyril Arthur **Right**, Miss Shirley Norway (Neville Chutes daughter) chats with instructor Bernard Sedgwick. Neville Chute (Norway) also the well known novelist was the founder of Airspeed Ltd. He was responsible for the design and production of the Oxford Airspeed, which Bill later flew in at AFU.

Having passed EFTS with flying colours, Bill was now ready for transfer under the British Commonwealth Air Training Plan to one of the EFTS bases located abroad. He set sail for Canada on the 13 September 1942, embarking on a remarkable adventure that took him half way around the world and back again.

# Chapter Three

## Gourock to New York

The British Commonwealth Air Training Plan, or BCATP, was also known in some countries as the Empire Air Training Scheme (EATS), and was a vast joint military aircrew training program created by Great Britain, Canada, Australia and New Zealand. It still remains the largest aviation training program in history. It was responsible for training nearly half the Pilots, Navigators, Bomb Aimers, Air Gunners, Wireless Operators and Flight Engineers who served with the RAF during the War. This included the Royal Australian Air Force (RAAF), Royal Canadian Air Force (RCAF) and Royal New Zealand Air Force (RNZAF). RAF aircrew were also trained in the United States, one of them being Flight Lieutenant (F/Lt) Jeff Gray* who trained at No. 1 British Flying Training School (BFTS) Texas, flying Boeing PT-18 Stearmans, Vultee BT-13 Valiants and North American AT-6 Havards.

*F/Lt Jeff Gray was a pilot in 61 Squ and a comrade of Bill North. He is an integral part of Bill's story and a fascinating connection between the two men will be revealed as the drama unfolds (see Chapter 10).

It may seem strange that a British pilot should have to cross the Atlantic to train to be an RAF pilot, but there were sound reasons for this. Britain was not the safest place for an airman to train, airfields being the targets for the Luftwaffe, as Bill had already experienced during air raids at Torquay. There were also the problems of heavy air traffic at British airfields, and the uncertain British weather. Canada was chosen as the main location for training RAF aircrew and was advantageous for a number of reasons. It was considered to be safe from air attacks and had large, open airspaces, good weather and ground facilities; also abundant fuel supplies and supporting aircraft industries for training aircraft.

RCAF AT16 T6 Harvard IIB, D-FRCP (source, *Noorduyn Aviation, J Klank)*

A Vultee BT-13 Valiant (source, *United States Air Force*)

Bill now travelled up to Scotland to embark for Canada on the RMS Queen Elizabeth, which left from Gourock on the Firth of Clyde. It would take Bill - and the other prospective airmen on the BACTP scheme - on a six-day voyage to New York, en route for Canada. It was anchored at the 'Tail of the Bank' north of Gourock and Greenock, under a heavy cloak of secrecy. The Firth of Clyde became one of the busiest estuaries in Great Britain during WW2. The Home Fleet had temporarily moved here from Scapa Flow after U-Boats had attacked it, and hundreds of Merchant ships from the Atlantic Convoys gathered here after the Blitz of London's Docklands rendered it unsafe to dock in. It was also home to the Free French Navy and became the busiest drop off point for US Soldiers disembarking from troopships. You can imagine the hustle and bustle of ships docking with troops and equipment loading and unloading day and night.

The voyage to New York would not be without its perils. A ship as large, fast and useful as the Queen Elizabeth was an obvious target for the Germans, and it was with some difficulty that it had reached the safe port of Gourock in the first place. The British Government had gone to great lengths to protect the whereabouts and well being of this very important new ship whose use was vital to the war effort. It was launched in the presence of Queen Elizabeth (later the Queen Mother) on 27 September 1938 from Slipway Four at John Brown & Company in Clydebank, Scotland (where, coincidentally, my grandfather Donald Sutherland had been a welder until he moved out to Barbados in the 1930's. He was to later repair ships here that had been attacked by U-Boats). The much needed dock space was immediately taken by the HMS Duke of York for fitting out; it was the only British dock big enough for this class of warship.

A cunning deception was deployed to fool German spies into thinking RMS Queen Elizabeth was to be moved to Southampton in 1940 to be fitted out. In fact she stayed in Scotland for her fitting out; Southampton was bombed on the day she was due to arrive. The danger was if anything even more acute by the time Bill set sail on 13 September, 1942. The world news report for that day, which Bill might well have heard, reveals how fierce the conflict was:

**Chronology of World WarII (www.onwar.com/chrono/index.htm) News Report 13 September 1942**

In North Africa, the airfields at Benghazi and Barce are attacked by British units of the Long Range Desert Group. The British also attempt an amphibious landing at Tobruk, it is repelled with heavy losses.

In the Solomon Islands, on Guadalcanal, the Japanese attacks intensify. The American forces hold them off with difficulty, aided by effective artillery support.

In the Arctic, Convoy PQ-18 leaves for Archangel. It is provided with a large escort including a carrier and fares much better than the last convoy (in June). It loses 13 ships in the course of the voyage (September 12-18); the Germans lose 20 planes and 2 U-boats.

The docking point at Gourock called 'The Tail of The Bank'
(source, *w:User:Dave souza*).

Bill was now on board RMS Queen Elizabeth which was painted in wartime colours, the hull was black and the remaining structure was battleship grey. The Battle of the Atlantic was raging during 1942 and with no decrypts from Enigma for most of the year there were huge shipping losses. In the first 3 months of 1942 alone, 1.3 million tons of shipping was sunk. Although the Queen Elizabeth was fast, with U-Boats roaming as far as the Eastern Seaboard of the United States (even reaching the port of New York) to sink ships, the danger was still real and ever-present. By July 1942 there were approximately 300 U-Boats operating in Wolf- packs causing mayhem in Allied shipping lanes. The United States had now fully entered the War after the bombing of Pearl Harbour and were finally organising Atlantic Convoys. The struggle to supply Britain was now at its most crucial stage as U-Boats decimated merchant shipping and the build-up of supplies essential for a European invasion. It was the WW2's longest continuous military campaign. Winston Churchill was later to state, 'The Battle of the Atlantic was the dominating factor all through the war. Never for one moment could we forget that everything happening elsewhere, on land, at sea or in the air depended ultimately on its outcome.' (BBC documentary series, Battle of the Atlantic (2003), The Royal Navy History website)

As Bill mentions (see letter below) a very common worry or concern amongst anybody sailing in those days was to be torpedoed whilst asleep below deck. Luckily for Bill and the rest of the trainee airmen and crew, the Queen Elizabeth's high speeds allowed them to outrun German U-boats and they made it safely across the Atlantic without escorts or convoys.

The following letter was written by Bill to his Mum and Dad at the beginning his voyage. Bill was a great letter writer and it has an innocent and endearing quality about it that is very much of its time, you also get a real sense of how close his family is. As he explains in his letter home he is not allowed to mention the name of the ship for intelligence reasons, but gives them a good idea anyway.

**Left**, the RMS Queen Elizabeth painted in wartime colours prior to her secret maiden voyage in 1940.

**Right**, approaching New York (source, *www.greatoceanliners.net*).

**13 September 1942** (Bomber Command target for the night, Bremen)

*Dear Mum and Dad,*

*I've just finished my first tea meal on board this ship and as I now feel very satisfied, I'm starting with this letter, to which I hope to add a little each day.*
*First of all I must tell you a little about the food I've had today. The quality and quantity of it has been so good that I'm really quite ashamed. For tea we had as much cooked ham as we liked (you can take the 'as much as you like' quite literally), together with a really superb salad. We had real 'white' bread and as much butter as we wanted. I personally had a lump of butter that must have weighed a quarter of a pound at least. All other items of food are equally abundant. I tell you the amount and quality of the food I've had today really makes me ashamed when I think of you at home. We've all been issued with a life jacket and we've been instructed to wear it on all occasions — even when we pay the W.C. a visit. Already we've had life boat drill and we've to make ourselves familiar with the emergency signals, air raid signals and other danger signals. Naturally I'll do all these things as my skin means quite a lot to me. The accommodation, as I told you is not so good. There are twelve of us in a small cabin, or state room, and we are sleeping in three tier bunks. I'm sleeping in the second storey bunk, but I wish I was on top — then nobody could be seasick over me.*

*Monday 14 September 1942*
*Well folks we're now a day's sail from the Old Country and it's quite a queer feeling to look around and see nothing except water. We sailed late last night (or rather early today) at 2.00am so you can see we're well on our way.*
*Already lots of chaps have succumbed to seasickness, but so far—touch wood—I'm all right. Remember Ilfracombe?*

*Tuesday 15th*
*As you will imagine we are now well away from England's shores. This thought, to be quite frank is a little disconcerting, but the eats on board are maintaining their high standard and in this event, all trials are bearable. When the ships canteen opened this morning—sorry to make your mouths water—I bought myself one dozen oranges and half a dozen apples. I would have bought some more, but this was all I could carry at one time. Still I've got a plentiful stock of fruit in my webbing equipment so I'm not grumbling. Provided they give me plenty to eat I can put up with anything—even sea*

*sickness. I've an idea that Dad would thoroughly enjoy himself were he here now. The waves are terrific and they keep hurling themselves right over the bows of the ship and into the huge guns. The ship, though a very very large one is being rocked about quite a lot and lads are still getting seasick. Last night the lad in the bunk below me was sick, but fortunately he did not wake me up—you know me, I can sleep anywhere and anyhow. All I'm afraid of is that if the ship's torpedoed during the night I might keep on sleeping—huh! What a thought!*

*Since I've been on this 'boat trip' I've realised why people use such adjectives as 'relentless' to describe the sea. Believe me, just now it most certainly does look pretty savage and 'relentless' with waves of about twenty to forty feet high coming over the ship. Still, I can still realise why it is that men love the sea so much that they decide to make their living on it. When you look at the sea it really does something to you.*

*Every time I go on deck 'for a blow'* [a smoke] *I lean over the rail, look all around me, and then try to picture myself back at an office stool in Wallingford. At the moment I just can't imagine myself going back, but I'll probably 'be sensible' and end up what I originally was—a clerk!!*

*This afternoon we've to parade on the Promenade Deck, Port Side, Aft—getting quite nautical aren't I?—in PT kit. However, if the ship keeps rolling as she is at present I've an idea that PT isn't going to be very successful. Still I'll tell you all about it in due course.*

*Well I've now just come back from half an hour's PT and I've thoroughly enjoyed myself. We've been tearing up and down the deck and doing all sorts of mad strenuous exercises. Still you know I always like doing mad things. Actually about fifty of us should have been on this PT stunt, but only about fifteen of us turned up. The remainder were 'incapacitated'—you know what that means don't you? Nothing more or less than that old complaint- seasickness! Anyway I'm still feeling fit as a fiddle and have just had a lovely salt water bath, so I'm feeling really fine.*

*By the way I haven't told you before, but we're not sailing in convoy. The reason is that this ship is very fast indeed as it does about 35 knots, so you can see that nothing Jerry's got could possibly catch us if it came to a race. When I come home (see I'm talking of getting home even before I've got abroad!) I'll certainly shake you people by telling you the name of the boat I've sailed on. It really is a world famous ship, so you can see I'm very lucky. Nowadays though, the ship is literally bristling with guns. Dozens of .303's, 3 inch guns and I believe there's even a 6 inch gun on the ship, so you can see we're well able to take care of ourselves.*

*You know I'm thinking of Iris* [Bill's sister] *today, she starts Cathays School doesn't she? Poor little 'form two swat'!! Just tell her not to worry though—everybody's got to go through it and just tell her not to cry too much!!* [Cathays High School is mentioned in the Chapter on Cardiff] *Well I'm now going to tea—lots of the fellows aren't going because they're 'incapacitated'—but you know me, I'll have my tea even if I get sick as a dog. Just think of all that beautiful white bread and real butter. Will write some more tomorrow so cheerio for now.*

*Wednesday 16th*
*It's now eventide and most of today I've spent in the galley of the ship depriving potatoes of their vision. I had to be on this job from 1am until 10am and from 2pm until 5pm. First of all I had grave doubts about this job, but I've liked it so much that I've swapped with a mate of mine so as to go on at 1am again tomorrow morning. The whole attraction is—food. Today I've fed like a fighting cock. For breakfast I had four fried eggs, bacon and mincemeat and fried tomatoes. You know I actually got up from breakfast feeling that I couldn't eat anymore. If I'd wanted I could even have had more eggs. Dinner and tea were equally good with such delicacies as peaches with condensed milk. In addition to all this I've made friends with the second cook—a strapping fellow—so you can see I'm fixed all right. Boy am I looking forward to tomorrows breakfast! All I hope is that it's another four eggs. I don't know, I'll be fat as a pig by the time I get home in nine months time.*
*The ocean today has been very calm indeed and consequently, very few cases of seasickness have arisen. We had more boat drill today, but nothing more exciting. To be quite frank I'd rather like to meet up with 'something or other' so as to have a little excitement—provided, of course, nothing serious happens. So far however this voyage has been very uneventful. We've streamed along all on our own without seeing a single other ship. Well it's bed time now and so I'll write some more tomorrow.*

*Thursday 17th*
*This morning I was again on potato pealing and again I made a pig of myself at breakfast. The usual four eggs, umpteen rashers of bacon and fried tomatoes. I don't know, I'm seriously thinking of remustering to the Merchant Navy. Still the Merchant Navy lads certainly earn all their food. By the way do you remember a boy by the name of Terrence Prickett? He lives in Whitchurch Road and is about two or three years older than I. I first met up with him when I was in the 'Life Boys'* [now the Boy's Brigade]*—that's going back some time now—and he was my 'Senior.' Mother will probably remember his name, with a memory like hers!! Well anyway this lad is now on this boat with me and is actually on the same section of the*

*draft as I am but, as he's a Navigator, we'll still be separated when we land. Still, it's good to meet up with these old friends occasionally.*

*We've been making pretty good speed today and the ocean, while it isn't calm as it was yesterday, most certainly isn't rough. There's just a very nice swell and the ship is rolling quite gently.*

*I've just this minute come back from having tea with 'my friend the second cook' and although by now my recital of our menus must be annoying you I must tell you what I've just had for tea. Here it is, about half a dozen slices of lean cooked ham, salad consisting of the usual tomatoes, beetroot, lettuce etc, two poached eggs followed by a plum duff pudding* [a suet pastry and plum desert related to Spotted Dick], *plenty of bread and butter and jam. Remember how I used to eat over Christmas time? Well since I've boarded this ship this is how I've eaten. How on earth I've not been sick goodness only knows. By all the laws of Nature, what with eating the things I've eaten and the pitching of the vessel, I should now be stretched out in sick quarters.*

*Tomorrow we've to hand in our currency for exchange. I'm handing in £9-10s which I raised by withdrawing from my P.O.*[Post Office] *savings book, but I spent the odd shillings on razor blades, apples, oranges, biscuits etc, from the ship's canteen. Actually I've got about five or six shillings in silver on me, but they will only exchange notes up to the value of £10 and the highest denomination they'll change is £1, so you see £5 and £10 notes aren't a scrap of good to me.*

*You know those pocket drafts which you gave me some time ago have come in very handy during this voyage. Quite a number of leisure hours have been whiled away at this game and incidentally, I've yet to meet my master at this game on board ship. The only other things I've done during this trip is eat, sleep, read and play cards. From this later game I'm glad to announce a profit of about one shilling and sixpence.*

*Friday 18th*

*Well folks tonight will be our last night at sea as tomorrow we are due to dock. We're to have all our kit packed by eight o'clock tomorrow morning although there is a possibility that we may have to spend another day on the ship.*

*The weather all day has been very hot and sultry and as it is raining now, it looks as though we may be in for a stormy night. Till today I've been wearing only my sports shirt and PT shorts—this being the only way to keep reasonably cool. This afternoon I spent reading and sleeping on the deck in the sun and as a result of all this my face and arms, plus the 'V' of my chest exposed has become quite sunburnt.*

*This morning I handed in my currency, but I'm not getting the required dollars until I get to my next Station. I don't like this idea really as I've no receipt at all for my money. Still all I hope now is that the RAF does not try to 'do' me. By the way, although this trip comes to an end tomorrow, I don't think I'll post this letter for a day or two until I reach this RAF Station of mine. I'll just keep on adding a little each day.*

*Saturday 19th*
*It's now ten o'clock but we are still out of sight of land. However a 'Flying Fortress' with the American markings has been escorting us on and off and so it looks as though we shall be on dry land today sometime.*
*Last night the weather was exceptionally hot and sultry. So much so that at 3 o'clock this morning I awoke and with a pal of mine, decided to go on deck for the rest of the night. We went to sleep in a life boat shaped something like an airman's rubber dinghy, but before going to sleep I thought a little of you at home. You see, as we're now five hours behind you, while I was wondering around the deck at three in the morning with a blanket draped over my shoulders, you lot were probably having breakfast and Dad, as usual, was probably late for work. What a family we are, it's a wonder we're ever early enough for anything.*
*You know now we've come so close to the 'New World' all the American and Canadian soldiers on board are becoming very excited—Hm! I wonder why? The rest of us chaps are certainly fairly excited—but not for the same reason as the Americans. The time when I shall get excited is on my return journey. I don't know, hark at me, here am I talking about the return journey when I haven't even reached this 'foreign land' yet.*
*Well folks we've now been in America for some hours although I'm still on board ship and shall be until tomorrow morning when we shall probably continue our journey by train. I obviously can't tell you the name of the town I'm in at present, but I don't think I'm giving any secrets away when I say I've already seen some wonderfully high buildings and statues. The roads here are also very wide and obviously built for fast traffic. Statistics say that there are twenty nine million cars in this port and from what I've already seen; I'm quite prepared to believe all this.*
*One of the things which I like most though is the absence of a black out. I'm really glad to know that Hitler hasn't forced this evil upon every free nation yet. Well I've to be up for breakfast at six tomorrow and so I'll close for now.* [In fact German U-Boats that were surfacing on the Eastern Seaboard at night to attack shipping were very surprised that there was no blackout in force and used the bright coastal lights to their tactical advantage by silhouetting their targets]

*Tuesday 22nd*
*Well folks you may wonder why I've not written since Saturday last. Well the reason is simple, on Sunday morning I left the boat and the next 30 odd hours were spent in a train speeding to Canada. The train was typically American (or Canadian) and so I was unable to write whilst we were on the move. I arrived at MONCTON yesterday late afternoon and by six o'clock I was on fatigues* [work duties, normally in boiler suits] *owing to an emergency.*

[Bill had travelled roughly 755 miles up the Eastern Seaboard and arrived at 31 RAF Personnel Depot (PD) at Moncton, New Brunswick. Due to its central location in the Canadian eastern Maritime Provinces it was, and still is, a major distribution centre with road and rail transportation hubs. This made it an ideal location for the holding centre for aircrews before they were transferred to EFTS or back to Europe.]

*However, as I was on fatigues last night and this morning, I am now free this afternoon and am taking the opportunity of looking Moncton over. It seems to be quite a nice little town and the people seem to be quite friendly. I shan't be here for very long however as I expect to be posting to an EFTS* [Elementary Flight Training School] *in about three weeks. Still I shall send you a cablegram today and will give you a YMCA address to write to.*
*On the train journey from the States to this place we were catered for as regards food, by the Canadian Pacific Railroad, whilst we travelled on the Pennsylvania Railroad. Note they call them Rail<u>roads</u> here, not railways.*
*During the train journey people waved to us and everybody is exceptionally decent towards us. This coupled with the fact that the food is still extra good augurs well for the future.*
*Well folks I'm just going to search for a post office and find out how much this little lot is going to cost.*

*Don't forget to write good and soon.*

*Your loving son, always,*
*Bill*

Bill's constant reference to food is amusing and had me in stitches, but I think there is a good reason for this. Dennis Bartlett's sister Daphne provides critical insight into pre-war life and when WW2 brought rationing: There were nine members of the Bartlett family, so having no food caused real problems!

**Daphne Pearce:-**

*'The War changed a lot of things socially in this country, before the War there was a big gap between rich and poor. The working classes suffered real poverty; it was really hard for the bread winners to find work especially on the back of the Great Depression.* [As explained in the Chapter 1 – Growing Up In Cardiff, large areas of the country were affected by the Depression. South Wales, where Bill and his family lived, was one of the worst hit areas and suffered great hardships] *We had nine children in our family and more often than not we had no food. Our Mum worked as a servant/cleaner in a big house and couldn't always get work, our Dad was a bricklayer.*

*One time we had no food to eat and were desperate.Mum took me down to the vicarage in Blackwater* [near Camberley where the Bartlett family lived] *which was a big beautiful house, to see the vicar. We were shown into a large room in the vicarage where the vicar asked us what he could do for us. Mum explained how desperate we were and that she had no money to buy any food for the children. After she had finished the vicar reached into a draw in his desk and gave Mum two shillings and said 'this is all you can have please don't come back again.' I was about five years old and can remember this and the impression it made on me like it was yesterday. I wasn't particularly enamoured with the church, but we did get something to eat. Food was a real problem - we were constantly hungry.*

*In those days you had to pay to see a doctor or a dentist, there was no NHS until 1948 when Aneurin Bevan, the new Labour Minister of Health, changed all that. When the war came, as terrible as it was, it did bring with it opportunity and hope in the form of jobs. I was slightly too young to enlist, but two of my sisters went to work in munitions factories. One girl they knew was blown up whilst carrying a box of detonators, there was nothing left of the poor girl. My brothers went into the Armed Services and as you know Dennis volunteered for the RAF and Mum and Dad both found work, all of a sudden we all had money which made a big difference to our lives.*

*Bananas and canned fruit were real treats; I can remember chasing a 'spiv' who was selling bananas illegally down Great Titchfield Street in London with a crowd of girls. Even though rationing continued for sometime after the war, the gap between rich and poor had closed and things steadily improved. From 1948 we had free health care and access to doctors and dentists, so for us the war brought a radical change in lifestyle.'*

W/O Peter Knox* recalls a fascinating conversation he had with new aircrew in their Nissen hut in May 1944 which highlights the wide spread poverty suffered at the time: *'One by one these young men told of their bitter experiences in the Great Depression of the 1920's and 1930's. There was scarcely one who had not suffered genuine hardships. Some recalled being turned away from food shops which could not give their families any more credit. Others talked of the despair of their unemployed parents, of the lack of money for clothes. All were determined that there should be no going back to those days—it was an evening that convinced me that the Conservatives would lose any post-war election.'*

*W/O Peter Knox was an RAAF Bomb Aimer, friend and comrade of Bill's Bomb Aimer W/O Norman Jarvis. Peter and Norman travelled from Australia to England together in 1943. He alongside the other mentioned Bomber Command Veterans provides some critical eyewitness accounts of the events surrounding Bill's training missions and Operations. These accounts are taken from his War Diary which came courtesy of his daughter Jane Knox.

Because of the intense shortage of food products rationing was introduced to try to ensure everybody got equal amounts of food. As previously mentioned, German U-boat fleets were decimating the merchant fleets bringing vital food supplies from America. Ration books were issued to everybody and the amounts of food allowed varied weekly depending on what was available. On 8 January 1940 bacon, butter and sugar were the first products to be rationed. Then followed meat, fish, cheese, tomatoes, rice, jam, eggs, peas, canned fruit, biscuits, cereal, milk, dried fruit and cooking fat (source - *Imperial War Museum*).

All the food products mentioned by Bill are on the ration list and, given the poverty that existed in South Wales before the war, it is no wonder he is like a kid in a sweet shop when he discovers the abundance of food on the QE. To be presented with this veritable feast after meagre rations at home must, as he explains, have been food heaven. At the same time though he admits his sense of guilt at having to keep mentioning the large amounts of food to his family at home. The RAF did in fact make sure that their training crews and airmen were well supplied with food compared to ordinary civilians as it was perceived they deserved it due to the extreme stress and hardship they would be put through.

Bill mentioned one of the treats they always looked forward to after Operations was bacon and eggs, which were always readily available to aircrews. Incidentally, rationing in Britain lasted for 14 years until 4 July 1954, a far reaching consequence the country endured long after the war ended.................................

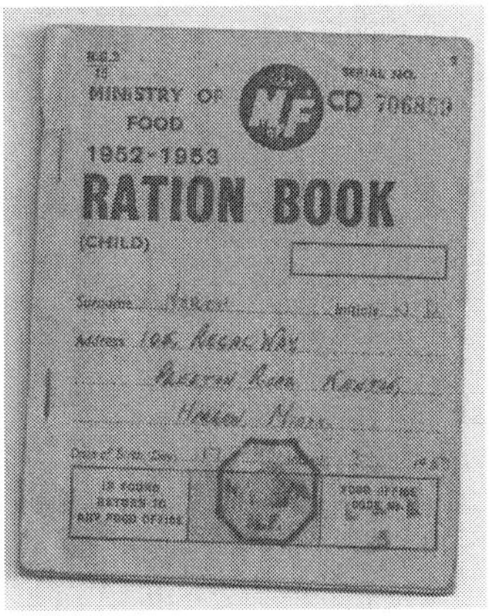


Copy of North family Ration Book.

After a four week break while held at 31 RAF Personnel Depot (PD), Moncton, Bill was transferred to 20 EFTS at Oshawa on the 25 October 1942. Oshawa, Ontario is located roughly 900 miles SW of Moncton by land journey and is near Toronto. This was the start of Royal Canadian Air Force flying training, to prepare him for perilous Night Operations with Bomber Command.

While Bill continued with his flying training in Canada, Bomber Command (BC) carried on with its visits to the German mainland but was undergoing some radical changes. By the end of 1942 BC received new technologies that would hone its effectiveness as a fighting force. The new Pathfinder Force (PFF)*1, had Oboe*2 fitted to its Mosquito force with H2S*3 introduced as well. Mandrel and Tinsel were two systems used to jam German radar and fighter communications, reducing efficiency of the German Night Fighter box defensive system called the Kammhuber Line.*4 By the beginning of 1943, with the expansion and reorganisation of Bomber Command and its new technology, it suddenly became a far more powerful and effective fighting force. The Main Force would also now be nearly doubled in size from an average of 250 planes to 450 planes per Operation.

*1 The PFF were new target marking Squadrons created within Bomber Command (see Chapter 11).
*2 Oboe was a 'blind bombing' navigational aid that used radio signals.
*3 H2S was a navigational aid and ground scanning radar system carried on board aircraft.
*4 The Kammhuber Line was the name given to the German night air defence system created in July 1940 by Colonel Josef Kammhuber.

# Chapter Four

## Canadian Flying Training

After the long train journey up from New York to 31 RAF, PD Moncton in Canada, and then on to Oshawa, Bill was now based at 20 EFTS, RCAF Oshawa. 20 EFTS was located in Oshawa from June 1941 to December 1944 and was one of the many training bases used in the British Commonwealth Air Training Plan. Trainees flew the de Havilland DH 82 Tiger Moth and were trained by civilian instructors from the Oshawa, Kingston, and Brant-Norfolk flying clubs (The airport is still in use today as Oshawa Airport).

**Left**, a Canadian DH-82C, Tiger Moth with perspex canopy. (source, *Canadian Forces*).
**Right**, a DH-82A, N81DH (source, *Towpilot*) The DH-82 Tiger Moth was in use by all Commonwealth training units and Bill flew in types A and C while in Canada.

On Sunday 25 Oct 1942 Leading Aircraftman (LAC) Bill North flew for the first time in Canadian airspace in DH 82 Tiger Moth serial no 5003 with Mr McFadden as his instructor. On his 13th flight (lucky for some) on 15 Nov, and after 10 hours flying time, he flew solo again. Bill had gone through sequences 1 to 16 which included: air experience, cockpit layout and drill, effect of controls, cruising straight and level flight, stalling, climbing and descending, medium turns, taking off into wind, engine failure, engine assisted approach and landing, spinning, climbing turns, side slipping and steep turns.

Bill flew 75 times in Tiger Moths at Oshawa, clocking up 69 hours and 30 minutes flying time. 30 of those flights were solo; the rest were with a variety of instructors, including Mr McFadden, Mr Carruthers, Mr Ozarko, and numerous others.

During Bill's stay at EFTS Oshawa from 25 Oct to 17 Dec 1942, two major WW2 battles took place that decisively influenced the course of the War. The tide of the War had now clearly turned, and the intense training Bill was now undertaking would help Bomber Command drive home victory in the final years of the War. As Bill took his much welcomed leave over Xmas from 17 Dec to the 28 Dec 1942, the German 6th Army at Stalingrad were teetering at the point of defeat after the Russian counter attack on the 19 November 1942. The German general population were stunned at this defeat after Field Marshal Friedrich von Paulus surrendered what was left (91,000 men) of the mighty 6th Army on 31 January 1943. The crushing defeat at Stalingrad was first time that the Nazi's had publicly acknowledged a failure in its war effort. The War for Germany was now at a turning point; on the Eastern Front it would be fighting a constant retreat back into its homeland.

In North Africa the Second Battle of El Alamein was taking place from 23 October to the 11 November 1942. Hitler's favourite General, Field Marshal Erwin Rommel (the Desert Fox), was defeated by the Allies, ending his intentions of occupying Egypt, taking control of the Suez Canal and gaining access to the Middle Eastern oil fields. Winston Churchill famously said, 'Before Alamein we never had a victory. After Alamein we never had a defeat.' El Alamein was the first land battle against the Germans in which the Western Allies were triumphant. Winston Churchill also famously summed up the battle on 10 November 1942 with the words, 'This is not the end, it is not even the beginning of the end. But it is, perhaps, the end of the beginning.'

These decisive battles shattered the myth that the German Army was invincible and were huge morale boosters to the Western Allies. I asked Bill what his impressions were at this time, when these victories were announced while he was training in Canada; *'I remember it being announced in the press and it was a huge boost to morale. It felt like there was a glimmer of hope and the training we were doing would make a real difference.'*

The devastated city of Stalingrad. Soviet soldiers attack a house, 1943. (source, *RIA Novosti archive, image #44732, Zelma)*

Bill North, next to DH-82 Tiger Moth at the RAF Museum Hendon, Sunday 28 Feb 2010 (CK).

*'I can remember taking off for the first time by myself in the Tiger Moth and looking back down at the airstrip; as I climbed away I thought that was easy. I then suddenly thought blimey I've got to land this thing by myself soon! Anyway I landed with no problems and really enjoyed flying in Tiger Moths. I loved that aircraft.'*

Part of preparing the trainee pilots for night flying was to practice in the Link trainer. This was the first Flight Simulator, designed by Ed Link, and focused on flying by instruments alone (blind flying), although basic by today's standards it worked extremely well providing invaluable life saving training. They were used by all the Allied Air Forces for basic instrument training. (The Link Company is now a part of L-3 Communications and still constructs flight simulators). Between 3 Nov to 13 Dec 1942 Bill spent 10 hours and 45 mins on the Link 'C' trainer. On 17 December Bill got a 61% mark from the chief Link instructor at Ontario County Flying Training School, Mr Dobson.

**F/Lt Bill North**

*'The pilot would get inside the Link, then the cover would be shut so you were in the dark. The instrument panel was lit up and the motion was controlled by pneumatic pumps that would make it move from side to side etc. The instructor would be sitting at an adjacent control desk monitoring your progress.'*

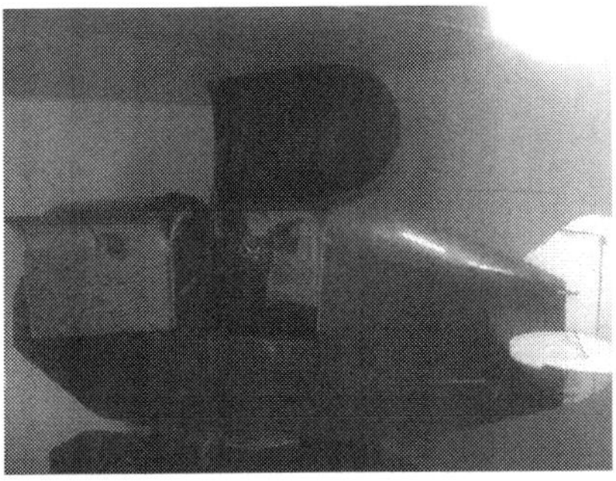 

**Left**, Link Trainer at Aviation Heritage Centre (CK) and **right**, at the Western Canada Aviation Museum (Photo by Bzuk).

Bill now went on a well-earned leave over Christmas from 17 Dec to 28 Dec 1942. He was then transferred to No 9 Service Flying Training School (SFTS), RCAF Centralia. This training base was located 156 miles SW of Oshawa and just outside the village of Centralia near Exeter, Ontario.

1943, No 20 EFTS Oshawa, Canada. Bill is top row, 5th from the right of the Tiger Moth.

This is the back of the photograph taken at 20 EFTS and is traditionally signed by those men present. At the top of the document third from the right is the signature of George Langford, Bill's mate from ITW and later Stalag Luft 1.

Now that Bill had completed his Elementary Flying Training, he moved up to the more advanced level of Service Flying Training, which was located at No 9 SFTS RCAF Centralia. The trainee pilots flew Ansons and Harvards - much bigger planes than the Tiger Moths Bill was used to.

After two weeks of lectures and theory Bill flew in the Anson Mk II (twin Jacobs engines) 704 for the first time, flying solo after 10 flights on the 5 Feb 1943. The Avro Ansons were used for advanced instrument training. Bill now proceeded onto sequences 16 to 27: Flying instruments, steep turns, low flying, precautionary landings, forced landings, taking off in and out of wind, aerobatics, night flying, cross country test, formation flying. He was now being prepared to fly on instruments at night for Bomber Command Operations.

Avro Anson, military trainer WD413, of the Air Atlantique Historic Flight, Hullavington Airfield, Wiltshire, England (source, *Arpingstone*).

From 14 Jan 1943 to 5 April 1943 Bill spent another 38 hours and 15 mins on Link E and D trainers, scoring 66% from Link Commanding Officer F/O Bennet. Up to the 29 April 1943 Bill flew in Ansons 137 times, clocking up 223 hours 20 minutes flying time and going solo 40 times.

On 26 April 1943 Bill North took and passed his wings test with F/Lt Huffman and became Sgt Pilot 13322055 (source, *Bill North*).

In Bill's Log Book was a notice: 'AN AIRCRAFT CRASHED THROUGH YOUR CARELESSNESS OR DIOSBEDIENCE WILL DIVERT WORKERS FROM BUILDING BOMBERS AND FIGHTERS TO REPAIRING TRAINING AIRCRAFT.'

Some of Bill's instructors at No. 9 SFTS (1 Squadron) were:-F/O Maffre, F/Lt Parish, P/O Patterson, P/O Dunbar (55 times) and a further 16 other men.

On the 5 May 1943 Bill was transferred back to 31 RAF Personnel Depot (PD) at Moncton. Moncton PD was a holding centre for RAF men on their journeys to and from the training bases in Canada and for the next three weeks Bill said he carried on with PE and other less intense tasks that were not to do with flying training.

Now that Bill's Service Flying Training was complete, he was to be sent back to England to continue with Operational Training, the last phase of training before he would be sent into action and fly missions. Bill's ship back to Britain was to leave from New York, but rather than wait for the official transport Bill and his mate Tedd Treeves left Moncton on 27 May 1943 and decided to hitchhike their way down to New York. Bill said they had a fantastic adventure on their journey, but he lost touch with Tedd during the war and always wondered what happened to him.

Bill thinks they travelled back across the Atlantic on the RMS Queen

Mary, which was the sister troop-carrying ship to RMS Queen Elizabeth. He said there were a lot of American servicemen aboard the ship as well. Again it was a dangerous voyage and Bill was well aware of this as they were still prime targets for the German U-Boats and Lufwaffe. Just one month earlier the troopship SS Banfora was in a Mediterranean Convoy alongside HMT Rhona, when the Rhona was hit and sunk by the first radio guided missile launched in a Lufwaffe bomber attack. (1015 American servicemen died in the sinking which was kept secret for 50 years. Bill's future comrade from 61 Squ, F/Lt Jeff Gray, had sailed to New York in the SS Banfora on 7 April 1942.) Bill arrived back at No 7 Personnel Reception Centre (PRC) at Harrogate on 4 June 1943 staying there until 5 July 1943. (Harrogate is a spa town located in North Yorkshire and has good rail and road links which made it an ideal transfer point for Allied Forces held at PRC.)

Troopship SS Banfora (Image from postcard by *Beken of Cowes, Simplon-The Passenger Ship Website*).

**<u>F/Lt Bill North</u>**

*'After I got back from Canada I flew in the Oxford Airspeed for the first time at an Advanced Flying Unit at RAF Chipping Norton. This was when the serious flying experience started. I was well aware of the constant air war being waged against Germany during my training and read about it in the press and heard about it through my training units. It was still a morale booster for the Country even though the aircrew losses were very high and I personally couldn't wait to get into action.'*

From the 6 July 1943 to the 15 September 1943 Bill clocked up another 83hrs 30mins flying time in Oxford Airspeeds at No 6 (P) Advanced Flying

Unit (AFU). Bill's comrade F/Lt Jeff Gray finished his Advanced Flying Training at No 6 AFU just 5 weeks before Bill arrived and provides a fascinating account of how these AFU's concentrated on training the men to use the aircraft's instruments. Bill had followed virtually the same path as Jeff Gray through training with both men eventually serving at 61 Squ. Jeff Gray arrived at 61 Squ on 26 Oct 1943, just over 6 months before Bill's arrival in May 1944. This is the first of some unique eyewitness accounts provided by Jeff Gray that add much colour to Bill's journey through Bomber Command.

**F/Lt Jeff Gray**

*'The CO at No 6 AFU really concentrated on training us to focus on our instruments when we were flying. This was to sharpen us up for flying in the dark. There was one particular method he used to simulate flying at night; this was practised during the day time. The perspex inside the cockpit would be covered up with sheets to darken the interior and then the instrument panel would be strongly illuminated. However, I didn't care much for this method as my flying goggles used to steam up from the lack of ventilation! This CO also pioneered a method of landing at night using a flare path down one side of the runway, so long as the flares were on your right coming into land you were ok. He later became part of the team that worked on FIDO* which was a system developed for landing in fog. He also had a mention in the Foreword of a book called 'Aircrew Unlimited.'*

*Fog Investigation and Dispersal Operation (see Chapter 13).

Oxford AS10 Airspeed (source, *Bob Brown, www.airline.net/photo/uk*).

No 6 (P) AFU used the airfields at Little Rissington and Windrush (both in Gloucestershire) Chipping Norton (in Oxfordshire), No 1517 at Chipping Warden (in Northamptonshire) for Beam Approach Training), and Chedworth (in Gloucs for Night Flying Training). Bill also continued with his instruction on the Link Trainer at these training bases. From the total on Canadian Link Trainers of 38hrs 15 mins, he added another 22hrs 45mins, totalling 60hrs 50mins on the flight simulator. Bill flew solo 34 times and some of Bill's instructors on Oxford Airspeeds were, P/O Bennett, Sgt Sessions, F/Sgt Ireland plus numerous others.

1943 saw Bomber Command return from a brief, but unsuccessful attempt at destroying the U-Boat bases in NW France in the first months of the year. Under AVM Arthur Harris' command, they now commenced a sustained and major effort against mainland Germany lasting for the remainder of Bill's RAF training.

Jeff Gray and Percy Cannings,* who flew 22 Ops with 100 Squadron, both served in Bomber Command during these daunting offensives against Germany. 5/6 March to 24/25 July 1943, Battle of the Ruhr, 24/25 July 3/4 Aug 1943, Battle of Hamburg, 3/4 Aug to 18 Nov 1943, Battle of Berlin 1st phase, 18/19 Nov to 31 March 1944, Battle of Berlin 2nd phase.

*Percy Cannings is another Bomber Command Veteran that I met and interviewed, who served with 100 Squ during 1943 and 97 Squ (PFF) during 1944. He like Jeff Gray has a fascinating connection to Bill North and his crew. He also provides some crucial eyewitness accounts of events linked to Bill's Operations (see Chapters 11 and 13).

We now one by one, meet Bill's crew, following them through the various stages of their RAF training, the paths that led to them meeting him and eventually forming a seven man Lancaster crew. The names of Bill's crew are mentioned below and will become very familiar as the story continues. Les Morton, (Flight Engineer), Dave Crowley, (Navigator), Norman Jarvis, (Bomb Aimer), Monty Montieth, (Wireless Operator), Dennis Bartlett, (Mid-Upper Gunner) and Eddy O'Shea, (Rear Gunner).

# <u>Chapter Five</u>

## War Diary, W/O Norman E. Jarvis

On 5 May 1943, 6 days before Bill's 21st Birthday, Bomber Command's target for the night was Mannheim. After the German Army's devastating defeat at Stalingrad at the beginning of the year, the Russians were forcing the Nazi's into a continuous, but hard fought retreat. As the War reached a turning point, Bill North's crew were slowly being drawn together from across 'the Empire'. This is the background to Norman Jarvis's journey to England from Australia and his eventual meeting with Bill North at OTU.

Norman Jarvis (source, *Pam Livingstone)*

The following is word for word as Norman Jarvis wrote it, except for some small spelling corrections to geographical references. One gets a real sense of the time, the history, the journey to and from home and the person himself. It is almost like being a fly on the wall, with his innermost thoughts and feelings laid bare. Having read this War Diary many times over and spent hours and hours typing it up from the original documents, I've found the more you read it the more you feel you get to know the man. I have woven his testament into the story and his eyewitness accounts of RAF training, Operations and POW life are fascinating. To begin with Norman Jarvis guides us through a sea journey from Brisbane to San Francisco, then by rail across America to New York and once again by sea to England. Throughout his diary his fascination with people, farming and places is endearing and his detailed description of the journey is colourful, eloquent and emotive.

**W/O Norman Jarvis**

*'It was 5 May 1943, when I struggled up the gangway of the Matson Liner,* the 17,000 tons U.S. Armed Merchantman to leave my native shores for the first time.*

**Matson Line's 'White Fleet'* included the *SS Mariposa, SS Monterey, SS Malolo and SS Lurline,* all were used by the US as fast Troopships.

*The kit we aircrew carry was no light burden and perspiration streamed down our faces when we finally got on deck with it, the temperature was high for the time of year, or maybe it was only because we had never been to such a latitude before. Brisbane was a very attractive little city and I think we were all just a little disappointed at not seeing more of it before setting out on our great adventure.*

*Once on board we skipped down below and changed our heavy blue uniforms and emerged in the more practical tropical wear of khaki shorts and shirt to explore the ship which was to be our home for the next sixteen days. Contrary to our expectations we did not leave harbour until the following morning, so the first night was spent below on our three tier canvas bunks. I was fortunate to be still with my three closest pals---Pete, Alan and Charlie. We all rose early on the morning of the 7th to watch our progress down the wide Brisbane River to the open sea, where we sighted a destroyer with our interests at heart. That was encouraging anyway, but as the Australian shores dipped below the horizon we all experienced a queer sort of sadness and for the very good reason that many of the keen young faces peering over the railing would never see Australia again, but find graves on the far distant shores, some Germany, some France and others in the sea or perhaps training in England.*

*I was not long in getting my sea legs on the calm old Pacific and never once during the whole trip did I feel at all sea sick. We were a day out from Brisbane when we passed the hospital ship Centaur* heading homeward with her big red crosses showing very prominently, but evidently the Jap subs were blind to them because it was sunk a few hours later by the cowardly dogs.'*

*The *Australian Hospital Ship (AHS) Centaur* was attacked and sunk by the Japanese submarine *I-177*, off the coast of Queensland on 14 May 1943. Of the 332 on board there were only 64 survivors who were rescued by the *USS Mugford.* There was widespread public outrage at the sinking, but Japanese Submarines continued to attack shipping off the Australian coastline. The *Matson Liner* which Norman was travelling on could quite easily have been sunk too.

AHS Centaur (source, *Australian War Memorial*).

*'We heard of The Centaur disaster on the radio the next day and it made us realise the peril that a lone ship was exposed to in the Pacific in those days. The destroyer was no longer with us, but we had heavy guards posted. The aircrew passengers assisted by taking watch in shifts which helped the American Merchant seamen, but the guns were manned by U.S. Naval personnel.'*

The I-176, was a KD7 type Kaidai class submarine. Japanese Rear Admiral Kaneyoshi Sakamoto, stated that Hajime Nakagawa and I-177 were responsible for the attack on the Centaur in his 1979 book History of Submarine Warfare. (source, Stille, Mark; Bryan, Tony (2007). *Imperial Japanese Navy Submarines 1941-45*. Osprey Publishing. p. 18. ISBN 1846030900).

*I was only on watch one night; it is a tiring, lonely job and I was glad when it finished and my turn did not come round again as Alan and I got ourselves employment in the ships stores; so we fared very well for grub on the remainder of the voyage. Entertainment on board was good. We had a small cinema, a good library and numerous deck games; the evenings were very quiet though because of the blackout regulations. Sunbathing was very popular. We used to lie there on deck watching the flying fish and as we moved further north, schools of flying fish and porpoises followed the boat. It grew hotter all the time and we stayed late on the deck in the evenings; those tropical nights are certainly wonderful, the moon and the various constellations of the stars. Nearing the equator the old Southern Cross was soon to desert us and we would soon be seeing the Big Dipper and the North Pole Star for the first time.*

*Crossing the imaginary line which is the equator was not celebrated with the usual custom of 'dipping' because we had no pool, but we were all given a certificate by the Captain. Boat drill was becoming a bind, two or three times a day the alarm was sounded and we all had to put on life belts and take stations for abandoning ship; they had got wind of a couple of subs skulking behind us, I believe. Our next big interest was crossing the International Dateline thus giving us two successive Sundays which is in itself a unique experience for land lubbers like myself. I only attended one Church service however, but on both occasions I heard our rather promising choir sing that very appropriate hymn 'For Those In Peril On The Sea.* [On each of the Sundays there was a Church service in which the choir sang 'For Those In Peril On the Sea', Norman only attended one service]

*On the 14 May we ran into some very bad weather and the ship was tossed about like a cork. The sea spray was coming up well above the deck and the terrific wind made it impossible for us to stay on deck. This meant to the seamen aboard that we were nearing the west coast of America, but the first indication we got was the sight of a Catalina Flying boat hovering out to our starboard.*

*On the evening of the 16 May we could see land, the first since leaving Brisbane and wondered where it really was. The behaviour of our sailors soon told us that it was the islands outside of San Francisco; by night we were sailing into that beautiful harbour, up under the Golden Gate Bridge with the now dim lights of the old Barbary Coast City* [An old name for the San Francisco Red Light district.] *silhouetted against the skyline high above us.*

*The remainder of the night was spent on board, but we awoke early the next morning to gaze at a fleet of naval craft in the harbour. Battleships, Cruisers, Aircraft Carriers and Destroyers were all there not to mention the smaller ships. Over the other side of the harbour was that famous prison island of Alcatraz and above us roared many different types of American warplanes.*

*It was somewhere about 11 o'clock when I first set my feet on American soil. We were moving straight away and were put into a ferry that took us across the bay to Oakland. It was a very interesting trip over and we passed under the second famous bridge, The Oakland, which is the longest in the world. At Oakland we boarded the train that was to take us right across the American continent. We found to our great satisfaction that we were travelling in Pullman sleeping cars and each little group of us had a Negro porter to look after our special requirements on the journey—ours proved a great asset and with small tips would do anything for us. At every station on the route he would bring in refreshments when we could not get off ourselves.*

*Our first day on the train was spent crossing the great red soil of California with its orchards and orange groves. I think the most attractive city we stopped at in this state was Sacramento, a lovely place with dark green avenues and clean white houses. The following day we were speeding across the prairies of the Nevada, mile after mile of sage and brush with the Great Plains rolling off to the snow-capped hills in the distance and studded here and there by cattle ranches. We got off the train to stretch our legs for a few hours at a place called Elko. Here we found the inhabitants resembled the movie versions of Western films and they gave us a good reception.*

*Utah was the next Western State to cross, but it differed from Nevada because of its great wastelands and salt lakes. Then later on the most interesting city where the Mormons settled so long ago, it seemed like an oasis to us and we could just see the Mormon church of Salt Lake City from where we were. My favourite state came next, Colorado, where we followed the river by the same name right up through the Rocky Mountains with the towering canyon walls on either side of the train; then the Royal Gorge which is magnificent and bridged by a structure 1000ft above the river bed.*

*We crossed the Rockies at Tennessee Pass at the altitude of 10,000 ft above sea level and still there were whole peaks towering above us on either side. Springtime in the Rockies is a sight that will stay in my memory for all time. We went down the eastern slopes following the fast flowing Arkansas River into the State of Kansas home of such famous old Wild West scouts as Ret Carson and others. It is now a land of fertile pastures and crops of all descriptions. We stepped off the train at Kansas City for a spell and had quite a good look around; the inhabitants found us something new and as we walked around we were mobbed and asked all sorts of questions. However the boys did not mind the forward advances of some of the female population.*

*Ohio was another agricultural state well blessed with rich soil and the waters of many rivers, but as we went eastwards we got more into the industrial parts of it and were very impressed with that modern city of Cleveland. Crossing Minnesota I can't remember a great deal except the twin cities of St Paul and Minneapolis with the Mississippi River flowing broad and full.*
*Illinois was next with its vast wheat fields and then the great inland fresh water lakes and the city of Chicago which we did not see too well because where we detrained was just in the coloured section. At the end of seven days we arrived at our destination, an American staging camp at Taunton Mass,* [Massachusetts] *south of Boston. This camp was different to any I had previously been in; the barracks were not dissimilar, but the camp administration and set-up was.*
*There were huge service clubs to which girls from the out-lying towns always came to act as hostesses and dance with the boys—the Australians soon became great favourites and we had a grand time and were invited into the homes of many people: these good looking stylish girls really showed the then bronzed and fit Aussie aircrew what hospitality was. We learned to appreciate their different customs and ways of living and had a very happy time. Perhaps I should mention here that we were not required to work, but had occasional parades and were waiting for transport across to England. There was a big lake near the camp where we used to swim and fish day after day, then go dancing or to a film in the evening—yes they were happy, lazy days!*
*Then came our turn to visit New York. We went up there by train one afternoon and stayed two days and three nights. Here we saw all that we could, in the time available, of the world's wonder city with its gay night life and rush and fare of daylight. My gang made their way to the Anzac Club on 49th Street and 6th Avenue, which is a pretty central place to operate. Here we obtained good rooms and an invitation to tour some of the night clubs, which we did that night. The night never seems to end in this great city; we dined, danced and finally slept a few hours, but the morning held too much for us, so we rose early and after seeing over the Rockefeller Centre we watched a show at the Radio City Music Hall, the largest theatre in the world; that night I saw The Stage Door Canteen* at which Ruth Hussey the film actress was a guest.'*

*Stage Door Canteen, was a musical film made in 1943, based on the famous New York entertainment centre for the Armed Services of the same name.

**Left,** *Stage Door Canteen* poster, courtesy of United Artists, MGM. **Centre,** Ruth Hussey, still from trailer, *The Philadelphia Story* (1940), courtesy of MGM. **Right,** *Radio City Hall,* New York, (source, adapted from original photo by *Matt H. Wade*)

*Next day we went to the top of the Empire State Building, the world's tallest skyscraper, then out to the Hudson River and many other sightseeing trips. We returned to camp tired but full of enthusiasm for New York and the way it treats the men of the fighting services. We also found that contrary to our expectations our draft was not yet sailing, so we could go off on leave, this time to Boston.*
*It would be difficult to describe all the places of interest we visited in this fine old city, but I must mention the people with whom Alan and I stayed during our time here. They took us into their home and treated us like their own sons. We visited Harvard College with them and also attended the College Girl's Graduation, which was very impressive and we were introduced to the young ladies afterwards and attended some of their parties. It was near the end of June 1943 that we said good-bye to our American friends and got ready to leave: I shall never forget sailing down New York harbour past the Statue of Liberty with the Manhattan skyline fading into the twilight. It was thrilling too, to think that we were at last on our way to England and on the world's greatest sea liner the Queen Elizabeth.'*

On the 13 Sept 1942 Bill North had sailed on the Queen Elizabeth from Gourock to New York and now 9 months later Norman Jarvis was on board the QE sailing from New York to Greenock which was next-door to Gourock on the Firth of Clyde. Both mention the speed of the trip and it is a testament to the great liner that she carried on transporting troops across the dangerous Atlantic Sea right through the war, carrying as Norman mentions up to 22,000 troops at a time. It is interesting to note that both Bill and Norman mention the ships defensive armament and that they both felt very safe on the QE.

**Norman Jarvis continues:**

*'The Atlantic crossing was of great interest to us, but the mighty liner was very crowded and the Australian Air Crew on board only made a small minority of the 22,000 troops it carried on that single journey. We watched the sailors doing their target practise and were quite reassured by the armament carried on it and confident that any enemy aircraft that could catch us would have to fight as well. The speed of that trip was amazing and we saw the Northern coast of Ireland after only four days out. By about two o'clock we were sailing up the Firth of Clyde and the quaint little stone houses and lovely green hills of that part of Scotland impressed us very much. As we made our way along half a dozen Spitfires came down to our deck level at terrific speed and did a roll before climbing speedily away into the blue. Then came the rush and bustle of disembarkation at Greenock; our heavy kit was already going ashore and we were not long following it. The customs officials did not worry us and there were the RAF looking smart and efficient in their lighter uniforms which we were to see so much of in the future.'*

We next meet up with Norman Jarvis in Brighton and then follow his journey to Bill's home country Wales. Coincidently the rest of Bill's crew were also doing their RAF training in Wales too.

# Chapter Six

## Bill's crew at RAF Training schools (Advanced Flying Training, Bomb Aiming, Navigation, Wireless Operation and Air Gunnery)

We now take a detailed look at Bill's crew and the journey they went on through their RAF training. Due to less information on Dave Crowley, Eddy O'Shea and Monty Montieth we use accounts here from Bill North, Dennis Bartlett, Les Morton and Norman Jarvis to follow the crew. To begin with we pick up Bill's Bomb Aimer Norman Jarvis as he arrives at Brighton after disembarkation at Greenock after his long journey from Australia. Again to help set the war time scene we look at some current news headlines.

### Thursday 8 July 1943, News Check

'On the Eastern Front, the battle of Kursk continues. The German advance in the north is less than one mile. To the south the German commanders remain hopeful of a breakthrough, but the rate of attrition remains high. Soviet strong points prove difficult to overcome. Meanwhile, Red Army counterattacks prevent substantial gains.

In the Solomon Islands, on New Georgia, US forces make some gains near the Barike River.

In the Atlantic, the British Home Fleet cruises off Norway, but the Germans fail to notice them. The British intention is to draw attention away from the Mediterranean operations.'

### W/O Norman Jarvis

*'My impressions of Britain up to now were very good, there did not seem to be a lot of bomb damage and they surprised us by giving us a very hearty meal as soon as we got on the train. This showed that the people were far from starving as we had for some time imagined.* On the journey south it was amazing to see the changes of terrain and scenery over such short intervals and everything looked just as I pictured in my imagination, small green fields surrounded by hedges, lovely old stone villages and towns. Later on down through the Midlands we got we got into the industrial fogs of those famous manufacturing towns and saw where the Luftwaffe had left their mark. We were in London soon afterwards and trying to see more of the 'Empire Capital' that day then was possible. Our destination was*

*reached when we got off the train at Brighton on the South Coast on the 8 July 1943. The billets soon proved highly satisfactory to us as they were two of the largest hotels on the sea front and would have cost perhaps £20 a week to stay at in peacetime; then we had a very good meal served in a neat mess by the first English WAAF's I had seen.*

*This was more to do with the RAF feeding its aircrew well, in 1943 the general population were on rationing and the country was still suffering from the affects of The Battle of The Atlantic.

*Our stay at Reception Depot was not very long, but we had a gay time in this famous old peacetime resort. It was here too that I experienced my first air raid, as 'Jerry' was only a quarter of an hour's flying time away we must expect a few bombs. The first time you hear the sirens go it chills your blood just a little, the low moan sounds almost like a death knell, but this time the bombs were dropped up the coast about a mile and the roar of the guns was terrific. My first impulse was to rush out and see what was going on, but wiser and more experienced veterans of the Blitzes warned us to stay in the basement of the hotel or take shelter.*
*With only one parade daily life was swell here and we learned to know the town inside out and in fact a lot of the south coast of Sussex, the South Downs are very pretty countryside, mostly agricultural. For our leave Charlie and I went to stay on a farm down in Malvern, Worcestershire, where we had an excellent time for about four days. During this time I was interested in the farming methods of England and noted how much they varied from ours at home and was very impressed with the amount of food produced per acre using these wartime measures.*
*Unfortunately we were recalled back to H.Q. and told that our postings had come through and we were to proceed straight away to RAF Penrhos in North Wales, where our Advanced Flying Training was to begin. Of course we were excited about the whole thing and had had a very good time for the past few months. Alan Duggleby was unlucky and had to have his appendix out so he could not join us; that meant his place was filled by Norman Page a lad who I did not know then, but has since been sharing experiences with me.'*

Norman Jarvis on leave. St Giles Cathedral, Edinburgh 1944.

RAF Penrhos, 70 Course Bomb Aimers, **Left**, top row, Peter Knox, 1st on the left, bottom row, Charlie Kroschel, 1st on left, Norman Jarvis 2nd on left, 1st on right Norman Page. **Right**, middle row, Norman Jarvis, 2nd from left, Norman Page is standing directly beneath him. Peter Knox is behind Norman to his right.

A large part of the Welsh coastline was requisitioned by the Air Ministry for training RAF aircrews and we will look at some of the bases mentioned by Bill's crew. Wales played a vital role in the War effort; it had virtually become one large RAF base with its airspace crammed with training flights and the towns full of trainee aircrew.

RAF Penrhos was an airfield located on the Llyn Peninsula near Pwllheli Gwynedd. It was operational from 1 February 1937 to 21 October 1946 for armament training, navigation, bombing and gunnery schools. In 1936 the Air Ministry also established an RAF bombing school at Penyberth; ideal for bombing practise this included an area of low plateau. RAF Hell's Mouth, 5 miles to the south west was also commissioned in February 1937 as a relief airfield and later an emergency landing drome for RAF Penrhos.

Bill North's crew were all in RAF Training School's learning their various trades. Bill was unsure if Norman Jarvis, Dave Crowley or Monty Monteith had ever crossed paths at all, but they were all on No. 70 courses. Dennis Bartlett was at the No 1 Air Gunnery School at RAF Pembrey, Norman Jarvis was at RAF Penrhos and Llandwrog and Les Morton was at RAF St Athans. We are not sure where Eddy O' Shea did his Air Gunnery Training, but it is quite possible that it was in the same schools.

No 70 Course, Navigators and Wireless Operators/Air Gunners. **Left**, Bill's WOP, Sgt Monty Monteith, top row, 2nd from left, 1st on left next to him is Sgt Thomas A Newbery, WOP from P/O Davis' ME846 crew. **Right**, Bill's Navigator, F/Sgt Dave Crowley, middle row, 1st on right, 1st row 2nd from right is P/O Davis' Nav, F/Sgt Leslie EJ 'Tag' Taylor.

A quick aside on the many 'coincidences' I have experienced while writing the book: As I was inserting the above photos into the script I discovered yet another connection between Bill's crew and Peter Knox's crew. Amongst the men in the pictures the name Newbery seemed to be familiar. I checked the photo of Sgt Newbery on the Knox family web site and it matched. I then did the same for F/Sgt Taylor in the WOP's course and that matched too. The Navigators, Bomb Aimers, Wireless Operators and Mid-Upper Gunners in the two crews were all training together at Penrhos and next to each other in the 70 Course class photos. It makes perfect sense that they all knew each other and had the same picture as Bill taken by the same Stirling at 1661 HCU in March 1944 (See Chapter 24 for ME846, Crew photo).

RAF Pembrey was located 17 miles west of Swansea and played a major role in Britain's defences as home to both fighter and bomber aircraft. The airfield had passed to No. 1 Air Gunnery School (AGS) on 15 June 1941. Bristol Blenheim's and Westland Lysander's were used as training aircraft initially and later replaced by Avro Ansons. Pembrey was also used for the testing of a/c and equipment and the Gunnery School ran some 114 courses before being disbanded on 14 June 1945. Penros and Pembrey both came under 25 Group RAF. (David Annand)

Dave Crowley (Navigator) and Monty Monteith (Wireless Operator) would both have followed a similar journey to the others. From volunteering, to medicals, Reception Centres, ITW, Navigator and Wireless Schools, to meeting Bill at OTU (See Chapter Seven for their crew duties).

Dennis Bartlett now explains some of his experiences volunteering and then training as an Air Gunner, the theory parts would have been the same ones that Bill studied on his WOP/AG course at ITW in Blackpool. As Bill's Rear Gunner Eddy O'Shea would have gone through the same schooling as Dennis. The Lancaster Bomber's Air Gunners needed a combination of essential attributes to be competent at their crew positions. Norman Jarvis also received Gunnery training and could operate the front gun turret if necessary. As well as the a/c defenders Bill's two main Gunners Dennis Bartlett and Eddy O'Shea were also lookouts for fighters and potential mid-air collisions, for this they would need 20/20 vision (Many potential crewmen would fail this part of the eye test) .Also essential was hand to eye coordination, judging distances and making quick decisions. As well as their knowledge of gunnery and turret manoeuvring, they also like Bill studied aircraft recognition. Gunners would also have to overcome air sickness and claustrophobia from the cramped turrets. For Eddy out on his own flying backwards looking into space for several hours required nerves of steel. All crew members would also require enormous reserves of concentration for the long fraught with danger journeys they would be making together.

**W/O Dennis Bartlett**

*'My journey in the RAF began early in 1943 when I was 18 years old. My 19th birthday was on the 5 July 1943, so I knew that I would receive call up papers soon and had been thinking about what I should do. I had a job at the aluminium sheet metal factory in Slough. One sunny day I was walking down Bath Road in Slough and I noticed a sign on the building next to the Three Tun Pub for RAF volunteers and on an impulse I thought, I'll join the RAF. I walked into the building and signed myself up without a thought for what I was getting involved in!*

*I got my call up papers a week later and went down to a recruiting centre opposite the bus station in Victoria in London. Here we did some maths exams and eye tests. The following week I was requested to attend the RAF Reception Centre at Lords Cricket Ground in St John's Wood. I got the train up from Camberley and got off at Oxford Circus. I then got hopelessly lost. Believe it or not it was only the second time I had been to London, Victoria was the first. Eventually after asking a few people I was kindly pointed in the right direction up towards Regents Park and Lords Cricket Ground.*

*It was here that I first met George Moggridge in the queue of excited recruits and we instantly became great friends. Our service numbers were very close and we stayed together until we were transferred onto Ops.* [Their service

numbers are only 17 digits apart:-Dennis, 1896762 and George, 1896779]
*We were given inoculations and uniforms and then later told that we would be training as Air Gunners. There was some disappointment among some recruits as a few had wanted to be Pilots, but got given other aircrew duties because they failed some of the tests. I can remember feeling really excited about the adventure we were about to go on the fact that we were going to serve our Country. A short time later we were then transferred up to ITW at Bridlington in East Yorkshire. I can't remember which one it was; it could have been No 14 ITW. We spent about 6 weeks up here doing Air Gunnery lectures/theory, PE, lots of parades and marching and then finally got transferred to No 1 Air Gunnery School at Pembrey on the South Wales coast.*
*During our Gunnery training we did some initial firing on fixed ranges with .303 rifles and Bren Guns. This also included stripping the weapons down, fault finding, cleaning them and putting them back together again. After this there were two main types of target practice. The first was 'air to air' and the second was 'air to ground', it was important to learn how to hit a moving target whilst actually moving. We used live rounds that were fired from moving aircraft which were covered with coloured paint; this would show which gunner had hit the target at all and how accurate they were. The range was normally up to about 300 yards and we would take turns to fire 200 to 300 rounds of ammunition. I can remember flying out over the Bristol Channel in Blenheims and following a drogue, which was basically a specially marked dummy aircraft that was being towed on a long cable by another plane. Sometimes it would tow a large flag that was a bit like a giant wind sock. We would shoot at the drouge from the Blenheim turrets and get marked by the instructor after the drogue had been dropped to the ground. The turrets were fitted with cine cameras, which also recorded accuracy and whether we were aiming above or below the target. However we had to be really careful not to shoot the aircraft that was towing the drogue, which would mean an automatic transfer off the course. The 'air to ground' targets were positioned on designated beaches and were also specially marked and similar in size to an aircraft fuselage.*

50 Squ Lancaster, VN-N (source, *warhistoryonline.com)*

Bristol Blenheim Mk I (source, *Canadian Forces*)

*Part of the course was on how to operate gun turrets, this included target practise in turrets mounted on the ground and powered by car engines. We also learned how the turret lifted the guns up and down and how to harmonise the guns. This meant how to aim the bullets in the centre of a moving target. When firing from the rear turret Eddy had four guns instead of my two guns and they were set so the bullets came out in a cone shape. Although it was all very intense George Moggridge and I had a lot of fun during these training sessions.*
*The range of the .303 Browning was limited to about 300 yards before you could see the tracers dropping away, so you had to be fairly close to a fighter for your bullets to do much damage. Although just firing the guns could scare a fighter off. In Gunnery School we were trained to calculate the rate of drop in order to put the bullets ahead of the aiming point. You would look through your sight and if it had a thirty-foot wingspan, it would be 300 yards away and you'd aim thirty yards in front. The American Gunners used a .50 inch calibre machine gun which had a far more effective range. These guns and their ammunition would have added a great deal more weight to the Lancaster, so I think that the powers that be decided against giving us the .50's.'*

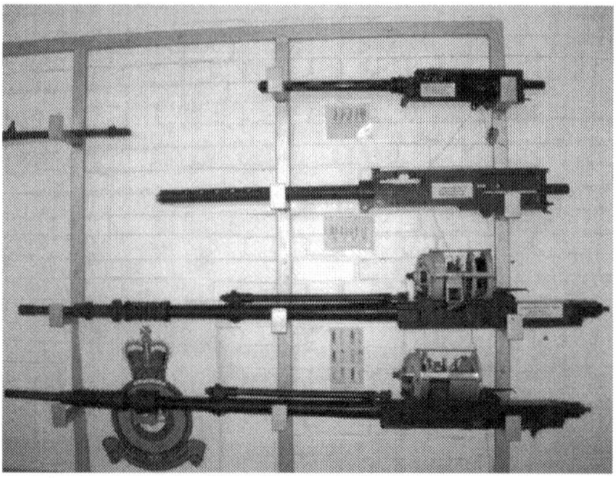

**Top of the picture**, RAF .303 inch (7.7 mm) *Browning*. **Second down** USAAF *B-17s* had .50 inch (12.7 mm) *M2 Browning* machine guns. **Next down** is 20mm Cannon of the type used by fighters, the difference in shell size is substantial and could cause catastrophic damage to the aircraft being attacked (source, *RAF Coningsby*, June 2012, CK).

## F/Lt Bill North

*'As a rear gunner, Eddy often felt very isolated and vulnerable at the back of the a/c. It was also the coldest crew position, but he did have a heated flying suit. He couldn't see anything that was happening up front and so was unaware of any danger ahead. He could however turn the turret to 90 degrees and lean out and look upfront. As I have mentioned before although against the rules, I would sometimes leave Les in charge of flying the a/c while I went down to see how Eddy was doing. One of his biggest fears was being injured or killed and no one coming to help him. Sometimes radio silence would be broken just so he knew we were still in contact. Contact during Ops over the intercom between the crew was discouraged though unless it was absolutely necessary.'*

Pembrey played a major part in the War effort, as well as the RAF training schools it supplied high explosives from the Royal Ordnance Factory to the War effort and was also a base for Fighter Command during the Battle of Britain claiming many kills.

## W/O Norman Jarvis

*'The weather up in North Wales was good and we soon started flying and working quite hard, but life was good and we enjoyed doing something. I*

*managed to get some very good bombing results on the practise ranges and enjoyed the map reading and navigational flights in the old Ansons up the very pretty west coast. After a month of day flying consisting of bombing, gunnery and navigation, plus ground lectures on bombs, ammunition, turrets and components, we moved over to another drome called RAF Llandwrog for our night exercises.*
*These proved far more hazardous and crews were persistently getting lost or crashing into the Welsh Mountains. Snowden, I think holds the secret to the cause of dozens of young airmen's deaths. On returning from a cross-country flight in a crash on the aerodrome, it was here that one of my first fellow students lost his life. Charlie contracted the mumps here and was put on a course or two behind us. I was very sorry to lose him as that only left Pete and I of the old four together.* [Alan Duggleby, Peter Knox, Charlie Kruschel and Norman Jarvis]

*I always had a wonderful time in my leisure moments there in Wales. We saw the grand old castles at Caernarfon and Harlech and went dancing in Pwllheli and parties all along the coast of North Wales. WAAF, ATS and WRENS made up the partners usually, but we did take a few of the girls out in Caernarfon and Pwllheli and were amused when they lapsed off into their native tongue and left us wondering what it was all about.*
*At the end of this course we were given a week's leave which I spent mostly in London. We found this grand old city crowded, drab and badly scarred, but nevertheless full of interest and a certain amount of beauty. We saw such places as London Bridge, the Tower, Westminster Abbey and St Pauls, then of course Buckingham Palace. There can be no doubt about what London suffered during the Blitzes of 1940-41, but they cleaned up the rubble marvellously well and life goes on now the same as ever. I should always have been lost there was it not for the brilliant Underground Railway System that goes under it and far out into the suburbs. One night we had an air raid there and hell, what a barrage they put up there. I would sure hate to bomb the place our guns made far more noise than the few bombs dropped that night.'*

RAF Llandwrog was opened in January 1941 as a Bomber Command airfield for training Air Gunners, Wireless Operators and Navigators; it was one of the largest RAF airfields in Wales. It was located 4 miles southwest of Caernarfon and Caernarfon Airport is now located on the site. The Air Observers School (AGS) flew Avro Anson's and Westland Lysander's (On 10 October 1941 two aircraft collided at RAF Llandwrog, killing seventeen people).

As Norman explains training crews and their aircraft were frequently crashing in the North Wales Mountains. The medical officer at Llandwrog, F/Lt G V Graham had an idea to help deal with the increasing number of crashes and in early 1942 the RAF Llandwrog Mountain Rescue Section was formed using local volunteers. As these essential teams gained recognition towards the end of 1943, the RAF Mountain Rescue Service was also formed in January 1944.

A quick point of interest:-Approximatley 71,000 bombs containing the nerve agent Tabun had been seized in Germany in the War and these were stored in the open at RAF Llandwrog, until 1954. During Operation Sandcastle they were transported to Cairnryan for disposal aboard scuttling ships at sea 120 miles north-west of Ireland.

**W/O Les Morton**

*'I volunteered at 18 years old for the RAF and completed a course as a Flight/Mechanic and Fitter 2A. My Flight/mechanic training was done at Morecambe, then based at Shetland Isle, Dyce and Northern Ireland. After a period of time servicing aircraft I volunteered for Flight Engineer duties. I was posted to St Athan, 15 miles west of Cardiff and completed my Flight Engineer's course. There were lots of WAAFs at St Athans, which was the first time I had seen so many women in uniform! From here I was posted to RAF Scampton for the Commando/Survival course that Bill and the rest of the crew completed in early 1944. I was then posted to 1661 HCU at RAF Winthorpe where I picked up Bill's crew.'*

RAF St Athan opened on 1 September 1938 and the first unit to take up residence was No 4 School of Technical Training. In 1939, the station's activities were expanded with the arrival of a fighter group pool, the School of Air Navigation, and a maintenance unit. During the War the station had over 14,000 personnel, and was used for training ground and air crew. It was linked to the aircraft storage and maintenance facility at RAF Llandow.

With their specialist RAF training completed each man now had a unique role to play. Bill and his crew were now destined to meet at an Operational training Unit and go through more intense training as they bonded as a seven man Lancaster Bomber crew.

# Chapter Seven

## Operational Training

At Operational Training Units men from all over the 'Empire' were brought together to form 7-man crews. English, Scottish, Welsh, Irish, Australian, New Zealand, Canadian, Rhodesian, South African, all fresh from 18 month to two year periods of training were all thrown together. In the mix were other European Nationals like Polish and Czech crewmen, all whose contribution was essential to the war effort. There was no class discrimination in Bomber Command as there had been in previous years in the RAF, the stuffiness was gone; the volunteers came from all walks of life, from Public Schools to working classes, anybody could become an Officer or pilot. This combination of men from the Commonwealth and Europe, with a cross section of classes and work titles gave Bomber Command a unique ingredient that functioned extraordinarily well throughout their service to the apocalyptic nature of the task they were charged with.

Pilots and Navigators were the high end of the crew spectrum, with Bomb Aimers now regarded as a specialist trade. The role of Observer was now split into Bomb Aimer and Navigator; there was no 2nd Pilot either and some recruits who had applied to be pilots were offered Bomb Aimer/Navigator roles instead. A large proportion of Navigators had been rejected from pilot training and moved to the next step down the ladder. Wireless Operators, Gunners and Flight Engineers went through meticulous equipment training.

Bomber Command's focus was now on assembling tight-knit crews that had integrity and mutual confidence in each other, hence the work hard and play hard philosophy evolved. The Bombing campaign required focused, bonded men who relied on each other and could trust their fellow Squadron members with their lives. The fate of freedom lay in their skilled and capable hands and night after night they would together conquer and overcome their fear and courageously fly into the dark face of the enemy. They all needed to know that in times of crisis they could rely on each other and Bill and his crew were put to the extreme test in their service with Bomber Command. The requirement was simple and informal:- that like-minded crew members could find each other and bond.

During Bill's Operational training period in late 1943 Bomber Command continued its offensive on the German mainland with visits to, Stuttgart, Frankfurt, Munich, Brunswick, Hanover, Duisburg and Mannheim. Some of these targets were places that Jeff Gray and Percy Cannings flew to and that Bill would soon visit himself.

Bill was now sent to one of the RAF's many Operational Training Units (OTU). He was now based at No.17 OTU at RAF Silverstone, and between 13 September and 6 October he met his crew and they began to shape up as an eventual seven man unit. This was done very informally on the basis of the men's own choices. In Bill's words:

**F/Lt Bill North**

*'I can remember crewing up like it was yesterday. It was quite informal and there was a large crowd of us in a room all with different crew titles. It was basically a big social for us to intermingle and find out who we got on with. The minute I saw Norman I knew he was going to be on my crew, we started chatting and got on like a house on fire. I asked him immediately if he would be my Bomb Aimer and he said yes straight away. We soon became best mates and it felt like we had known each other forever. Monty and Dave joined us a bit later in the week and then Dennis, we all got on really well. Eddy joined us at RAF Turweston and Les Morton was attached to the crew at RAF Winthorpe HCU.'*

**And in the words of Bill's Bomb Aimer, Warrant Officer Norman Jarvis:**

**W/O Norman Jarvis**

*'I reported to RAF Silverstone* in the Midlands for my operational training on about 20th September with ten other Australian bomb timers. Here we were to be crewed up and trained for Operations with Bomber Command. The Wellington aircraft looked large and formidable to us in those days and we were keen to start flying them. This Station was very dispersed and we were to live in Nissen huts for the first time. These are very comfortable in the summer, but cold and dreary in winter unless you have a good fire. Within a few days of our arrival I met Bill North, a good looking young Welsh Sgt. pilot and I was very pleased when he asked me if I would be his Bombardier, as I knew there were no Australian pilots at the time and I knew I would like his quiet manner and capable looks. Later in the week he had a Wireless Operator Sgt. Monteith, a nineteen-year old lad from Northern Ireland and Dave Crowley, another Welshman, for a Navigator.'*

*After the War Silverstone became the home to British Grand Prix racing, which was first hosted there in 1948. It was built on the site of RAF Silverstone, where Bill did his training. The airfield's three, classic triangle shape WW2 runways, lie within the boundaries of the present racetrack.

## THE 'NORTH CREW'

**Left to right:** 174326 Pilot Officer W. North (Bill) Cardiff, Wales. (Pilot/Captain/Skipper) Born 11/05/1922, died 15/12/2011

410413 Flight Sergeant N.E. Jarvis (Norman/Norm) Cudgewa, Upper Murray, Victoria,
Australia. (Bomb Aimer) Born 28/07/1920, died 24/08/1949

1422158 Flight Sergeant H. E. Crowley (Dave) Merthyr Tydfil, Wales. (Navigator) Died in the 1980's.

1518174 Sergeant G.I.W. Monteith (Monty) Ballymoney, County Antrim, N. Ireland.
(Wireless Operator) Died October 2007.

Second temporary Flt/Eng Jock 'Pork', not a crew member.

1527796 Sergeant L. Morton (Les) Woodlands, Nr Doncaster, South Yorkshire, England.
(Flight Engineer) Born 16/06/1922 died 04/04/2013

1813944 Sergeant P.E. O'Shea (Eddy) Limerick, Irish Republic. (Rear Gunner, AG2) Died 9/08/1984

1896762 Sergeant D.A. Bartlett (Dennis/Denn) Camberly, England. (Mid-Upper Gunner, AG1) Born 5/07/1924

Bill's crew was made up of 2 Englishmen, 2 Irishmen, 2 Welshmen and 1 Australian and although that sounds like the beginning a joke, it actually is a reflection of the geographical diversity that made up the crews of Bomber Command and the random nature in which they selected themselves. Bill explained that Monty and Eddy were both from opposite parts of Ireland and got on just fine, there was no political tension between them whatsoever and no prejudice from anybody they came across. Although there was a general mix of Nationalities from the Empire across the Squadrons in Bomber Command there were also all Australian, Canadian (6 group), Polish and New Zealand Squadrons too.

The crew would wear a badge on their uniform that would indicate their trade title or qualification called 'Brevets'. Bill wore the full set of wings indicating he was the pilot. The rest of the crew wore a 12 feather half-wing brevet with a laurel wreath surrounding the letters that applied to their trade. O, was for Observer, N, was for Navigator, B, was for Bomb Aimer, AG was for Air Gunner, E, was for Flight Engineer and WAG, was for Wireless Operator/Air Gunner.

F/Lt Bill North's RAF Wings and Brevet badges for a Navigator, Bomb Aimer and Air Gunner, Flight Engineer and Wireless Operator/Air Gunner.

**The crew positions in the Lancaster consisted of:-**

**The Pilot, P/O Bill North** who was in charge of flying the aircraft and leading the crew. The alternative titles for this position were Captain or Skipper.

Bomber Command's pilots shared a combination of duties that set them slightly apart; in no other branch of the RAF did such a responsibility fall as on those young Officers and NCO's. As well as flying the finest and most powerful machine in the RAF, the 'perfect heavy', Bill regardless of rank was also the leader of his crew and he combined authority and discipline with great friendship. To his crew, 'Example was the key to confidence and to secure confidence was the essence of leadership.'*

Bill possessed the perfect balance of qualities required by a Captain. He was without doubt a fine leader and outstanding friend, who had the full confidence of his specialist crew to make lifesaving decisions in the many unexpected emergencies they experienced. Bill's crew like many of Bomber Command's finest were a well oiled machine, all relied upon and respected each other's abilities.

*(Quote from p51 *Lancaster At War 2*, Mike Garbett and Brian Goulding)

619 Squ Lancaster III, LM446, PG-H (Source, *Charles E. Brown*, Feb 1944. Expired Crown Copyright, public domain).

Maximum level speed with full load at 15,000ft was 275mph. Maximum level speed at sea level was 245mph. Cruising speed was 200mph. Maximum permissible diving speed for example during the 'Corkscrew' manoeuvre was 360mph. Stalling speed at 50,000lb weight with undercarriage and flaps up was 110mph.

The Pilot and Flight Engineers view (CK).

The pilot sat in a seat on the left or port side of the cockpit with the only piece of armour plating on the a/c was behind his head. The Flight Engineer sat on the right or starboard side on a pull-out seat that could swivel in and out, although most of the time he would be standing up. Immediately behind the pilot sat the Navigator, sealed in by a curtain that pulled across to keep out any light interference. Immediately behind the Navigator's position sat the Wireless Operator with the main spa directly behind him.

**The Flight Engineer, Sgt Les Morton** whose duties consisted of being responsible for the aircraft's engines and fuel systems, also implementing any possible repairs to the aircraft whilst in flight. The Lancaster power units were 4 *Rolls Royce Merlin* engines XX, 22 or 24, fitted with 3 bladed, constant speed variable pitch airscrews. Bill flew the Lancaster Mk III which had the American built *Packard Merlin* engines. Jeff Gray told me that the *Packard* power plants didn't overheat as much and didn't leak oil so much. This was because the *Packard's* surfaces were machine finished and Rolls Royce were hand finished with files. The maximum fuel load was 2,154 gallons (15,509 lb) of standard octane petrol held in 2x580 gallon, 2x383 gallon and 2x114 gallon fuel tanks in the wings.

**Left-** the view from WOP's port window and **right-** the port view from the pilot's seat.

The Navigator, F/Sgt Dave Crowley who was in charge of the safe passage of the aircraft to and from its target, this included the use of maps and electronic technology like *Gee* and *H2S*. The range of the aircraft varied according to the weight of the bomb and fuel load. 2,530 miles with a 7,000 lb bomb load, 1,730 miles with a 12,000lb load and 1,550 miles with a 22,000lb load.

The Navigator's position where his maps and instruments would sit on this steal desk lit by a small lamp, a curtain separated the position from the cockpit to keep it dark.

**The Bomb Aimer, F/Sgt Norman Jarvis** who was in charge of the bomb load and its accurate delivery to the target. This would include the use of the *Mk 14 bomb sight* and other equipment related to dropping the bomb load. He would also take charge vocally of the direction of the aircraft whilst on the bombing run. He would also operate the front gun turret by standing up from his prone position over the bomb site and act as a lookout too.

Bomb Load: The maximum load was 18,000lbs, but reduced to 10,000lbs or less for long range targets. They could carry a mixture of 500lb or 1000lb high explosives, incendiaries and 4,000 or 8,000lb blast bombs,'Cookies'. The mix of bombs could be modified according to what the target was and the drop sequence varied according to this mix to allow smooth exit from the bomb bay. The crew would generally feel a wobble throughout the aircraft as the bombs dropped and an uplifting of the aircraft as the weight of bombs fell away. Specially modified Lancaster's could carry the 22,000 lb *Grand Slam* 'Earthquake' bomb and 18,000lb *'Tallboy'*. This would stress the airframe to the maximum limit and the crew could actually see the wings bending upwards during flight.

The armament was a *Frazer-Nash FN5A* nose turret fitted with two, *303 Browning* machine guns. **Left,** looking out of the Bomb Aimer's compartment and **right,** looking up into the bomb bay, BA's compartment and front turret.

**The Wireless Operator, Sgt Monty Monteith** who was in charge of providing wireless communications, to operate electronic and other radar equipment like *Gee*, *Monica*, *Fish Pond* and *H2S*, and also to carry out any repairs necessary whilst in flight. The WOP was also trained to operate the guns as well. Above the WOP's position was the Astrodome which was the bubble shape on the back of the Cockpit glass and he would use this as a lookout position or to track the stars. His duties also consisted of administering first aid or morphine injections to injured crew members.

View from the Astrodome down to the Mid-Upper turret and view of the Wireless Operators position.

**The Mid-Upper Gunner, Sgt Dennis Bartlett** who was in charge of operating the gun turret located in the top middle of the fuselage. His duties also consisted of being a lookout for enemy fighters, bombs falling from above, flak intensity, damage to the aircraft, calling out for evasive manoeuvres and returning fire. The armament consisted of a *Frazer-Nash* hydraulically operated turret with 2, .303 *Browning* machine guns.

View of the Mid-Upper turret and Rear turret giving an indication of their combined field of fire. Although not shown here, a flared cowling surrounding the Mid-Upper turret prevented the Gunner from shooting away any part of the tail section by accident and streamlined the turret. The bubble on the fuselage underneath the Mid-Upper turret housed the *H2S* ground radar system (CK).

**The Rear Gunner, Sgt Eddy O'Shea** who was in charge of operating the gun turret located on the far end of the rear fuselage between the two tail fins. His duties also consisted of being a lookout for enemy fighters, bombs falling from above, flak intensity, damage to the aircraft, calling out for evasive manoeuvres and returning fire.

Sgt Eddy O'Shea.

The Rear Gunners armament consisted of a *Frazer-Nash* hydraulically operated gun turret fitted with four.303 (7.7mm) *Browning* machine guns. The rate of fire was 1150 rounds per minute, 76 rounds per second from all four guns and a muzzle velocity of 800 metres per second.

External and interior view of the Rear Gunners position. The turret on the left has two guns, the right photo shows the correct figure of four. He had to slide feet first over the tail spar to gain access to the turret. I did this myself in 'Just Jane' and it is a tight fit.

Whilst flying these seven men would be working as a highly trained team all carrying out intricate tasks to and from the target zones.

Bill's Mid-Upper Gunner Warrant Officer Dennis Bartlett also adds in his own words what the view was like from the Mid-Upper Turret:

**W/O Dennis Bartlett**

*'The view from the Mid-Upper Turret was incredible, you had a 360 degree view of the top of the aircraft. You could see up and down the fuselage and out across the wings, also the whole of the surrounding airspace. Later on we wore electrically heated suits in the Gunners positions as the temperatures often went below freezing point. Although they were warm inside I would get a sheet of ice forming down my front from the condensation freezing. At the same time on Operations it could be quite a nerve wracking place to be, you could see all the flak bursting around you and all the tracers and blinding searchlights coming up from below. At night the flak burst in orangey coloured explosions and in the day bluish grey puffs, these came so close to the aircraft you could feel the blast and sometimes feel bits of shrapnel hitting the fuselage. You could even feel the aircraft shudder from the slipstreams of other Lancasters passing close to us. There was a hole blown in the fuselage not far from me once. I also saw one of our engines on fire once trailing a long line of smoke and fire behind us. I also saw other aircraft exploding around us and once immediately in front of us on the*

*bombing run, it wasn't a nice thing to see. When Bill did the 'corkscrew' and the aircraft was thrown around all over the sky it was like being on a rollercoaster, he really was an extraordinary pilot.'*

Sgt Dennis Bartlett and Sgt Les Morton with their RAF Brevets in 1944. A 57 Squ Mid-Upper Gunner at his post, 1943 (Source *P/O NS Clark, CH 8795 IWM*).

The Main Spar was the connecting structure between the front wings and ran at waist height through the middle of the aircraft. Bill told me that with all their flying kit on it was a bit of a struggle to climb over this structure, but they were young and fit and didn't think too much of it in those days. In an emergency situation the Main Spar could prove to be a major obstacle to climb over if the need arose to do so.

View from the Navigators position looking towards the rear showing the size of the Main Spar, with Sean Taylor kindly demonstrating the Spar dimensions inside NX611, 'Just Jane' at The Aviation Heritage Centre,East Kirkby. Sean Taylor again sitting on another obstacle, the smaller Rear Spa located just behind the Main Spar in which the huge aeriolon bars are located.

Most of the crew could double as Air Gunners and had a fairly good knowledge of each other's duties. W/O Norman Jarvis explains in his War Diary that he familiarised himself with all the functions of the other crew positions. Although there was no second pilot the Flight Engineer Les Morton could fly the a/c in emergencies. Bill mentioned to me that during their training periods on flights out over the North Sea he would spook the crew by exiting the cockpit leaving Sgt Les Morton in charge to go and talk to Rear Gunner Sgt Eddy O'Shea to see how he was. The crew would get all jittery and tell him to hurry up and get back to the front.

We now follow Bill and his crew through more training in Wellingtons and Stirlings. The two near death experiences they all had whilst flying in Stirlings made them somewhat 'Legendary' at 1661 HCU and gave Bill the nickname 'Prang 'a' North'.

# Chapter Eight

## Wellingtons, Stirlings and 'lucky escapes.'

With the crew nearly complete, the serious business of training for Operations began. Bill and his crew moved to RAF Turweston, a satellite base of Silverstone's, and from 6 October to 12 November 1943, they began their training in Wellingtons, nicknamed 'Wimpeys'. It was here they picked up their Mid-Upper Gunner Sgt Dennis Bartlett and Rear Gunner Sgt Eddy O'Shea.

The Wellington was a twin engine medium bomber built by Vickers-Armstrong. Bill said he remembered this aircraft with great affection. He said it had a geodesic fuselage design covered in a fabric coated in many layers of dope resin. This was an aluminium lattice framework invented by the famous aircraft designer Barnes Wallis that gave it incredible strength and resilience. When I visited RAF Hendon with Bill I saw this for myself, while he proudly explained this unique feature I took his photo in front of the resident Wellington Bomber. Many battle damaged Wellingtons returned home with the outer skin burnt off giving it a ghostly skeleton like appearance. Dennis Bartlett explained that when boarding a Wellington you had to be careful to stay on entrance platform, one wrong foot either side of it and you would end up with a leg poking through the fabric covering.

Whilst at RAF Hendon we found out that this aircraft that Bill was now training in had been responsible for the first RAF bombing attack of the war four years earlier, against German shipping at the Port of Brunsbüttel on 4 September 1939. More ominously for Bill the Wellington was also the first aircraft shot down on the Western Front, on that same raid.

Wellingtons in formation based at Malta flying to bomb Italian ports in 1941 where the Afrika Korps were supplied (*Lie In The Dark And Listen*, W/C Ken Rees).

Throughout the rest of this chapter, I tell the story in the words of Bill and his crew wherever possible:

**<u>W/O Norman Jarvis</u>**

*'We finished ground lectures at the home drome after two weeks and proceeded to the satellite RAF Turweston to commence flying as a crew. It was here that we picked up our Rear Gunner Sgt. Eddy O'Shea (Eddy was from The Irish Republic) and it seemed that we should have the luck of the Irish on our side; he was a smart looking lad but rather wild and irresponsible. Then we added Sgt. Dennis Bartlett as the Mid-upper Gunner; he was the first English member of the crew and was also very young and quiet.*
*Bill soon got off solo in the old 'Wimpey' and we had a good time flying around together, starting off with an instructor then doing circuits and bumps, later on we did bombing and gunnery. At the end of the month we won the practise bombing contest, a good indication that we had crew co-operation and were fairly efficient as a crew generally. By the time we got back to the main aerodrome to commence our long night and day cross-countries we all got along well and used to go out together to the local village.'*

**<u>W/O Dennis Bartlett</u>**

*'When I first met Bill he made a real impression on me. When he picked me to be his Mid-Upper Gunner I thought to myself, 'You poor sod, you picked me!'*

The boys would often go into the local pubs like The Stones Arms or the Plough Inn on the High Street in Skellingthorpe. Bill's girlfriend WAAF Sheila Randall and Norman Jarvis's WAAF girlfriend were good friends and they also often went out together, but as a rule the boys would eat, sleep and go out on the town together. I spoke on the phone to Roger Morley a local resident and later met him on the 12 June 2011 for the 61 Squadron Memorial service on the 12 June 2011. His Mother and Father were the landlords of The Plough Inn and he has passed on fascinating insights into the antics the crews got up to on their days off or when they were stood down from Ops and rushed off to the nearest pub.

In 1944 The Plough Inn was run by Pop Morley, Roger Morley's Grandfather and was only licensed to sell beer. After closing time the crews would move to local resident's houses and carry on drinking spirits. Roger

Morley said that their belongings often got left in houses in the village only to be collected by the RAF Police the following day when they failed to return from Operations. Once his mother was hanging out the washing early one morning when a badly shot up Lancaster which was on fire came in low over the village and clipped the chimney pot on her house. She watched it pass overhead and then burst out crying as it exploded whilst trying to land. One night in The Plough Inn some crew from 'Skelly' were getting roaring drunk. One of them went outside and put Pop Morley's pyjamas over his uniform which were hanging up to dry. He then proceeded to do cartwheels from one end of the pub to the other. When relaxing the crews really let themselves go because they were always aware of the ever-present shadow of death.

Dennis Bartlett mentioned to me that they would also go into Lincoln and Nottingham if they wanted a bit more fun with the girls and sometimes even Northampton. The journeys back to Skellingthorpe from these places was an adventure on its own with them often carrying Eddy O' Shea because of the huge amounts of alcohol he had consumed. If they missed the last bus and they were lucky they would get a lift back from a passing car or someone based at 'Skelly' or one of the other bases. On one occasion they even got a lift off Wing Commander Doubleday.

## W/O Norman Jarvis

*'The Midlands suffered a lot from industrial fog and haze, consequently our drome was often shrouded in a blanket of it and we were grounded, but apart from an occasional night out in Northampton we worked hard and got very tired flying right the way out over the North Sea and down to the SW to Plymouth and even Cornwall, over the Irish Sea and North of Scotland. We had a few very thrilling experiences, but our confidence in Bill was growing. Once after a big Operation by Bomber Command over Germany we had a Lancaster land on the drone badly shot up and we listened with interest to the stories from the crew; they told us of the life they led and what we were to expect within the next few months.'*

Some of the instructors who flew with Bill and his crew in 'C' Flight were:- F/Lt Hughes, F/Lt Crump, F/O Harsenfus, P/O Rhys, F/Lt Wynne, P/O Goodwin, F/Sgt Bone, F/O McRea,. On the 18 Oct 1943 Bill flew solo in the Wellington for the first time. Training exercises included fighter affiliation, cine gun, bomb practise, and many flights out over the North Sea. On the 13 Dec 1943 he received his assessment certificate for Wellingtons Mk III and X and an above average summary of flying certificate on 6 Jan 1944.

Bill and his crew Crowley, Jarvis, Bartlett, Monteith and O'Shea had flown in Wellingtons 43 times and Bill had clocked up 384 hours and 45 minutes flying time by the time their training at Silverstone was over.

The crew were given nine days off at this point in their training. Bill seems to remember going home to Cardiff for leave and thinks that all the others except Norman Jarvis went home as well.

**W/O Norman Jarvis**

*'Just before Christmas of 1943 we had finished our OTU so were given 9 days leave, the RAF got generous like that whenever they thought you were nearly flown to death. I went with Peter Knox up to London for the first few days as he was representing his father at a big amalgamated Newspaper dinner and I went along as his friend. It was quite an affair and we met some extremely interesting people. The climax was when we had to sing 'Waltzing Matilda', but we had a lot of fun.*
*Our destination was then Scotland. We went on the night train from Euston and arrived up there about mid-day following and stayed at the home of the Elliot's. This visit was arranged for us by Lady Frances Ryder* [Isles Dominion Hospitality Scheme], *who arranges private billets for Dominion Forces overseas. The Elliot family gave us a particularly interesting and enjoyable time over Xmas on their rather large estate. It was hard to have to return to work, although we were keen to do our conversion on to four engine aircraft. The task of flying training for war is heavy and we were pleased when we heard that we were not going until after New Year.*
*The New Year party in the mess was something I will not forget in a hurry, everyone let themselves go, regardless of what 1944 held for us. All the WAAF from the station were invited, the ATS from the town and the Local Land Girls, so there was no shortage of girls. What a gay carefree lot we all were then—living for the present and getting the best out of life.'*

Even now, Bill's training was not over. He was now an experienced solo pilot, but still he and his crew had to undergo, first, Commando training, and then training at a Heavy Conversion Unit (HCU) where Bill and the crew would get used to flying four-engined heavy bombers.

The Commando Training course was held at RAF Scampton from 4 January 1944 to 20 February 1944.

**W/O Norman Jarvis**

*'About the 4 January 1944 our crew went and did a Commando Course,*

*which was the procedure to toughen us up physically; it lasted about 3 weeks and was a great deal of fun and we had a lot of entertainment. The nearest big town from here was Lincoln, which was to become our local leave place until we gave up the flying game 6 months later. How tired the people there must be of aircrew and I wonder how many hearts have been broken there, because the boys all go on leave there and heavy bombers scream out just over the city before setting off on bombing missions.'*

Bill and his crew were then sent to RAF Winthorpe near Newark in Nottinghamshire to 1661 Heavy Conversion Unit (HCU). It was here they picked up their Flight Engineer Sgt Les Morton, this was a common practise with Flt/Engineers. At OTU the Wellington had a five man crew and at HCU the Stirling required a seven man crew, up until this point Norman Jarvis had been performing the Flight Engineer's duties alongside his Bomb Aiming practise. Starting with the Short Stirling they learned how to fly and operate the huge, four-engined aircraft that they would be sent on bombing raids over Germany in. This final phase of training ran from 20 February to 22 April 1944. It would prove to be by far the most dangerous stage of training. The flight codes for Winthorpe were KB and GP. These were the letters on the side of the aircraft that identified which RAF Squadron it belonged to.

The Short Stirling would prove to be Bill's least favorite aircraft to fly in. Alongside the Halifax it was the first of the four-engined heavy bombers used by the RAF in WW2. The Stirling was designed and built by Short Brothers and entered service in 1941. The Stirling's operational career as a bomber was fairly short and it was gradually replaced by Lancaster's and Halifax's from 1943. It was also used in other roles, one being to tow gliders during the D-Day landings, also minelaying, electronic countermeasures and dropping agents behind German lines. It could carry a 14,000 lb bomb load and had an operational ceiling of 15,000 ft for 2,000 miles (Bill North and Arthur Smith, an ex 50 Squadron Flight Engineer I interviewed, who also provided critical eyewitness accounts).

Short Stirling cockpit. (source, IWM, CH 17086)

Arthur Smith at the 50 and 61 Squadron Memorial Day, Skellingthorpe Village, 10 June 2012.

1661 HCU was where Norman Jarvis' fellow Australian Bomb Aimer Peter Knox was also sent with his crew Captained by P/O 'Dave' Davis. Dennis Bartlett's best friend Mid-Upper Gunner George Moggridge was also in this crew. They would later go to 619 Squ to fly in Lancaster ME846, splitting up the band of friends. An interesting recollection of Stirlings is provided by Peter Knox:

**W/O Peter Knox**

*'Stirlings were huge planes, which stood high off the ground. They had only recently been taken off Operations—they could not compete with the Lancasters and Halifaxes in general performance. The popular story was that they had been designed before the War and their wingspan had been reduced so that they could fit more easily into the hangars used then. Whatever the truth in the story they were cumbersome and hard for the pilots to handle. Our month or so on Stirlings tested us to the full.'*

Peter Knox and Gwen Copeland on their wedding day after the war.

April 1942, Stirling N6101 from No. 1651 Heavy Conversion Unit at Waterbeach, Cambridgeshire, being 'bombed up' (Photo, *Charles E. Brown, TR8, Imperial War Museum*).

At 1661 HCU RAF Winthorpe the crew were practising corkscrews, banking searches, fighter affiliation, flying on 3 engines and bomb aiming. These next experiences recalled by Bill, Norman, Les and Dennis are astounding given that both events happened virtually one after the other in Stirling IIIs.

**W/O Norman Jarvis**

*'In February we were introduced to the four engine aircraft for the first time, the largest of them all too, the Stirling and here we were given the last member of our 7 man crew, our Flight Engineer Sgt Les Morton. It was Bill's first time as a Captain of one of these big bombers that we got our first real shaking; some hydraulic trouble developed and we could not get our undercarriage down, so they told us from the ground to bring her in for a crash landing. We all took our crash positions and he put the 50,000lb monster down on the runway; the shock of such a mass of metal on its belly was terrific, but apart from a few bruises the whole crew walked away pretty fast out of the wreck and stepped into the waiting ambulance that took us for a routine medical inspection.'*

**F/Lt Bill North (Stirling III, code GP-H, serial no.LK537)**

*'The first crash occurred on Monday 20 March 1944 at Winthorpe and was due to the fact that the port wheel of the undercarriage wouldn't lock. We had an instructor called P/O Ball (DFM) with us on this training flight. My*

*recollection is that when I lowered the undercarriage as part of my landing procedure, a red warning light showed—something which indicated that the undercarriage had not 'locked'. In these circumstances I took the normal action: 'rocking' the aircraft alternately port to starboard: going into a reasonably steep dive and pulling up sharply, etc. All to no avail. The red light remained 'on'. I was of course in contact with the Control Tower and was requested to fly at a low level near to the Tower for observers to view the situation. Although everything appeared normal—the warning light remained 'on'. I was given permission to land, adopted the recognised emergency procedure, ordered the crew to get into pre-determined drill positions whereby they could brace themselves for the impact should the undercarriage collapse, as proved to be the case. On the ground and near the runway an ambulance and fire engine were standing-by. The crash landing was uneventful and no-one was hurt.'*

## W/O Les Morton

*'The cable which operated the motor for the landing gear malfunctioned, then I had to carry out the emergency landing procedure, having done that with the help of Dave Crowley we proceeded to turn the handle which lowered the under carriage, but the up lock hadn't released the screw jack and with the extra pressure on the handle it broke the up lock which resulted in the port wheel swinging. On the second attempt Bill put the aircraft down on a one wheel landing. On later inspection it was found that the star wheel had become corroded.'*

Three Stirlings in formation (source, *Histomil.com*).

Bill and the crew had an instructor called P/O Ball (DFM) on board with them during this crash landing and it is intriguing to see that they all flew again the next day on another training mission in a Stirling. It was business as usual; Bill was unfazed by the experience.

**W/O Norman Jarvis**

*'We flew again the following day 21 March 1944 completing all of our exercises and then a short time afterwards we had another much worse crash then the one on Whit Monday. This time two engines failed on the port side not long after take-off on a night cross country, then a third caught fire. It was a hell of a predicament and just on dark. We were losing height rapidly and it seemed almost too low to risk baling out, when suddenly out of the evening gloom appeared an aerodrome runway as if by magic. Bill swung the crippled kite and pointed it at the black stretch of runway, but the controls were dead as we were nearly at stalling speed and it was too late to drop the wheels, so in we went, touching down about halfway up the runway and then skidding through the far fence. I can still see the high bank of a gully looming up in front of us, but we stopped just short of it. I helped Bill out and when we stepped from the top hatch it was good to see the rest of the crew safe again, but this time more shaken and trembling. An ambulance was right on the job again, so once more we visited the MO (Medical Office). The track we ploughed was plainly visible and the propellers were lying along it; later she blew up and caught fire.*
*In those days there were some very unfortunate accidents in other crews, many of them fatal. On one occasion we saw a Stirling go straight in from 1000ft killing the whole crew in front of our eyes, but it was only to be expected and it did not bear thinking about too much; personally I always liked flying and learned to do nearly everyone else's job in the aircraft. Our crew always got along quite well, but Bill and I were the only two who were very close and on and off duty, we had a lot of good times. His girlfriend* [WAAF Sheila Randall] *and mine were great friends as well.'*

**W/O Peter Knox recalls the same accident at 1661 HCU:**

*'On one of our final flights we witnessed for the first time a fatal crash. We were doing routine training in the vicinity of the airbase when a Stirling several hundred feet in front of us suddenly dived towards the ground from a height of 1,000ft. We saw one person try unsuccessfully to bale out—the whole crew perished as the plane hit the earth and burst into flames. There was an eerie silence in our plane as we came into land ourselves. Mercifully*

*flying was cancelled for the day—our base Commander did not follow the WW1 precept of sending pilots straight back into the air after a crash.'*

In 1980 I had my own experience of watching a WW2 Bomber crash and explode and it left an indelible mark on my emotions.

On the 21 of September 1980 my father and I went to the Biggin Hill air show, I was 16 years old and a keen photographer and took my camera with me. We wandered around the air strip looking at the various aircraft that were on display. I was in my element I couldn't think of a better way to spend the day. The sounds of the engines, the smell of the aircraft and to actually touch them and get up close was sensational. One of the aircraft I came across was the A26 Douglas Invader N3710G. I stood in front of this aircraft and was enthralled by it. My nose was pressed up against the Bomb Aimer's glass as I stared down inside the aircraft wondering what it would be like looking out the other way as it was in flight. I also thought, and I'm not sure why, wouldn't it be awful to be looking out of that glass nose section if it was about to crash into the ground! My father was also chatting to the crew men who were standing beside the aircraft. My thoughts were interrupted by somebody saying 'It's a fantastic aircraft isn't it?' I replied 'Yes it is.' The man I was talking to was one of a few men my father was talking to and who seemed to be in charge of or looking after the wonderful machine. I later realised that this must have been Don Bullock and I only knew this later, because when I asked him if he was something to do with the aircraft he replied that he was the Pilot and would be flying it shortly. I stepped back from the nose of the Invader and was about to take a picture looking up into the glass of the nose when somebody bumped into me and for some reason or other I didn't take that picture.

However, when the invader took off I was awestruck, the sound of the engines especially throbbing through the air and through my chest. My father and I watched closely as it flew past the crowd and then started to climb into a barrel roll, as it reached the top of the roll the nose dropped and an older gentleman standing next to us said 'He's not going to make it.' I looked over at him curiously and wondered what he meant. We then watched as it dived into the valley at the end of the runway, there was a pause and we saw a slight orange flash and then a huge pall of smoke. There was an awful silence which seemed to last forever, then I heard a woman say 'Oh my God it's crashed' and the silence was broken. I immediately started to take pictures with my camera and rushed off towards the end of the runway, eventually getting right up close to the crash zone where I took more pictures.

Barney Case was sitting in the valley at the end of the runway, he witnessed and took pictures of the A26 crash into the ground and explode. He said he felt the intense heat wave hit him full on even where he was standing half way up the hill (original photo by Barney Case).

This whole sequence of events has stayed with me all these years and what has moved me especially is that I was standing right in front of the A26 and spoke to Don Bullock just minutes before this tragedy. It gave me a clear idea of what Bill and his crew witnessed when they saw the Stirling go straight into the ground (I spoke to Squadron Leader Russ Heath at the 2012, 10 June 50/61 Squadron Memorial Day about this crash and discovered we had been standing just a few feet away from each other at Biggin Hill that day).

I remember speaking to Bill a few days later back at Regal Way about the crash and again years later when we spoke at Regal Way in early 2010; his view on it was this. *'That when pilots perform stunts at a low altitude especially at air shows and the aircraft malfunction there is no time to recover the machines. If this particular manoeuvre had been implemented higher up there is a strong possibility it would not have crashed or could have had a more controlled crash landing; but it probably should not have been tried in the first place.'*

Three pictures from the sequence I took that day. The rest can be seen on the A26 Invader web site run by Martin Simpson.

## F/Lt Bill North (Stirling III, code GP-K, serial no. LK485)

*'The second Stirling crash took place on Friday 7 April 1944 and potentially this mishap was far more serious. We were taking off at dusk on a night exercise when one of the engines caught fire. We attained a height of not more than 1000/1200 ft. A second engine began to lose power; we were too low for me to instruct the crew to bale out and I was losing height fast. I used a procedure called feathering the engines which altered the pitch of the props to fine to create the least wind resistance or drag, which could make it harder to control the aircraft. However a third engine caught fire as well which we feathered too.*

*The situation was desperate and as Norman Jarvis said 'we were in a hell of a predicament'. I ordered the Flight Engineer Sgt Les Morton to re-start one of the engines; he didn't want to re-start the feathered engine as it might explode. I said, 'If you don't start it I won't have enough power to continue and we will drop like a stone. After our slight disagreement Les successfully re-started the engine. The crew were ordered to get into their emergency positions and I prepared to crash land when, very luckily, I spotted a runway ahead that just seemed to appear out of nowhere and decided to immediately attempt a landing.* [This was RAF Ossington about 10 miles NW of RAF Winthorpe] *I took action to lower the undercarriage. My intention, hopefully, was to save the aircraft-and avoid a crash landing. There was insufficient time for the undercarriage to get into the 'locked' position. Consequently when we 'landed' we sped along the runway at quite a speed and for quite a distance before the undercarriage collapsed and we finally came to a halt. I learned later on that I had landed downwind; I had come in the wrong way down the runway, a consideration which was not uppermost in my mind! Luckily for us there were no aircraft taking off at the same time as we were coming in. The crew all very quickly left the aircraft because of the danger of the fuel igniting and causing an explosion. I was the last one to leave and was banging my fists in frustration on the cockpit control panel shouting out loud, 'These bloody Stirling's have nearly killed us twice they're bloody useless', and that was the polite version of what I said. Norman Jarvis came back for me and said, 'Hurry up Bill if you don't get out now she's going to blow!' Shortly afterwards the aircraft exploded.'*

**W/O Dennis Bartlett**

*'I remember both our crashes in Stirlings during HCU really well. On the first crash Bill couldn't get the port undercarriage to lock. He tried a few tricks like rocking the aircraft from side to side and the diving steeply and pulling up sharply, but none of this worked and the warning light stayed on. We flew past the control tower for a visual and they gave us the all clear to land. The undercarriage collapsed as we were landing and the Stirling hit the runway with a hell of a bang. We were all thrown around and had some bruises, but we got out of the wrecked plane pretty quickly and all agreed that it was a close call.*

*The second crash came shortly afterwards and was a more shocking experience. We had only just taken off on a night exercise when an engine caught fire. I could see the whole drama unfolding from the Mid-Upper Turret and could see the flames and smoke trailing off behind us. Bill feathered the engine and then another engine failed and we started to lose power and height. Bill feathered this engine too and then another engine caught fire, we only had one engine left and were rapidly losing height. Bill managed to restart an engine and then suddenly out of nowhere a landing strip appeared. With just enough power to land Bill brought the Stirling in down the wrong way on the runway, luckily nothing was taking off. When we hit the ground the noise of the aircraft crashing down the runway was deafening. We went through a fence and finally came to a stop by a bank in a ditch and all piled out as quickly as we could. Norman had to go back and get Bill out of the cockpit and we all saw the wreckage scattered down the runway, the emergency crews were standing by to help us. We were all really shaken up and realised we had come very close to being killed. Bill kept his nerve and stayed calm right through both these crashes, he really was an outstanding pilot. I don't think we would have made it without him. He was nicknamed 'Prang 'a' North' on the base after this second crash which he took in good spirits, it was something we could not dwell on, but just laugh about.'*

**W/O Les Morton**

*'We had just become airborne when the port outer engine malfunctioned*

*and then the port inner caught fire. The aircraft wouldn't maintain height on 2 engines and breaking through the cloud at about 1,000 ft we sighted an airfield which appeared from out of the cloud, we were descending rapidly. Bill wanted to unfeather the port inner engine, but I advised him not to. I managed to restart an engine and it gave us just enough power to land. Then I selected under carriage down and then we hit the deck, the undercarriage being half way down took the initial shock then collapsed. We careered along the runway until the aircraft came to a stop and then there was a mad scramble to get out.'*

Just to add some more colour to the drama of the already desperate situation of the second Stirling crash. I have discovered that after Bill feathered the Port engines he tried to immediately un-feather them but couldn't. This was because of an oil leak to the CSU-Constant Speed Unit-located inside the hub and used to automatically adjust prop pitch. In the Port Outer there was metal found in the induction pipe of no. 7 cylinder and the big end bearing of the Port Inner had broken up. Bill was recommended for a 'Green Endorsement' to be added to his log book for his actions in saving the crew that night. 'A Green Endorsement is given 'For the avoidance or loss of aircraft and crew by exceptional flying skill'. Mike Smith, the curator at Newark Air Museum explains that 'Evidently these are rarely given.' The day after this crash the Station was visited by Air Vice Marshall Ralph Cochrane, Air Commanding Officer of 5 Group (Bill mentioned he remembered speaking to a senior Officer who visited the base the day after this crash, but couldn't remember his name).

I asked Bill how he stayed so cool and calm in all of his intense emergencies with the crew; given the extreme stress and tension of these situations and with them being so close to death. Bill then explained to me that in relation to his three crash landings, two in Stirlings and one in a Lancaster that he was fully aware of the fact that they could die at any moment in those emergencies. However his RAF training took over and he followed the procedures he had been taught in the hours and hours of flying training. Bill never mentioned the Green Endorsement to anybody and considering what it is given for, that makes perfect sense too. Bill always underplayed his role in saving his crew on many occasions, even all these years later he still got quiet satisfaction from knowing that he did. In his own words, *'I could make the Lancaster do whatever I wanted it to do.'*

Bill really was an outstanding Bomber pilot. He had a true understanding of and a real natural gift to control an aircraft in whatever situation (good or bad) that presented itself to him. They lost 3 engines and nearly all died, but yet again Bill's exceptional skill and calmness saved them all again. Even his family didn't know he had been awarded a 'Green Endorsement' and were delighted to be informed of the latest twist in Bill's story.

Bill was so humble and unassuming and was uncomfortable with the 'hero' attention. This however was the Bill I got to know over the last 40 years of his life. It is the same Bill who was the Father and Grandfather that his family and friends knew and loved so well (Further details of all the training crashes at 1661 HCU RAF Winthorpe can be found in Bill Taylor's book on *RAF Winthorpe*, courtesy of Howard Heeley, Newark Air Museum).

Stirlings, as the above demonstrates, were unpopular and most certainly not one of Bill's favourite aircraft to fly. Many of the training units at HCU and OTU were given clapped out Bombers from Operational Units. It is no wonder that so many accidents occurred during RAF training when there were malfunctions with inexperienced crews. Jeff Gray explains that Stirlings were so big that they wouldn't fit in the hangars and the ends of the wings were clipped slightly. The undercarriage was also extended in height otherwise the propeller blades would hit the ground. The undercarriage design was weak and would often give way as happened to Bill. Arthur Smith a Flight Engineer with 50 Squadron, explained to me that most of the systems worked on electric motors which were always burning out. It had a maximum ceiling height of 17,000 ft which again was unpopular with crews and the engines were extremely unreliable as Bill and his crew found out for themselves too. *'It was a bit like flying a double-decker bus and was quite a clumsy aircraft,'* said Bill.

Another crew at 1661 HCU RAF Winthorpe that trained at the same time as Bill was P/O Mark Davis' crew, who went on to serve with 619 Squadron in Lancaster ME846. This crew had members who were best friends with the 'North Crew'. One was Bomb Aimer Peter Knox who had left Australia with Norman Jarvis and attended 70 Bomb Aimers Course in Wales. The other was the Mid-Upper Gunner Sgt George Moggridge who was Dennis Bartlett's best friend (See Chapter 24, Lives Lived And Lives Lost, for 'coincidences' with the two crews).

16, 250lb bombs being loaded onto 7 Squ N6101 of 1651 HCU, Waterbeach. (source IWMTR36) .

ME846 Crew by Stirling. **Left to right**: F/S Peter E Knox (RAAF), Sgt Thomas A Newbery, Sgt W Dennis 'Geordie' Belshaw, P/O Mark AH 'Dave' Davis, F/S Leslie EJ 'Tag' Taylor, Sgt George H Moggridge, F/S John ER 'Porky' Bowering (RCAF).

The accident rate at OTU was horrendous, from 1939-45, 5,327 officers and men were killed and a further 3,113 injured in training accidents. With some courses losing 25% of their trainees; 'tour expired crew posted to instruct in tired and under maintained bombers soon found out it was no rest cure' (Max Hastings, *Bomber Command*).

While Bill and his crew were at OTU during 1943 the losses on two engine aircraft in were as follows: 425 Wellingtons, (201 of them Wellington IIIs), 72 Whitley Vs and 6 Ansons, totalling 503.

During 1944, losses at HCU were 41 Stirling Is and 99 Stirling IIIs: 140 lost in total. 26 were from 1661 HCU, 2 of these Stirling crashes were those involving Bill, with the 'North' crew walking away from both accidents.

158 Halifax IIs, 5 Halifax IIIs and 123 Halifax Vs: 286 lost. Lancasters were the lowest with 9 losses, only one of them a Lancaster III, proving the Lancaster III was by far the safest aircraft to fly in. Although there were 20 Lancs lost at LFS, all were Lancaster Is. The total was 467 losses at HCU in 1944 (WR Chorley, *1944 Losses*).

Part of the reason for such high losses in Halifaxes is explained by Leonard Cheshire, the CO of 76 Squadron. From August 1942 to April 1943, No 76 Squadron was commanded by W/C Leonard Cheshire. Cheshire noticed that very few Halifaxes were coming home on three engines. He would do nothing his crews wouldn't do and flew regularly on some of the most dangerous missions to gain as much technical and practical information as possible so he could pass this onto the crews. He took a Halifax up to find out what the problem was and found out that if a Halifax stalled after losing an engine it went into an uncontrollable spin. After falling for a terrifying minute from the sky, luckily and skilfully Cheshire recovered the aircraft to land and report the problem, which was caused by a fault in the rudder design. Handley–Page, refused to interrupt aircraft production to modify the design. Leonard Cheshire was furious and the changes were only made after a Polish test pilot was killed investigating the same problem. Leonard Cheshire was an inspirational Commander who saved many aircrews lives by his dedication to air training, safety and technical procedures. (Max Hastings, *Bomber Command*)

Some of the instructors who flew with Bill and his crew in 'A' Flight were: F/O Coxhill (DFC), F/O Gifford (DFC), F/O Price (DFM), P/O Ball (DFM). On the 20 March 1944 Bill received a High Average Certificate from 1661 HCU, with 419 hours and 55 minutes flying time under his belt.

1661 HCU RAF Winthorpe is where the famous picture I saw as a child of Bill's crew standing by the Stirling Bomber was taken; each of the crew had a copy of this photo.

From 22/04/1944 to 06/05/1944 Bill and the boys moved to No 5 Lancaster Finishing School (LFS) at Syerston. The boys flew Lancaster Bombers in 'A' Flight for the first time and learned all the technical procedures unique to this aircraft. Flying in Lancaster's Mk I and III, codes F, A, T, M and S, his instructors at Syerston were F/O Cuelenaere and 61 Squ's F/Lt BC Fitch (435hrs and 30mins flying time).

**W/O Norman Jarvis**

*'In April we went to change over on to Lancasters, the aircraft which we were to take on Operations a month later. This was a very busy time; we had to learn all new Dinghy drills, new instruments, parachute drill peculiar to Lancs and many new sets of equipment to get used to, but we thought at the end of that we knew it all and could give a good account of ourselves with the immortal Bomber Command of the RAF.'*

Peter Knox was also transferred to Syerston and gives his first impression of the Lancaster:

*'On the first flight, the instructor cut two of the four engines and demonstrated how the Lancaster could still fly safely and keep its height. We only did about 15 hours of flying on this particular course and it was pure pleasure after the Stirling experience. This was a plane that inspired confidence.'*

Bill was now flying the Avro Lancaster and it was an aircraft that Bill truly loved. Many design successes helped the Allies to win and shorten the war: the Spitfire, the Mosquito, the Mustang and the Rolls Royce Merlin engine that powered them all. One of the most important of these masterpieces of technical design was surely the Lancaster Bomber - a vast improvement on the old Stirlings. As soon as Bill began to fly it he felt at home. He could make this aeroplane do anything he wanted it to.

**F/Lt Bill North**

*'When I first flew the Lancaster it was like flying a Rolls Royce, it responded perfectly, it was beautiful to fly and very forgiving. The stick on Wellingtons had to be held in place or it would come back at you, so you needed some physical strength to fly it; the Lancaster was a dream and looked amazing.'*

The Lancaster Bomber, beautifully menacing, full of authority; iconic symbol of freedom and technology (Source, *Bomber Command Museum of Canada*).

When we took Bill to RAF Hendon on 28 Feb 2010 it was arranged that we could pass the cordon ropes and go right underneath the resident Lancaster S for Sugar. It was an emotional day with Bill's family and my family present. When we approached the Lancaster and stopped next to it Bill's eyes filled with tears. I asked him if he was ok and he said, *'I haven't been this close to a Lancaster for a long time. I can't quite believe that I actually flew it, it looks so big, but then again we were young fit men in those days. This brings back so many memories it has made me feel very emotional.'*

Bill North next to 467 Squ's 'Ton up' Lancaster at RAF Hendon, 28 Feb 2010. A Mk I, R5868, S for Sugar is the oldest surviving Lancaster and flew 137 Operations during its faithful service to Bomber Command. It was the 2nd Lancaster to complete 100 Ops and has 467 Sqn's (RAAF) PO-S code (*Claims To Fame, The Lancaster,* Norman Franks) Dennis Bartlett, London Guildhall, 27 June 2012 (CK).

It was here at RAF Hendon that I found out more about the Lancaster's birth and Operational history from Bill, our guide Bev Rickson and information present in the museum. The Lancaster had evolved from a twin engined aircraft designed by Roy Chadwick called the Manchester which was powered by 24 cylinder Rolls Royce Vulture engines. These engines proved to be extremely unreliable with many Manchesters lost. Chadwick realized that the aircraft had serious design flaws and made plans to modify it. He managed to get hold of four Rolls Royce Merlin Engines which were extremely hard to come by due to their allocation to Fighter Command. He added twelve feet to the wingspan and replaced the two troublesome Vulture engines with the four Rolls Royce Merlins and the Lancaster was born. In true British wartime style he had snatched success from the jaws of defeat in the most ingenious way and then delivered an aircraft to Bomber Command that Bill and his comrades loved and had the upmost respect for.

The new bomber was immediately regarded as a complete success and large production orders were placed. Avro's production facilities were soon overwhelmed, and many other companies and contractors joined the effort to produce Lancasters. Consisting of 55,000 separate parts, some half a million different manufacturing operations were involved to produce just one aircraft. Peak production was achieved during August 1944 when 293 aircraft were produced. Of the total of 7,377 Lancasters built (430 of them in Canada), 3,932 were lost in action. The superior capabilities of the

Lancaster gave it good flexibility and allowed it carry a variety of bomb loads. Weighing 36,900 lbs empty, the Lancaster was capable of taking off with an additional 33,100 lbs of fuel and bombs, it could carry almost its own weight again. Bill's 5 Group had a close working relationship with Avro and Rolls-Royce during the development of the Lancaster as it evolved from the Manchester, so that by 1942 it was often referred to as 'Avro's Air Force.'

Lancasters flew a total of 156,308 sorties, dropping 608,612 tons of bombs and placing over 12,000 mines in enemy waters (Photo, *Stephen Elsworth*).

Winston Churchill had a firm understanding of the concept of superior air power and effective control over air space and made this famous comment. *'The Navy can lose us the war, but only the Air Force can win it. Therefore our supreme effort must be to gain overwhelming mastery in the air. The Fighters are our salvation, but the Bombers alone provide the means of victory.'* The Government and the Air Ministry were now committed to maximum effort in the production of heavy bombers and the training of aircrew to fly them.

While Bill was going through Initial Training Wings in early 1942 the War Cabinet agreed to the 'area bombing' of German cities. In February 1942 Arthur Harris was appointed Commander in Chief (CinC) of Bomber Command, taking his place at Headquarters in High Wycombe. Two months before Bill's 20th birthday Lancasters flew on their first Operations in March 1942. Harris had been tasked with implementing Churchill's policy and fervently supported the development of tactics and technology to perform the job more effectively. Harris now assisted Chief of Air Staff Charles Portal in carrying out some of the most devastating attacks on the

German war machine. A quote from Arthur Harris that Bill remembers well and became one of his more famous comments was:- *'The Nazis entered this war under the rather childish delusion that they were going to bomb everyone else, and nobody was going to bomb them. At Rotterdam, London, Warsaw, and half a hundred other places, they put their rather naive theory into operation. They sowed the wind, and now they are going to reap the whirlwind.'*

On 6 May 1944 Bill and his crew moved to RAF Skellingthorpe to commence their tour of 30 Operations for Bomber Command. Training was over and Bill and his crew were about to witness the true horror of war. Their first Operation together to Lille in France would be a baptism of fire.

# Chapter Nine

# Into the fire

The Royal Air Force Flag.

## W/O Norman Jarvis

*'On 7 May 1944, just a year after leaving Australia I arrived on 61 Squadron of the RAF to commence my Operational career. The whole crew were a bit excited as we stepped out of the van that had brought us from Lancaster Finishing School. It was good to know that we had really made the grade though and were to be members of such a famous Squadron, face to face with the grim purpose of helping to carry on the greatest striking power the world has ever known. Being an Aussie I was disappointed a little at not being able to go to one of the Australian Lancaster Squadrons as they had such a brilliant record. However this one was equal in every way and its commander was an Aussie Wing Commander* [A.W. Doubleday] *who met us and gave us a good welcome, but said he was very short of crews and wanted us to become Operational as soon as possible.'*

When I was interviewing Bill for this book, most of the questions I asked would be answered immediately and in much detail. The odd question here and there would not be answered, or answered very briefly, and we would skip onto the next subject. One such question was, 'Were you ever scared, Bill, or what did you fear the most?'

Bill's immediate answer was, 'No, I was never scared, although many would say you were a liar if you said you weren't.'

That was it. There was no elaboration and we moved onto other topics. Six months later, on the 14th August 2011 Bill unexpectedly answered this question at a much deeper level. The original question had sat there with him for all that time; he had obviously been mulling it over and had finally come up with this answer.

**F/Lt Bill North**

*'Chris, I've been thinking about your question about what did I fear. I wasn't scared or didn't fear going on Operations or the danger that came with it. I actually enjoyed flying and the challenges it presented. What I feared the most was letting my crew down.'*

Well, this brought tears to my eyes. I really had to hold on tight to the waterworks as I sat in front of Bill and wrote this down. It was an answer I could not have predicted and again represents the bond, friendship and respect Bill's crew had for each other. Bill certainly never ever let his crew down!

It is astonishing that he never felt scared amid such acute danger and the ever-present threat of death, but his own words as well the words of his comrades and the evidence of his record testify that this is the case. His determination never to let his crew down is proved by his heroic actions.

The first time Bill's crew flew together at 61 Squadron was on the day after they had arrived, on a training mission. The Movement of Crew Records shows them arriving on the 6 of May 1944. In Bill's Log Book the training missions are written in dark blue ink, the night bombing Operations are in red ink and day Operations in green ink, here however all are written in black. They are marked accordingly.

From 25 October 1942 when Bill first flew a Tiger Moth in Canada to the 7 May 1944 when he first flew a Lancaster at an Operational Squadron, a period of just over 18 months had passed. He had clocked up an incredible 435hrs 30mins flying time. Add the 15 months from when he passed his medical exam on the 14 July 1941 and we have a time span of just over two and a half years. This was the average period of time it took the RAF to train their potential pilots, more often than not they would be lost in their first few Ops.

7 MAY 1944, LANCASTER QR-M (Mickey the Moocher). SELF. 6 CREW. X COUNTRY + BOMBING (Cross country was a navigation and crew coordination exercise on which they would fly from A to B to C etc and return to base, using map, compass and navigational equipment. They would be timed in and out to monitor their crew efficiency).

**W/O Norman Jarvis**

*'The very first night there were no Operations, so we were sent out on an 8 hour cross country trip and the next day the crew were all interviewed by the various section commanders. Then we heard for the first time the saying 'There is a war on tonight.' Our pilot Bill was going with the 'A' Flight Commander, F/Lt Farmiloe on his 'second dickie' trip just to get an idea, hopefully saying 'Oh that's not possible.' Just before Bill went to briefing the whole crew wished him good luck and perhaps chaffed him a little bit. I was watching a movie when I heard them take off that night and I felt a little bit queer as one after another I heard the bombers roar down the runway and off we knew not where.'*

**F/Lt Bill North**

*'Although I had Dave Crowley with me as Navigator on this Op. it was a strange feeling to be flying without the rest of my crew, as we had all become very close by then and they were naturally wary of the fact that Dave and I might not return which upset all of us.'*

The so-called 'Second dickie' trip was a compulsory introduction to flying on real Operations for all new pilots. The new pilot would sit in on an Operation with a veteran crew (usually with their own Navigator) to get a feel for what went on and what to expect. Bill was lucky, in that the pilot on his 'second dickie' mission was the skilled, experienced and highly courageous pilot Howard Farmiloe.

F/Lt Farmiloe and his crew took Bill and Dave Crowley off to Brest, a sea-port in France on the far north-west tip of Brittany, nearly a five hour journey there and back. This was a familiar target for Bomber Command, was heavily defended and had received many previous visits. It was an important strategic Naval base and home to some of the Kriegsmarine's Battleships, Cruisers and Destroyers. The Germans also maintained a large U-boat base at Brest allowing them quicker access to the Atlantic shipping lanes and convoys. Only the 12,000lb Tallboy bomb could and eventually did pierce the 7m thick concrete U-Boat Pens located here (The city was totally destroyed during the Battle for Brest in 1944 after the D-Day landings, with barely more than three buildings left standing. After the war the West German Government paid compensation to help rebuild the devastated town).

Right through all Bill's Operations I will mention 3 of 61 Squadron's 4 famous 'Ton-up' Lancasters. ED860, QR-N for Nan, (130 Ops), EE176,

QR-M, 'Mickey the Moocher', (128 Ops), JB138, QR-J 'Just Jane', (123 Ops), and the fourth was LL843, QR-P for Pod, (118 Ops). This last a/c joined 61 Squ from 467 Squ, beginning Ops on 20/21 July to Courtrai with F/Lt S Parker and later in July was also flown by W/Cmdr AW Doubleday. It was also up in the air for the remainder of Les Morton's Tour of Ops. All I will do as a reference is put the a/c serial number alongside the name of the pilot that flew it on Bill's Operation. Flying alongside these 4 famous a/c were a number of workhorse Lancasters, one of them being Bill's EE186. Many of these Lancs had reached 50, 60, 70 Ops before they were 'fail to returns' and should not be forgotten.

I think this is a convenient place to quickly run through an average day on Operations at 5 Group HQ and its relationship with Bomber Stations like Skellingthorpe, also the duties the staff and crews went through. So we begin on an average Operational day in May 1944 at 5 Group's HQ Morton Hall, Swinderby, this was located approx 9 miles SW of Bill's base at Skellingthorpe.

The whole Bomber Command structure was complex and relied upon an efficient chain of communication and coordination between the CinC at HQ in High Wycombe and the various Groups with their affiliated Bomber Stations, which were located all over the country. The day would begin at Bill's 5 Group HQ with AVM Ralph Cochrane analysing and evaluating all the bombing results of the previous night's raids while waiting for the 'target for the night' signal from Bomber Command HQ. Swinderby would be a hive of activity with WAAF Officers studying bombing photographs and plotting all the release points over the target, civilian statisticians then preparing reports of last the night's raid for the strategists at High Wycombe. Senior staff would all be buzzing around attending to their various duties; then as soon as the signal was received for 'The target for the night', it all began again. The distance to the target would be measured; fuel and bomb loads worked out, tactics for PFF target marking discussed, then all this detailed operational information contained in a form B would then be transmitted via teleprinter to all the Group Squadron Commanders located at the associated Bomber Stations all around Lincolnshire. Precise plans would be worked out to coordinate the Group's a/c with a/c from other Groups including weather, courses, timings, altitude and speed, all of which would all help to avoid collisions and concentrate the Bomber Stream with anything up to 600 a/c over the target in a 20 minute time frame.

Bill's Station Skellingthorpe itself was also a part of this hive of 24/7 activity, from passing on their bombing results and debriefings to Swinderby, to preparing the RCM (Radio Counter Measure equipment (H2S, Gee, Oboe, Monica etc), the constant 24 hour servicing and maintenance of a/c by ground crews (mostly at dispersal points), also the constant repair of battle damage to its 40 odd Lancasters from 50 and 61 Squadrons by 58 Maintenance Unit.(A Merlin engine could be replaced by ground crew in 5 hours, a job which would normally take a week. In WW2 an average operational life of a Lancaster was 40 hours flying time!). All the Lancasters would be fuelled, armed and bombed up, which often gave any curious crews an idea of where they were flying to if they wanted to know. The fusing of the bomb load and bombing up of the a/c by the Armourers was also an extremely technical, physically demanding and dangerous job.

So Bill and his crew who made up some of the 2,600 or so service personnel located on an average Lincolnshire Bomber Station, were all a component of this complex machine with each trade attending to their own specialist roles. After individual trade briefings the crew would then attend a joint briefing in which 'The target for the night' would be revealed. A variety of specialists would all speak and share vital information like the Armourers, Met Officers and Flying Control Officers. This included info like aiming points, PFF target indicators, icing levels, flak concentrations, window deployment locations, searchlights, Night Fighters and above all precise timekeeping and altitudes. The Station and Squadron Commanders would all have a final word wishing them all good luck and the last thing crews would do before going to the locker rooms to draw their flying gear, parachutes and Mae Wests, etc would be to synchronise their watches.

We now follow Bill on his first Op, flying '2nd Dickie' to F/Lt Tommy Farmiloe:

**The Transportation Plan (31 March to 5/6 June 1944)**

**Operation No. 1. (Night mission)**

**8/9 May 1944, '2nd Dickie' to F/Lt HH Farmiloe, DSO. Seaplane Base, Brest, France.**

**Detailed bombing height 8,000ft, detailed bombing load unknown, 11 Lancasters detailed. Meteorology Report, no cloud, visibility good.**

**Lancaster, ME719, QR-F for Fox or FrEddy was the 5th a/c to take off and the 2nd a/c to return** (This a/c was eventually transferred to 1661HCU).

**F/L HH Farmiloe (DSO), P/O W North (2nd Pilot), Sgt GA Berry,**

**F/S H Crowley (Navigator), F/S K Vowe, F/S EA Davidson, W/O AE Patchet, SGT R Noble.**

Up---**21:27**---Down---**02:16**---Time out---**4hrs 49m**.

The abbreviations in the debriefing reports are as follows:- MPI, is for 'Mean Point of Impact', a term for the centre of bombing concentration. RSF, is for 'Red Signal Flare' and is a parachute type sky target marker (Wanganui), dropped above cloud. GTI, is for 'Green Target Indicator', a green ground target marker. American GP, is 'General Purpose Bomb'. a/c stands for aircraft and (7/7) means 7 crew members and their a/c were a complete loss. The Meteorological reports were provided by PFF (8 Group) and codenamed 'Pampa'. These were unarmed Mosquitoes of the Met flight No. 1409 stationed at RAF Wyton, that flew virtually 24/7 as and when requested by the CinC, they faced extreme danger while penetrating deep in to Germany (p179 *Pathfinder*, AVM Don Bennett).

**Debriefing report: -** F/Lt Farmiloe bombed west corner of main hangar at 23:58 hrs from 8,500ft. Other bombs seen dropping across target area, no markings seen at all. RSFs seen clearly from the attack 1 mile west from about H+5. R/T control very bad. Bombing winds not received until H+5. PHOTO: Good detail.

**Squ Ops. report:-** No cloud, good visibility. Eleven aircraft were detailed on the night to bomb the Lanvedoc-Poulmic Seaplane Base at Brest. The target was identified visually and a large hangar, slipways, barracks and other buildings were attacked. The bombing appeared to be well concentrated in the target area, light and heavy flak was active mostly on route to target. Once again all the aircraft obtained photos of ground detail. Bombing height ranged from 7,250 – 9,500ft.

58 Lancasters and 6 Mosquitoes of 5 Group attacked the seaplane base at Brest, with others attacking railway yards and gun emplacements. For the 452 sorties this night 12 aircraft were lost, 1 over Brest. The one Lancaster III lost on the Brest mission was from 83 Sqn. ND818, OL-T, flown by F/L AP Whitford (RAAF), who was on his 40th Op. It was lost over the target area, disintegrating after being hit by light flak (F/Lt Jeff Gray reported the target was illuminated by an a/c exploding on the run up to the target). The whole crew perished, proving that any crew (even veterans), anytime could succumb to the ever-present shadow of death. A further 2 aircraft and their crews were complete losses (14 men) and 1 Lancaster from 35 Squ was lost with 1 survivor, Sgt WG Lawrie who evaded capture. The large number of

2nd Pilots lost on their 1st 'second dickie' Ops is also very sobering fact too. After forming up and bonding these poor crews having lost their leader would now be 'headless' and have to reform with a new Captain.

Some of the other 61 Squadron pilots who flew alongside Bill that night and would become familiar names, flying with him on many subsequent missions were:- P/O Jeff Gray (who was 2nd to take off and 1st to return just ahead of Bill, beating Tommy Farmiloe again by just one minute), F/S EJ (Jack) Goodyer (1st to take off), P/O JA Forrest, P/O F Norton in EE176, F/S J Kramer (RCAF), P/O EW Hallett, P/O D Street, Sgt HW Cooper and P/O EA Stone in ED860. The whole Squadron (11 a/c) returned safely, all landing at Skellingthorpe within 30 minutes of each other. This was a remarkable achievement and testament to their courage, skill and crew co- ordination given the near 5 hour journey there and back.

**W/O Norman Jarvis**

*'That first trip of Bill's was not a long one, but he said that he had a good knowledge in what the various types of flak looked like and of the conditions in the target area. We heard all this when he returned about two in the morning, then we rolled over and slept much sounder for the rest of the night.'*

BBMF Lancaster, PA474. The Flypast at 50 and 61 Squadron Memorial Day, 10 June 2012, Skellingthorpe Village (CK).

Bill's Captain on this his first 'second dickie' mission, was F/Lt HH Farmiloe who was a distinguished pilot (F/Lt Jeff Grey who knew him well called him Tommy Farmiloe). I was saddened to discover this Obituary as I was writing this chapter.

**Headline from Daily Telegraph Airforce Obituaries. 7 June 2010. Flight Lieutenant Howard Farmiloe**

'Flight Lieutenant Howard Farmiloe, who has died aged 88, brought his bomber back from Berlin on two engines in 1944 and was awarded an immediate DSO, an extremely rare award for a Pilot Officer, the most junior of the RAF's commissioned ranks'.

F/Lt HH Farmiloe (Source, *Daily Telegraph*).

At the height of Bomber Command's winter offensive, Farmiloe and his crew had twice pressed on to Berlin to drop their bombs despite losing one of the four engines of their Lancaster before reaching the target. On the night of March 24/25 1944, his eighth visit to the 'The Big City', Farmiloe's skill and determination were put to an even sterner test.

En route to the target, the port outer engine failed and caught fire. Shortly afterwards the port inner had to be shut down. Farmiloe would have been fully justified in jettisoning his bomb load and turning for home, but he decided to continue despite steadily losing height and speed. After dropping his bombs on the target he chose to take the most direct route to England. An SOS was sent and the crew jettisoned all the loose equipment, including the guns, ammunition, some of the navigation equipment and the portable lavatory.

The failed engines provided much of the aircraft's electrical power and hydraulic functions, so most of the aircraft's 'services' were not functioning. The Lancaster was returning alone and away from the main bomber stream, it was continuing to lose height and it had no means of self-defence. Farmiloe had great difficulty holding the aircraft on course but received crucial assistance from the bomb aimer who, for two hours, locked his arms around the rudder pedal to ease the load on Farmiloe's leg. The crew prepared to ditch in the North Sea, but the Lancaster finally reached the East coast – where a searchlight directed it to the nearest airfield, Little Snoring in Norfolk. Farmiloe managed to get the undercarriage down, but with no flaps he had to land faster than normal and, without brakes, the aircraft ran off the end of the runway into a field before tipping on to its nose in marshy ground. The citation for Farmiloe's DSO concluded: 'This gallant pilot displayed outstanding determination in pressing home his attack and his great skill and coolness in the face of increasing difficulties on the homeward flight set an example of the highest order.' His navigator was awarded a DFC and the bomb aimer and wireless operator received DFMs.

Howard Hatherall Farmiloe was born on 21 August 1921 in Birmingham and educated at Chipping Camden School and Birmingham University. A keen motorcyclist, he intended to join the Royal Signals but responded to a call for volunteers to be aircrew. He joined the RAF in 1940 and trained as a pilot in the United States.

His first operations over Germany with the Lancasters of No 61 Squadron coincided with Bomber Command's 'Maximum Effort', when the German night fighter forces were at their strongest and the casualties among bomber crews were very high. After his desperate return flight from Berlin, Farmiloe completed another 12 operations, some against communications targets in France in the build-up to D-Day. During the early hours of 6 June 1944 as the invasion forces landed in Normandy, he attacked the gun batteries on the French coast. A few days later he flew his final bombing operation of the war.

Farmiloe left the RAF in 1946 and qualified as a chartered surveyor. He spent many years as an estate agent and auctioneer in the Tewkesbury area. In retirement he and his wife were intrepid travellers, and when he was in his sixties he learned to ski and windsurf. Howard Farmiloe died on June 7th. He married, in 1948, Moira Williams; she died in 1999, and he is survived by their two daughters.'

This was another fine example of the tenacious and courageous nature of the men who flew on Operations with Bill North in Bomber Command's 61 Squadron. For a more detailed account of Tommy Farmiloe and crew's dramatic brush with death on 'the night of the strong winds':- p73, Chapter 8, The Big City, *Thundering Through The Clear* Air by Derek Brammer.

**<u>W/O Norman Jarvis</u>**

*'Training schools had ended, but aircrews are always learning new methods and the ever changing tactics of the enemy keep you learning something*

*fresh all the time. We realised the grim purpose ahead of us, but we also knew with luck on our side we would fly to glory in the skies 'Per ardua ad astra.' And flying back at sunrise watching the colours of the east and the nights of stars and beautiful clouds is something of a sight that only the aircrews see and few appreciate.'*

*Per ardua* **ad astra** ('Through Adversity to the Stars') or ('Through Struggle to the Stars') is the motto of the RAF and other Commonwealth air forces such as the RAAF, RNZAF and the RCAF. It dates from 1912 and was used by the newly-formed Royal Flying Corps.

One more training exercise now followed on the 9 May. In-between missions the Bomber Command crews were still kept busy with training operations and tactics especially night flying to constantly update their capabilities. From Feb 1943 enigmatic Scotsman Air Chief Marshal Ralph Cochrane took over command of 5 Group and was constantly pressuring his Squadrons to keep training in between operations.

1944 9 MAY. LANCASTER, QR-E (Easy) SELF. 6 CREW. FIGHTER AFFILIATION/BOMBING (Fighter affiliation was when the crews practised evasive manoeuvres like the corkscrew generally with a Hurricane acting the part of a Night Fighter. Bombing was dropping dud practise bombs generally coloured yellow on bombing ranges, they would be marked accordingly to how close the bombs fell to the target).

1944 10 MAY. LANCASTER, QR-M (Mickey the Moocher) SELF. 6 CREW. BOMBING – N.F.T.

NFT (Night Flying Test). This was an Operations precheck of the Lancaster to make sure everything was working as it should be.

Bill and his crew now fly on their first mission together: a bombing raid over German-occupied Lille, inland on the French/Belgium border. For the first time, he came under fire, and saw his comrades being shot down around him. As Bill returned to Skellingthorpe in the early hours of the 11 May 1944 it would be his 22nd birthday. There were no real celebrations; there was no time, just a quick drink with his crew and onto the next mission!

Here is his own account of what he called his baptism of fire, in an almost literal sense of that expression:-

**Operation No. 2. (Night mission)**

**10/11 May 1944. Marshalling Yards, Lille, France.**

**'The North Crew':- P/O W North, F/S H Crowley, F/S NE Jarvis, Sgt G Monteith, Sgt PE O'Shea, Sgt DA Bartlett, Sgt L Morton.**

**Detailed bombing height 12,000ft, Bombing load 10,000lbs, 15 Lancasters detailed. Meteorology Report, haze with no cloud, visibility above good.**

**Lancaster III, EE176, QR-M, 'Mickey the Moocher' was the 4th a/c to take off and the 8th a/c to return. Later in this Lancaster's lucky life it became a member of the 'Ton up' Club, 100 plus Operations. This was 'Mickey's' 61st mission.**

Up---**21:56**---Down---**01:15**---Time out---**3hrs 19m**

Below I give Bill's debriefing report as recorded in the Operational Record Book (ORB), along with Squadron Operations report of the Lille mission - a procedure I follow throughout where I list all the missions flown by Bill and his crew.

**Debriefing report:-** P/O North bombed one RSF at 23:38 hours from 10,000ft. Excellent observation at 23:36 hours just short of R.S.F. Large amount of smoke up to 8,000ft. Attack did not seem to be particularly concentrated as there were three fires going on in the target area. PHOTO: Ground detail.

**Squ Ops report:-** Met: Ground haze with no cloud.Vis above good. Fifteen a/c were detailed for bombing Ops against Lille, all of which successfully bombed the target. Twelve a/c obtained photos of ground detail. The remaining three had photo flash failures. RSF's were bombed from heights between 14,500-16,000ft. Several bombs were seen to explode in a close proximity to the markers. Ground defences were negligible, although one a/c was hit by heavy flak.

**Flying alongside F/Lt Bill North and F/Lt Jeff Gray to mark the target and on his 11th Op with 97 Squ PFF was W/O Percy Cannings and his crew:-** Skipper, F/O WM Reid, FE, Sgt W Richards, NAV, F/O RD Parker, BA, F/ Sgt GD Moir, WO, F/Sgt B Harthill, MUG, F/Sgt DP Cannings, RG, Sgt G Brown, 97 Squadron PFF marked this target for Bill in Lancaster ND807, OF-P, 'B' Flight, 97 Squadron PFF Coningsby (**BI**).

**PFF Debriefing report:-**

T/o Coningsby. Up 22:03, Down 01:12 (almost exactly the same Up and Down times as Bill North). Bomb and marker load:- 6x7' clusters, 1x4000lb HC, 8x500lb MC, 3x4.5 reco flares. Weather clear, ground haze. Identified target on H2S. Re-marking became necessary and more flares were asked for. Fresh lot of reserve flares went east of target, so we were asked to drop our internally stowed flares to the west of these. Main Force came in after second marking and did some very good bombing resulting in several good explosions around 23:55 hours; there was no scatter of bombs noted.

EE176, QR-M, 'Mickey the Moocher at Skellingthorpe dispersals in 1944. In the background the shape of Lincoln Cathedral can just be made out (source, *original photo by F/Lt Jeff Gray*).

Lille was part of a group of 5 railway targets to be attacked that night with 506 aircraft; 291 Lancasters, 187 Halifaxes and 28 Mosquitoes. It was a baptism of fire for the young 'North Crew'; death cast a long shadow over the whole Operation. 14 aircraft were lost, 12 from Lille, 1 from Dieppe and 1 Halifax lost on minelaying. 11 of them were complete aircraft and crew losses (7/7s) and one 467 Sqn Lancaster III, LM 475, PO-B was 6 out of 7 crew lost. The skipper S/L DPS Smith RAAF was ejected as the bomber exploded mid-air, landing relatively unscathed and evading capture. Two 50 Sqn Lancs and crews were completely lost and in terms of aircrew casualties the Lille raid was a horrific operation, with 83 dead and 1 survivor. The majority were claimed by heavy night fighter activity, most shot down and lost in large ground or mid air explosions over the target area as witnessed by Bill and his crew. Two of 5 Groups PFF Lancaster's from 97 Squ Coningsby F/Lt JB Smith, DFC, (RNZAF) in JB708, OF-J and P/O SA Edwards in ND813, OF-Q were also complete losses in large explosions over and near the target (Both these a/c had taken off just before Percy and his crew). Skellingthorpe Station Commander W/Cmdr AW Doubleday also flew alongside Bill on this Op and his debriefing report also confirms: 'Numerous explosions in the air'.

There was some uncertainty over Lille due to incorrect bombing winds and quite a time period when the target was unmarked by the PFF backing up crews (A cease bombing signal was received at 23:42, but the crews still bombed anyway). This turned the bomber stream in all directions as some came in again for the bombing run, W/Cmdr Doubleday made 3 bombing runs. This increased the collision rate as witnessed by F/Lt Farmiloe at 23:41, who reported the target illuminated by the light of an explosion from a collision between 2 a/c (Possibly either 463 Squ HK535 and 467 Squ LL788 who both crashed on a factory in SE suburbs of Lille, or 467 Squ's EE143 and LM475 who both crashed at Lezennes Ronchin in SE suburbs of Lille. *WR Chorley*). P/O RA Dear also reported a collision with his a/c by another Lancaster turning across him from port to starboard, shearing 2ft of his port rudder. Despite the horrors of mid-air collisions, explosions and Night Fighter attacks, the whole Squadron miraculously returned safely to base between 00:55 and 01:37, P/O Dear limping in last at 02:00.

Some of the other 61 Squ pilots flying with Bill that night were: W/Cmdr AW Doubleday, F/L HH Farmiloe, F/O GA Berry (RCAF), P/O JA Forrest (RAAF), P/O CJ Gray (who again was the first pilot to return), F/S Kramer (RCAF), P/O RA Dear, P/O D Street in ED860 and P/O WE Jeavons. Forrest, Gray and Kramer all took off in that order immediately after Bill. I asked Bill if he remembered any of these pilots and he said F/L Farmiloe really well from his 1st Op and Forrest, Kramer, Goodyer and Jeff Gray from the briefing sessions.

There now follows eye witness accounts from Bill and his crew explaining the Lille Operation:-

**W/O Norman Jarvis**

*'Next morning we reported to our various sections and did the daily inspection of our machine. At eleven o'clock we heard that there was a 'War on' again. This meant us. The whole crew would be going out tonight to drop bombs on the enemy and do battle for the first time. We did our night flying test early and at the evening meal in the mess I felt a little tense and excited, but did not want to show it. In the mess there were men with tired eyes, but they all had that determined look about them which made them appear much older than their years.'*

**W/O Peter Knox recalls the emotions felt before crews left for an Operation:**

*'In the afternoon we went back to our living quarters for a rest period. A strange quietness descended on our huts even though each housed a dozen or more men. This was a time for reflection. Letters home were written. I can recall saying a few prayers in the privacy of my bed. I imagine others did the same. I would not have known. This was a very personal time—— the one occasion when you asked yourself if this was to be your last living day. For an hour or two there was little conversation or fraternisation. For a short time we lived in our own world. Most of us were young and without responsibilities. This made it easier to live with the inner fear we obviously all experienced.'*

The names of the crews on operations that day were generally put up on a board outside the mess, also in the course of my research and talking to veterans the general feeling was that although service personnel went through varying degrees of nervousness they would not share their apprehensions and kept these to themselves. I will touch more on this later on. The next stage was the briefing sections and final group briefing. The crews generally arrived at dispersals an hour before takeoff time to prepare themselves and double check all their equipment. Before taking final charge of the a/c from the Ground Crew at dispersal point Bill had to sign a form 700 to say he was happy with the aircraft and its flying condition. A final wee over the back wheel of the a/c was a good luck ceremony for some crews.

**W/O Norman Jarvis**

*'I got up to the briefing room early and had a good look at the target maps and the route there and back. I began to put the tracks in on my topographical maps, then I helped Dave (Navigator Sgt. Dave Crowley) with his charts. Then I went in with all the bomb aimers to hear from the bombing leader; the load and types of bombs and the procedure to be adopted by us. We went back in and waited for our pilots to tell us what they had been instructed, then came the main briefing of all the crew. The meteorological men told us what weather to expect, the intelligence men gave us our escape aids; then Wing Commander Doubleday wished us all luck. I stacked up my gear and we all moved into the locker room to dress.*

*The first trip of ours was not going to be a long one and we were going in to attack the target from 10,000ft, so I wouldn't need a lot of clothes; but I wasn't taking any chances tonight, so put on my inner flying suit and heavy aircrew sweater over my battle dress and of course the usual fur-lined flying boots and two pairs of socks. The only gloves I ever took though were a pair of silk ones covered by leather gauntlets. Then I collected my Mae West, put it on, then drew my parachute and harness from the racks. By this time the crews were all moving out to their kites, so we asked a pretty little WAAF driver to take us out to ours. This we learned was Anne, who was to perform the same duty for us many more times and wave goodbye from the top of her little van. I examined the bomb load on our aircraft and got quite a shock to see that we were actually going to try and take off with it, it looked so big and deadly looking; eight 1000 pounders and four 500 pounders. When I was satisfied with the way they were loaded I climbed into the aircraft and made the necessary settings on my panel and tested the circuit, then arranged my maps and stacked the parachute while the skipper and Les (Sgt. Les Morton) ran up the engines. Then I hopped out again to wait on the soft green grass around the dispersal area with the other boys. If I remember correctly we did not take a lot that night. The crews all had prearranged take- off times and we were around the middle, so we saw the first boys taxiing around on their way to take off before we were wished good-luck by our ground crew and climbed in. We did our harnesses up, stored the chutes and re-tested the oxygen and intercom etc. We then joined the great circle of bombers going around the perimeter track on their way to take off. It was a very inspiring sight seeing them taxiing slowly around; the propellers of the one behind us was only a few yards from the rear gun turret of our machine. As soon as one Lancaster left the ground another went tearing down the runway with full power to lift a full-up weight of 65,000lbs off the deck. We got our green flash from the 'aldis lamp' at the taxi post; this ok'd us to take off. Bill swung our kite around and there they all were, the boys who were not going and many ground staff waving goodbye with their thumbs up. It felt really good to be going out on something really important and all those interested spectators made us feel at last we were doing a job. I could feel the power of those four 1250bhp engines as the revs. were increased and down the great back track we went. Forty, fifty, sixty, eighty mph, then the far boundary fence coming up at a hundred miles per hour and we were off the ground. The fence and the trees were below us and we climbed quite rapidly to 1,000ft, where we all breathed a sigh of relief. Bill was climbing all the time, but still circling the drome until it was time to set course. Everyone has to have his eyes open at this time because there are so many of you in the air doing the same thing as you are that a collision means the end of both parties. We set course and noted with satisfaction the navigation lights of our comrades in the stream of bombers. As we crossed the English coast the lights must be put out. I stood up and cocked my two guns in the front turret, then settled down in my compartment. It was dark, but on the horizon in the west, the last red reflection of the sun could be seen on the clouds. I reported crossing the English coast to our Navigator Dave Crowley and fused my bombs, then came half an hour over the sea. Far below I could see the French coast coming up and what were those strange red and orange bursts? It must be flak, yes it was flak and soon it was bursting off to the port side, but not too close.'*

BBMF Lancaster PA474 in flight at Coningsby 30 Sept 2012. She is marked here as KC-A, 'Thumper Mk.III' of 617 Sqn to commemorate the 12 Nov 1944 mission to sink the Tirpitz (photo, *Stephen Elsworth*).

Two of the immediate dangers to crews were flak and Night Fighters. Sometimes even to the most experienced and alert crews death could strike instantly and without warning. Discipline and coordination between the crew was paramount whilst facing these dangers. We now take a slight diversion from the Lille Operation to explain what Bill and the crew experienced and the danger of flak to a 'Heavy Bomber':-

Flak batteries (*Flakartillerie* or anti-aircraft artillery) were a part of the Luftwaffe and organised into light, heavy and searchlight companies, with calibres ranging from 20mm to 128mm. The 88mm Flak Gun (*Flugzeugabwehr-kanone* or Flak 18) and its variants was one of the most reliable, accurate and effective heavy weapons in WW2. It could fire from its semi automatic breach system high-explosive or armour piercing shells, at up to 15 rounds per minute to a height of 32,482ft. The German gunners were experts at laying a carpet of flak at whatever height they choose too and the unfortunate bomber streams would be literally be buffeted by these relentless orangey black puffs from these 88mm shells exploding and showering the surrounding air space with shrapnel in varying sizes. Any of these deadly pieces of red hot metal could pierce or pass through the Lancaster's body causing catastrophic damage to vital equipment and serious injury or death to any crew members unlucky enough to be in its path. If there was a direct hit it was game over and the aircraft would explode in a sickening ball of fire (RAF Hendon and Imperial War Museums).

Nobby Clark a Wireless Operator with 61 Squadron in 1943 who's skipper was P/O Ward Parsons (RCAF), recalls his last mission on his tour of 30 was to Gelsenkerchen on 9/10 July 1943 (A target Bill was to later fly to in 1944). This mission ended in tragedy for Nobby Clark's crew and proves how lethal flak could be (Derek Brammer, *Thundering Through The Clear Air*).

**Nobby Clark**

*'Shortly after we had bombed the target, we ran into heavy flak and our Navigator, P/O R.S. (Bob) Dyson, was hit by the only fragment of shrapnel that penetrated the fuselage and he died shortly afterwards.'*

**W/O Norman Jarvis**

*'We were hit by heavy flack one night. It slammed with a bang, just like someone shutting a train door in your ear above the roar of the engines. Fortunately no one was injured and the only damage was a large hole in the fuselage between the Mid-upper and Tail Gunners.'*

**F/Lt Bill North**

*'On one occasion when we had returned to base there was a large piece of the fuselage missing, the Lancaster airframes were robust and could take a lot of punishment. Flak was a curious thing, you could feel it buffeting the plane, you could see it and smell the acrid cordite, but not hear it as the roar from the four Merlin engines drowned out most other noise.'*

**W/O Dennis Bartlett**

*'I can remember on one low level mission over France we were hit by flak in the fuselage between my position in the Mid-Upper Turret and the Rear Turret. I saw it slam into us with an almighty bang leaving a gaping hole, it was unnerving, I felt the thump go right through me.'*

A Lancaster explodes mid-air after a direct hit by flak (IWM).

Now back to the Lille Operation and Norman Jarvis guides us again:-

**W/O Norman Jarvis**

*'Then came one or two alterations of course and the gunners and I were searching the skies and I kept on thinking down below is an enemy who is going to take a pretty dim view of us up here. Another half an hour and there were two flares going down in the target area, perhaps thirty or forty miles away, within a few minutes we were getting close and I saw the red markers go down to indicate the target right in amongst the flares. As we approached I could see nothing but a mass of lights of various colours and size and it was not all going down; quite a lot of it was coming up towards us.* Now came the time for me to take over the directing of the bomber. I got Bill to turn approximately on the briefed heading for bombing. I selected what looked like the centre of the target area and sang out, left, left, steady. Bomb doors open, left, left, steady, steady. Hell what was that! It's ok, steady, steady, bombs going, bombs gone; ok skipper, they're all gone, smack on.'*

* The tracer bullets and cannon shells that came up from the varying sizes of anti-aircraft guns seemed to move in slow motion as they criss-crossed and lit up the skies.

**F/Lt Bill North**

*'The bombing run was one of the most intense times of many for the crew. For a few minutes Norman was in charge of directions and I had to hold the air-craft straight and steady no matter what. I would fly the aircraft on instruments alone at this point, so I was not distracted by what was going on outside. It was the longest few minutes of our lives and each time we did the bombing run we all held our breaths. The minute the bombs were gone the tension was released and someone would normally shout, let's gets the hell out of here. However we still had to hold steady for a little bit longer until we had taken our bombing pictures, if you didn't take these you could get in a lot of trouble as this proved you had reached the target and dropped your bombs.'*

**W/O Norman Jarvis**

*'Someone said 'Let's get out of here,' then I heard Dave say 'turn on course so and so' which was the way home. A searchlight or two flashed past us and there was a bit more flak, but we had done our first job and must not relax, the bigger danger from Night Fighters came usually after bombing. We were now out of the target area and the first thing everyone wanted to know was what was it that blew up right in front of us on the bombing run. Most of the boys thought it was another aircraft, but Bill and I were of the opinion that it was a 'scare-crow' put up by the Jerries as we ran right through the wreckage of it without doing any harm to ourselves.'*

Another quick diversion from this Operation to explain to the reader the perilous experience they just went through and the danger to Bill and his crew from Night Fighters that were fitted with upward firing cannons.

There is some debate over the use and tactics regarding 'Scarecrows.' The aircrews were aware of their presence and use as is illustrated in Norman and Bill's testament. They were reported in the press at the time, but there is no official German record of them being named as such or their use. Technically they were said to be a type shell which had a large explosive device attached to it that would simulate an aircraft blowing up without evidence of attack (tracer bullets etc). It obviously as is mentioned made an unholy noise; which in turn along with all the other chaos going on had the desired psychological effect of unnerving or distracting the aircrews.

An alternative view and one that is more likely to be accurate is that these 'Scarecrows' were actually aircraft that had mysteriously exploded.

They had actually been attacked by Night Fighter's codenamed *Schräge Musik* or 'Strange Music'. The codename was a derivative of the German colloquialism for 'Jazz Music' (the German word *schräg* means slanted or oblique and refers to the angle of the guns). The Luftwaffe had installed twin upward firing 20 mm cannons in the cockpits of their Night Fighters like the Ju 88, Dornier 217 and Bf 110's. It was first operationally used with devastating consequences during Bomber Command's Operation Hydra, the raids on the V2 research establishment at Peenemünde on 17/18 August 1943. Bomber Command lost 40 aircraft out of 596 on this Operation.

Night fighters could now approach and attack the Bomber Force from below, where they would be outside the crew's field of view. Approaching from below provided the Night Fighter's with the advantage that the bomber crew could not see or hear them; often thinking the resulting attack was ground fire; if they even lived to tell the tale. RAF Bombers had no defensive turrets under the fuselage (although some RCAF Lancs were specially fitted with belly turrets). Crews could not see the night fighter against the dark ground or sky, but the German pilots could observe and identify the silhouette of the aircraft they were about to attack. The only defensive action pilots could use was to perform banking manoeuvres. By 1944 a third of all German night fighters carried these upward-firing guns and 70% of RAF aircraft lost were due to night fighter attacks. Aiming for the petrol tanks in the wings, the result of an attack would often be the complete loss of the aircraft and its crew in a huge explosion and fireball.

This is testified by Oberleutnant Rolf Ebhardt of 3/NJG1 based in Holland who achieved 8 kills using *Schräge Musik.* He explained that the blind spot for a British Bomber was underneath. He would approach unseen and unheard from below sometimes only 120 yards away, close enough to note down the aircraft's serial number. He would then aim and fire at the middle of the fuselage. If the petrol tanks in the wings were hit or the bomb load was still onboard the aircraft would instantly explode. On one particular occasion one second after firing the aircraft he was attacking instantly exploded, it was so bright he was blinded and could not see for 5 minutes. His first kill was on the 26 April 1944 just before Bill and his crew started flying on Operations. The technique required precise timing and swift evasion; a fatally damaged bomber could fall directly onto the Night Fighter if it did not move away quickly. They used a lethal combination of special tracer, explosive and armour piercing ammunition.

During the 1943–1944 Battle of Berlin the RAF lost 82 of 823 bombers that attacked Leipzig on 19 February 1944, and 95 of the 795 bombers that attacked Nuremberg on 30 March 1944(A further 10 were lost in home crashes). The sudden increase in bomber losses had often been attributed to flak and Bomber Command was slow to react to the threat from *Schräge Musik.* Crews had reported being stalked by Night Fighters as early as 1943, but it was not proved until much later. A 61 Squadron Lancaster R5734, QR-V piloted by P/O J A Haste (RAAF) was lost on the Nuremburg Raid to *Schräge Musik.* A Ju 88 piloted by Major Rudolf Schoenert tracked its H2S Radar using Naxos (aircraft location equipment) and fired into its right petrol tank from below causing a huge fire, the whole crew perished. The 'Scarecrow' myth could have been created to stop the crews getting freaked out at witnessing their comrades perishing in huge fireballs which were the result of an unseen night fighter attack from below. It is quite probable that Bill and his crew witnessed the aircraft in front of them explode as a result of such an attack, it could quite easily have been them (Jeff Gray, Max Hastings, *Bomber Command, Bomber Boys*, documentary).

Junkers Ju 88 G-6, with two MG151/20 upward firing cannons set mid way down the fuselage (Source, *German Luftwaffe photographer, Junkers Ju 88* in action part 2, by Brian Filley).

Junkers Ju 88 G-6, with upward firing cannons set immediately behind the cockpit (Source, *wartime Irish photographer*).

Bill now leads us back to the Lille Operation:-

**F/Lt Bill North**

*'On the 10 May 1944 we flew on our first Operation together as a crew in EE176, Q-M, 'Mickey the Moocher' to attack marshalling yards in Lille in France. It was an eventful journey, our bombing height was 12,000 ft and there was a lot going on around us, there was a huge blinding explosion right in front of us on the bombing run and we flew right through it without any damage to us. The crew were a bit rattled by the explosion. I thought it was a 'Scarecrow' shell, but I have later learned that this was probably an attack by a night fighter using upward firing cannons. We saw explosions all around us on the way there and back; it was an awful feeling to know that your comrades were dying around you in huge fireballs. Two 50 Squadron Lancasters were lost that night both crews 7 out of 7 lost, that night was a baptism of fire for us all. Les Morton suffered terribly with his nerves after that night. I witnessed many of my comrades having similar experiences, given the traumas we went through it is quite understandable; nowadays the term for this is post traumatic stress. The RAF called it LMF (Lack of Moral Fibre) which I thought was a bit unkind. We didn't know much about it then and didn't have time to think about it; we all had to carry on regardless to get the job done. We all helped and encouraged Les Morton and Wing Commander Doubleday spent a lot of time with him and the other men, he was a great Commander often flying with us on Operations. Les flew on 8 Operations with me and then went to fly for another crew in 'A Flight' piloted by P/O Gerry Taylor who was a Canadian.'*

**W/O Dennis Bartlett**

*'The first Operation we flew on together was to Lille in France to attack railway marshalling yards. The journey there and back was a shocking first experience of Ops. I saw many aircraft exploding in big orange balls of fire all around us. I could see the sky all around us from the Mid-upper Turret lighting up with all sorts of things. I saw a huge explosion right in front of us on the bombing run and we flew right through it. It was a sickening feeling to know that our comrades were dying around us in these explosions.'*

Norman Jarvis now explains the journey home during the Lille Operation:

**W/O Norman Jarvis**

*'On into the night and we flew back over the French coast again; the stretch of the North Sea and then the dear old coast of England. By Dave's calculations we were getting near base, so we looked out ahead at the dimly lit ovals which were the bases of the various squadrons in our group. Then our letters were recognised, so we flew over and joined the circuit, called up control and they told us to wait and gave us a landing number. This meant we were stacked pretty high and a lot of crews would be landing before us, but after a while our turn came and in we went. Bill did a lovely landing. This was the end of our first hop. He swung off the runway and we were guided by the ground crew to our dispersal, where we closed the engines down and piled out one after another. The waiting transport congratulated us and we went in for interrogation. Over a cup of tea* [often laced with brandy] *we told the intelligence men just what we saw and all the details. I handed in my report and camera magazine to the bombing section. This was to be proof of our night's work. Later on we arrived at the mess and did justice to the bacon and eggs; the crews were now talking excitedly and chattering about their experiences and had seemingly forgotten about sleep, but about 4 am they broke it up and I hit the pillows and slept a dead sleep for about eight hours. The photographs of our bombing which I examined the next day were very good and I had obtained direct hits on the target on important marshalling yards. We had a day or two to recover from this first trip then went out to bomb another place, where we experienced slightly less opposition, but nevertheless made a successful raid.'*

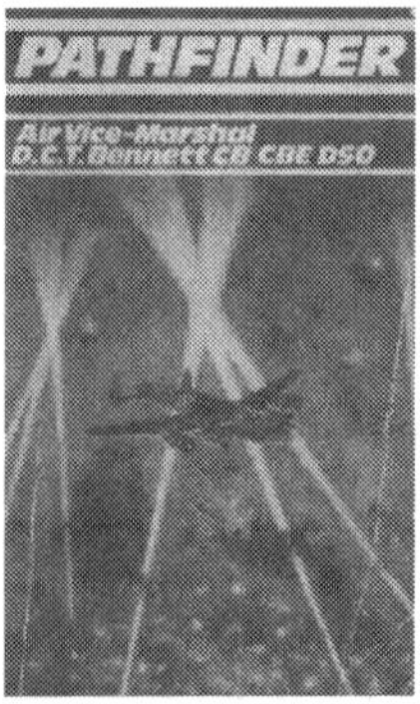


AVM Don Bennett's Pathfinder book, showing Lancaster over target with searchlights in a cone.

I found the following poem by Noel Coward handwritten in Bill's POW Diary. It is about British civilians listening to bombers departing on raids and pays tribute to the heroism of the men who took off these perilous bombing missions night after night, while civilians lay safe in their beds.

## LIE IN THE DARK AND LISTEN

**by**
**Noel Coward**

**Lie in the dark and listen,**
**It's clear tonight so they're flying high**
**Hundreds of them, thousands perhaps,**
**Riding the icy, moonlight sky.**
**Men, materials, bombs and maps**
**Altimeters and guns and charts**
**Coffee, sandwiches, fleece-lined boots**
**Bones and muscles and minds and hearts**
**English saplings with English roots**
**Deep in the earth they've left below**
**Lie in the dark and let them go**
**Lie in the dark and listen.**
**Lie in the dark and listen**

**They're going over in waves and waves**
**High above villages, hills and streams**
**Country churches and little graves**
**And little citizen's worried dreams.**
**Very soon they'll have reached the sea**
**And far below them will lie the bays**
**And coves and sands where they used to be**
**Taken for summer holidays.**
**Lie in the dark and let them go**
**Lie in the dark and listen.**

**Lie in the dark and listen**
**City magnates and steel contractors,**
**Factory workers and politicians**
**Soft hysterical little actors Ballet dancers,**
**'reserved' musicians,**
**Safe in your warm civilian beds**
**Count your profits and count your sheep**
**Life is flying above your heads**
**Just turn over and try to sleep.**
**Lie in the dark and let them go**
**Theirs is a world you'll never know**
**Lie in the dark and listen.**

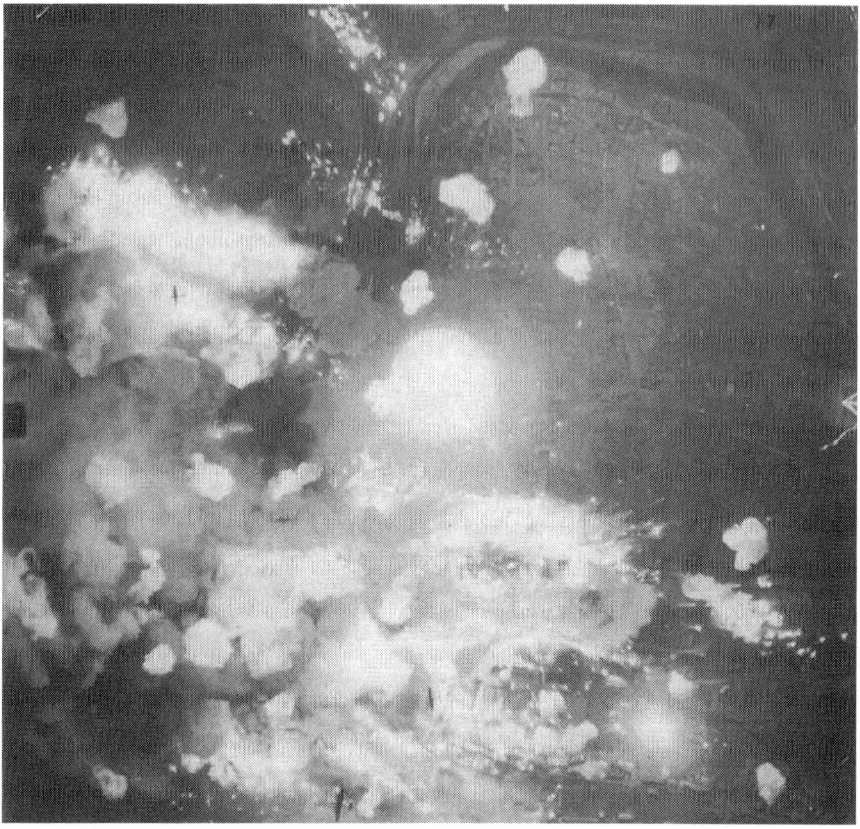

5 Group photo of bombs hitting a target, far below are three or four Lancasters over the target. 'Bombs from above' were an ever present danger (IWM).

Norman Jarvis says they had one or two days off to recover, but it was slightly longer than that. This time was filled up with more intense training missions before their next Op which was on the 19 May 1944 to Tours, a city located on the Loire River in central France.

# Chapter Ten

## 50% Chance of survival

As Bill and his crew testify their first Operation together to Lille was a baptism of fire and although they knew that they had a 50% chance of survival it was still a violent introduction to Ops. Bill asked me to demonstrate to the reader the fact their survival statistics were extreme and they were well aware of the catastrophic losses Bomber Command had suffered in the few months prior to the start of his Operational service with 61 Squadron. To do this we agreed to go back in time to 1943 and use Bill's comrade Jeff Gray's service with 61 Squadron to lay bare the facts. We thought here would be a good place to take a slight break from Bill's Ops and time travel slightly.

F/Lt Jeff Gray, 1943

Dennis Bartlett and right Jeff Gray. Burnham Beeches, 13 Sept 2011 (CK).

By an odd chance, my research for this book uncovered the flying record of another bomber pilot in Bill's Squadron, F/Lt Jeff Gray, and in this chapter I turn aside to record his astonishing story. F/Lt Jeff Gray served in Bomber Command during one of the most intense periods of time with astounding casualty rates. He relentlessly flew Operations to some of the most heavily defended areas of Germany and occupied territories, flying to Berlin 9 times, also Nuremburg, Dusseldorf, Leipzig, Stettin, Stuttgart, Frankfurt, Essen, Sweinfurt, Mailly le Camp and Brunswick, all were heavy losses for the RAF. Miraculously Jeff Gray and his crew survived through this period of some of the heaviest losses in Bomber Commands History. When I interviewed Jeff Gray and offered this information to him he again, just like Bill, had full awareness of his mortality, but totally played it down. I felt utterly in awe of this remarkable man. Jeff kindly lent me his precious Log Book to research for the book. Again this has been one of the most important documents I have handled and felt honoured to do so; thank you Jeff.

It was a strange twist of fate that brought Jeff Gray to my attention, during the course of writing this book. I went to visit Dennis Bartlett and his sister Daphne on the 17 April 2011 in Camberley and Daphne mentioned that her next-door neighbour Jeff Gray was interested in the book and meeting me. She said he was in the RAF during the war and they had known him for 50 years; he had also written a book, about a WW2 bomber that had crashed nearby in Farnham called, *The Stain On The Glass.*

I finally got to meet Jeff on 13 September 2011 at Daphne's house in Burnham Beeches and he brought his Flying Log book along with him. I asked him what Squadron he served with and he said, '61 Squadron.' I then looked at Dennis and said, 'He was at 61 Squadron with you, Dennis.' Dennis said, 'I had no idea that we served in the same Squadron.' Dennis, as I have already mentioned, didn't talk much about his wartime experiences.

Jeff then said 'Dennis, we've known each other all these years and didn't know we were in the same Squadron!'

I asked Jeff if I could look through his Log Book. I then quickly discovered that not only were they in the same Squadron, but they also flew on 4 missions together to bomb the same targets. The room was silent for what felt like forever as it all slowly sunk in. We were all astounded by this revelation, even Daphne and Jeff's wife Joan couldn't quite believe it. Jeff then mentioned that he remembered Bill North as well from the briefing sessions at Skellingthorpe. It never ceases to amaze me that these men who were in their late eighties could remember so much detail from so long ago. Even as I am writing this I am getting goosebumps; through the corridors of time a fascinating web of coincidences regarding Bill, Jeff, Dennis and later on Percy Cannings kept revealing themselves to us. Extraordinary men, all of them!

Jeff Gray took part in some of the deadliest operations of the war. His 21st Operation with 61 Squadron was to Nuremburg in Lancaster LM478, QR-K. Nuremberg had marked the end of Bomber Commands Battle for Berlin, losing 8,000 aircrew and 1,100 aircraft which equated to 60 bomber Squadrons. These were the most highly trained personnel in the British Armed Services. (Derek Brammer) Air Chief Arthur Harris had promised Berlin would be obliterated and the will of the German people to fight would be broken for good. Unfortunately this was not to be and nearly proved to be the finish of Bomber Command as an effective fighting force due to the catastrophic losses involved. During the Battle for Berlin 61 Squadron's F/Lt Jeff Gray visited the 'Big City' 9 times on his tour of Ops. Other famous pilots that went to Berlin with 50/61 Squadron were Sir Michael Beetham, F/Lt Tommy Farmiloe and the tenacious F/Lt William Reid who was awarded a Victoria Cross (VC).

Jeff Grey and three of his friends from No. 1 BFTS, (*British Flying Training School*), Terrell, Texas, May 1942. Walking from camp into Terrell town, left to right:- Gordon Walker, Bill Lowe, Jeff Gray and John Alstan. On the journey over on the SS Banfora, Bill Lowe couldn't stand sleeping below deck; so he slept in a life belt box on deck!

Jeff Gray's tour of Operations included several successive bombing raids on Berlin, the most heavily defended of all German cities, where as mentioned Bomber Command casualties were incredibly high. In his own words:-

**F/Lt Jeff Gray (61 Squadron)**

*'Berlin was a challenge to say the least and was considered to be a failure in Bomber Commands history. There was a combination of factors that explain the reason for this. Berlin was a large city spread out over a wide area. The Pathfinder Force used H2S to get a fix on approaching the city; from the west the lakes could be picked up on H2S as it was easy to tell the difference between land and water. However the Germans knew this and put boats and other obstacles around the lakes to mask off the definition making them difficult to identify. On the way to, and over the target, bad weather often was a major contribution to failure in accuracy. Berlin was made up of a combination of wide streets and tall buildings with steep rooftops. The 4000 lb 'Cookie' or blast bomb's job was to blow the roof tiles off allowing incendiaries a chance to penetrate and spread fire and high explosive bombs would cause structural damage. However a lot of the time we didn't carry the right combination of explosives to obtain maximum effect on Berlin because of these factors. Berlin also had some of the heaviest air defences in Germany. Another thing that had changed was that Goring had very cleverly taken the Night Bomber crews who were trained to fly at night and put them into a/c like the Ju 88 with the bomb bays removed. These heavily armed a/c would infiltrate the 'Bomber Stream' and fly alongside it to the target; let them drop their bombs while leaving them to AA units, then refuel and fly back with them with devastating consequences. I experienced this tactic on the Nuremburg raid which I will explain later.'*

Whilst researching the 61 Squadron ORB I noticed that Jeff Gray was often the first Lancaster to return to base with Tommy Farmiloe landing very close in time behind him. I asked Jeff if he made a conscious effort to return first and this was his answer:

*'Some crews held back on the throttle to conserve fuel, but I always went full throttle on the way home. I liked to be back first from Ops to get the debriefing over and then get to the mess first for bacon and eggs, before all the other crews came piling through. There was also a bit of a competition going on between Tommy Farmiloe and I to see who could get back to base first during Ops. As you have found out I was often the winner, it was all very friendly though.'*

BBMF Lancaster PA474 Flypast at 50/61 Squ Memorial Day service, 10 June 2012. Lancasters were made from some 55,000 parts, using half a million manufacturing operations; nearly half the Avro work force were women. Lancasters flew 156,000 sorties and dropped 608,612 tons of bombs during WW2. 35 Lancasters completed more than 100 Operations, joining the 'Ton Up' club and of the 7,377 made 3,249 were lost in action (photo, CK).

**Below is the list of Jeff Gray's completed tour of 30 Operations:-**

**F/Lt Jeff Gray, 61 Squadron 1943.**

**Crew members:- Jeff Gray (Pilot), John McCulloch (Flight Engineer), Ron Jones (Bomb Aimer), Geoff Ward (Navigator), Norman Jackson and W Green (Wireless Operators), Paddy Morrison (Mid-Upper-Gunner), Jock Hay (Rear Gunner).**

**No 1. Dusseldorf.** 3/4 Nov 1943. 2nd Dickie to P/O APE Strange in DV312, QR-Z (See Op 25 for story on P/O Strange). This a/c was transferred to 207 Squ and then back to Skellingthorpe to 50 Squ, coded VN-J, it was a (6/7) loss on 18/19 July 1944 to Revigny with Skipper F/O WJ Long (RCAF). Also lost at Revigny was 61 Squ's P/O HW Cooper in DV304, QR-V. The previous 61 Squ QR-Z, DV401 was lost on Ops to Berlin 2/3 Jan 1944.

This was the night 61 Squadron's F/Lt William Reid was awarded the VC for his courageous and tenacious flight to and from the target after being badly shot up. Excerpt taken from The *London Gazette* 14

December 1943. 'Wounded in two attacks, without oxygen, suffering severely from cold, his Navigator dead, his Wireless Operator fatally wounded, his aircraft crippled and defenceless, F/Lt Reid showed superb courage and leadership in penetrating a further 200 miles into enemy territory to attack one of the most strongly defended targets in Germany, every additional mile increasing the hazards of the long and perilous journey home. His tenacity and devotion to duty were beyond praise.'

**No 2. Modane.** 10/11 Nov 1943. EE176, QR-M, 'Mickey The Moocher', the famous 'Ton Up' Lancaster. Bill North also flew in Mickey on Operations and training missions. This was 'Mickey's' 23rd Operation in its fairly younger days. (On the 19 Nov Jeff and his crew did a dinghy search in the North Sea, this counted as half an Operation)

While Jeff was on leave throughout the rest of November, 61 Squ suffered its single biggest loss. Three Lancasters were FTR's all (7/7s) on 26/27 Nov to Berlin. P/O AJD Eaves and crew in W4198, QR-H. P/O APE Strange and crew in DV297, QR-O and P/O JG McAlpine (RAAF) and crew lost without trace in DV339, QR-W.

F/Lt Tony Bird who was flying with 61 Squ at the same time as Jeff had also flown '2nd dickie' with P/O Strange. He remembered seeing him sitting alone in the crew room before this Op with 'a look of great sadness'. *'I feel sure that P/O Strange had experienced a strong premonition that he would not return, and I was to treat such premonitions with great respect during the coming weeks'* (p 48, *A Bird Over Berlin*, Tony Bird DFC).

On the 16 Nov 1943, 61 Squ moved from RAF Syerston to RAF Skellingthorpe.

**No 3. Berlin.** 2/3 Dec 1943. JB-129, QR-G for George.

**No 4. Berlin.** 16/17 Dec 1943. EE-176, QR-M, 'Mickey the Moocher' This was Mickey's 29th Operation. This night Thursday 16 December 1943, became known as 'Black Thursday' due to the heavy losses mostly on home territory due to the bad weather. Jeff Gray made it home in 61 Squadron's lucky 'Mickey'. 97 Squadron suffered its single biggest loss with 8 Lancasters (36 aircrew dying and one sixth of its total losses for 1943), and four of 100 Squ were lost, fortunately W/O Percy Cannings (100 Squ) was not flying this night.

One of the ever-present dangers the crews faced was mid-air collisions. The crew of another Lancaster witnessed what happened this night. 9 Squadron Lancaster, DV293, WS-Y for York, piloted by P/O RA Bayldon had completed its bombing run and turned towards the Baltic for its return to RAF Bardney. It collided with 619 Squadron Lancaster JA867, PG-X, piloted by P/O GB Loney (RCAF). Locked together the two aircraft plunged towards the earth in flames, crashing in woodland 30 miles NE of Berlin. Both crews were all killed, 14 men. All are buried in the Berlin 1939-1945 Commonwealth War Cemetery, Charlottenburg, (3198 identified and 396 unidentified casualties). 23 other Lancs were lost over Germany and 29 crashed in fog near their bases. Over 300 men were killed and it was called 'Black Thursday' (Patrick Otter's father F/O B Otter was the Navigator on DV293, WS-Y for York and had left home without his lucky green scarf, this crew was a (7/7) loss over Berlin and all crew rest in the Berlin 1939-1945 War Cemetery. Patrick Otter, Lincolnshire Airfields in the Second World War).

**No 5. Frankfurt.** 20/21 Dec 1943. JB129, G for George.

**No 6. Berlin.** 23/24 Dec 1943. JB129, QR-G for George.

**No 7. Berlin.** 29/30 Dec 1943. JB129, QR-G for George. 50 and 61 Squ had one FTR each, both a/c were (6/7s). 61 Squ's F/Lt GH Harvey (RAAF) in DV399, QR-R.

**<u>1944</u>**

**No 8. Berlin.** 2/3 Jan 1944. EE186, QR-A. (Bill's trusty Lanc is recorded as A instead of D here) 61 Squ lost one Lancaster with its crew of 7, F/O GA Tull in DV401, QR-Z. 83 Squ PFF lost 4 of its Lancasters with all their crews, 49 men. The previous night 1/2 Jan, 61 Squ lost 2 a/c on Ops to Berlin, both (7/7s). F/O RP Cunningham and crew in DV344, QR-V and F/O GE Sharpe (RCAF) and crew in LM377, QR-F.

It is worth noting here that Jeff and his crew had now flown to Berlin three nights in a row. Given the heavy losses around Jeff this was an achievement of outstanding courage and skill.

**No 9. Stettin.** 5/6 Jan 1944. DV294, QR-K for King (This a/c was a (7/7) loss over France on 25/26 Feb to Augsburg, F/O FJ Dixon and crew). W/ Cmdr RN Stidolph in JB138, 'Just Jane' is ferociously attacked by ME210 losing two engines and emergency landing at RAF Matlaske in Norfolk. 97 Squ PFF lost 2 a/c, both (6/7s).

While Jeff was on leave from 12th to the 25th, 61 Squ had one (7/7) FTR on 21/22 Jan to Magdeburg, Sgt T Martin and crew in R5565, QR-S. 97 Squ also lost a further 3 a/c, 2 of them (7/7s).

**No 10. Berlin.** 27/28 Jan 1944. ME596, QR-H, 'Hells-A-Poppin' Jeff received a promotion to Flight Sergeant (This a/c was later flown by Jeff's good friend F/Lt Tommy Farmiloe on Bomber Commands last heavy Bomber visit to Berlin 24/25 March 1944, where losses totalled a horrific 72 a/c; 44 Lancasters and 28 Halifaxes to flak and NF's. See Bill's 1st Op to Brest for details of Tommy Farmiloe's astounding ride through death's shadow in ME595. Like EE186, ME595 was one of 61 Squadrons many workhorse Lancasters and had some remarkable escapes, it was eventually a (6/7) loss on the 12/13 Aug 1944 to Rüsselsheim, Skipper P/O GM Taylor).61 Squ had 2 FTR's this night with P/O EA Williams in W4315, QR-Q ditching near Guernsey (3 crew lost) and F/O RA West a (7/7) loss in DV400, QR-Y.

'Twilight take-off' at Coningsby, BBMF, PA474 (photo, *Stephen Elsworth*).

**No 11.** Berlin. 28/29 Jan 1944. JB129, QR-G for George.

**No 12. Berlin.** 30/31 Jan 1944. JB129, QR-G for George. 'Maximum Effort', Berlin 3 nights in a row again. It was virtually non-stop for Jeff and his crew; they flew an incredible 7 training missions before returning to Berlin again on the 15/16 Feb. Jeff was up in the air on the 12 Feb training in JB129, QR-G when 50 Squ's Sir Michael Beetham had a catastrophic accident in Lancaster W4119, VN-Q. There were 10 crew on board, with 4 extra Air Gunners on gunnery training. During steep diving whilst on Fighter Affiliation the port outer engine caught fire and the abandon a/c order was given. Before all the crew had left the port wing broke off sending the a/c spinning to earth and killing the four remaining crewmembers.

Jeff Gray:-'*I was up in the air training when this happened, but I didn't see it happen. The whole base was talking about the accident. Tommy Farmiloe's Navigator P/O FJ Davis told me what happened and I said, 'That man (F/Lt Beetham) will make an Air Vice Marshall one day!"*

Hawker Hurricanes were used for Fighter Affiliation exercises. This is Hurricane Mk I, UP-W, R4118 and is the only Battle of Britain Hurricane still flying today (source, *www.airpowerworld.info*).

**No 13. Berlin.** 15/16 Feb 1944. JB129, QR-G for George.

Again Jeff and his crew flew to Berlin this time four nights in a row. I cannot think of anything more daunting. Bomber Command's motto was 'Press on Regardless', and the senior officers at 61 Squadron certainly adhered to this philosophy; Jeff also confirmed this to me. During maximum effort which was normally three nights in a row the boys did not even had time to think! This was now the 9th time they had flown to Berlin and survived whilst many around them were 'Fail to Returns'.

**No 14. Leipzig.** 19/20 Feb 1944. JB129, G for George. There was more drama for Jeff as his Port Inner Engine was shot up and failed, he was awarded an immediate DFM (Distinguished Flying Medal). Two 61 Squ Lancs were lost at Leipzig. P/O H Wallis a (5/7) loss in HK538, QR-F and P/O JW Golightly a (7/7) loss in ME591, QR-C.

**No 15. Stuttgart.** 20/21 Feb 1944. R5734, QR-V. (This a/c was a (7/7) loss at Nuremburg 30/31 March, shot down outbound by NF Ju 88 flown by Major Rudolf Schoenert of NJG10 over Belgium. P/O JA Haste (RAAF) and crew.The previous QR-V, DV344 was lost over Berlin 1/2 Jan 1944).

**No 16. Sweinfurt.** 24/25 Feb 1944. JB129, G for George. 35 Aircraft were lost on this Operation including one 61 Squ FTR with F/L ND Webb

(RNZAF) in LM310, QR-E (6 of this crew including the skipper survived being shot down from 20,000ft).

During a short 5 day break for Jeff 61 Squ lost a further 2 a/c on 25/26 Feb Ops to Augsburg. F/O FJ Dixon a (7/7) loss in DV294, QR-K and F/L JW Einarson DFC DFM (RCAF) a (6/7) loss in LL775, QR-O.

**No 17. Stuttgart.** 1/2 March 1944. JB129, G for George.

14 March 1944, EE186, QR-A (Bill's trusty Lanc is again flown by Jeff Gray on training mission under Squ code QR-A). On the 15 March Jeff received a promotion to Pilot Officer.

**No 18. Stuttgart.** 15/16 March 1944. LL777, QR-S for Sheila. This a/c was also flown by F/Lt Bernard Fitch DFC on a tour of Ops, who passed away on 9 August 2011 (LL777 was lost on 6/7 Dec 1944 to Giessen after crash landing in Belgium. P503, WR Chorley *1944 Losses*).

On the first Op of his second tour W/O Percy Cannings from 97 Squadron PFF helped mark the target this night. In Lancaster JB708, OF-R, his Captain F/O W (Bill) Reid provides a fascinating debriefing regarding marking by 8 Group's PFF. T/o Bourn, Up 19:35, Down 02:25. 5 x 2000lb. Stuttgart bombed from 19,300ft. Vis fair. The first Wanganui went down at 23:10hrs, but this was not backed up for about 5mins. Later three separate concentrations appeared to form **(SUPP, Supporters)**.

Percy Cannings flew 22 Ops with 1 Group's 100 Squ based at RAF Grimsby, from 1 March 1943 to 27 July 1943. Their Squ badge was a 'Skull and Crossbones'. His 2nd Op was to Nuremburg on the 8 March 1943 in ED564 and his last Op was in ED815 on 27 July 1943 to Hamburg; the night of the famous 'Firestorm'. 100 Squ's EE169, HW-O, pilot W/O R Gafford was lost without trace this night. Then after serving as a Gunnery Instructor for 6 months at 83 OTU Peplow from 21 Aug 1943 to 14 March 1944, he was transferred to 8 Groups 97 (Straits Settlements) Squ at Bourn for a 2nd Tour of Operations.

**No 19. Frankfurt.** 18/19 March 1944. JB129, QR-G for George. 61 Squ had one FTR with P/O L Cannon a (7/7) loss in ND727, QR-C. 50 and 97 Squ had one FTR each (Whilst Jeff went on a week's leave 61 Squ lost 2 more a/c. His faithful JB129, QR-G was claimed by a NF, a (7/7) loss over Berlin on 24/25 March, F/O JG Cox (RNZAF). P/O D Carbutt was also a 6/7 loss over Berlin in DV397, QR-W). On the night of March 24/25 1944, on his eighth visit to the 'The Big City', Tommy Farmiloe had his remarkable brush with death.

**No 20. Essen.** 26/27 March 1944. LM476, QR-E (This a/c was a (6/8) loss over Lügde in Germany on 22/23 April to Brunswick, see Brunswick Op for details. The first production Lanc L7527 was also lost this night. It served as an Avro development a/c, then to 1654 HCU and finally to 15 Squ in March 1944 for a very short service. Thought to have exploded over Aachen, the crew are all commemorated on the Runnymede Memorial).

**No 21. Nuremburg.** 30/31 March 1944. LM478, QR-K (This a/c was written off in a crash at Skellingthorpe when returning from the Bourg Leopold Op 11/12 May 1944, with F/S CJ Woolnough (RAAF).

This was the most infamous night in the history of Bomber Command, with the highest losses ever of 105 (95 shot down, 10 lost in crashes in England). Jeff recalls, *'Our CO Wing Commander AW Doubleday DFC had famously commented that 'Jerry got a century before lunch today!' He was hauled before the CinC and given a dressing down for this comment. HQ had tried to keep the loss numbers under 100 for propaganda purposes, but the real figure was soon well known and controversial.'*

The bombing had been ineffective due to adverse weather conditions and part of the Bomber Stream had been blown off course, also *'Creep back'* had also resulted in missing the main target by the part of the Main Force that actually reached the target. Some thought it was a step too far, but Churchill and the Air Ministers wanted to hit the historic home of the Nazi Party. Jeff Gray contributed to Martin Middlebrook's excellent book *The Nuremburg Raid.* Jeff was one of 120 aircraft that had mistakenly bombed Schweinfurt as a result of badly forecast winds and his Lancaster QR-K for King had taken drastic evasive action after two Night Fighters attacked it. As he explained to me, *'We were shadowed by two Ju 88's on the way into the target, one on port and one on starboard side. I corkscrewed and went all over the place before we finally got rid of them, but we were hopelessly lost. We reset course adding 10 minutes on before I turned to starboard to what I thought was the target. We were then conned by searchlights and still unsure where we were I thought we had better bomb something rather than nothing at all. We aimed at the searchlights and knocked them out and I think the other crews who were experiencing navigational problems saw the explosions and honed in dropping their bomb loads. I thought we would get in serious trouble for bombing the wrong target, but when we got back because of the unprecedented losses they were just pleased that someone had returned at all! We later found out that we had bombed Schweinfurt. Part of the reason for the heavy losses was also due to the fact that we were briefed to fly in a straight line to the target, which was not something I was happy about. Don Bennett had opposed the idea saying that it would be a disaster, it proved to be so!'*

I came across some fascinating evidence relating to what went wrong on the Nuremburg raid from AVM Don Bennett and W/C AW Doubleday in the ABC (Australian Broadcasting Corporation) 1986 documentary, *Wings of the Storm-Part 2, The Survivors.* The friction experienced between AVM Don Bennett and OC 5 Group, Sir Ralph Cochrane is evident and confirms Jeff's own concerns about flying in a straight line to and from the target.

## AVM Don Bennett (RAAF) CB, CBE, DSO

*'We laid down the usual tactics, diversions, raids by the Mosquito force to take the enemy fighters away and so on in the usual way and everybody was happy. But by midday the deputy CinC Saunderby rang me up and said, 'The CinC wants to overrule your plans for the day, he thinks that the OC 5 Group* [Sir Ralph Cochrane] *should have a chance of proving that he is right, he wants to go straight in and straight out.' And so I immediately burst a blood vessel and said, 'Well that's just crazy, it's a clear moonlit night, the casualty rate will be enormous!'* [Saunderby replied], *'Oh no, he doesn't think so and he'd like to try it.'*

**Left,** AVM Don Bennett and **right,** W/C AW Doubleday. Stills taken from the 1986 Australian Broadcasting Corporation documentary, *Wings of the Storm - Part 2, The Survivors.*

## W/C Arthur Doubleday (RAAF) DSO, DFC, MID

*'And I said to the boys, 'Look it's on for young owl tonight, now keep your eyes on the sky!'Because they started to fall, as I say, within 20 minutes anyway, or probably less than that, 10 minutes of crossing the coast. And from then to the target the air was not only a good visibility,*

*but seemed to be bright, the moon was shining brightly, although it wasn't a full moon. I was first back at Waddington and was called up to the control tower by Sir Ralph Cochrane who said, 'Well, how did it go?' And I said 'Jerry got a century before lunch today!', and he didn't quite, he got 96.'*
Both these quotes were taken from the ABC 1986 documentary, *Wings of the Storm-Part 2, The Survivors.*
(Doubleday flew in Lancaster LL843, on the Nuremburg raid. LL843 was transferred to 61 Squ where he flew it again; it was then passed onto 1659 HCU. Doubleday flew an astounding 53 Operations completing two tours of duty. He passed away in 2001)

S/L Arthur Doubleday and his crew were posted to 467 Sq on 8 Dec 1943, most of the crew like Doubleday were on their 2nd tour of Ops, he had completed his first Tour with 460 Sq and after a rest was posted to 467 Sq as a Flight Commander. On 22 April 1944 he was promoted to W/C and posted to command 61 Sq at Skellingthorpe. His crew were, Sgt J Slome, F/O RB Murphy, P/O FJ Nugent (DFC), P/O H Sinnamon, P/O B Gray and P/O AA Taylor.

Two of the fourteen 61 Squadron Lancasters dispatched to Nuremburg were complete losses after failing to return. Lancaster DV311, QR-P flown by S/L EH Moss DFC and R5734, QR-V flown by P/O JA Haste (RAAF). Four 50 Squ and two 97 Squ Lancasters were also lost. The 97 Squ Lancs were (7/7s), with a Veteran of the Dambusters raid F/Lt RAD Trevor-Roper (who flew with W/C Guy Gibson) lost with ND390, OF-S.

Nuremburg marked the end of the Battle for Berlin, phase 1 and 2 and the beginning of the Transportation Plan. If I have done my sums correctly, during this apocalyptic period of service to Bomber Command, 50 Squ lost 19 a/c and 61 Squ lost 18 a/c. However, 97 Squ PFF lost an incredible 33 a/c; over 70% higher losses, with 14 more a/c than 50 Squ, proving that the Pathfinder Force were at even greater general risk whilst they circled the skies through death's dark heart.

4 April 1944, EE176, QR-M, (Mickey) is flown with P/O Farmiloe, P/O Norton and P/O Gray on an air test.

**No 22. Toulouse.** 5/6 April 1944. LM-478, QR-K (This a/c was written off in a home crash at Skellingthorpe on 11/12 May to Bourg Leopold, Skipper F/S CJ Woolnough (RAAF), all ok).

**No 23. Tours** (Marshalling Yards, France) 10/11 April 1944. ME725, QR-G for George (A new G for George returns here with serial no. ME725, first flown by Jeff on 7 April, Air Test). Bomb load 14 x 1000 HE. Bombing height 6,750ft.

ME725, QR-G for George with 42 Ops painted on the nose
(original photo, *F/Lt Jeff Gray*).

**No 24. Aachen** (Marshalling Yards) 11/12 April 1944. ME725, QR-G for George. One 61 Squ Lanc JA695, QR-W, was a (6/7) FTR with Skipper EA Williams DFC, the only survivor was F/S ADM Anderson (POW). Williams and Anderson had already survived ditching in the sea off Guernsey after flak damage on 27/28 Jan, in W4315, QR-Q, on return from Berlin. One 50 Squ Lanc was a (7/7) loss and two 83 Squ PFF Lancs were lost. On the 15 April 1944, 61 Squadron transferred from Coningsby to Skellingthorpe. This was the last time Jeff flew with his Wireless Operator Norman Jackson.

**<u>F/Lt Jeff Gray</u>**

*'My Wireless Operator Norman Jackson had been with me from the beginning and had flown on about 20 or so Operations with me. One of the WOP's jobs was to read the onboard radar system called Monica. This allowed us to see in quite a basic way if there were any Night Fighters stalking us. I had felt that Norman was having trouble reading the signals correctly and the crew were feeling very uncomfortable about this. After we transferred to Skellingthorpe from Coningsby we all agreed that it might be best if Norman went for some retraining. We were then given another Wireless Operator, Warrant Officer W Green who flew with us for the rest of our Tour. After some more training Norman then went onto fly with F/Lt Jeavons and finished his Tour. It was only later on that I found out that Monica was quite an unreliable piece of equipment and the Night Fighters were actually using the signal it gave off to track our Bomber Force. Some crews were actually switching it off because they felt safer without it on. For a long time afterwards I felt uncomfortable about this decision with Norman, but in the heat of war we did what we thought was best for us at the time.'*

After a brief retraining period in which he also flew with Bill North on the 7 May, Norman Jackson flew again with P/O Kramer alongside Jeff on his last Operation to Tours on 19 May 1944; the day of the fatal explosion at Skellingthorpe. Bill, Jeff and Kramer/Jackson all flew to Tours. Jackson then flew with F/Lt Jeavons another 15 times completing his Tour with 34 Ops (7 of these were alongside Bill North). However, there was a further tragedy to follow after Norman Jackson had completed his Tour. (See Chapter 24 Lives Lived and Lives Lost)

**No 25. Brunswick.** 22/23 April 1944. ME725, QR-G for George.

This was the night 61 Squ's F/Lt Tony Bird failed to return from Brunswick. His Lancaster LM476, QR-E in which Jeff had flown to Essen was a (6/8) loss over Lügde in Germany. It disintegrated in a mid-air explosion, throwing clear the only two survivors:-Skipper F/L A Bird (who had only just been given back his 'lost' pilot's parachute) and Bomb Aimer P/O FJ 'Lucky' Davies (who uncannily seconds before the explosion had retrieved and half clipped his parachute on), the 2nd pilot was F/L HCC Goodyear (RCAF), (*A Bird Over Berlin*, Tony Bird). The next QR-E lost was ME783, curiously with an almost identical crew name, P/O Jack Goodyer on 15/16 June 1944 (Quick note:- When crewmen were ejected from Lancasters that unexpectedly exploded mid-air, if still in one piece, the pilots would often survive as they had their parachutes on already. The other crew members most likely not surviving ejection, as they had to retrieve and clip their chutes on to their parachute harness first).

I asked Jeff if he remembered Tony Bird as they were flying on Ops at the same time. *'No I don't recall Tony Bird. It's funny what you do and don't remember, sometimes recollections are clear as a bell and other times not.'* I then mentioned Tony Bird's memory of P/O Strange having a premonition on Jeff's 2nd Op on 10/11 Nov 1943. *'Ah yes, now I do remember P/O Strange as I flew '2nd Dickie' with him on my first Op to Dusseldorf on 3/4 Nov 1943. It was a very dramatic initiation to Ops! P/O Strange was weaving all the way to and from the target. When we were on the bombing run he continued weaving instead of flying straight and level, which I thought was a bit 'strange'. There was flak exploding all around us, the black puffs were eerily highlighted by the fires below and searchlights. The Bomb Aimer was doing his nut over the intercom saying, 'for God's sake keep it steady will you!' P/O Strange then to my utter astonishment said, 'Ok I'll go round again.' He then turned to port right across the path of the Bomber Stream and came back around to repeat the bombing run. I could not believe what I was seeing, there were a/c all over the place and we were flying right across them all! Well I shut my eyes, I just couldn't look. Needless to say, I was extremely happy to make it back to base.'*

On his 4th Op with 97 Squ PFF, Percy Cannings and his crew helped mark this target in Lancaster ND807, OF-P. Up 23:52, Down 05:12. 12x cluster flares, 1x target flare, 1x green TI. Target Brunswick thin layer cirrus cloud approx 19,000ft with thick haze below. Identified target by another a/c. H2S failed approx enemy coast. Dropped flare on another illuminator later seen to be two miles south of target. Several red spot fires seen, but one stood out with green TI adjacent. Heard order to bomb by VHF. Initial bombing appeared accurate (**FD**, Flare Dropping).

The following night 24/25 April to Munich one 61 Squ Lanc LM359, QR-B was a (6/7) FTR with P/O CWJ Newman. One 50 Squ Lanc was a (7/7) FTR.

Tony Bird next to the Bomber Command Memorial, 7 Oct 2012
(Thank you to *Sue Foll* for supplying this photo).

**No 26. Mailly-le-Camp. (Tank training centre)** 3/4 May 1944. ME725, QR-G for George. (42 Lancasters were lost, 237 aircrew) Four 50 Squ Lancs were FTR's, one a (8/8) totalling 24 aircrew lost.

**No 27. Lanvedoc-Poulmic (Brest- Seaplane Base)** 8/9 May 1944. ME725, QR-G for George. P/O Bill North and his Navigator F/Sgt Dave Crowley flew alongside Jeff Gray on this Operation. Hit by flak in port main frame and starboard outer engine. Flew home on two engines.

As it happens, Jeff's 27th mission was also Bill's first, 'Second Dickie' mission, when Bill and his navigator F/S Dave Crowley flew with Tommy Farmiloe to Brest. Light and heavy flak was active mostly en route to target.

F/Lt Jeff Gray's trusty Lancaster QR-G for George was also hit by flak in the Port main frame and Starboard Outer Engine rendering it useless.

**No 28. Lille (Marshalling Yards)** 10/11 May 1944. ME725, QR-G for George.

P/O Bill North and Sgt Dennis Bartlett also flew on this Operation in EE176, QR-M, Mickey the Moocher alongside Jeff and his crew. 97 Squ PFF, Percy Cannings and his crew helped mark this target. Two 50 Squ and two 97 Squ Lancs were all (7/7) FTR's.

On 4 April Jeff flew with P/O H Farmiloe and P/O Norton on an Air Test in QR-M Mickey the Moocher. Jeff mentioned that he became really good friends with Tommy Farmiloe and this friendship continued after the war.

**No 29. Bourg-Leopold (Military Camp)** 11/12 May 1944. ME725, QR-G for George. Return to base, dumping bombs at dump site over the North Sea. The 'North Crew' also flew alongside Jeff on this mission. One 61 Squ Lanc was a (7/7) FTR with P/O JH Eastwood.

**No 30. Tours (Marshalling Yards)** 19/20 May 1944. ME725, QR-G for George, Jeff's last Op. The 'North Crew' also flew alongside Jeff on this mission. One 50 Squ Lanc a (3/7) loss in home crash.

EE186, QR-A, is flown F/Lt Tony Bird and by P/O Jeff Gray in Jan 1944 and F/Lt GA Berry on Ops during Feb, March 1944. EE186 takes a break from Ops during April, presumably for a refit. The Squ code changes to QR-D when Bill North arrives at 61 Squ in early May and is given his new charge, continuing its Ops with Bill on 21/22 May 1944 to Tours.

This was the fourth Operation that P/O Bill North had flown on alongside F/Lt Jeff Gray in the Bomber Stream and the third one with Sgt Dennis Bartlett, it was also Jeff's last mission. Jeff Gray and his crew had now completed a tour of 30 Operations.The choice now was to either volunteer for a second tour of duty or to transfer to a training Squadron (OTU). Jeff was posted to 14 Operational Training Unit, *'a nice touch',* as this is where Jeff Gray trained himself in 1943. Here he passed on his invaluable experience to pilots and their crews who were still in training. Jeff's trusty Lancaster ME725, QR-G was eventually lost on Ops 6/7 Dec 1944 to Giessen in Germany (Crash site Ilschhausen). The pilot was F/O CA Donnelly (RAAF) who survived with four of the crew, the other two rest in Hanover War Cemetery. LL777, QR-S was also lost this same night after an attack by a NF it crash landed on an Allied held Belgium airfield with the loss of one crew member Sgt GF Cartwright.

61 Squadron, Skellingthorpe, 1 March 1944. Lancaster JB129 'G' for George with ground crew. 1st on right 'Lofty' Bennett, 4th from right S/L Beard and crew, 5th from right F/Lt J Anderson. JB129 was a FTR on 24/25 March 1944 to Berlin (source, original photo, *F/Lt Jeff Gray*)

F/L/t Jeff Gray's WW2 medals. Left to right:- DFM (Distinguished Flying Medal), 1939-1945 Star, Air Crew Europe Star, Defence Medal and 1939-1945 War Medal. (The new Gold Clasp award attaches to the 1939-1945 Star)

**At this point, in the early springtime of 1944 just as Bill and his crew were embarking on Operations, they were fully aware of the heavy losses suffered by Bomber Command and the fact that they only had a 1 in 3 chance of surviving a tour of 30 Operations.**

# Chapter Eleven

## One in Three Chances, an Operational background.

In the early years of the war, after the evacuation of Dunkirk, and with Great Britain standing alone in Europe against Nazi tyranny, we had no means of fighting back except by using the limited number of outdated aircraft of Bomber Command to attack Germany. Besides, retaliation in kind for the Blitz of London and other major cities seemed only natural and justified. In June 1941 Winston Churchill delivered his famous speech concerning the focus and direction Great Britain would follow regarding the Bombing Campaign: 'We shall bomb Germany by day as well as night in ever increasing measure, casting upon them month by month a heavier discharge of bombs and making the German people taste and gulp each month a sharper dose of the miseries they have showered upon mankind.'

The complexities of the bombing campaign and the evolution of tactics and technology that made Bomber Command an effective fighting force have been well documented (Max Hastings and Richard Overy, Bomber Command, amongst many worthy publications), so there is no attempt here to do so. To understand what I am writing about and the way Bill's service fits into the WW2 jigsaw puzzle, however, it has to be touched on briefly as we follow Bill's journey.

I asked Bill what his view on the evolution of tactics in Bomber Command was at this point in the War. (1941/42) *'At this point in the War we had no effective way of fighting back except for the aircraft of Bomber Command. The Germans had to be beaten, it was all out war. We could not have done this without the strong characters which we needed to deliver the fight back to them. Winston Churchill and Arthur Harris were two of the strong men we had available and thank goodness we did. We all had the upmost respect for Arthur Harris. We also had a remarkable collection of scientists and technicians from across the board that helped us with technological breakthroughs. The best kept secret of the War was the work done by the Code Breakers at Bletchley Park and as you know Margaret* [Bill's wife] *worked there with Alan Turing.'*

Bill and I examined a lot of the research I did regarding Bomber Commands Operational history and again WR Chorley has sections in his book that explain this that we looked at together. Bill had a huge collection of books to do with Lancaster Bombers, Bomber Command and the RAF. His books on the Lancaster Bomber have also been used in our research as well. I mentioned this fact to Bill once when we had books and papers lying all over his living room floor.

*'You have a lot of books on the Lancaster here Bill?'*

*'I know Chris I loved that aircraft so much and still have a great affection for it.'*

Just before we launch into Bill's Ops he also felt it would be a useful to explain the role of the Pathfinder Force which helped guide him to and mark his targets. Bill and his crew entered Operational service with 61 Squadron during a change in Bomber Commands tactical history. Bill had just missed the 'Battle of Berlin' (Second Phase 1 January to 24/25 March 1944), and the high casualty rates of the infamous Berlin raids and the Nuremburg mission we described that 61 Squadron's F/Lt Jeff Gray took part in. Nuremburg marked the turning point between the old and new order in Bomber Command. On 14 April 1944 it came under control of Supreme Allied Commander in Europe Dwight D. Eisenhower. Bomber Command's services were now required to take part in the 2nd Front Offensive (Operation Overlord or D-Day Landings).

This was called the Transportation Plan, (31 March to 5/6 June 1944) and Tactical Support, (6 June to 15 September 1944). The Transportation plan targets included communications, coastal defence batteries, supply dumps, military camps, rail centres, roads and bridges in France and Belgium. This also included a continuation of Operation Crossbow to take out German V weapons. These raids were meticulously planned to avoid civilian casualties and forewarning the Germans of where the Allied landings might take place. These targets that Bill and his comrades attacked slowly ensured that the infrastructure of the entire network feeding the essential supply lines into Normandy was being eroded; in-between these missions there were some raids to the Ruhr Valley (WR Chorley, Max Hastings, Richard Overy, Bill North, Jeff Gray).

One example of such tactics was the Mailly-le-Camp Operation on the 3/4 May 1944, which was 4 days before Bill's first mission. As Jeff Gray who also flew on this Op explains, 5 Group was still in the early stages of experimenting with extreme low level target marking and this sometimes led to a delay in the Main Force being called in for the bombing run while the target was marked. Group Captain Leonard Cheshire was the Master Bomber in 5 Groups PFF and the raid involved Squadrons from 1 and 5 Group. 346 Lancasters and 14 Mosquitoes attacked the German military camp situated near the village of Mailly-le-Camp located directly south of Reims. Although the target was accurately marked, communication difficulties alongside the disruption in marking led to a delay in the Main Force attack, during which Luftwaffe fighters intercepted the force with devastating consequences. Most of them were shot down just before, on and just after the bombing run. Subsequently, 1500 tons of bombs were dropped with great accuracy, causing extensive damage to buildings, weapons and equipment. RAF losses were heavy, 11.6%, all in all 42 Lancasters were lost, 25 of them 7 out of 7 losses (175 aircrew), four 6 out of 7 losses (24 aircrew). Four 50 Squadron Lancasters were lost with only 6 survivors, 5 evading capture. 237 aircrew were lost, all are buried at various French cemeteries surrounding the town, 7 are commemorated at Runnymede. F/Lt Jeff Gray flew on this Operation in Lancaster ME 725, QR-G for George. Again Bill and his crew were fortunate enough to just miss this Operation. None of 61 Squadron's aircraft were lost this night and was for them considered a successful attack due to good initial marking and their precise bombing times. All 14 detailed a/c bombed in a 23 minute period from 00:10 to 00:33 and landed in a 49 minute period from 03:11 to 04:00. Jeff Gray was second to land. Although Kramer reports orbiting the target they didn't seem to get caught by the serious delays that affected the Main Force. However, the crews did report heavy opposition and seeing many 'Scarecrows' over the target. As we all know now these were in fact aircraft exploding.

I have used Jeff Gray's rank as a F/Lt in all his quotes, this is as all the other men quoted, their highest rank achieved on leaving the RAF.

**F/Lt Jeff Gray**

*'You will be aware that the Mailly-le-Camp Operation was led by Cheshire himself and it turned into something of a disaster. It did however spell the end of the notion that the French trips were to count as one third of an Operation. Many years later I discussed Mailly with the great man himself and asked if he remembered it. He looked at me for a moment and then said, 'Shall I ever forget?'*

WR Chorley's Bomber Command Losses series books have played an important part in my relationship with Bill and our understanding of the astounding casualty numbers. Bill had a copy of the 1944 Losses book on his living room bookshelf. I can remember as clear as a bell the moment I first looked into the pages of this moving book. It is a series including the complete record of all the aircraft and men lost during Bomber Command Operations in WW2. Bill had been explaining to me in the late 1990's how lucky he was to have survived on the 4/5 July 1944 St Leu Ops. As we sat talking he said, 'Can you get that book down off the shelf for me Chris, it's the one with the black binding.' I got it down not quite sure what I was really looking at. Bill said, 'Open it up on the page that has a marker on it and look down the page. There is a 61 Squadron listing for Lancaster EE186, QR-D, 4/5 July. Look at it carefully and tell me what you see.'

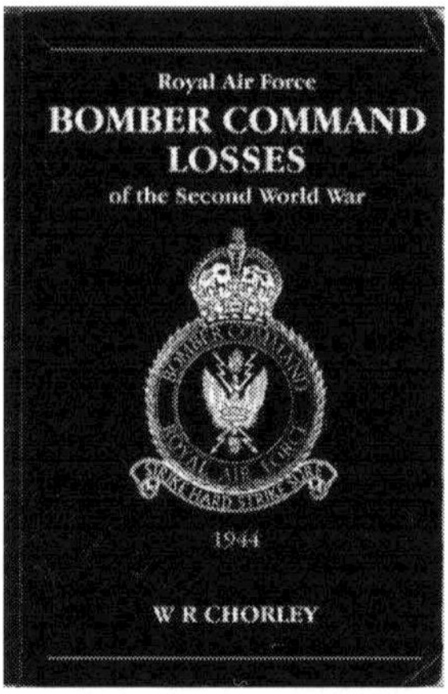


My well worn copy of WR Chorley's *Bomber Command Losses, 1944.*

I told him exactly what I saw. Under the listing was Bill's name, P/O Bill North, then the names of each of his crew. Next to their names were some abbreviations, *pow* and *evd,* short for Prisoner of War and evaded capture. He then said, 'That shows my crew all survived the crash that night. Now look at the 3 listings for Lancasters immediately above it and tell me what you see.' All I could see was row after row of little black crosses alongside the names of the crews. I looked back up at Bill and said 'Does this mean that all these men died?' Bill looked me right in the eyes and said 'Yes, all those crews were 7 out of 7 lost. Now look at all the rest of the aircraft losses for this night.' I was absolutely stunned at the number of crosses. As I turned page after page trying to digest the enormity of these losses, Bill sat there in silence watching me. I was completely captivated by this book and the short moving explanations by WR Chorley against most of the lost aircraft. It compels one to turn the pages and examine in more detail. I finally looked back up at Bill and said 'This is unbelievable; all those men died on Operations, many of them 7 out of 7. Now I understand what you have been saying about you and your crew surviving and being lucky to be alive.'

After discussing each of his Operations Bill and I would always talk about the number of Lancasters and crews that were lost. The statistics we talked about were from Bill's copy of WR Chorley's 1944 Losses book, The Bomber Command War Diaries by Martin Middlebrook and Chris Everitt and my copy of the ORB that I originally obtained from PRO; then later on from Alan Wells at 61 Squadron Forum. We used this combination of sources to cross reference these loss figures. The 61 Squadron ORB is notorious for mistakes and typing errors. I use Middlebrook and Everitt, then the ORB and then I hand count the losses from WR Chorley's losses series. This does present some slight differences in figures sometimes, these can be due to a fact as simple as an a/c crashing at a home base or one or two losses totally missed out. Usually a hand count of WR Chorley will on occasions add 1 or 2 to the figure from the Bomber Command Diaries. Alan Wells has also confirmed that sometimes even the reference books can be wrong as well. My journey with Bill has unearthed errors here and there; hence the hours and hours I have spent cross referencing everything.

Bill was fascinated by WR Chorley's Losses book, each time he looked at it I would quietly observe him and mentally note his own astonishment at his survival. Even though he was aware of the high losses Bomber Command had suffered this book somehow fully confirmed what he already knew. Our discussions would include how many Lancasters were (7/7s) and the number of crewmen lost etc and this had a direct bearing on the common theme that Bill would always mention. This was that given the severe losses on Ops he had flown on, especially (7/7s) and what he had witnessed he always felt that he shouldn't be here and was lucky to be alive. We also discussed the pilots from 61 Squadron that Bill had flown on Ops with and I had also recorded their names from the ORB for this purpose. I would mention certain names to Bill like, 'Do you remember F/Lt Jeff Gray?' and Bill would comment on the name in question, sometimes he would say 'No I don't remember him,' and other times he would say 'Oh yes, I remember him'.

Bill North and Jeff Gray explained some of the technological background and how they had faced flying in outdated aircraft with very crude Navigational methods. When Bill finally started Ops he had far more reliable Navigation equipment and of course was flying the trustworthy Lancaster.

The early bombing campaigns that took place while Bill was in early training however were not very effective and RAF losses were high. Bomber Command had been a sleeping giant that was about to be angrily awoken when it was finally given the new technology it desperately needed. Jeff Gray explains that navigational techniques and equipment were basic using 'Dead reckoning' to find targets (time and distance to target using compass, maps and visual points of recognition). Winds and bad weather would often push the aircraft way off their targets. There was also no accurate method of calculating how accurate the bombing was and Lord Cherwell, Churchill's friend and chief scientific advisor commissioned an investigation in the spring of 1941 called the Butt Report.

The report used reconnaissance and aiming point photographs for its data and highlighted how inefficient and inaccurate the early bombing missions were. Using only crews who reported bombing the target, it concluded that 1 in 3 aircraft were bombing within 5 miles of their target during full moon periods. 1 in 20 bombed within 5 miles during moonless periods and one third of crews admitted not even bombing the main targets with bombs falling in open country. The results were a huge shock to everybody as Britain stood alone against Hitler's tyranny (Max Hastings, Derek Brammer). So while Bill was training there was a huge push to modernise RAF training, tactics, equipment and technology taking priority over Army and Navy. Bill and Bomber Commands crewmen would now become the most highly trained and specialised personnel in the British Armed Forces.

Mr. Justice Singleton, a High Court Judge, was asked by the War Cabinet to study the conflicting opinions in the execution of tactics. In his report delivered on 20 May 1942, he concluded that: *'If Russia can hold Germany on land, I doubt whether Germany will stand 12 to 18 months continuous, intensified and increased bombing, affecting, as it must, her war production, her power of resistance, her industries and her will to resist (by which I mean morale).'*

The Area Bombing Directive was issued on the 14 February 1942. It listed the primary industrial targets that were within 350 miles from 5 Groups Headquarters at RAF Mildenhall. This was the distance slightly over the maximum range of the radio navigation aid GEE. The objective of the directive was 'To focus attacks on the morale of the enemy civil population and in particular the industrial workers.' Arthur Harris took charge of Bomber Command on 22 Feb 1942 and was tasked with implementing Churchill's policy and unwaveringly supported the development of tactics and technology to perform the task more effectively. Alongside the Chief of the Air Staff, Marshal of the Royal Air Force Charles Portal, he relentlessly maintained one of the most devastating strategic bombing campaigns in history. The first major target attacked in the campaign was Essen on the night of 8/9 March 1942. On the 14 June 1943 it was agreed that the USAAF (United States Army Air Force) and the RAF would work together (Point Blank Directive). The Americans were bombing by day at oil and industrial targets including German aircraft production and the British hitting the industrial cities by night. The first USAAF raids were on the 4 July 1942 to the Netherlands (Max Hastings, Richard Overy, Derek Brammer).

By the time Bill reached 61 Squadron in May 1944 the rapid advances in technology from the scientific community had allowed Bomber Command to improve its methods. Electronic navigational instruments like Gee, Oboe, G-H (a reverse form of Oboe operated by USAAF, whereby the aircraft carries the pulses instead of the ground force transmitting the electronic beam they rode on. AVM Don Bennett's book, Pathfinder) and the ground mapping radar codenamed H2S, all helped to improve bombing accuracy for his missions. Bill said these improvements to Navigational techniques and the development of the Path Finder Force was crucial to his successfully reaching and accurately bombing his targets.

As mentioned at the end of Chapter 4, I by coincidence had met another Bomber Command Veteran called Percy Cannings, who shared some fascinating accounts of bombing missions. I felt honoured to meet Percy who served with 97 (Straits Settlements) Squadron, Pathfinder Force on Wed the 10 Oct 2012. Bill would have been fascinated to meet Percy and I can only hope that he somehow or other was with us in spirit. The meeting came about through his daughter Sandy Cannings who had contacted me through the social networking site Twitter. The site has proved invaluable as a promotional and research tool with many people on the 'WW2 Aviation Trail' networking each other. Amongst many were the BBMF at RAF Coningsby, NX611 'Just Jane' at the Aviation Heritage Centre in East Kirkby, which also included staff members Sean Taylor and Louise Bush. Steven Elsworth also provided much assistance through his connections at 97 and 61 Squadrons old base RAF Coningsby, also donating some outstanding Lancaster photos.

Percy Cannings was a Mid-Upper Gunner and is one of the 'extraordinary men', who at 89 years old provided me with some unique eye witness accounts of PFF marking techniques. I took Bill North's and Jeff Gray's Log books with me to our meeting and had an overwhelming feeling that through the corridors of time, some 'coincidences' would reveal themselves to us.

Percy flew 22 Ops with 100 Squadron during 1943, part of which were the 'Battle of Berlin' (as mentioned above Jeff Gray also flew to many of the targets where Bomber Command losses were horrific and survived to tell the tale). Percy then served with 83 OTU at Peplow as a Gunnery instructor, flying in Wellingtons as the 'screen' gunner to the training Air Gunners. He was then transferred to 97 Squadron PFF at Bourne and then Coningsby to fly another 25 Ops, after which he was transferred to Bill's old unit 17 OTU at Turweston, gaining the award of a DFM.

Percy completed an incredible 47 recorded Ops and notched up an unbelievable tally of flying hours in his service to Bomber Command. Sure enough on comparing the three men's Log books we found he was marking targets for 61 Squadron's F/Lt Jeff Gray (15/16 March 1944, Stuttgart and 22/23 April 1944, Brunswick) and five targets for F/Lt Bill North and his crew during May and June 1944. Percy remarkably also flew alongside Bill's Flt/Eng Sgt Les Morton.

Percy Cannings, courtesy of the *Cannings family.*

Bill North, Arthur Smith, Jeff Grey, Percy Cannings and Alan Wells all helped explain this next section regarding Pathfinders and Bomber Streams. It is also cross referenced with my research from Max Hastings and Richard Overy's publications Bomber Command, also Don Bennett's, Pathfinders and various documentaries listed in the Bibliography. It also helps to explain Bill's debriefing reports and tactics on Operations.

Bill explained that after the switch from day to night bombing the development of the Pathfinder Force became a critical tool in helping the main Bomber Force to locate their targets from August 1942. After studying German electronic techniques for the devastating bombing of British cities like Coventry, the outstanding scientist Dr RV Jones advised that the radio directional equipment should be located in the leading Bomber Force. During the Blitz the Germans had unwittingly revealed to us their extraordinary electronic beam techniques used in locating, marking and bombing a target.

Much to the chagrin of the old school Air Commanders the specialist Pathfinder Force was formed and commanded by the young charismatic Australian, Air Vice Marshall Don Bennett. Don Bennett was appointed to command the Pathfinders on 5 July 1942. The PFF was formed in mid August 1942 with an initial five ordinary Squadrons from each of Bomber Command's 5 Groups, 156, 109, 7, 35 and 83 respectively. Arthur Harris had initially opposed the idea of elite Squadrons being formed and absorbing experienced Bomber Command crews. Although reluctantly supporting Bennett he transferred these 5 regular Squadrons with no experience in target marking to him, they began service straight away and Don Bennett refined their techniques as they went along. After a shaky start PFF improved its performance through the last months of 1942 with the 3 groups of markers proving their efficiency in the successful 4/5 Sept 1942 attack on Bremen.

AVM Don Bennett (source *B-G-AABE-GOLDEN-AGE AVIATION in...*).

The PFF used a combination of aircraft, Wellingtons, Stirlings, Halifaxes, the superfast de Havilland Mosquito and also the Avro Lancaster. Leonard Cheshire eventually had the use of a Mustang for his 5 Group low level marking technique. It was later expanded in January 1943 to become its own number 8 Group. Don Bennett's intense rival was the AOC of 5 Group Ralph Cochrane who alongside the CO of 617 Squadron, Leonard Cheshire were both pivotal in refining 5 Groups own PFF marking techniques. W/O Percy Cannings service with 97 Squadron began in the middle of this rivalry between Bennett and Cochrane. The CinC and Bennett had disagreed on a low level marking technique to be used over Berlin. Bennett having peeved the CinC due to his refusal to use the system was shocked to be ordered after the 5/6 April 1944 raid to Toulouse, that 83 and 97 Squadrons (to Coningsby) plus one Mosquito Squadron 627 (to Woodhall Spa with 617 Squ) were to be immediately transferred back to their original 5 Group with Ralph Cochrane. Proud of their Pathfinder status and achievements their loyalty remained with 8 Group. However on arriving at Coningsby instead of a warm welcome, the base Commander AC Bobby Sharpe rubbed salt in the wound and gave the two Squadrons a humiliating lecture in the briefing room on the error of 8 Group ways.

Thus Percy Cannings flew two Ops with 97 Squadron to Stuttgart and Berlin in March 1944 with PFF 8 Group at Bourne and then from early April was part of the transfer back to 5 Group's Coningsby. He flew his first Op with 5 Group to Paris, La Chapelle Marshalling Yards on the 20/21 April 1944 as an FD (Flare Dropper), (P175, 176 *Pathfinders*, Don Bennett. *The Bomber Command War Diaries*, P490. P. 80, *5 Group Bomber Command*, Chris Ward and W/O Percy Cannings).

Bill said these crews had to fly 45 Operations (15 more than Bill) to complete their tour of duty (It originally had been set at 60 Ops by Arthur Harris).

**W/O Percy Cannings**

*'The PFF Tour was 45 Ops, this was equivalent to 2 Tours for the Main Bomber Force (The 1st 30 missions, the 2nd 20 missions). Don Bennett didn't like using incendiaries for marking because of 'flare back' over the target. These meant that PFF wouldn't be blinded by the glare of the burning incendiaries and thus hinder marking efficiency. However when we rejoined 5 Group we started using incendiaries again.'*

The PFF flew ahead of the main Bomber Stream in which Bill would be flying in to mark and identify the target with a system of coloured flares and markers. Don Bennett's exceptional PFF Mosquito Squadrons would also locate obscured targets by using blind marking navigational equipment Oboe (Don Bennett makes constant reference throughout his book, Pathfinders to the importance of Oboe and how it was a critical technology that helped PFF locate targets in varying weather conditions). The large number of aircraft sent to targets was organised into a formation of varying heights and speed over a common route, the intention being to overwhelm the German defences. This was called the Bomber Stream. The first time the Bomber Stream was put into operation was before the birth of PFF on the famous '1000' Bomber Raid to Cologne on 30/31 May 1942 which was an overwhelming success. Bomber Command's techniques were given a huge push forward through Don Bennett's aggressive lobbying and would soon to become the effective fighting force it wanted to be; a sleeping giant had been awoken.

The PFF carried a mixture of coloured Target Indicators (green and red TI's) and marker flares. These brightly concentrated markers could be identified from high above the target areas even through smoke and sometimes cloud. Bill said the target was often a jumble of different colours as the markers went down, bombs exploded and AA fire came up at them. The tactics were as follows, there were 3 groups of marker aircraft.

The first group was called the 'Illuminators' whose job was to find the target and light it with white flares, route markers would also be dropped. The second was called the 'Visual Markers' who found the target aiming point dropping coloured flares and incendiaries on it. The third group was called the 'Backers Up', who would be distributed at points within the main Bomber Stream; their task was to remark the original TI's as required.

These refined marking techniques also helped to prevent 'creepback' from the target. The Bomber Stream would follow in behind the PFF in carefully timed waves dropping a mixture of incendiaries, high explosive and blast bombs (cookies). If the target was covered in cloud bright red and yellow flares called Wanganui would be used as sky markers.

Percy Canning's crew had a flexible role with regard to these tactics and performed a variety of these PFF techniques with 97 Squ. Alongside Percy's debriefing notes are some abbreviations for what tactic his crew performed on the given night. **SUPP** (Supporters), **VBU** (Visual Back Up), **FD** (Flare Dropping), **BI** (Blind Illuminator) and **BMI** (Blind Marker Illuminator). These abbreviations are all marked at the end of his debriefing notes.

Another improvement in marking technique came on 20/21 June 1943 with the introduction of the Master Bomber (Grp/Cpt LC Slee) in the attack on the Zeppelin Works at Friedrichshafen (Bomber Command War Diaries p399). Also used effectively in Operation Hydra, the attack on the V2 secret research establishment at Peenemunde 17/18 Aug 1943, the Master Bomber was Grp/Cpt JH Searby of 83 Squadron. The Master Bomber was equipped with High Frequency Radio allowing it to communicate with his Deputies and the Main Force; it circled the target redirecting marking and requesting extra markers to be dropped.

A new and much more flexible Automatic Bombsight called the MK 14, was also introduced in 1942. This gave Bill's Bomb Aimer Norman Jarvis even greater accuracy whilst dropping their bomb loads on the PFF markers and targets. As mentioned on Bill's first Op to Brest the essential meteorology reports were provided for him and the Bomber Command crews by 8 Groups PFF, Met flight No. 1409 at RAF Wyton with their Mosquitoes flying over the target areas prior to Bombing Operations.

**Left:** de Havilland Mosquito and **right:** a 105 Squ Mosquito with crew painting on the 203rd Op (*CH15100 IWM*).

**W/O Percy Cannings**

**3 Codenames for PFF Ops** (these techniques were coded by Don Bennett and were given the names of towns in England, Australia and New Zealand).

**Newhaven** where target was visually identified and marked with TI's Target Indicators of red or green.

**Parramatta** where target was marked after identification by H2S or OBOE with TI or red spot fire with OBOE by Mosquito.

**Wanganui** – this is a sky marker which was on a parachute with a steady main colour with dropping stars of different colours, red or green at required intervals, placed so that when bomb aimer got this flare in his sight on a precise height and speed and a particular heading would deposit his bombs or flares on the target. See illustrations attached. The reader must appreciate that wind plays a very critical role. Assumed for clarity the plane has to go to B from A (your base) to B (your target) is a straight line, but because of how the wind controls where the plane goes the pilot has to turn towards the wind to actually travel in the required direction (see sketches). The critical placing of flare is vital to success and would need to be replaced as soon as it is blown off course and timed depending on wind strength and height by barometric fuse to ignite at right height. Not the most reliable system of marking, but some chance of success when no other method available (TI's often could not be seen through thick cloud cover).

97 Squadron (Straits Settlement) Pathfinder Force 1944 (source *Percy Cannings)*

The history of 97 Squ can be read in Kevin Bending's excellent book, *Achieve Your Aim* (Woodfield Publishing). On 25/26 April 1945 97 Squ completed its final Operation. It lost 123 a/c on Ops and completed 4,066 sorties. It won 18 DSOs, 1 OBE, 228 DFCs, 41 Bars to the DFC, 1 BEM, 163 DFMs, 2 Bars to the DFM, 2 USA DFCs, 2 Belgian Croix de Guerres and 1 Russian Medal of Valour.(source, *97 Squadron Association)*

**Sketch of Wanganui:-**

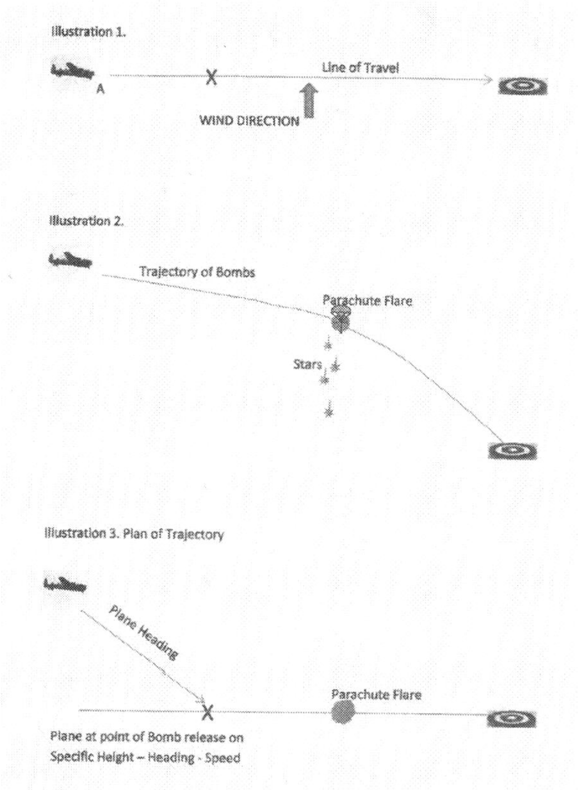


Drawing of Wanganui technique by *Percy Cannings.*

**W/O Percy Cannings**

*'After completing 22 ops with 100 Squadron with the last one going to Hamburg on the 27 July 1943 (why only 22 before being screened from Ops I don't know). I then spent 6 months as a Gunnery Instructor at 83 OTU Peplow, Shropshire up to 15 March 1944. I was then posted to 97 Squadron at RAF Bourn, Cambridgeshire. I arrived at about 6pm on the 15 March 1944 and reported to the Guard Room. I was told 'We have been waiting for you leave your kit bag with us and report to F/O Reid in the Briefing Room now'. I was duly introduced to my 2nd tour crew and learned that I was in a PFF Squadron and off to Stuttgart. I was told by F/O WM Reid that I had replaced their original Mid Upper Gunner who had eyesight trouble. I was only vaguely aware what PFF was having been on a non operational station for 6 months.*

*I had no time to find my billet and had also missed the bacon and egg pre-op meal and had to draw a parachute and borrow flying gear and head off to our Lancaster taking off at 7.35pm. 6 hours 50 minutes later we landed and attended the debriefing and post-op meal, bacon and eggs (much needed having missed pre-op one while travelling from Peplow to Bourn). I was advised to sleep in the Guard Room and find a billet the next day. I imagine my bed must have been in one of the cells, but time has dimmed that memory. I soon got to know the crew and we quickly became an efficient team. This new role meant instead of just going to target, bombing, and getting back to base we had to do other things as well. Initially we dropped flares to light up the area for aiming point to be marked with a TI and also learned later part of our job was to help deflect defences from concentrating on the very few marker aircraft. While cross referencing my Log Book with Bill North and Jeff Gray's Log Books, Chris Keltie found out that I had flown alongside 61 Squadron's F/Lt Jeff Gray on this first Op with 97 Squadron to Stuttgart. Then subsequently also flying alongside F/Lt Bill North on five of his Ops.'*

140 Squ Mosquito warms up engines for night photo-reconnaissance mission, Melsbroek, Belgium, 15 Feb 1945 (*CH1500 IWM*).

Jeff Gray now recalls a fascinating story to do with PFF and AVM Don Bennet CB CBE DSO:

**<u>F/Lt Jeff Gray</u>**

*'Don Bennett was a very gifted and charismatic man who didn't get the recognition he deserved. I met him a few times after the War as he lived fairly close by to me in Farnham Common. He became a little bit*

*reclusive after the collapse of British South American Airways* [BSAA] *and I sensed he was also a bit disillusioned. A lot of the pilots from BSAA were ex PFF and most of them came to British Overseas Airways Corporation* [BOAC] *where I was working. During the War Don Bennett was always scouting for volunteers from other Groups to join the PFF. He constantly kept his eye on the Operational performance of other Bomber Command aircrews. This involved him looking at crews that were about half way through their tours, had a good record of reaching and bombing the target and had no early returns. In early 1944 my crew and I were scouted by Don Bennett to join PFF. However, this meant that our crew could be split up as Don Bennet often took the core of Pilot, Navigator and Bomb Aimer only. My crew and I agreed to have a meeting and decide whether we would stay where we were at 61 Squ or join the PFF. We arranged to meet up at the Leagate Inn near Coningsby, where I had reserved a table for us all. The barman was told to expect the 'Gray Crew' and direct them to the table where I was sitting which was all on my tab. We all proceeded to talk about it over a fantastic meal and the drinks were soon flowing. However what I didn't know was that whenever anybody came into the Pub in RAF uniform the barman called out, 'Are you with the 'Gray Crew' the drinks are on them?' Anyway my crew all voted and it was decided that we would all stay with 61 Squ. My Navigator noticed that I hadn't voted and asked me why. I said, 'That in view of there being a deadlock, I would have had the casting vote', to which he replied, 'What would you have done?' My reply was, 'That if it had come to it I would have voted to go to PFF.' So there you go I didn't have to face that situation in the end and we stayed with 61 Squ. However the sting in the tale of this particular episode was that my tab came to 25 quid because everyone else's drinks had been put on it. The 25 quid was the money that had been awarded to me with my DFM. I'll never forget that, it was a lot of money in those days, it totally cleaned me out!'*

I myself had sat in the Leagate Inn with my wife Wendy for dinner and drinks twice on my travels around Lincolnshire without knowing that Jeff and his crew and many other aircrews had graced its four walls. The Inn has a long history of hosting guests dating back to 1542 and is just up the B1192 Leagate Road from the wonderful Laburnum House B+B where we stayed. It only clicked when Jeff told me this story recently that this was the same place. It hasn't changed much since those turbulent days and I could just imagine Jeff and his crew meeting there. Its four walls have many stories to tell, and I by chance found one of them to share. The Bluebell Inn, 617 Squ's Petwood Hotel in Woodhall Spa, East Kirkby, which was home to 5 Group's 57 and 630 Squadron's and the BBMF at RAF Coningsby; all these places and the area are steeped in WW2 aviation History, and all have an atmospheric presence about them.

When Bill and I were researching the loss figures we found that there were slight variations in the records obtained from The Bomber Command War Diaries and WR Chorley's Bomber Command Losses. For each Operation flown on by Bill North and his crew I hand-counted the losses in WR Chorley's book and compared it to losses recorded in The Bomber Command War Diaries. Sometimes these figures matched exactly and other times they varied slightly. The Bomber Command Diaries also include a/c written off in crashes at home bases and we have also included losses for other Ops on the dates we have recorded, to demonstrate the full extent of the dreadful odds against Bill's crew survival.

Each Operation Bill flew on is recorded here and is followed by his own debriefing report which was given to the debriefing Officer on return to Skellingthorpe. This was Top Secret. This is followed by the Squadron Ops report; both of these reports are recorded in the 61 Squadron Operational Record Book (ORB). This is kept at the Public Records Office (National Archive under AIR 27) at Kew and 50/61 Squadron Association also has a copy of the ORB which can be obtained by contacting Alan Wells. Finally I have given the total number of aircraft detailed for Bomber Command Ops and supporting information from the Bomber Command War Diaries. To this I have added some points discovered in my own research and added the exact number of aircraft and men lost that I counted from WR Chorley's Bomber Command Losses book.

Just a quick note now from Bill in relation to the history of Operational Tours in Bomber Command. Bill bookmarked p520-527 in his book *The Right Of The Line* by John Terrain for me to look at. Very briefly these pages reveal the evolution of the Tour of duty, how many Ops it should be and the way this affected morale in Bomber Command. Like infantry men and officers on the Western Front in WW1 the task set to the aircrews was relentless, demanding and of an 'unprecedented and peculiar nature' (quote, John Terrain). These men displayed extraordinary degrees of stamina and resolution in the face of adversity and this phenomenon appeared in the same wide cross section of people who had volunteered and served in the RAF. 'On Operations they had to fly long distances at night and generally in bad weather, much further than most pilots ever flew before the war, and also suffer enemy attacks, cold and discomfort, fatigue and fear as a matter of routine' (quote p51, *Lancaster at War 2*, Mike Garbett and Brian Goulding). One of the main moral effectors was the high loss of experienced crews and potential leaders which created sub factors like fear of flying on Operations.

To combat the loss of morale a psychological defence mechanism would be required to give the men a point in time where an end could be visualised.

Discussions and meetings took place early in 1943 between the Air Ministry, Air Chiefs, CinC Arthur Harris and Group and Squadron Commanders to access breaking down the Operational service into manageable portions of time. Originally tours had been set at 60 sorties with 2 tours of 30 Ops and an 8 to 9 month break in-between to serve on OTU. The second tour often resulted in the loss of experienced crews towards its end, so it was agreed a reduction to 20 Ops would reduce this factor. In the Air Council Room on the 4 February 1943 a meeting took place with Portal in the Chair and the CinC present. Portal asked Harris what length of tours Bomber Command recommended. Harris replied, 'The first tour should consist of 30 sorties and the second tour should not normally exceed 20 sorties. The PFF should be on a different basis and these should consist of 45 sorties, but crews could be withdrawn at any time after completion of 30 sorties' (a tour of 30 equated to an average of 200 hours flying time). Generally the men wouldn't look beyond this set figure of 30 to a second tour of 20, so it was considered to be a good defence mechanism. In the Air Ministry letter dated 8 May 1943 the chain of Command was thus instructed; first tour, 30 sorties, second tour, 20 sorties. So 'the tour of Operations, with its definite promise of relief, was a sheet anchor of morale in Bomber Command.' John Terrain, *The Right Of The Line.*

On my travels I came across another very sobering yet fascinating record of the way in which Bomber Command compiled their statistics for aircrew survival. It is taken from a French book called, *Aircraft Battle in County Vienne (Fr) 1939-1945* by Christian Richard. The translation from French to English is as follows. 'Thus, the Bomber Command of the RAF compiled a number of points (120 in 1944 and 144 in 1945) that was calculated as 3 points per mission if the target was west of longitude 6 degrees east, or 4 points if it was east or towards Germany. At every mission the RAF was losing 5% of the committed forces. The risk of being killed was statistically reached at 100% at the 20th mission'.

**W/O Peter Knox**

*'After a night of Operations by 5 Group a report was circulated on the Group's activities and posted on the Squadron's bulletin board. Missing crews were identified. There was full disclosure of casualties. No one was under any illusions that the odds of completing a Tour of Operations were poor.'*

Another fact Bill also mentioned was that on the following day from Operations, BBC News Reports would mention the number of a/c that had failed to return from the whole Bomber Force; *'It was obvious to anybody who could add up two plus two that the survival odds were stacked against us!'* This, then, is the background against which Bill flew his Operational Missions for Bomber Command, where there was a one in three chance of surviving a tour of 30 Ops. Next we take a quick look at the base that Bill flew his Operations from and his and the crews memories of it.

A very young looking Percy Cannings, 2nd on the right, 2nd row from bottom. RAF Reception Centre, Lords Cricket Ground, St John's Wood, 1943. (source, *Percy Cannings)*

# Chapter Twelve

## RAF Skellingthorpe

The 'North Crew' had arrived at RAF Skellingthorpe. This Station was home to two elite Bomber Command Squadrons, 50 and 61 Squadron and under the command of the auspicious 5 Group. The 61 Squadron CO during Bill's service was Wing Commander Doubleday DSO DFC who proved to be an outstanding leader. He had completed a tour of 30 Ops with RAAF 460 Squadron and a 2nd tour with 467 Squadron. He was posted from 467 Squ on 22 April 1944 to command 61 Squadron until 25 September 1944. He eventually completed 53 missions whilst flying Ops with 61 Squ; an amazing total given that the chance of surviving two tours of duty was only 2 per cent.

**Left to right**, 61 Squadron badge with the Lincoln Imp mascot and their motto, (Per *Purum Tonantes*),'Thundering Through The Clear Air' The Bomber Command badge and motto 'Strike Hard Strike Sure. The 5 Group badge and motto 'Undaunted'.

During WW2 there were over 700 Bomber Command airfields that as Churchill put it 'Speckled the English countryside'. Of these there were 30 Bomber Stations surrounding the city of Lincoln and Lincolnshire itself was nicknamed 'Bomber County'. The nearest base was Skellingthorpe, two miles south-west of the outskirts, originally a satellite airfield for Waddington. Lincoln Cathedral could be seen from the base and was a familiar landmark on take-off and landings. It was located on an area of pasture known as Black Moor, 2½ miles south of the village of Skellingthorpe and by several large woods and bordering the B1190. RAF Skellingthorpe was nicknamed 'Skelly' and its call sign was 'Black Swan', named after the local pub. It was surrounded by a perimeter fence and was made up of a combination of perimeter track, dispersal areas, hangars, technical buildings, offices and accommodation in Nissen huts for the personnel who lived on the unit. The base could house 1,803 men and 295 women including WAAF (Women's Auxiliary Air Force) and some 40 Lancasters operated from the base. The RAF crews at Skelly were a mixture of men from 'the Empire' and included British, Irish, Australian, New Zealand and Canadian's.

Bill said there was nothing luxurious about 'Skelly', the Nissen huts were very basic with simple beds and a table. The huts could house two crews (14 men), often after returning from missions the seven beds of the other crew would be empty where they had 'failed to return' from Ops. There was a small coke fire, but they were still cold and draughty in the winter. The airfield consisted of the standard pattern of three runways, with one Type B1 and two Type T2 hangars. There is a small portion of the original runway left and it is where the aircraft turned around on the journey from dispersals to the take off point. When taking off and landing Bill said they got a fantastic view of Lincoln and the Cathedral.

The control tower at East Kirkby, 21 June 2011 (CK).

**W/O Percy Cannings**

*'The most heartbreaking memory of those days is seeing the empty beds of fellow comrades who didn't make it back.'*

**James Flowers (50 Squ Rear Gunner)**

*'I well remember the hairy times taking off and landing at Skelly. As a rear gunner I seemed to be constantly warning Skip about other aircraft*

*at our height. With Waddington's circuit, and others, nearby, many unlit aircraft crossed our path. With the main runway in a direct line towards the Cathedral, which is itself on top of Lindum Hill, taking off fully loaded made the ring twitch a bit. I always breathed a sigh of relief when we reached a thousand feet. When there was a lot of activity, i.e. with Ops on and many a/c around, whilst in the circuit I used to swing my turret from beam to beam, at the same time leaning forward and almost putting my head through the opening in front of me. With the turret swung to beam and by leaning well forward I could see almost to the front of the aircraft. Those were the days. Millions of people now love to hear the roar of the remaining veteran Lancs even though (I'm told) only 60 percent throttle is ever used. How they would have loved to hear the roar of four Merlin engines on full throttle as the aircraft strained to lift 14,000lbs of bombs and 2,200 gallons of fuel off the ground. The whole frame of the aircraft used to vibrate with the stress. The tension and excitement was unbelievable. What memories.'*

James Flowers. 50/61 Squadron Memorial Day, 10 June 2012 (CK).

After Operational service in WW1 and being disbanded 61 Squadron was re-formed in 1937 as a Bomber Squadron and moved around various bases in Lincolnshire (Hemswell, North Luffenham, Woolfox Lodge, Syerston, Coningsby and Skellingthorpe twice). It eventually ended up at Skellingthorpe in November 1943 after transferring from Syerston, also returning again in April 1944 when Coningsby became the headquarters of No. 5 Group's Special Duties Operations. It was one of the original 5 Group Squ's and flew Audax, Anson, Blenheim, Hampden, Manchester and Lancaster's. Its first Operational sortie was on 25 Dec 1939 and dropped its first bombs on 7 March 1940.

After the War, RAF Skellingthorpe was home to No. 58 Maintenance Unit RAF and salvaged crashed aircraft were stored at the base. Today the site is in the area known as Birchwood and is covered by the Birchwood

Housing estate where there is a Memorial to 50/61 Squadron and a small Museum.

**Left -** the two D for Dog Skellingthorpe Lancasters flying over the base with runways in the background. 61 Squadron's QR-D was flown in by Bill North and his crew and 50 Squadron's VN-D was flown in by Sir Michael Beetham and his crew. This picture was in Bill's collection and is a copy of a painting by *Reg Payne* who was Sir Michaels Beetham's Wireless Operator.

**Right -** vertical aerial shot of Skellingthorpe (*50/61 Squ Association*).

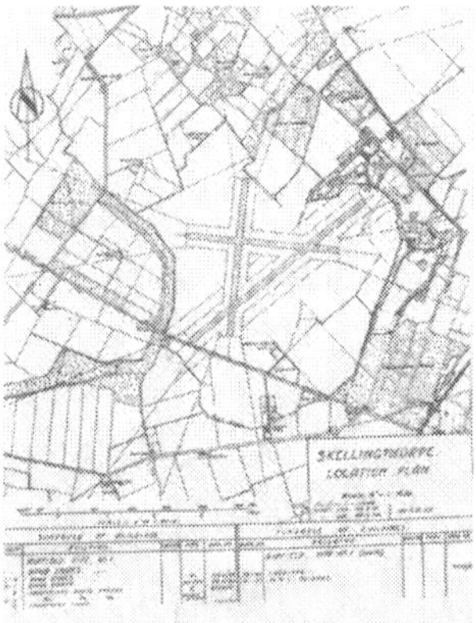

A copy of the *Air Ministry map* of the base supplied by Roger Morley of Skellingthorpe Village. 50 Squ badge and motto, *From Defence To Attack* and 97 Squ badge and motto, *Achieve Your Aim*.

Part of the RAF Skellingthorpe runway outside the Birchwood Community Centre. The spires of Lincoln Cathedral can just be seen on the far right. (CK)

Chris Keltie standing next to the 50/61 Squadron Memorial on Memorial Day 12 June 2011. At the base is a wreath I laid for Bill North and his crew. (CK)

There now follows a list of the all the remaining Operations Bill flew on; with the first two, the catastrophic night mission to Lille marshalling yards and the port of Brest already described. Again I also include eye-witness accounts from Bill and his crew and other named Bomber Command Veteran's, based on the interviews I conducted, to supplement and add colour to the missions and their debriefing reports. This, then, was the base from which Bill and his crew were to fly 17 missions- the last of which ended in disaster.

# Chapter Thirteen

# Operations, 'A' Flight, 61 Squadron.

**Operation (Night mission)**

**11/12 MAY 1944. BOURG-LÉOPOLD (German Army Barracks, Belgium) 'The North Crew'. F/S H Anthony replaces Sgt Les Morton as Flight Engineer and Sgt CC Scrimshaw is on board as an AG3 (Third Air Gunner making it an 8 man crew).**

**Detailed bombing heights 14,500-16,000ft. Bombing load unknown, 11 Lancasters detailed. MET: 10/10ths C.U. Tops. 14,000ft.**

**Lancaster III, EE176, QR-M (Mickey the Moocher) was the 2nd a/c to take off and the 1st a/c to return due to equipment failure.**

(BOOMERANG-NAV. ERROR)

Up---**22:19**---Down---**00:41**---Time out---**1hrs 22m**

**Debriefing report:-** P/O North returned early owing to compass trouble. Bombs jettisoned at 5527N 0240E (Approx 40 miles directly west of Leiston on the Suffolk Coast).

**Squ. Ops report:-** MET: 10/10ths C.U. Tops. 14,000ft. 11 a/c were detailed to bomb BOURG-LÉOPOLD Military Camp. 6 a/c bombed RSF's from heights between 14,500 to 16,000ft and many sticks of bombs were seen to hit the target. Considerable fighter activity was observed, but otherwise ground defences were practically nonexistent. FOUR a/c did not attack the target as W/T instructions to cease bombing were received. The single remaining a/c [EE176, P/O North] returned early owing to compass trouble and bombs were jettisoned at position 52.27N 02.40E. 6 a/c obtained photos which recorded Ground Detail.

The Master Bomber in the Pathfinder Force gave a 'cease bombing' signal at 00:28hrs followed by 'a return to base'. This was because of bad haze over the target and the risk of inaccurate bombing to civilians nearby.

**W/O Peter Knox (Bomb Aimer, 619 Squ and friend of Norman Jarvis)**

*'Weather conditions were bad at Bourg-Leopold and it was a rule that there should be no bombing of towns in Occupied Europe unless the target could be clearly identified. If you were turned back when flying over Germany you dropped your bombs in any event in the hope they might find a target. The Germans were the enemy. Since it was forbidden to drop bombs indiscriminately over Occupied Europe and it was too dangerous to land planes laden with bombs, in this case they had to be jettisoned over the Channel.'*

190 Lancasters and 8 Mosquitoes of 5 Group and 3 of 8 Group, were dispatched to attack this large military camp in Belgium. Haze hampered the marking of the target and the master bomber ordered the raid to be abandoned, for fear of hitting nearby civilian housing, after 94 Lancasters had bombed. 6 Lancs were lost on the Borg-Leopold Op. One a home base crash at Skellingthorpe, two (7/7s), one (8/8), one (6/7) and one (5/7. A further 9 Lancasters and 3 Halifaxes were lost from other Ops, two of them (8/8s), six of them (7/7s).

This mission was not written in red in Bill's Log Book and hasn't been added to his tally of Operations. The reason for this Bill explained was his early return, a *'Boomerang',* due to compass trouble, therefore not completing the Op.

Some of the other 61 Squadron pilots flying with Bill that night were: 'A' Flight Commander, F/L HH Farmiloe, P/O CJ Gray (The competitive race between Grey and Farmiloe to get back first continued. Discounting Bill's early return, Tommy Farmiloe was first back beating Jeff Gray by 1 minute who was second back). Also F/O GA Berry (RCAF), F/S J Kramer (RCAF) and P/O RA Dear. There are two recorded losses for 61 Squadron this night. One was F/S CJ Woolnough (RAAF) who overshot the runway at Skellingthorpe on his return. The crew were all ok, but the Lancaster was written off. Although not recorded in the ORB at all P/O Jack Hilton Eastwood* is mentioned in WR Chorley's Losses book as the (6/7) loss at Bourg-Léopold and would have been the 12th a/c detailed for this Op, taking off last at 22:39. I have since confirmed with Alan Wells at the 61 Squadron Forum and the CWGC (Commonwealth War Graves Commission) that this is the case and a mistake was made in the omission of this crew in the ORB.

*P/O Jack Hilton Eastwood, 171333 was the son of Percy and Emily Eastwood, who lived on Kingsway, Gatley. He attended Cheadle House School and King William School, Isle of Man, volunteering for the RAF when he was 18 and trained in the USA, arriving in Alabama in December 1942. His Lancaster LM454, QR-Z was a (6/7) FTR and 21 year old Jack is buried alongside F/O Kayser in Schoonselhof Cemetery, Antwerp. There was only one survivor Sgt RO Willis, the rest of the crew are commemorated on the Runnymmede Memorial.

**Training Ops:-**

14 MAY 1944. LANCASTER D. (Dog) SELF. 6 CREW. N.F.T. – BOMBING.

15 MAY 1944. LANCASTER D. (Dog) SELF. 6 CREW. CROSS COUNTRY.

16 MAY 1944. LANCASTER D. (Dog) SELF. 6 CREW. AIR FIRING – LOW LEVEL BOMBING.

18 MAY 1944. LANCASTER D. (Dog) SELF. 6 CREW. AIR SEA FIRING.

19 MAY 1944. LANCASTER D. (Dog) SELF. 6 CREW. N.F.T.

Discounting the Bourg-Léopold Op for the reasons Bill explained, we now look at his third Operation. The first was to Brest and the second was to Lille as already described. His third Op was now to Tours in France.

**Operation No. 3. (Night mission)**

**19/20 MAY 1944. TOURS, FRANCE. 'The North Crew'**

**Detailed bombing height 7,000ft, Bombing load 13,000lbs, 18 Lancasters detailed. Met.Rep, no cloud, some haze.**

**Lancaster III, EE186, QR–D for Dog was the 9th a/c to take off and the 12th a/c to return.**

**(Received no back wind so returned to div. pt. with bombs)**

Up---**22:22**---Down---**04:45**---Time out---**6hrs 23m**

**Debriefing report:-** P/O North received signal at 01.05hrs to cease bombing and return to base. 3 x 1000 American GP Jettisoned at 49.07N 02.44W 02:07 at 10,000ft to reduce weight. 8 x 1000 Am GP AND 4 X 5000.P. brought back to base. [Jettison point is in English Channel SW of Jersey]

**Squ. Ops report:-** Met: no cloud, some haze. Attack on TOURS Marshalling Yards was carried out by 18 aircraft of this Squadron, SIXTEEN aircraft successfully carried out the Operation, bombing RSF's from heights ranging from 5,500-12,000ft. Marking and bombing was well concentrated and the attack was considered a good success. Several explosions were seen with much smoke rising from the target area. Defences were very light indeed. Several photographs were taken which showed ground detail. One aircraft received 'Cease Bombing' signal at 01:05 [this was EE186, Bill's Lancaster] and returned to base with 8x1000 American GP and 4X500 GP, the remaining 3x1000 American GP were jettisoned at 49.07N 02.44W [SW of Jersey, Channel Islands]. The remaining ONE aircraft [P/O D Street] returned early with Bomb Sight u/s and jettisoned full load at 50.08N 00.40W [This was in the middle of the English Channel, half way between Worthing and Caen].

Bill received no Back wind radio communication report, so returned to base with part of the bomb load. The broadcast for wind report was originally designed for the Berlin trips and other missions over Germany. They were intended to keep the Bomber Streams together, so if they went off course they went off course together. Jeff Gray explained that probably due to Bill's inexperience on Operations, when his Navigator failed to pick up the signal he didn't realise that they could have carried on; at this point the Back wind reports weren't relied on so much in Operations history. The bomb loads were part or fully jettisoned to lighten/correct the weight of the aircraft on landing and also to reduce the risk of fatal explosions. It was extremely dangerous to land with a full bomb load.

Tours was one of 5 railway targets detailed to be attacked this night, also 2 coastal gun batteries and a radar installation with other minor Ops. 113 Lancasters and 4 Mosquitoes of 5 Group were tasked to attack railway installations in the centre of Tours. No fighters appeared and no aircraft lost at Tours, 7 aircraft were lost for the whole night's Ops of 900 sorties. 4 a/c and crew were complete losses. 2 Lancs were lost from 7 Squadron Pathfinder Force to le Mans, including the highly distinguished Master Bomber Wing Commander JF Barron (RNZAF) and his 7 crewmen. It was a grave night for the Pathfinder Force with a third 7 Squ Lanc lost at Mont de Couple. Lancaster III, ND736, MG-G was hit by light flak and exploded ejecting the pilot S/L ID Oliver (DFC), he was the only survivor out of the 8 man crew.

This target was located slightly deeper in central France and nearly a 7 hour journey. Tours is a city situated on the lower reaches of the river Loire, between Orléans and the Atlantic coast. Some of the other 61 Squadron pilots flying with Bill this night were: 'A' Flight Commander, F/L HH Farmiloe, with 2nd Pilot P/O WR Sinclair (RAAF), P/O CJ Gray, with 2nd Pilot P/O DW Simmons (RAAF), (Jeff was the first back again and this was his last Op, Tommy was 4th), F/O GA Berry (RCAF), F/S J Kramer (RCAF), F/L BM Acott, with 2nd Pilot P/O RH Passant, F/L WE Jeavons, with 2nd Pilot F/O ER Church (RCAF), F/S EJ (Jack) Goodyer (RNZAF) landing 5 mins before Bill , P/O RA Dear, P/O D Street, P/O EA Stone in ED860, P/O DF White (RCAF) in EE176 with AG3, and P/O HW Cooper. This mission was a success and all a/c returned safely except P/O Auckland, who suffered a collision 10 seconds before the bomb drop damaging the port engines/frame and made an emergency landing at 02:51. Four 2nd pilots were flying on this Op, a huge risk to the Squadron, but as Norman Jarvis mentions they were short of pilots and were much needed.

Earlier in the day the boys had all witnessed a fatal explosion which killed some Ground Staff at Skellingthorpe. Whilst the flights were being prepared for that night's Operations a bomb fell off a bomb trolley and exploded, rocking the whole base (See Chapter 14, Tragedy at Skellingthorpe).

18 MAY 1944. LANCASTER D. (Dog) SELF. 6 CREW. WESTCOTT – BASE.

Bill's next Op was the crew's first visit to Germany and 'the target for the night' was Duisburg. Duisburg was a major logistical centre in the Ruhr Valley and was a familiar target for Bomber Command. Located in the Rhineland on the Dutch German border North of Cologne it had the world's largest inland harbour and was the site of chemical, steel and iron industries vital to the German war effort. This made it a primary target in the Bombing Campaign and it is considered to be one of the most heavily bombed German cities during WW2. The city was badly damaged again from the 2,000 tons of bombs dropped on 22 May 1944. A total of 299 bombing raids had almost completely destroyed the historic city with two thirds of the buildings destroyed or partly damaged. After the War almost the whole of the city had to be rebuilt, most of the historic landmarks had been lost.

'Patiently awaiting take off time'. The Battle of Britain Memorial Flight (BBMF), Lancaster PA474 at RAF Coningsby 9 June 2012 (CK).

**Operation No. 4. (Night Mission)**

**21/22 May 1944. Duisburg, Ruhr Valley. 'The North Crew'**

**Met.Rep 10/10ths cloud. Detailed bombing height 22,000ft, bombing load 13,750lbs. 16 Lancasters detailed.**

**Lancaster III, EE186, QR-D for Dog was the 9th a/c to take off and the 12th a/c to return.**

Up---**22:38**---Down---**03:39**---Time out---**5hrs 01m**

Bill's Bomb Aimer Norman Jarvis leads us into this Operation:-

**W/O Norman Jarvis**

*'My third trip was to Duisburg and the most heavily defended area in Germany, the dreaded 'Happy Valley' or Ruhr in Germany. The preparations for this trip were more elaborate than the previous ones; the tactics and the bomb load were also different. This time we were to carry for the first time the 4000 pounder or 'Cookie' and Incendiary bombs. We crossed the North Sea quietly as the twilight faded into darkness, then on across Holland where the Germans had dropped fighter flares on both sides of our track in and we saw an occasional combat. This made our Gunners uneasy and everyone was tense. We pushed on into Germany and around us above and below us were violent puffs of orange. Then we swung*

*into the 'Happy Valley' and great masses of searchlights were stabbing the sky and it was like day up there up there at 22,000 ft. We could see other aircraft 'coned' by the searchlights as they ran in and getting hell from the ground defences. Now and then we could see air-to-air tracers which indicated to us that one of our comrades was fighting it out with one of their deadly Night Fighters; often these terminated in a ball of flame rushing towards the earth, with one of them going down. Bill battled on and I assisted by looking out underneath us and advising him on the searchlights which never held us in a cone. Each time they streaked towards us we turned towards them and they lost us.*

*I saw the target area ahead and we had barely commenced the bombing run when Eddy the rear Gunner called, 'Fighter, fighter, down port!' There was a great lurch as Bill put our ship into a steep bank and down to port; we went into a corkscrew which was a violent evasion manoeuvre used in such emergencies. Bill kept it up for a few moments when the Gunners reported that the Fighter had broken off his attack; so we then resumed the run into the target. Flak was now intense and bursting all around us, as I gave the directions and just below us was a bomber on fire going down in a sickening spin. At last the target came into my bomb sight and I let the bombs go. Just after closing the bomb doors I was attempting to relieve the Flight Engineer of his job 'windowing'* when I accidentally pulled my oxygen tube off the supply. At this height 22,000 ft, I soon began to pass out, but before doing so I mentioned a few things to Bill that had absolutely no bearing on our present predicament, so he guessed what had happened and sent one of the crew to investigate. As soon as I was plugged in again I was ok, but had rather a heavy head. We were clear of the target area by this time, but just beginning the long trip home, where eternal vigilance was the price of our safety. Bomber Command lost fairly heavily on that occasion and it was very disconcerting to hear that so-and-so's crew had failed to return, but the Duisburg industrial works and the great inland dock at the junction of the Ruhr and the Rhine had received a heavy battering. I always felt sorry to hear of our losses, but one suddenly became hardened and found ourselves not worrying about it.'*

*Window was strips of aluminium foil which was pushed out of the aircraft through the flare chute in the Bomb Aimers compartment to confuse the German Radar systems. The job would be shared by the Bomb Aimer and Flight Engineer and these bundles of 'window' took up much of the space around the nose section.

**F/Lt Bill North**

*'Yes, I remember this Op very well. I have read Norman's account from his War Diaries many times and it always brings back vivid memories. The Ruhr Valley was extremely well defended and we seemed to have everything thrown at us this night. There was a NF attack and I had to 'corkscrew' after the Gunners called out the move, fortunately we lost him. From 22,000 ft we could see a lot going on, there were searchlights, AA bursting all over the place, we saw a/c exploding in the sky, air to air tracers and the target itself was a mass of burning fires. I had to try and ignore all the drama going on around us and concentrate on flying straight and level for the bombing run. Then Norman pulled off his oxygen line and started talking nonsense over the intercom. I sent Les down into the front section to see what was going on and he plugged Norman's supply back in again.'*

**Debriefing report:-** P/O North reported target well marked and heavily defended with fighters. Saw glow of fires over target. Bombed 5 Wanganui flares at 01:12hrs from 22,000ft. PHOTO: Target conditions.

**Squ. Ops report:-** Met report. 10/10ths cloud. Tops. 1,500ft. 16 aircraft, all of which successfully bombed the target as detailed at Duisburg, bombed from heights ranging from 18,250ft-21,500ft. The success of this Operation was doubtful. Wanganui flares were used for identifying the target. Defences were moderate, several aircraft obtained photos of ground conditions.

510 Lancasters and 22 Mosquitoes of 1, 3, 5 and 8 Groups were detailed to attack Duisburg this night. It was the first heavy raid for a year on this target and it was covered by cloud with Oboe and Sky Markers (Wangahui flares) being used. The Oboe sky-marking was accurate and extensive damage was caused in the southern parts of the city.

Bill and his crew rode through the dark heart of death's shadow yet again. Heavy Night Fighter activity claiming most of the 31 Lancasters lost, with 3 more lost on Minelaying. 17 Lancs and their crews were complete losses (119 men) including one 50 Squ Lanc. 6 Lancasters were 6 out of 7 crewmen lost (36 men) and a further 41 men were lost with the rest becoming POWs or evading capture. The total fatalities that night were 196 aircrew from 716 sorties.

Some of the other 61 Squadron pilots flying with Bill this night were: F/L HH Farmiloe, F/O GA Berry (RCAF), F/S Kramer (RCAF) attacked by ME109, MUG fired at it, P/O WE Jeavons, F/S EJ (Jack) Goodyer (RNZAF) Bill landed 5 minutes after Jack, P/O HW Cooper, P/O RA Dear, F/L BM Acott (2nd Dickie F/O BS Turner), P/O EA Stone in ED860 and P/O RH Passant. Most of these pilots reported high cloud swamping Wanganui flares and poor marking hampering aiming points with F/L Jeavons bombing on ETA (estimated time of arrival) because there were no markers seen. Despite the heavy Bomber Command losses that night, the whole Squadron unbelievably returned to Skellingthorpe landing between 02:46 and 04:14.

Bill's next Op was the crew's second visit to Germany and 'the target for the night' was the city of Brunswick which was located in central Northern Germany near Hanover. This made three Operational nights in a row, Tours, Duisburg and Brunswick. The term used by Bomber Command to describe this practice was, 'Maximum Effort'.

The bomb bay of a 9 Squ Lancaster, 5 Jan 1944
(Source, F/O SA Devon, CH 18554 IWM).

**Operation No. 5. (Night mission)**

**22/23 May 1944. Brunswick, Germany. 'The North Crew' (Flt/Eng Sgt Les Morton is replaced by P/O Simmons' Flt/Eng, Sgt GR Candy)**

**Detailed bombing height 21,250ft. Bombing load 8,000lbs. 17 Lancasters detailed. Met.Rep 10/10ths cloud.**

**Lancaster III, EEI86, QR-D for Dog was the 5th a/c to take off and the 10th a/c to return.**

Up---**22:27**---Down---**04:48**---Time out---**6hrs 31m**

Again Norman Jarvis leads us in with his eye witness account of this extremely hazardous and dramatic mission to Germany:-

**W/O Norman Jarvis**

*'On 22 May 1944 the night following the Duisburg raid we had another great nightmare of a trip to Brunswick. We had had very little sleep in between and this time we were going further into the Ruhr than ever before, but somehow I was quite thrilled about it and did not care. Our Flight Engineer Les Morton had been a bundle of nerves up to now and did not want to go, but we encouraged him not to let it get him down and when we took off he was with us. I felt very tired and drowsy on the way out and wished I had taken more 'wakey wakey' tablets*, but as we crossed the coast of Europe I was keen on my toes. The Zyder-Zee passed below us and the usual coastal batteries gave us a welcome for a while. All was quiet for a while until away in the east we could see a great barrier of searchlights, put there it seemed to defy us a passage through to our objective. From the Baltic Sea down they stretched and there was no way around them. By much skill, weaving and manoeuvring we got through and pressed on dropping our bombs without a great deal of opposition. We then had to face that barrier of lights again which was studded with heavy flak. We were temporarily coned many times and the flak bursts shook us when they slammed in close by. All around us we saw others in greater difficulty and we finally came out of it past the circle of defence that was Hanover and then the long vigil until we got home. Being coned by searchlights is a horrible uncomfortable feeling; it seems as if you are naked in the midst of*

*a crowded street and so big that the whole world can see you exposed and they are all throwing stones into the bargain.'*

*These tablets were amphetamines and during WW2 they were distributed in pill form as a precautionary measure. Allied Air Forces advised aircrew to take them only if they needed to, to stay awake on long missions, where the risk of long periods of inactivity and the constant droning of the engines could induce sleep.

**F/Lt Bill North**

*'We were coned temporarily many times on this raid. There was a master radar controlled searchlight that was a bluish colour, this just pointed straight up in the sky and would then just suddenly lock on to us automatically. The rest of the searchlights were white and they would then follow and swing onto us, sometimes as many as twenty searchlights could cone us. We had to twist, dive and turn all over the place and eventually shook the lights off. During this time the lights were so bright they would blind the whole cockpit and the other crew positions, you could not see any of the instrument panel and it was quite disorientating. We felt very alone and exposed and the flak batteries would then all start aiming and firing at us. Once in a cone it was very difficult to escape and aircraft wouldn't last longer than a few minutes before they were blasted out of the sky or shot down by a Night Fighter.'*

**Debriefing report:-** P/O North reported target poorly marked in view of what we were briefed to see. At zero hour no markings whatsoever seen. Large incendiary fires in target area. Bombed Green TI at 01:28hrs from 21,000ft. Photo Ground detail.

**Squ Ops report:-** Met report 10/10ths cloud. Tops. 5/6000ft. Some ground haze. 17 aircraft were detailed for bombing Operations against Brunswick. All the a/c bombed the target successfully with the aid of RSFs, TI's and Wanganui flares. The success of this attack was rather doubtful and numerous incendiaries were observed burning in fields, although fires were seen in the target area. Defences were active all along the route and countless search lights were observed. Night Fighters were also in the vicinity, which seemed to be working in conjunction with the searchlights. 6 a/c only had photos of ground detail. Bombing heights were from 19,250-22,000ft.

W/O Peter Knox also provides a fascinating eyewitness account of the condition of the skies over the target area:

*'We were at our appointed bombing height of 22,000 feet. There were planes milling around above and below us waiting for the Pathfinders to drop their markers. The target area became more crowded as new waves of planes arrived. The pre—plotted staggered bombing times had lost their meaning. Instructions were coming from the plane in charge of the operation in clear voice transmissions—there was no longer any secrecy about the target. The airwaves were buzzing. I recall hearing one pilot pleading for permission to bomb saying 'this is the last mission of my tour and I want to get the hell out of here.' Other pilots were warning that they had not been able to make their bombing height. In addition to the ever present danger of collisions they faced the peril of having one of our bombs drop on them.'*

**Flying alongside F/Lt Bill North for the second time to mark the target and on his 13th Op with 97 Squ PFF was W/O Percy Cannings and his crew:-**

Skipper, F/O WM Reid, FE, Sgt W Richards, NAV, F/O RD Parker, BA, F/Sgt GD Moir, WO, F/Sgt B Harthill, MUG, F/Sgt DP Cannings, RG, Sgt G Brown, in Lancaster ND807, OF-P, 'B' Flight, 97 Squadron PFF Coningsby **(BI, Blind Illuminator)**.

**97 Squ, PFF Debriefing report:-**

Up 22:53, Down 04:22. One flare red/green stars, 1x2000lb HC, 1Xti green No4, 11x'J' type clusters. 8/10ths cloud and haze. Tops approx 7,000ft. Target identified by H2S. Heard markers trying to contact controllers. Flares estimated east of target. Waited to release sky markers, had orders to release so bombed. Order for Wanganui received at 01:24hrs, returned and released own skymarker; approx 3 seen; Controller not heard; Deputy took over at H+2.

Pathfinder Force, 97 (Straits Settlements) Squadron, Lancaster B Mk III, PB410, OF-J, 8 Aug 1944 (source, *Alliot Verdun-Roe, 1000 aircraft photos*).

225 Lancasters and 10 Mosquitoes of 1 and 5 Group were detailed to attack Brunswick. This raid was a failure, although clear weather had been forecast over the target it was unexpectedly completely covered by cloud. There was interference on the Master Bomber's radio communications which would explain the poor marking reported by Bill. Most of the bombs fell outside the city with no civilian casualties and one hour later the cloud had cleared. 14 Lancasters were lost at Brunswick, with 6 complete aircraft and their crews (42 men). One 50 Squ Lanc, LL744, VN-B, was a complete loss and 4 Lancs were lost with 6 out of 7 crew (24 men). The remaining crew losses were 14 men dead and the rest were POWs or evaded capture. 1x 97 Squ lost (7/7).

19 Lancs were lost at Dortmund with one 408 Squ Lanc LL723, EQ-H, piloted by 408's Wing Commander DS Jacobs DFC (RCAF), a complete loss with its 9 man crew. 8 Lancs were (7/7s), 56 men. 1, (6/7), 6 men and a further 29 men dead, the rest were POWs or evaded capture. The Ops to Rail yards; 4 Halifaxes 1, (7/7) and 1 Whitley, (6/6), this was the last Whitley lost on Ops. A further 15 were dead and the rest POWs, all in all 38 aircraft. Dortmund had some residential damage in the SE of the city. The Ops to Brunswick and Dortmund this night were the last heavy Bomber Command raids on German cities until after the Normandy invasion was firmly established. All in all 206 RAF Bomber Crewmen were lost at Brunswick and Dortmund; these were heavy crew losses for little damage done to the German War machine.

Some of the other 61 Squadron pilots flying with Bill this night were: F/L HH Farmiloe, F/O GA Berry (RCAF), F/S Kramer (RCAF), P/O WE Jeavons, F/S EJ (Jack) Goodyer (RNZAF), who took off and landed just before Bill, P/O HW Cooper, P/O RA Dear, F/L BM Acott, P/O RH Passant (RAAF), P/O DC Freeman, P/O R Auckland in ED860, P/O DF White in EE176 and P/O Sinclair. Again there was heavy cloud and most of these pilots reported poor marking. Also confirming Norman Jarvis' account, Acott, Goodyer and Farmiloe reported heavy defences including flak, Night Fighters and countless searchlights constantly active along their route from Osnabruck-Hanover-Bremen. P/O's Freeman and Jeavons Lancasters were both hit by flak over Hanover. P/O Cooper reported Night Fighters co-operating with searchlights, but little trouble due to good co-operation between his Gunners and Bomb Aimer. P/O Sinclair was hit by heavy flak at 24/25000ft approaching Hanover, causing damage to 2 engines, fuselage, wings and tail (even at this altitude German AA was effective). This, and the heavy crew losses, all proving that the Ruhr Valley really was the 'Valley of the shadow of death.' The first home was P/O J Gibberd (RAAF) at 03:17am. The remainder of the battle weary and flak damaged Squadron, 16 Lancasters, miraculously returned between 04:02am and 05:25am.

24 MAY 1944 LANCASTER QR-D FOR DOG, SELF AND 5 CREW TRAINING MISSION, LOCAL FLYING.

**W/O Norman Jarvis**

*'Our first Operational leave was due now,* [25 May 1944] *so off I went for nine days of glorious relaxation and freedom—how good I felt then, confident that we were capable of coming through any emergency.'*

Whilst Bill and his crew were on leave Ops continued with F/Lt Jeff Gray's 2nd Pilot from Tours, P/O DW Simmons flying in Bill's faithful EE186, QR-D for Dog. The trusted famous 'Ton-up' trio, 'Nan', 'Mickey' and 'Jane' continued their relentless service to Bomber Command. ED860 and JB138 both went to the Phillips Radio works at Eindhoven on 24/25 May 1944, with F//Sgt Percy Cannings from 97 Squadron PFF helping to mark this target in ND807. Also on the 27/28 May ED860, EE176, JB138 and EE186 flew Ops to Nantes and 31/1 May/June all 4 flew again to Saumur with all returning safely. EEI76, EE186 and JB138 all flew together again on 3/4 June to Ferme d'Urville and 5/6 June to St Pierre du Mont. Bill and the boys were now back from leave and as Norman Jarvis mentions he only just made it back in time for Ops on D-Day 6 June 1944.

## Start of Bomber Command's Tactical Support Operations to the D-Day Landings, Operation Overlord.

### W/O Norman Jarvis

*'On 6 June I just made it back to the Squadron in time for Operations on D-Day. 5 Group had all sorts of targets such as gun positions, aerodromes, railways and one particular job was to smash the lines of communication at a big function near the Normandy Bridge Head. Our D-Day job was no different from any of the previous ones, but it held a new significance. Down below us just around the Normandy peninsula were our own soldiers fighting to maintain their hard won positions and pressing inland.*
*Then over the next few weeks we pounded important marshalling yards, ammunition dumps, troop and Panzer concentrations. One night we successfully wiped out a full Armoured Division* [Aunay-sur-Odon, 14/15 June]*; all these were precision targets and required great accuracy in navigation and bombing. I got some lovely hits on some of them, but they were all pretty deadly and the losses were heavy because we had to go in low, anything from 2,000 to 10,000 ft. The light and heavy flak were intense and Night Fighters were also taking a heavy toll.'*

The 'North Crew' were now intensely involved in Bomber Command's Battle of Normandy 5/6 June 1944 to 16 August 1944, which was the tactical support to the (2nd Front) D-Day Landings and Normandy Bridge Head. F/Lt Jeff Gray explained to me that these trips to France were quite short in time and distance compared to the heavy raids over Germany. As Jeff previously explained Bomber Command had thought of making 3 trips equal 1 Operation to compensate, but there had been enormous resistance to the idea, due to Mailly-le-Camp, so it was rejected very quickly.

Percy Cannings had a chilling experience that coincided with the start of the Battle of Normandy. He had flown in Lancaster III, ND739, OF-Z four times from the 17 May to the 19 May on local flying trips. The last two trips had been as a Gunner to W/C Jimmy Carter DFC with Percy's Gunnery Leader S/L M Bryan-Smith DFC & Bar MID (who had a fine handlebar moustache) on board. Percy went on leave for 2 weeks from 30 May 1944. While he was gone the Battle of Normandy began with 97 Squ taking part in a mission on 5/6 June to soften up the defences on the coast at St-Pierre. On the return journey the same a/c he had flown in ND739 was lost without trace with W/C Jimmy Carter and his Gunnery Leader S/L Bryan-Smith. This crew of 8 was one of the most senior and highly decorated crews lost during Bomber Command's history. To have such a close connection to this event was certainly a thought provoking moment for Percy. The crash site of this a/c was recently discovered with personal effects of the crew, it was this discovery that led to me eventually meeting Percy Cannings.

**<u>Operation No. 6. (Night Mission)</u>**

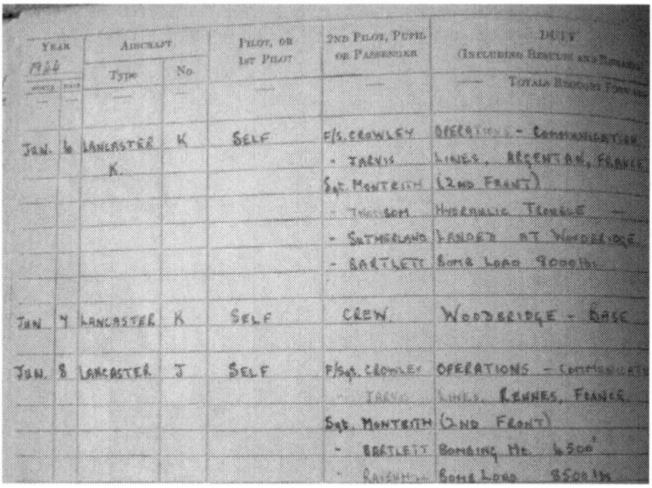

| Year 1944 Month | Date | Aircraft Type | No. | Pilot, or 1st Pilot | 2nd Pilot, Pupil or Passenger | Duty (Including Results and Remarks) |
|---|---|---|---|---|---|---|
| JUN. | 6 | LANCASTER K. | K | SELF | F/S. CRAWLEY | OPERATIONS – COMMUNICATION |
| | | | | | - JARVIS | LINES, ARGENTAN, FRANCE |
| | | | | | SGT. MONTEITH | (2ND FRONT) |
| | | | | | - THOMSON | HYDRAULIC TROUBLE – |
| | | | | | - SUTHERLAND | LANDED AT WOODBRIDGE. |
| | | | | | - BARTLETT | BOMB LOAD 9000lbs |
| JUN | 7 | LANCASTER | K | SELF | CREW | WOODBRIDGE – BASE |
| JUN. | 8 | LANCASTER | J | SELF | F/SGT. CROWLEY | OPERATIONS – COMMUNICATIONS |
| | | | | | - JARVIS | LINES, RENNES, FRANCE |
| | | | | | SGT. MONTEITH | (2ND FRONT) |
| | | | | | - BARTLETT | BOMBING HT. [illegible] |
| | | | | | - [illegible] | BOMB LOAD [illegible] |

Bill's entry to his RAF Log Book for D-Day 6 June 1944.

**<u>D-DAY, 6/7 June 1944. Argentan, France. The 'North Crew' (Flt/Eng Sgt Les Morton is replaced by Sgt Thomson and Rear Gunner Eddy O'Shea is replaced by Sgt Sutherland, (Bill's Log Book); although Sgt FA Scales is mentioned in ORB here as replacement Flt/Eng)</u>**

**Detailed bombing height 4,000ft. Bombing load 8,000lbs. 18 Lancasters detailed. Meteorology Report 10/10ths cloud, base 7,000ft good visibility below.**

**Lancaster III, JA872, QR-K for King was the 12th a/c to take off and the 3rd a/c to return.** This a/c came from 630 Squ and finished its service at 46 MU. The next QR-K, LM718 was an FTR at Ladbergen, 23/24 Sept 1944 with S/L HW Horsley. (See Chapter 17 on W/O Les Morton)

Up---**<u>23:46</u>**---Down---**<u>03:19</u>**---Time out---**<u>3hrs 27m</u>**

**<u>Debriefing report</u>:-** P/O North bombed MPI of several RSF's and 1 red TI at 01:35hrs from 4,000ft. Consider raid a success as both bombing and marking appeared concentrated and accurate. Photo Ground detail.

**Squ Ops report:-** 18 aircraft were detailed for bombing Operations against ARGENTAN. Met: 10/10ths cloud, base 7,000ft, good visibility below. All a/c successfully bombed the target using TI's and several explosions and fires were seen to be started. Believed to have been a very good attack. Several of the aircraft were attacked by A/A fire from the Royal Navy although colours of the day were fired. Enemy defences were scarce in the target area, but flak and fighters were encountered along the route. Photos, revealed ground detail, fires and smoke. This attack was carried out by 61 and 50 Squadrons only.

Some of the other pilots flying with Bill this night were: The Squadron Commander W/Cmdr AW Doubleday, F/L HH Farmiloe, F/O GA Berry (RCAF), P/O Granthan, P/O Forrest, S/L J Woodroffe, F/L BM Acott, F/S EJ (Jack) Goodyer (RNZAF), Jack took off just before and landed shortly after Bill, P/O PH Martin, P/O RA Dear, P/O Street, P/O RH Passant (RAAF) in JB138, S/L SJ Beard in EE176 and P/O HW Cooper. W/Cdr Doubleday reported the main force was ordered down 2,000ft because of scattered cloud, but marking was good. P/O Cooper was attacked 3 times by 2 Fw 190's injuring his Rear Gunner and Berry and Farmiloe both saw large explosions.

Farmiloe, Grantham, Forrest, Woodroffe, Acott, Goodyer and Martin all reported being fired on by a Royal Naval Convoy in the English Channel even though they showed colours of the day. They all were extremely upset as they saw another Lancaster shot down in flames and crash into the sea, proving that 'friendly fire' was also one of the unexpected dangers they faced. The Lancaster they all saw crash into the sea was most likely 115 Squadron's LM533, KO-T, piloted by F/O JM Wesley, returning to RAF Witchford from Lisieux; it was recorded as lost without trace (WR Chorley's *1944 Losses Book*). Bill and his crew missed witnessing this crash because they had their own drama going on. They were hit by flak over Argentan and had to perform an emergency landing at RAF Woodbridge with damaged hydraulics (Another quick point of interest:- with the exception of Bill North and P/O HW Cooper, who both made emergency landings at other bases due to battle damage; the remainder of the Squadron, 16 Lancasters, all landed safely back at Skellingthorpe between 03:15 to 04:01. This was a time period of 46 minutes, averaging nearly 3 minutes between each aircraft landing, not bad going for the battle weary crews. All 18 Lancasters had taken off in a 42 minute time frame).

1,065 aircraft, 589 Lancasters, 418 Halifaxes, 58 Mosquitoes were detailed to bomb lines of communication behind the Normandy Bridgehead area. All of the targets for 6/7 June when Norman Jarvis and his best friend Peter Knox flew, were in or near French towns to bomb railway and road centres and communication lines. Achères, Argentan (Bill and Normans target), Caen (Peter Knox and P/O Davis' target), Châteaudun, Condé-sur-Noireau, Coutances, St-Lô, Lisieux and Vire.

These Second Front targets were all low level attacks from 4,000 to 6,000 ft which as Norman Jarvis explains was a dangerous height to bomb from because low level flak was intense. Bill's Lancaster JA872, QR-K for King was hit by flak loosing hydraulic power which prevented them from closing the bomb bay doors and they had to make an emergency landing at a base called RAF Woodbridge; this had an extended runway to allow for these emergencies. 10 Lancasters and 1 Halifax were lost. 6 Lancasters were lost over Peter Knox' target Caen where he flew in below 3,000 ft, many of the roads in the town were blocked preventing German Mechanised units from moving.

BBMF Lancaster PA474, landing at RAF Coningsby (photo, *Stephen Elsworth*).

All in all this night 14 Lancasters and I Halifax lost, 6 Lancs and their crews were complete losses (42 men), 2 Lancs were 6 out of 7 crew lost (12). 17 other men were lost with the remainder POW or evading capture. Total effort for the night was 1,160 sorties. It should also be mentioned that during Operations on 5/6 June many of which took place in the very early hours of 6 June the number of sorties flown was a new record at 1,211 and with 5,000 tons of bombs dropped was the greatest tonnage in one night so far in the war. These were the attacks to soften up the Normandy Coastal Batteries for the landing forces and also Diversion Operations to conceal the true location of the invasion for as long as possible.

13 a/c were lost, 2 of them were home crashes and 8 of them complete losses. Three Lancasters were lost at St-Pierre (Pointe du Hoc), one 50 Squadron a 6/7 and a heavy night for 97 Squadron with two a/c complete losses. One of these was an 8 man crew flying in Lancaster III, ND739, OF-Z. This crew was captained by 97 Squadrons CO, W/Cmdr EJ (Jimmy) Carter DFC. This crew was one of the most highly decorated and ranking

in Bomber Command losses, with 4 DFC's and 3 DFM's for gallantry. The ranks were 1 W/Cmdr, 1 Squ/Ldr, 3 F/Lt's, 1 F/O, 1 P/O and 1 W/O, all are commemorated on the Runnymede Memorial. I have just recently found out from Richard Smith at The Daily Mirror that all three a/c were shot down together by the same Luftwaffe pilot. ND739 had set off from RAF Coningsby at 2.56am on June 6, 1944, but at around 5am just after bombing the target Pointe du Hoc, west of Omaha Beach, the Lancaster was among the three shot down in five minutes by Oberleutnant Helmut Eberspacher. This horrific attack is a shocking example of how deadly an experienced Night Fighter Pilot could prove to be with 21 dead and 1 survivor from 50 Squ, Sgt SK Reading. The final resting place of ND739 and its 8 crew has also just been discovered in a field near Carentan, Normandy by outstanding aviation archaeologist Tony Graves. With it are many poignant reminders of the crew. With German pilots like this flying at night what sort of chance did Bill and his crew have?

Spitfire MK356, Mk LFIXe, flew Ops on 7 June 1944 and during a beachhead cover patrol, F/O 'Gord' Ockenden's (RCAF) flight engaged four ME Bf 109Gs 'on the deck'. He fired at one of the '109's and saw his rounds hitting the enemy aircraft. His wingman finished it off and each pilot was credited with a half share of the kill (BBMF, RAF Coningsby, 9 June 2012. photo, CK).

The whole air support operation for D-Day was complex and involved many Operations. The RAF dropped dummy parachutists to confuse the German defences and real Paratroopers were deployed from Dakota's and Horsa Gliders over Normandy. The RAF and USAAF established complete air superiority over the Normandy battlefield shooting down many German aircraft heading for the beaches. German ground troops were overwhelmed by Allied fire power from above and deeper inland Bomber Command hit the transport network paralysing German reinforcements. The RAF contribution was decisive, 2 TAF (Tactical Air Force) flew 4386 sorties on 5/6 June while ADGB delivered 1246 sorties on D-Day itself. Bomber Command flew 1211 sorties on the night of 5/6 June. Bill North and his crew flew on the night of 6/7 June in the 1160 sorties carried out by Bomber Command. The sheer firepower and flexibility helped ensure the successful opening of the whole Western Front and the eventual downfall of the Third Reich. P/O Bill North and his crew played a part in one of the most critical campaigns of WW2.

Norman, Dennis and Bill explain their emergency landing at Woodbridge and how a system called FIDO was a life saver:-

**W/O Norman Jarvis**

*'On one occasion* [D-Day 6 June] *we limped back after being hit on a low level raid; the hydraulics were all gone, so the bomb doors remained open greatly reducing our speed. There was a likelihood of our wheels not coming down so we landed at an emergency drome called Woodbridge with a two mile long runway. We made it quite successfully and stayed the night there, getting the necessary repairs the next day before returning to our Squadron.'*

**W/O Dennis Bartlett**

*'We had to make an emergency landing at RAF Woodbridge which had an extended runway. I seem to remember Woodbridge being equipped with FIDO because as we came into land the bright fires were burning either side of the runway.'*

**F/Lt Bill North**

*'It was an extremely satisfying feeling to know that we were supporting our troops on the ground at the D-Day landings, however we had more drama unfold on this Op. We had to make an emergency landing at RAF Woodbridge because we were hit by flak at about 4,000ft, damaging our hydraulic systems. The runway at Woodbridge was much longer and wider than standard airfields allowing damaged bombers to land safely. I seem to remember Woodbridge being fitted with FIDO as well.'*

The runway at RAF Woodbridge was constructed as an emergency landing airfield and was operational from 1943. The runway was 5 times the normal width and 3,000 yards long with additional overshoots at either end. By the end of the War 4,200 aircraft had made emergency landings there, including Bill North and his crew. One third of the emergency landings were caused by bad weather, especially fog and Dennis and Bill mentioned the FIDO equipment installed at Woodbridge was used to assist their emergency landing. (In late December 1980 there were a series of reported sightings of unexplained lights and the alleged landing of UFO's witnessed by many USAF personnel who were based there. The dramatic episode became known as 'The Rendlesham Forest Incident').

**F/Lt Bill North**

*'We made a couple of emergency landings in heavy fog. One base we landed at was located at RAF Metheringham which was not too far from Skelly, this was fitted out with FIDO. FIDO was an invention that burned the fog away from the airfields. It was quite an impressive sight to see the huge walls of flames below us lighting up the runway and dispersing the fog.'*

Fog Investigation and Dispersal Operation (FIDO) was a system used for dispersing fog from an airfield so that aircraft could then land safely; it was developed by Arthur Hartley for RAF bomber stations. When fog prevented aircraft from locating or seeing their runways they would be diverted to FIDO equipped aerodromes. The device allowed the safe landing of aircraft returning from Operations in poor or zero visibility, by burning vaporised fuel in rows on either side of the runway. Two pipelines were located along both sides of the runway; petrol was then pumped through them and forced out through burner jets positioned at regular intervals. The fuel from the burner jets was then lit, sometimes by a jeep with a flaming brand attached to its rear as it drove down the sides of the runway, or ignited by men on bicycles or by runners on foot. The result was a spectacular row of flames along the sides of the runway that could be seen from a great distance in the air. The heat from the flames evaporated the fog creating a chasm that the aircraft could then see clearly to land in. FIDO used huge quantities of fuel, but the heavy cost was outweighed by the large number of aircraft and their crews (1000) that landed safely using the system. (Source:- Bill North, Dennis Bartlett, Jeff Gray and *Now It Can Be Told! - 'Operation Fido': Beating Airfield Fog, The War Illustrated, Volume 9*, No. 210, Page 140, July 6, 1945 and *Pathfinder*, Don Bennett, P. 180-183).

**Operation No. 7. (Night mission)**

The 'Just Jane' nose art on NX611 at the Aviation Heritage Centre, East Kirkby, 3 Nov 2012 (CK).

**8/9 June 1944, Rennes, Brittany, NW France, (Railway Yards/Lines) The 'North Crew'(Rear Gunner Sgt Eddy O'Shea is replaced by Sgt EW Ravenhill)**

**Detailed bombing height 4,500ft. Bombing load 8,500lbs. 17 Lancasters detailed. Met Rep. 10/10ths cloud, base 8,000ft. Vis below, very good.**

**Lancaster III, JB138, QR-J, 'Just Jane' was the 15th a/c to take off and the 16th a/c to return. Later in its life this lucky Lancaster would also became a member of the 'Ton up Club'. This was 'Just Jane's' 52nd mission.**

Up---**23:16**---Down---**06:45**---Time out---**7hrs 29m** (at over 7 and a half hours, this was the second longest time out for the crew)

**Debriefing report:-** P/O North Bombed 2 GTI's at 01:44 from 4,000ft. There was considerable smoke over target, but marking was visible and bombs were seen bursting. I should imagine target was well pranged. Bombs slightly overshooting as planned. PHOTO. Target conditions. Ground detail on frame 5.

**Squ Ops report:-** Attack on RENNES. Met: 10/10ths cloud, 8,000ft visibility below good. 17 a/c were detailed for bombing Ops against this target, all of which successfully bombed the target from heights of between 4,000 and 9,000ft. Considerable smoke was seen over the target, but the marking was visible and the bombing was concentrated around them. Much light flak was encountered in the target area. Photos: Ground detail.

483 aircraft- 286 Lancasters, 169 Halifaxes, 28 Mosquitoes attacked communication lines (railways/roads) to prevent German reinforcements from the south reaching Normandy. All the raids appear to have been successful. 6 aircraft were lost, 3 Halifaxes, 2 Lancs, 1 Mosquito (33 men lost). One 50 Squadron Lancaster and crew was complete loss with its pilot, P/O J Gilmour and Navigator, F/S GH Wright (For anybody into Pink Floyd coincidences).

Some of the other 61 Squadron pilots that flew with Bill that night were:- F/L JA Forrest, F/L GA Berry (RCAF), P/O WE Granthan, S/L J Woodroffe, F/L BM Acott, P/O EJ (Jack) Goodyer (RNZAF), P/O PH Martin, P/O RA Dear, P/O D Street, P/O RH Passant and P/O HW Cooper. (Small note there have been some promotions in rank to F/L and P/O) 14 Lancasters from the Squadron returned to Skellingthorpe in a 59 min period from 04:56 to 05:55. The other 3 Lancasters including Bill landing close to 07:00, it is possible like Bill the other 2 were diverted because of the heavy weather to and from the target. All had taken off in a 36 minute time period. (The first Tallboy bombs were used by 617 Squadron on the Saumur railway tunnel).

Bill and Norman explain the drama of losing an engine and being diverted to Siloth on this mission to Rennes:-

**F/Lt Bill North**

*'We were hit by flak again on this Operation. This was one of the dangers of flying low over these targets in France. We lost our Port Inner engine and I followed the usual procedures and feathered the engine. We lost the use of a generator, but had back up power on the Starboard Inner and also lost hydraulic power to the Mid-Upper turret. However, I had no problem flying on 3 engines as we had practised this many times in training. The weather was really bad as well and we ended up diverting right up to RAF Silloth, which was up near Scotland for an emergency landing. As Norman mentions we nearly crashed into Ailsa Craig that night, it suddenly appeared out of the fog as we were trying to land!'*

## W/O Norman Jarvis

*'On some occasions after returning from Operations we got over our own drome, but it was impossible to land because of the weather clamping down and visibility was nil. We would call up and be often told that we had been diverted to another drome which was usually up north. I remember one night we called up after a very exciting trip to Rennes and feeling very tired. They told us we would have to go to a drome up in Scotland to land; this meant an extra 200 miles. On our arrival up there it was impossible to get down because of the weather. We heard a crew bale out because they were out of petrol and found that we too would have to do something soon or we would be in the same position. We descended far lower in that Highland country than was healthy for us, then went out to sea a little way to try and make an approach, but Ailsa Craig loomed out in front of us from the fog, so the only thing to do was to try and make a drome we knew of down the coast called Silloth. We made this successfully just in time, the dawn was breaking and we had been airborne nearly ten hours. We also lost an engine on this Operation, but the Lancaster fellow flew us home on three without a lot of trouble.'*

RAF Silloth was located on the coast of West Cumbria near the Scottish border just down the coast from Ailsa Craig and was home to No. 6 OTU from 1943. Silloth was one of the last 'Expansion Period' airfields to open just before the War. It remained in service after the war as an RAF station before closing in the 50's; a few scenes from the film 'The Dambusters' were filmed here.

463 Squadron's JO-P, 'Piratical Pete'. This was in *Norman Jarvis's photo album*. The third 'Piractical Pete' DV229, JO-P was a FTR on 10/11 June 1944 to Orleans. The only crew member lost was the Skipper P/O JJ Fletcher (RAAF).

**Operation No. 8. (Night Mission)**

**10/11 June 1944. Orléans, France, (Marshalling Yards) The 'North Crew'**

**Detailed bombing height 6,000ft. Bombing load 8,550lbs. 18 Lancasters detailed. Meteorology Report 10/10ths cloud, base 7,000ft good visibility below.**

**Lancaster III, ND865, QR-A for Able was the 13th a/c to take off and the 8th a/c to return.**

Up---**22:39**---Down---**03:36**---Time out---**3hrs 27m**

**Debriefing report:-** P/O North BOMBED 3 RSFs at 00:43hrs from 6,000ft. RSFs were well placed and in good concentration, two sticks of bombs appeared short, but bombing on whole was well concentrated. PHOTO: Heavy smoke. Target conditions.

**Squ Ops report:-** 18 a/c were detailed for bombing Ops against Marshalling Yards at ORLEANS. Met: slight cloud, visibility fair. All the a/c successfully bombed the target with the aid of RSF's and GTI's, much light flak was encountered en route, but over the target area defences were practically non-existent. Bombing appeared well concentrated and a large explosion was seen at 00.51½hrs. Enemy fighters were in evidence along the route in, but none over target. Photos taken revealed ground detail.

432 aircraft flew on Ops this night, 323 Lancasters, 90 Halifaxes and 19 Mosquitoes attacked various railway targets in France. 15 Lancasters and 3 Halifaxes were lost. 8 Lancasters and their crews were complete losses (56 men), 2 Lancs and 1 Halifax were lost with 6 out of 7 crewmen (42 men). One Lancaster from 463 Squ DV229, JO-P, 'Piractical Pete' was lost. P/O JJ Fletcher (RAAF) stayed on board to allow the rest of the crew to bale out safely and died when the aircraft crashed at Ste-Gemmes-le-Robert (Mayenne).

This target was a bit deeper in to France, about 130 km southwest of Paris. Orléans is located on the Loire River where the river curves south towards the Massif Central. Some of the other 61 Squadron pilots who flew with Bill that night were:- F/L JA Forrest, P/O F Norton in JB138, P/O RJ Auckland, P/O WE Grantham, P/O EJ (Jack) Goodyer (RNZAF) Bill landed 11 minutes after Jack, P/O D Street, P/O RH Passant and

P/O W Cooper. We also see some near all Canadian crews flying that night:- F/O FO Gilmore (RCAF), P/O DE White (RCAF) in EE176, F/O ER Church (RCAF) and F/O BS Turner's crew. The weather, marking and bombing was all good with light defences, the whole Squadron returned safely. P/O DW Simmons successfully thwarted an attack by a Night Fighter after 'corkscrewing' for nearly 15 minutes. 17 Lancasters took off from Skellingthorpe in a 37 minute period and landed between 03:20 and 04:20, indicating excellent Squadron and ground staff coordination and efficiency. All in all a perfect raid for Bill and the boys.

12 JUNE 1944 TRAINING MISSION, LANCASTER A FOR ABLE, THE 'NORTH CREW' AIR FIRING AND BOMBING

**Operation No. 9. (Night Mission)**

**12/13 June 1944. Poitiers, France. The 'North Crew' (Troops de-training nightly, Communications, Railways)**

**Detailed bombing height 9,000ft. Bombing load 10,750lbs. 18 Lancasters detailed. Meteorology Report 5/6ths cloud, clear, good visibility below.**

**Lancaster III, ND865, QR—A for Able was the 9th a/c to take off, and the 2nd a/c to return.**

Up---**22:34**---Down---**04:20**---Time out---**5hrs 46m**

**Debriefing report:-** P/O North bombed 1 RSF and 1 GTI at 01:48hrs from 9,000ft. Large flash orange in colour, seen in target area at 01:47. The markers did a fine job and the target should be well and truly hit. There were no defences of opposition of any kind. PHOTO: Ground Detail.

**Squ Ops report:-** 18 a/c were detailed for bombing Ops against POITERS. Met: clear, good visibility, 5/6ths cloud, Tops 17,000ft. All the a/c again successfully bombed the target. Bombing and marking were both considered very accurate and the attack was most successful. Large explosions were seen and a good deal of black smoke was seen to rise. No defences were encountered over target, although some flak was seen on outward journey.

671 aircraft flew on this Operation, 285 Lancasters, 348 Halifaxes, and 38 Mosquitoes of 4, 5, 6 and 8 Groups to attack communications, mostly railways at Amiens/St-Roch, Amiens/Longueau, Arras, Caen, Cambrai and Poitiers (Bill's target for the night). These targets were the sites of famous WW1 battles, bar Caen, which would soon see bitter fighting. The Poitiers attack by Bill's 5 Group was the most accurate of the night. However, 26 aircraft were lost, 6 Lancasters, one (8/8), two (7/7s), with a Victoria Cross posthumously awarded to P/O AM Mynarski from 419 Squadron over Cambrai. The Halifax Squadrons were hard hit with 20 Halifaxes lost, eight (7/7s) and one (6/7) with a total of 119 men dead. On the adjoining Operation Gelsenkirchen, 17 Lancasters were lost; ten (7/7s), four (6/7s), with a total 108 men dead. Although 43 aircraft and 227 crewmen were lost from these two Operations, 50/61 Squ had no fail to returns this night. (WR Chorley, *1944 Losses Book*) Again when Bill and I were looking through WR Chorley's 1944 Book for 12/13 June, we were overwhelmed by the amount of crews that were 7 out of 7 losses. Bill shaking his head said, *'I had no idea that this many men were lost on these Operations, it just goes to show again how close to death we all were.'*(This was the night P/O AC Mynarski of 419 Squ was awarded a posthumous VC for his valiant attempt at saving the trapped Rear Gunner).

Poitiers was again an attack that took Bill deeper into German occupied French territory. It is a city on the Clain River in west/central France. Some of the other 61 Squadron pilots who flew with Bill that night were:- F/L JA Forrest, P/O EJ (Jack) Goodyer (RNZAF), (Bill took off 12 mins after and landed 3 minutes before Jack), P/O F Norton in JB138, P/O DE White in EE176, P/O RJ Auckland, F/L WE Jeavons, P/O HW Cooper, P/O D Street, F/O FO Gilmore (RCAF), P/O DW Simmons (RAAF), and P/O RH Passant. Bill was the second pilot to return. 18 Lancasters took off in a 34 minute period and 17 landed between 04:19 and 05:00, virtually 1 to 2 minutes between each aircraft. The last to land was F//L BS Turner at 05:32.

Despite the horrendous overall losses to Bomber Command that night from its 1,083 sorties, the whole of 61 Squadron returned safely. Riding in and out of death's shadow, this again was another perfect mission for Bill and his crew with Poitiers the most accurate bombing and marking of the night. (A quick point of interest:-5 minutes after Bill landed at 04:25 the first V1 attack took place in London. A strange sound was heard in the sky with some seeing the burning flame from the V1's Pulse engine streaking through the air. It dived and exploded in Grove Road, E4 damaging a railway bridge and tracks. It was one of five to hit London that night and was 48 hours before the next wave of V1's came over. It is odd to think that as Bill and the remainder of 61 Squadron were returning to Skellingthorpe from France, that they were flying alongside V1's. British Intelligence had codenamed them '*Diver*'.

The damaged railway bridge used by the Great Eastern Railway Company from Liverpool Street at Grove Road in East London. (*flyingbombsandrockets.com*).

Norman Jarvis' mate from 619 Squ Peter Knox was on a weeks leave from the 6 June. He was down below in London as Bill and Norman passed overhead on their return to Skellingthorpe and the V1's crashed to earth. Peter mentions a retaliatory daytime mission to Berlin which was cancelled at the last minute.

**W/O Peter Knox**

*'I had a break from the War and returned to Lincoln via London spending a couple of days with the Steels. London was in the grip of a wave of air attacks by the V—bombs, but none fell near the area that I was in. We were quickly thrown into activity on our return to the Squadron. We had been back only a day or two when we were put on alert for a daytime raid. The ground staff had to change all the ammunition in our machine guns from night tracers to day tracers. It was a hot sunny day and they were sweltering in the turrets. We were warned to be ready for a briefing shortly after midnight. There was an air of excitement because it was most unusual for RAF Bomber Command to operate in daylight. When the briefing came we learned that the target was to be Berlin. Then almost immediately we were stood down. The whole operation was cancelled. The story that went the rounds was that Prime Minister Winston Churchill had ordered a massive attack on the German capital as a reprisal for the V—bombs*

*falling on London. We did not know why it was cancelled——perhaps the weather, perhaps the RAF persuaded Churchill that the losses would be too great.'*

14 JUNE LANCASTER ND865, QR-A (Able) SELF CREW NIGHT FLYING TEST

'Throttles open for takeoff.' Lancaster NX611, 'Just Jane' 3 Nov 2012, Aviation Heritage Centre (CK).

**Operation No. 10. (Night Mission)**

**14/15 June 1944. Aunay-sur-Odon, France. The 'North Crew' (Bottleneck and Panzer Division)**

**Detailed bombing height 8,750ft. Bombing load 13,500lbs. 19 Lancasters detailed. Meteorology Report 10/10ths AT, no cloud, clear, good visibility below.**

**Lancaster III, ND865, QR-A for Able was the 9th a/c to take off, and the 2nd a/c to return.**

Up---**22:41**---Down---**02:38**---Time out---**3hrs 57m**

**Debriefing report:-** P/O North saw sticks of bombs fall across markers just prior to bombing leaving only the remains of RTI visible. Town about 5 miles north (Villiers?-) seen to be burning. Another good show with Marker Force doing an excellent job. Defences were negligible. Bombed remains of RTI at 00:39 from 9,000ft. PHOTO: Ground Detail (Quick note: Villiers is questioned as the town burning 5 miles north; it is most likely that this indeed was the other 'target for the night'- Évrecy, near Caen. Villiers is further south near Bill's previous target Poitiers).

**Squ Ops report:-** Attack on AUNAY. Met: No cloud, clear, good visibility.19 a/c were detailed for bombing Ops against this target. All the a/c once more successfully bombed target with aid of RSFs and TI's. The markers were all well placed and the bombing very concentrated around them. Several large explosions were seen as bombs landed and fires were burning all over the target area. Defences were very light and this should prove a very successful attack.

337 aircraft were detailed this night to attack German troop positions. 227 Lancasters, 100 Halifaxes and 14 Mosquitoes of 4, 5 and 8 Groups attacked troop and vehicle positions at Aunay-sur-Odon and Évrecy, near Caen. Allied Forces reported details of the presence of major German units at Aunay-sur-Odon and Bomber Command quickly prepared and executed these raids. The weather was clear and both targets were successfully bombed. Aunay-sur-Odon where the marking was shared by 5 and 8 Groups was particularly accurate. There were no aircraft lost at Aunay-sur-Odon, although 3 Halifaxes and 2 Lancasters were lost at other railway targets in France. Two of the Halifaxes were (7/7s), the crew of the other Halifax all survived after baling out. The 582 Squadron Master Bomber F/L JH Hewit (DFC) was a complete loss with his 8 man crew at Douai. The other Lanc was lost with only 1 survivor who evaded capture. (28 crew men)

Some of the other 61 Squadron pilots who flew with Bill that night were:- newly promoted F/L F Norton in JB138, P/O DE White in EE176, P/O WE Grantham (was first down followed by Bill who had landed 2nd two times in a row), F/L WE Jeavons, P/O EJ (Jack) Goodyer (RNZAF), Jack took off 5 minutes after Bill, P/O RJ Auckland, P/O HW Cooper, P/O D Street, F/O FO Gilmore (RCAF), P/O DW Simmons, P/O DE White and P/O RH Passant. The whole Squadron took off in a 38 min period and all 19 Lancasters returned safely landing in a 58 minute period between 02:36 and 03:34am. For a hastily prepared Bomber Command raid, 61 Squadron had responded promptly and efficiently, offering another perfect mission with excellent PF marking and bombing results.

**F/Lt Bill North**

*'This was another low level mission to support our troops and attack German Armoured reinforcements trying to reach Normandy. I can remember seeing our bombs falling and exploding right across the target. Norman got very excited and called out that we got some direct hits on the units below. This was a very satisfying feeling knowing we were helping our invasion force.'*

**W/O Norman Jarvis**

*'One night we successfully wiped out a full Armoured Division (Aunay 14/15 June). This was a precision target requiring great accuracy in navigation and bombing. I got some lovely hits on this one.'*

**Operation No. 11. (Night Mission)**

**15/16 June 1944. Châtellerault, France. The 'North Crew' (Fuel Dump) This was the last time that Sgt Les Morton flew with Bill.**

**Detailed bombing height 8,000ft. Bombing load 13,000lbs. 17 Lancasters detailed. Meteorology report, no cloud, good visibility.**

**Lancaster III, ND865, QR-A for Able was the 14th a/c to take off, and the 8th a/c to return.**

Up---**21:37**---Down---**03:50**---Time out---**6hrs 13m**

**Debriefing report:-** P/O North reported exceptionally large explosion, red in colour, seen at 00:59hrs and lasting for 2/3 seconds. Black smoke seen to rise to 8,000ft, shortly afterwards. Bombing to left of markers appeared to do most damage. Bombed MPI of RSFs and 2 GTI's at 01:04hrs, from 8,000ft. A good show all told, but a poor view is taken of our London defences opening up on us. PHOTO: Failure. (There were a couple of typing errors I corrected in this report. The time of the large red explosion
01:59 is changed to 00:59 and the time length 20/30 seconds, to 2/3 seconds, both these changes are in line with what the other pilot's witnessed in their debriefing reports. Bill also confirms this himself saying, he would have been well on his way home at 01:59 if he had bombed at 01:04.) All the pilots reported being attacked by the London defences and were all extremely annoyed about this. P/O Simmons reports: that there was more flak over the English coast at 6,500ft than the target. The ORB for 463 and 467 Squ's also confirm a/c attacked by the London defences.

**Squ Ops report:-** 17 aircraft were detailed for bombing Ops against CHÂTELLERAULT. Met: no cloud, good visibility. 16 of the a/c bombed the target with considerable success. Very large explosions and fires were seen and bombing and marking was well concentrated. Several instances occurred of our a/c being engaged by London A/A defences on their return journey. Although Colours of the Day were fired these had little effect, though this may be accounted to the 10/10ths cloud. Two of our a/c were damaged by this flak. The remaining one a/c failed to return. (ME783, QR- E, Captained by Jack Goodyer)

**Flying alongside F/Lt Bill North for the third time to mark the target and on his 16th Op with 97 Squ PFF was W/O Percy Cannings and his crew:-**

Skipper, F/O WM Reid, FE, Sgt W Richards, NAV, F/O RD Parker, BA, F/Sgt GD Moir, WO, F/Sgt B Harthill, MUG, F/Sgt DP Cannings, RG, Sgt G Brown, in Lancaster ND807, OF-P, 'B' Flight, 97 Squadron PFF Coningsby. (**BI**)

**97 Squ, PFF Debriefing report:-** Up 21:34, Down 03:23. 9x7x4.5' clusters, 9x500lb MC, 3 reco flares. Weather clear. Identification of target by H2S and ETA. Dropped flares orbited to starboard. Mosquito went in right away. His red marker was assessed as being on the corner of the road. Controllers called in to back up which was done very quickly. Flare Force called in to bomb, markers told to go home with exception of Marker Leader. 00:47 hours Flare Force told no more flares needed. Main Force called in to bomb. Wind received 350/19 knots.

50 and 61 Squadron Memorial Day, 10 June 2012. Battle of Britain Memorial Flight Lancaster PA474 performs a rooftop flypast over Skellingthorpe Village. PA474 has been with the BBMF since1973. It was built by Vickers-Armstrong Ltd in 1945 and destined for Tiger Force in the Far East. (photo, CK)

## W/O Norman Jarvis

*'One night we were returning from the south of France and our route brought us just to the east of London over the Thames Estuary. The boys ahead of us seemed to have started up the London defences, because we saw a terrific barrage of flak. We thought 'Hell, I hope they know we are not Jerries'. It kept up though and most of us shied round it as best we could, but were very resentful. The next day we heard that it was the first few nights that the V1 Bombs came over.'*

'Returning home'. BBMF, Lancaster PA474 (photo, *Stephen Elsworth*).

227 aircraft were detailed for Operations. 119 Lancasters, 99 Halifaxes and 9 Mosquitoes from 4, 5 and 8 Groups attacked ammunition and fuel dumps at Châtellerault and Fouillard. The all 5 Group raid at Châtellerault destroyed 8 fuel sites out of 35 in the target area. (These fuel supplies were essential to the Nazi war effort and the lack of fuel eventually brought German war machinery grinding to a halt.) 14 aircraft were lost this night with Six Lancs (7/7s), including ME783 P/O Jack Goodyer. 4 Lancs were (6/7s), the sole survivor of each all evading capture. A further 13 men were lost, with their comrades POW or evading capture. 1 Mosquito and 1 Halifax were also lost. A heavy toll was incurred as a further 83 highly trained crewmen died on Operations.

The 61 Squadron pilots who flew to Châtellerault that night in the order they took off in were:- P/O EJ (Jack) Goodyer (RNZAF), who unusually took off first, P/O JE Gibberd, P/O DW Simmons, P/O WE Grantham, P/O D Street, F/O ER Church, F/L WE Jeavons, P/O DE White in EE176, F/O FO Gilmore (RCAF), F/L JA Forrest, P/O RH Passant (RAAF), P/O WR Sinclair, P/O HW Cooper, P/O W North, P/O EW Hallett, F/L BS Turner and F/O DE Stone. The whole Squadron 17 Lancasters took off between 21:07 and 21:42 in a 35 min period, with 16 returning safely and landing in a 70 minute period between 03:15 and 04:25am. Bill and his comrades in 61 Squadron had taken part in another traumatic mission and performed with great coordination and efficiency. There was excellent PF marking and good concentrated bombing. The Operation however was stained with sadness as deaths dark shadow stole another 61 Squadron crew.

**There now follows a sub-section to this Chapter, in which we look at the loss of Jack Goodyer and his crew. It reveals the danger of bombs falling from above and the emotional connection that is still present nearly 70 years later between families and lost crews. Bill felt that this was a poignant example of how lucky he was to survive the War.**

When Bill and I were first discussing the losses for this Operation in 2010, I mentioned that there was one loss recorded in WR Chorley's book and the ORB for 61 Squadron. ME783, QR-E, piloted by P/O EJ Goodyer (RNZAF), a complete and the only loss at Châtellerault. I said to Bill, 'Bill there is one loss for 61 Squadron I found; it is a NZ pilot called P/O EJ Goodyer, he is also mentioned in the ORB quite a few times. Can you have a look and do you remember him?' I handed Bill the Losses book and sat quietly observing. After a long pause while he looked at the page Bill said, *'Oh yes, I remember him his name was Jack. He was from New Zealand, he was a good pilot. I remember him from briefing sessions and the mess at breakfast time after Ops, he was always smiling. The next day he was posted in the Flight Room as the only one who was missing from Ops and this is why it made an impression on me. The other men were saying have you heard about Jack he's missing? I can see that the crew was a 7/7 loss, I didn't know this until now.'* When I originally asked Bill this question a whole other story revealed itself. It unravelled a close Operational connection between the two pilots. I went back through the ORB with Bill and examined the record in much more detail. Bill had flown alongside Jack Goodyer on many Operations, both of them taking off and landing very close in time to each other.

**<u>Pilots who saw the Lancaster ME783 explode and bombing times</u>:-**

Jack Goodyer and Bill North were always very close in their take-off, landing and bombing times; which also puts them very close together in the bomber stream and on their bombing runs. As we have seen from examining the ORB and comparing each of Bill's Operations, 61 Squadrons close Operating times indicate how efficiently it worked together as a unit.

Their take-off, landing and bombing times were all generally extremely tight which meant they were all flying close together to and from the target.

The following details help us to understand Jack Goodyer's tragic loss and yet another lucky escape for Bill. Four PFF Mosquitoes marked the target at 00:43hrs, the markers landed on the corner of Junction of the A46 and the Controller immediately called Backers Up to remark. Satisfied the target was correctly marked the Main Force was called into bomb by the PFF Controllers just after 00:47. 6 minutes later the first of 61 Squadron's 16 a/c dropped on the bombing run from 00:53 to 01:04. They all bombed from heights between 7,000 to 10,000ft, with many matching bombing times putting the Lancasters bombing at lower heights at high risk of being hit from above. This was not an unusual thing and was considered to be a 'run of the mill' risk on Operations. There were many other a/c from 5 group detailed for Châtellerault that night. These wouldn't necessarily have bombed at exactly the same time as they travelled in Squadron waves and there was no disruption to the Bomber Stream that night which could have mixed up the bombing run. However we do have evidence that 463 and 467 Squ's bombed at virtually the same time.

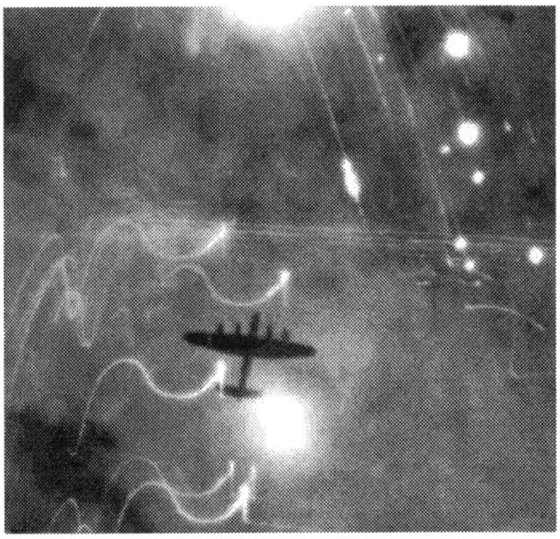

A Lancaster over Hamburg in July 1943; caught by the photo flash of the aircraft above it on the bombing run (*IWM*).

Again from Olivier Roelly I have 467 Squ nearly identical from 00:53 to 01:01 and 463 Squ were from 00:55 to 01:09. All these bombing times were right on top of each other, it was a crowded sky and they also carried nearly identical bomb loads and types (9,000lb av per a/c of 500lb and 1,000lbs). We know that Forrest was the first to see the explosion at 00:55, the next pilots saw it at 00:56, at the same time as 463 Squ dropped their first bombs. We don't know for sure but can only make a logical assumption from the evidence that Jack was hit from above by falling bombs possibly from 463 Squ or from any of the above Squadrons in the Main Force who released their bombs in the time frame, 00:53, 00:54, 00:55, 00:56, 00:57.

The joint first to bomb were Gibberd (8,000ft) and Hallet (9,500ft) at 00:53. Second was Jeavons (7,500ft) at 00:54. Joint third were Granthan (8,500ft), Forrest (7,500ft) and Passant (10,000ft) all at 00:55. (Any crews below these bombing heights at this moment would have been at risk of being hit from above. Since we don't know what Jack Goodyer's bombing height was, we can only assume it was below 8,000 to 7,500ft as Forrest was the first to see and the closest to the explosion). It was now at this point that the first three of the Pilots flying witnessed a large deep red mid-air explosion lasting for 3 seconds. Forrest at 00:55, Gibberd and Church at

00:56. Turner now saw the explosion too at 00:56½, followed by Street, Jeavons and Sinclair 00:57. Fourth to bomb was Church (9,750ft) at 00:57. Joint fifth to bomb were Street (7,750ft) and Turner (9,250ft) at 00:58. Joint sixth were Gilmore (9,000ft) and Cooper (7,000ft) at 00:59. Seventh was Simmons (7,250ft) at 01:00. Joint eighth were White (9,250ft) and Sinclair (8,000ft) at 01:01. Ninth was Stone (8,000ft) at 01:03. The tenth and last to bomb was P/O Bill North (8,000ft) at 01:04. Bill and his crew saw the explosion too and recorded it at 00:59. F/Lt Forrest mentions there was no flak or obvious night fighter activity over target which also had a clear sky; also the fact that it was an a/c that exploded.

On the night of this Operation to Châtellerault most of the crews including Bill North unknowingly witnessed their comrade Jack Goodyer and his crew perish in a huge mid-air explosion on the bombing run. (8 pilots witnessed this deep red explosion). This was the only loss at this target. Châtellerault is in the Poitou-Charentes region of France and the wreckage was scattered over the south borders of the village of Besse which is located slightly north of the target. The bodies of the crew are buried at Escoublac-la-Baule War Cemetery near St Nazaire.

There are two likely main possibilities for the explosion given the fact that no one experienced any flak in the area and no obvious Night Fighter activity:-one is that it was hit from above by bombs from another Lancaster, this would indeed have caused the catastrophic explosion. This was a known risk as mentioned and sometimes falling bombs could either go straight through or smash pieces of the a/c off. The other possibility is that ME873 was a victim of *Schräge Musik* which I explained in an earlier chapter. An attack from below by a Night Fighter with upward firing twin 20mm cannons into the wing petrol tanks/bomb bay usually ended in a huge explosion and instant loss of the a/c. Bill and his crew were no strangers to witnessing a/c explode in the airspace around them. One third possibility is that there was a malfunction in the bomb bay which would have been unusual. Jeff Gray explained what the bombing load would have been on a target like this.

**F/Lt Jeff Gray**

*'We didn't carry 'cookies' on this type of Operation, but 500lb and 1,000lb General Purpose high explosive bombs, generally armour piercing for these tactical support missions. When these bombs exploded they would send shrapnel high into the air, because we were at low altitude this could sometimes damage the Lancasters. I lost two engines when we bombed Brest because of this. These bombs were stacked all around the dispersal points at Skellingthorpe in those days and weren't very nice to look at.'*

Jack Goodyer's bombing load was as follows:- 2 x 1,000 lbs + 12 x 500 lbs = 8,000 lbs. Light compared with Bill North's load of 13,000lbs.

**F/Lt Bill North**

*'We had seen other aircraft explode on bombing runs before, it happened at Lille. We were well aware that we had seen a Lancaster explode at Châtellerault and how it made us feel. I didn't know however that this was Jack Goodyer and his crew until you explained this to me Chris. We also saw many big orange explosions on the ground and could still see fires burning half an hour after we had left the target.'*

This one has given me goose bumps; Percy Cannings as mentioned flew on the Châtellerault Operation in which Jack was lost and is of the opinion that P/O Jack Goodyer was most likely hit from above by bombs from another Lancaster. He himself witnessed a Lancaster explode mid-air right next to him after it was hit by bombs from above that just missed his Lancaster. The exploding a/c damaged his Lancaster and one next to him. This was a daylight raid and as Bill and Dennis both mentioned on their first daylight raid they were all horrified at how close the bombs from above fell to them, something which they would not have seen at night-time! Percy Cannings now shares his eyewitness account of how 'bombs from above' destroyed the Lancaster next to him on his last mission and nearly took his crew with it.

**W/O Percy Cannings**

*'My last Operation was a daylight raid to Deelan, Holland, on 15 August 1944 in ND961, OF-N. We knew this was our last Op and were really keen to get it over and done with. However it was shockingly nearly the end of our crew. On these daylight raids we flew closer together and it was plain to see how near the bombs from above actually fell to the a/c below and not something we would have been aware of at night-time. During the bombing run the Lancaster behind us was hit by bombs from above and instantly exploded in a huge fireball. These bombs literally passed within 5ft of our Lancaster and just missed hitting us as well. The explosion was a terrible thing to see and it shattered our rear turret and put holes in our fuselage. Bob Lasham from 97 Squadron was in the formation above us and said one of his Gunners saw the bombs from above fall past hitting this same aircraft below them. The rear turret was completely severed and his Gunner vividly remembers the aircraft fall apart and the turret tumbling down, with the rear gunner still inside it!' The other 97 Squadron Lancaster in our formation PB358, OF-J which was flown by F/O BB Lindsay had two engines damaged by the explosion as well. This a/c ditched in the sea off the Dutch coast and a German E-Boat was dispatched to pick up the crew. This E-Boat was chased off by an American Thunderbolt that was escorting the formations and the crew were then all rescued by one of our High Speed Launches (HSL). The whole of this crew were back on base at Coningsby the next day and when we arrived back safely I breathed a huge sigh of relief that my second tour of Ops was now finally over.'*

Again this eye witness account from Percy Cannings demonstrates the extreme dangers that Bill and his crew faced during their Operational service to Bomber Command and also yet again how lucky they all were to survive at Châtellerault. The lost Lancaster that Percy Cannings and his comrades witnessed exploding on his last Op to Deelan, 15/16 Aug 1944 was most likely to be the only (7/7) loss over the target, a 207 Squ Lanc I, KB263, EM-N, pilot F/L GAC Overgaauw, Dutch, from Amsterdam. (Peter Gould, *The Best Twelve Years*, WR Chorley, *1944 Losses Book*, Percy Cannings and Bob Lasham)

61 Squ's LM481, QR-O, Skippered by F/O H Watkins and crew were on their 10th Op when they also had a tragic experience related to the ever-present danger of bombs falling from above. On the 25 July 1944, 61 Squ took part in a daylight raid to St Cyr airfield near Tours. Whilst on the bombing run their Lancaster LM481, QR-O, was hit by 3 bombs from

above damaging the starboard wing, tail-fin and rudder forcing it into an uncontrolled dive. The third bomb had completely severed the rear turret sending it plunging to earth with F/S CJ Foy in it. F/O Watkins regained control of the seriously damaged a/c and made an emergency landing on home soil. Needless to say the shocking loss of their Rear Gunner had a profound effect on the whole crew. Harold Watkins Tour of 30 ran from 19th June to the 27 September 1944. (*Thundering Through The Clear Air*, Derek Brammer)

Châtellerault was a dramatic raid with big orange ground explosions and fires that could be seen 100 miles or half an hour after leaving the target, there was also the horrific, large deep red explosion in which P/O Jack Goodyer was lost. Many of the crews flying witnessed this explosion. The devastating loss of 7 crewmen and 1 Lancaster is heart wrenching and one that is repeated thousands of times during Bomber Command's Operational history. The awful sense of loss and pain is still felt now nearly 70 years later by crew member's families. You only have to read all the poignant messages placed at the Bomber Command Memorial to perceive and understand these emotions.

Whilst researching this Operation I became good friends with Noeline Arnott who is Jack Goodyer's cousin. Noeline met him when she was a child has been on an emotional journey to record Jack's story and to piece together the sequence of events on the night he was lost. She like me has experienced an overwhelming desire to follow this journey wherever it takes her. I have met and corresponded with many other people who have been on similar journeys to immortalise and recognise their loved one's ultimate sacrifice. For Noeline Arnott, Jack's death is deeply personal and not an academic exercise. *'Jack's ghost walks with me every step of the way.'*

At 31 years old Jack would have been one of the older crew members at Skellingthorpe. The average age of Bomber Command crewmen being 22, his two gunners were both 19 and Bill North was 22. Jack Goodyer's mature, strong personality would have been a crucial positive influence on the spirits of these younger men. Like Norman Jarvis and many other crews from the Commonwealth these men played a crucial part in Bomber Command's history.

Olivier Roelly who lives near the French cemetery at Escoublac-la-Baule where the crew are buried has visited it frequently over the years laying flowers at the graves. Olivier has felt a strong emotional connection to the crew and has wondered many times who they all were. He got in touch with Noeline and I on the 23 Sept 2012 and provided a moving French report of the crash of ME783 taken from the French book, *Aircraft*

*Battle in County Vienne* (fr) 1939-1945, by Christian Richard. It is as follows:- 'The Lancaster Mk I, code QR-E, serial ME783 crashed on the south border of the Besse village, Châtellerault borough, between the houses and farms and the railway at Châtellerault-Lencloître, near the Envigne river, a few hundred metres from the north of the target. The next morning, bodies were found inside and near the wreckage scattered around a small intersection. Robert Burns managed to gather witness statements and Jack Creuzé realised that it was a four engine aircraft. A body was still in the wreckage, another one near a big piece of the plane and one of the engines was lying near the Besse Bridge on the railway; a wing was also resting near Gérard Beauvillain's farm. It is likely that the 6 bodies from the aircraft found on the 16 June were buried in Châtellerault. A week later, a worker working on an electric mast discovered the body of the 7th crew member hidden in a wheat field in a village called Le Moulin-Neuf. He was buried in the north cemetery in Châtellerault and today all 7 bodies rest at Escoublac-la-Baule in the military cemetery' (Le Moulin-Neuf is a short distance west of the crash site on the south borders of Besse).

This sent shivers through me, Jack and his crew were lost on their 20th Operation. (1 in 3 chance of completing a tour of 30) Corresponding with the way that Bomber Command compiled their loss statistics mentioned in the French book, where points reached 100% at the 20th Op. Bill North went down on his 17th Op and confounded the odds by surviving (1 early return and 1 recall not counted make it 19 times).

Because of their close proximity on missions it could quite easily have been Bill who was lost in that huge explosion that was most likely caused by bombs falling from above. The fact that Jack was lost and Bill wasn't demonstrates the very sentiment that is the constant theme right through this book. It is again that Bill North quite knowingly rode in death's dark shadow, passed right through it and survived to tell the tale.

P/O. E. J. Goodyer, of Inangahua Junction, missing, believed killed in action.

## Noeline Arnott

*'It was a year ago yesterday* [Wed 15/08/2012] *since we visited and placed sunflowers on the graves of Jack and the crew of ME783 at the CWGC at Escoublac-la-Baule, and a year today* [Thu 16/08/2012] *since we went back for a second visit. It was very hard to tear myself away from the place where Jack is buried, knowing that the chances of my ever returning are very slim. There was a tremendous sense of not just Jack's, but the whole crews' presence but as it has turned out, since coming back to New Zealand and through my contact with so many good people like yourself, who have helped to widen the scope of my knowledge, I've never really left the place. It is a small but very beautiful cemetery with only about 230 graves. Besides RAF aircrew, some were the victims of the sinking of the Lancastria on June 17, 1940, others casualties from the Commando raid on St Nazaire in March 1942, mostly from the ill-fated motor launches.'*

The 7 grave stones of a Lancaster crew, a moving scene that is repeated in many cemeteries across Europe. Noeline Arnott visited the above graves of Jack and the crew of ME783 at the CWGC at Escoublac-la-Baule on 15 Aug 2011. She placed a sunflower at each of the headstones. P/O Jack Goodyer (RNZAF) is third from the right. The rest of the crew are: F/Eng, Sgt W Stovold, Nav, F/O BA Clack, B/Aimer, F/O E Jones, WOP, Sgt J Hughes, MUG, Sgt GV Foyle and R/Gnr, Sgt EF Price (61 Squadron revisited Châtellerault on the 9/10 Aug 1944 with no Fail to Returns, also flying to this Target was W/O Percy Cannings).

W/O Norman Jarvis also lost one of his best friends on the following night's Ops, 16/17 June to the Synthetic Oil Plant at Sterkrade. F/S Alan Duggleby (RAAF) from 102 Squ was the Bomb Aimer in Halifax III MZ642, DY-U (See Chapter Stalag Luft 7).

18 JUNE LANCASTER ND865 QR-A (Able) SELF AND 4 CREW BOMBING AND NIGHT FLYING TEST.

(Earlier that day at 11:00 a V1 destroyed the Guards Chapel at Birdcage Walk in London killing 121 people. Up to 60 V1's a day were now reaching the Capital).

**Operation (Night Mission)**

**19/20 June 1944. Flying Bomb Store, Watten, Pas-De-Calais, France. The 'North Crew' (V1/V2 Site) Flight Engineer Sgt Les Morton is replaced by Sgt GE Gaunt. Gaunt would later fly with F/S GM Taylor on his first 3 Ops. This is the first Op that Sgt Les Morton flew on alongside Bill, but with another crew, S/L SJ Beard in EE176, QR-M.**

**Detailed bombing height unknown. Bombing load 13,300lbs. 22 Lancasters detailed. Meteorology Report unkown.**

**Lancaster III, ND865, QR-A for Able was the 11th a/c to take off, and the 13th a/c to return.**

Up---**22:32**---Down---**00:55**---Time out---**2hrs 23m**

At 2hrs 23m, this was the second shortest mission Bill flew on due to the complete Squadron recall owing to bad weather; it was therefore again not added to his tally of 30 Operations. The first shortest being, 1hrs 22m to Bourg-Léopold. This made the next mission Operation no 12.

**Debriefing report:-** P/O North returned early owing to W/T recall. 4 x Amer. GP .025 + 3x500 GP LD 6hrs 1x500 GP Inst. Jettisoned at 53.40N 02.10E at 00.18hrs from 6,000ft. 7x1000 Amer. GP returned to base (In North Sea 50 miles east of Mablethorpe 60 miles north of Norwich).

**Squ Ops report:-** Attack on WATTEN, Met not known, 22 a/c detailed to bomb the construction works at WATTEN. This attack was a complete failure, all aircraft being recalled. Part of bomb load was returned to base. Jettison point, 53.33N 01.30E. (Directly east of Skellingthorpe and 30/40 miles east of the coastal town Skegness in the North Sea)

Some of the other 61 Squadron pilots who flew with Bill that night were: the now familiar Officer Commanding 'A' Flight, F/Lt F Norton in JB138, P/O J Kramer with the first appearance of fellow Canadian F/S GM Taylor as 2nd Pilot (Taylor had to repeat his '2nd Dickie' with Kramer again the next day at Gelsenkirchen as this whole mission was not counted as an Op) Jeavons, S/L SJ Beard in EE176 with Bill's Flight Engineer Sgt Les Morton, also Forrest, Street, White, F/Lt BS Turner in ED860, Stone, Cooper and Church. (Three of 61 Squ's famous 'Ton Up' Lancs were flying) After standing by for three days waiting for cloud to clear over the Pas de Calais conditions were too difficult for accurate marking at the concrete flying bomb store in the woods at Watten, near St-Omer. The whole of 61 Squadron were recalled due to the bad weather, with no one attacking the target except 617 Squadron who dropped a number of 'Tallboys'. Bill and his comrades jettisoned part or in some cases the whole of their bomb load over the North Sea.

Bomber Command was now directing its resources into attacking Hitler's Vengeance weapons again. The V1 launch and storage sites were located along the French and Belgium coastlines within easy striking distancc of thc South of England. Bill and his crew were now involved in the continuation of Operation Crossbow, to take these flying bombs out. No losses are recorded for this night.

A V-1 is rolled to its launch site (source, *Bundesarchiv*, Bild 146-1975-117-26 / Lysiak / CC-BY-SA).

**W/O Norman Jarvis**

*'We were given the job of blasting these flying bomb emplacements and their maintenance units, as they were a deadly weapon and knocking London and the South of England about with their indiscriminate landing.*

*These trips were short, but lively and the Germans had brought a lot of defences and fighters into the area; so the cost in our Bombers alone made them a profitable weapon.'*

**Bill:-** *'Les now started flying alongside us on Ops with other crews, eventually settling down with the Canadian pilot Gerry Taylor whom we became quite familiar with.'*

For the next Operation Bill and his crew now returned to Germany and the Ruhr Valley again. This mission was part of the 'Battle of The Ruhr' and the combined Allied Air Offensive called 'The Oil Campaign', the objective of which was to try and starve the German war machine of fuel. Bill and his crew would be attacking one of the two targets for the night, the Synthetic Oil plants at Wessling and Scholven-Buer. This was a different type of Operational experience returning to the high altitude bombing heights and was fraught with danger as they again 'ran the gauntlet' through the 'valley of the shadow of death', facing some of Germany's heaviest defences.

**Operation No. 12. (Night Mission) (NORDSTERN SYNTHETIC OIL PLANT, SCHOLVEN-BUER, GELSENKIRCHEN, NORTH OF ESSEN).**

**21/22 June 1944. Gelsenkirchen, Ruhr Valley, Germany. The 'North Crew' Flight Engineer Sgt Les Morton is replaced by W/Cmdr Doubleday's F/Eng, F/Sgt J Slome** (21st of June was the longest day of the year).

**Detailed bombing height 19,250ft. Bombing load 13,400lbs. 21 Lancasters detailed. Meteorology Report 10/10ths cloud, tops 3,000ft.**

**Lancaster III, ME732, QR-P, 'Ali Oop!' was the 13th a/c to take off, and the 14th a/c to return. (ORB has ME752, but this is a typing mistake) This a/c was a (6/8) loss at Ladbergen 23/24 Sept 1944 with F/Lt DER Stone)**

Up---**23:22**---Down---**04:10**---Time out---**4hrs 48m**

**Debriefing report:-** P/O North bombed centre of glow of red and green TI's at 01:44hrs from 1,9250ft. Ground detail could not be seen owing to cloud. Fighter activity prominent, also moderate flak over target area.

**Squ Ops report**:- 21 a/c were detailed for bombing Ops against GELSENKIRCHEN. Met 10/10ths cloud, Tops 3,000ft. 20 of the a/c successfully bombed the target from heights between 17,000-20,000ft. Very heavy opposition was encountered from heavy flak and searchlights and fighter activity was plentiful. Several combats were observed and one of our a/c was damaged. Thc bombing attack was considcrcd good, but hindered by low cloud over the target. Several glows were observed through the clouds. The one a/c which was unsuccessful returned early from position 53.03N 03.30E [North Sea] owing to starboard inner engine catching fire, bombs were jettisoned. [JB138, 'Just Jane', F/L F Norton]

**Flying alongside F/Lt Bill North for the fourth time to mark the target and on his 17th Op with 97 Squ PFF was W/O Percy Cannings and his crew**:-

Skipper, F/O WM Reid, FE, Sgt W Richards, NAV, F/O RD Parker, BA, F/Sgt GD Moir, WO, F/Sgt B Harthill, MUG, F/Sgt DP Cannings, RG, Sgt G Brown, in Lancaster ND807, OF-P, 'B' Flight, 97 Squadron PFF, Coningsby **(BI)**.

**97 Squ, PFF Debriefing report**:-

Up 23:10, Down 03:12. 4 x TI yellow No 16s, 9x7' clusters, 3 reco flares. 10/10ths low stratus, tops 2,500ft. Target seen visually-Oboe markers and H2S. Told to drop flares. Yellow Oboe 01:32.5hrs. Headed towards this to back up. Another yellow down 1 ½ miles north of previous yellow: orders given to back up second one. Backed up the greens and returned to base. Large explosion in target area at 01:45hrs. (F/L Jeavons mentions 'PFF should be praised for not dropping flares or target would have been like daylight.')

In fact only 19 a/c successfully bombed as there was a second near tragic early return at 02:50 to Woodbridge by P/O RH Passant in JB351 who was attacked and damaged by a Night Fighter. They couldn't jettison the bomb load as the bomb bay doors were jammed. Shortly after clearing the runway the Lancaster was hit and totally wrecked by a 214 Squadron B-17 Flying Fortress Mk II which was also performing an emergency landing after also being severely damaged by NF's. With only a couple of injuries it was a lucky escape for all concerned.

In January 1944, 214 Squadron was converted to special operations, joining No. 100 Group RAF for electronic countermeasures in support of the main bombing operations.

The Squadron used the B-17 Fortress Mk II and Mk III and Stirlings. They used the jamming system codenamed 'Airborne Cigar' (ABC) to block German night fighter communications. German speaking radio operators would identify and jam the ground controller's broadcasts and also pose as ground controllers themselves with the intention of steering the NF's away from the Bomber Streams. Photo of B-17 Mk III) This technique reduced the risk of NF attack to Bill and his Bomber Command comrades.

A 214 Squadron (ECM) Flying Fortress at Prestwick 1944.
(Source, *ATP 13090B IWM*).

**W/O Norman Jarvis**

*'Then came another trip to the Ruhr Valley and perhaps this night was one of the blackest in the whole history of Bomber Command. The losses for this trip were 47 Lancasters out of 256 taking part. My best pal Peter Knox* [619 Squadron, ME846] *was shot down on this raid; also a lot more of my 'cobbers' were missing as a result of it. There seemed to be flares, rockets and air combats all the way into the target and back. Many times we saw an orange glow in the sky as a Bomber was hit; sometimes they went up with all their bombs—this was a beautiful, but horrible sight. The target area too is one of the grandest sights I ever saw from up above, the green and red target indicators cascading down, the chandelier flares, the bomb bursts, searchlights and flak.'*

**F/Lt Bill North**

*'As Norman mentions this was a horrific night for aircrew losses, we saw many orange explosions in the air to and from the target. The Night Fighters had a field day on this Operation and we were all were thankful to make it back to Skellingthorpe in one piece.'*

Some of the other 61 Squadron pilots who flew to Gelsenkirchen that night with Bill were:- OC 'A' Flight, F/L F Norton in JB138, F/L WE Jeavons, F/L JA Kramer (RCAF) with 2nd Pilot F/S GM Taylor (RCAF); Les Morton's future Skipper. F/L JA Forrest, F/Lt BM Acott with 2nd Pilot P/O DG Bates, P/O RA Dear, P/O JE Gibberd, P/O D Street, F/O S Parker, P/O DW Simmons (RAAF), P/O HW Cooper, F/O ER Church, F/Lt BS Turner in ED860, P/O DE White in EE176 and P/O RH Passant (RAAF). The whole Squadron 21 Lancasters took off between 22:54 and 23:33 in a 39 min period. Bar JB138, 'Just Jane's early return and P/O Passant's lucky escape at Woodbridge, 19 returned safely to Skellingthorpe, landing in a 92 minute period between 03:07 and 04:39am. 19 a/c bombed in a 9 minute period between 01:38 and 01:47 with PFF Oboe used to aid sky-marking; the bombing results were hard to see because of heavy cloud. Amidst the shocking tally of losses on Ops this night, Bill and his comrades in 61 Squadron still maintained their close Operating times. They had taken part in yet another harrowing mission witnessing many mid-air explosions with numerous NF attacks in and out and had yet again performed with great coordination and efficiency.

Gelsenkirchen was steeped in sadness for Bill's Mid-Upper-Gunner W/O Dennis Bartlett. It wasn't until 2011 when I first met Dennis that we found out exactly what happened to his best friend Sgt George Moggridge. All he knew was that George had been lost on Ops shortly before he got shot down himself; yet again another heart-wrenching story revealed itself. Norman Jarvis' best mate Peter Knox was also on this same 619 Squ Lancaster ME846 (See Chapter 24 Lives Lived and Lives Lost).

The combined 5 and 1 Group attacks experienced horrendous losses this night with the joint attacks on Gelsenkirchen (123 Lancasters and 9 Mosquitoes dispatched) and Wessling (133 Lancasters and 6 Mosquitoes dispatched). The two Ruhr Valley targets were approximately 40 miles apart with 38 a/c lost at Wessling. 20 of these were complete losses (217 men), 27.8% of the force. 9 Lancasters were lost at Gelsenkirchen, 3 were complete losses and a total of 47 crewmen lost (A 20% loss in oil production is recorded here). All in all 47 a/c were lost this night with 264 crewmen, a heavy contribution in lives and equipment to the Oil Campaign (There were some heavy Squ losses; 6 x 44 Squ, 6 x 49 Squ, 6 x 57 Squ, 6 x 619 Squ, 5 x 207 Squ and 5 x 630 Squ) In this combined Bomber Offensive Sir Arthur Harris had agreed to divert spare effort to oil targets. Adolf Galland, Herman Goring and Albert Speer all mentioned later that the Oil Campaign helped lead to the collapse of the Luftwaffe as its fuel supplies slowly dwindled. Bill and his crew had yet again experienced seeing many a/c explode in the sky around them, most lost due to heavy NF activity. The Ruhr Valley again proved to be 'The Valley of the Shadow of Death' and Bill's Guardian Angel was without doubt watching over him again.

Bill's next mission went slightly deeper into German occupied French territory. Bomber Commands targets for the night were 4 flying bomb sites and the railway yards at Saintes and Limoges, which were fairly close to each other and slightly north of Bordeaux in west-central France. Bill's target was Limoges, the administrative capital of the Limousin province and an important railway hub for the German Army.

**Operation No. 13. (Night Mission)**

**23/24 June 1944. Limoges, France. (Marshalling Yards) The 'North Crew' Flight Engineer Sgt Les Morton is replaced by W/Cmdr Doubleday's F/Eng, Sgt J Slome. Second Op that Sgt Les Morton flew on alongside Bill as F/Eng to P/O Don Street in ME595, QR-Y, also first main Op for his future Skipper RCAF Pilot F/S GM Taylor.**

**Detailed bombing height 5,750ft. Bombing load 8,200lbs. 21 Lancasters detailed. Meteorology Report 10/10ths cloud, tops 3,000ft.**

**Lancaster III, EE186, QR—D for Dog was the 8th a/c to take off, and the 10th a/c to return.**

Up---**22:41**---Down---**05:12**---Time out---**6hrs 29m**

**Debriefing report:-** P/O North reported a really good attack, markers were on time and accurately placed and bombing was well concentrated around these markers. Bombed MPI of 3 GTI's at 02:03hrs from 5,500ft. PHOTO: Ground detail.

**Squ Ops report**:- Attack on Marshalling Yards at LIMOGES. Met: clear, good visibility. 21 a/c were detailed for bombing Ops against the target, all of which successfully bombed the Marshalling Yards. This attack appeared to have been extremely successful and munitions appeared to be going up continually and the whole area was ablaze. The bombing was well concentrated and photos taken reveal ground detail.

**Flying alongside F/Lt Bill North for the fifth time to mark the target and on his 18th Op with 97 Squ PFF was W/O Percy Cannings and his crew**:-

Skipper, F/O WM Reid, FE, Sgt W Richards, NAV, F/O RD Parker, BA, F/Sgt GD Moir, WO, F/Sgt B Harthill, MUG, F/Sgt DP Cannings, RG, Sgt G Brown, in Lancaster ND961, OF-N, 'B' Flight, 97 Squadron PFF Coningsby. **(BI)**

**97 Squ, PFF Debriefing report**:-

Up 22:54, Down 05:02. 9x7' clusters, 8x500lb MC, 1x500lb MC LD (12hrs), 3 reco flares. Target seen by flares, H2S and visually on RSF. Flares down on time and excellently placed. Markers down one minute afterwards, backed up with green and red TI. First stick of bombs blew up RSF and a terrific explosion 01:57hrs. Bombing excellent, very great number of explosions continued after we had left the area. (Again Percy and Bill's takeoff and landing times were very close. This is the last time Percy Cannings flew alongside Bill. Percy would now fly alongside Les Morton for another 5 Ops.)

203 Lancasters and 4 Mosquitoes of 1 and 5 Groups attacked and very successfully bombed the railway yards at Limoges and Saintes. There was excellent marking from PFF and extremely accurate and concentrated bombing by the Main Force resulting in a number of large ground explosions at Limoges as munitions went up and followed by many more with fires burning 35 mins after the attack. 7 Lancasters were lost this night and 2 Stirlings on 'Gardening' Ops. Two 7 Squ Lancs were (7/7) at the flying bomb site Coubronne, one 156 Squ 6/7 loss. One 12 Squ Lanc was a (7/7) lost without trace at Saintes. One Stirling a (7/7) loss near Brest. 38 crewmen lost, 12 POW 14 saved. A comparatively low figure compared with previous Ops.

Some of the other 61 Squadron pilots who flew to Limoges that night with Bill were:- OC 'A' Flight, F/L F Norton in JB138, F/Lt BS Turner in

ED860, P/O DE White in EE176, F/L JA Kramer (RCAF), 1st Op for F/S GM Taylor (RCAF); Les Morton's future Skipper, with Sgt GE Gaunt as F/Eng, F/Lt BM Acott, P/O RA Dear, P/O JE Gibberd, P/O DW Simmons, P/O HW Cooper, F/O ER Church and P/O D Street with Sgt Les Morton as his F/Eng. It is interesting to note that P/O Don Street and Bill's takeoff, landing and bombing times were very close, Don Street and Les Morton landing 1 min after Bill. Bill was also bombing at 5,500ft with the majority of the Squadron bombing from above him! Don Street and Sgt Les Morton were above Bill at 6,750ft. This was another perfect Operation for Bill and 61 Squadron. There were no Fail to Returns and their timing and efficiency were excellent with great coordination with PFF. 21 a/c took off in 40mins from 22:22 to 23:02, bombed in 9 mins from 2:00 to 02:09 and all landed back at Skellingthorpe from 04:54 to 05:43 (Just quick notes on coincidences, Percy Cannings and Bill North's up and down times are virtually identical putting them up in the air at the same time!).

As Bill North, Norman Jarvis and Percy Cannings have explained training exercises carried on in-between Operations and even without the presence of NFs and Flak there were still dangers to be faced even on home ground! On 23 June 1944 shortly before Bill's Op to Limoges 97 Squ's Percy Cannings now recounts a horrific example of how Bill, Percy and the Bomber Command crews still faced extreme dangers even on these training missions, nowhere was safe from deaths dark shadow.

Whilst interviewing Percy on the first occasion that I met him on 10 August 2011, I had put down WR Chorley's Bomber Command 1944 Losses book on the coffee table in front of him. I was explaining to Percy and his daughter Sandy how the book recorded lost Bomber crews and right in front of our eyes the book flipped open by itself to page 298. I picked it back up and looked at it and said, 'Oh, look Percy there are two losses for 97 Squ here for 23 June 1944' and before I could say another word Percy virtually told us word for word what was written on the page. We were all a bit spooked by this, Percy then explained in more detail what happened that day whilst training before the Op to Limoges later that night. As Percy was recounting what happened that sad day in 1944, I quietly checked Bill's Log Book and discovered that they had both flown on this Op together. The hairs on the back of my neck stood up on end and when I looked up Sandy had tears in her eyes which set me off as well. Just like Bill, Percy's voice was steady and his eyes set in the distance far beyond the living room, he was right back in his Lancaster as if it were yesterday.

Percy Cannings and Bob Lasham reflecting at the 2012, 97 Squadron Association Reunion (photo, *Sandy Cannings*).

## W/O Percy Cannings

*'One of the vivid memories I have are of the tragic training exercise accident on the 23 June 1944 before we flew later that night on Ops to Limoges. This day is also Sandy's birthday so I am constantly reminded as the years have gone by. We were on a formation flying exercise with 5 other Lancasters from the Squadron including my crew Skippered by Bill Reid. The formation was flying in two 'V' shapes, with my crew in the second 'V'. F/Lt HS van Rhalte's Lancaster ME625 was ahead of us to the right in the first 'V' formation and suddenly got caught in the slipstream of the leading a/c. The result was that van Rhalte's Lancaster side-slipped over F/ Lt ELJ Perkins Lancaster ND981, which was slightly below him. Then as everyone in the formation watched in utter horror, van Rhalte's Lancaster then dropped suddenly and collided with Perkins Lancaster.* [It removed the entire tail section from Perkins plane and smashed the nose section of van Rhalte's a/c]. *Both aircraft disintegrated and plunged into the fields below, they missed us by inches! We saw one parachute open as the two a/c went down. Out of the 2 crews (8 in van Rhalte's and 6 in Perkins) there was one survivor from the Perkins crew. It was Sgt Cowan* who had managed to bale out, but he never flew again. The Station hushed it all up and the surviving crew member was posted as LMF.'*

Although Percy wasn't involved, some of the Squadron had all been laughing and joking minutes earlier when F/Lt Perkins car had been lifted up onto an air raid shelter. After the crash, the mood was somewhat darker as Perkins car had to be removed from the shelter.

*Sgt Cowan was later to die from TB; the shadow of death unyielding to all concerned!

**Sandy Cannings**

*'So sad. On checking dad's log book I see he was up again the same day on the Op to Limoges. It just goes to prove that these brave young men suffered so much heartbreak and saw so much tragedy yet they still managed to carry on with their duties. Absolute heroes, all of them. I am so unbelievably proud of them all. Even after this terrible accident that they had all witnessed and the close shave with the a/c falling within inches them, they still flew on Ops the same day.'*

Some of the wreckage from these 2 a/c is on display in the Museum at the Aviation Heritage Centre, East Kirkby. I walked around the display on our visit on the 3 November 2012 with Percy and Sandy Cannings. Percy was lost in thought as he looked at the wreckage of two Lancasters that he saw crash 67 years ago. (The crash site was at Cloor House Farm on Deeping Fen, Cloot Drove, Crowland in Lincs. A tenth of Bomber Command's overall losses were in training accidents.)

This was now the last Op that Percy Cannings flew on alongside Bill North. He now took a break from Operations and was thrown back into more intensive training. From the 26 June to 20 July 1944 his crew practised, Fighter Affiliation, more Formation Flying and Special Exercises etc. Bill was a FTR during this period of time as were many more crews; 50 Squ lost 6 a/c, 61 Squ also lost 6 a/c. 97 lost 1 and 83 Squ lost 2 a/c. However this was not the end of Percy's association with Bill and his crew though. When he returned to Ops on the 20/21 July he started flying alongside Bill's Flt/ Eng Sgt Les Morton and his new Skipper P/O Gerry Taylor.

**Operation No. 14. (Night Mission)**

**24/25 June 1944. Prouville, Pas de Calais, France (Flying bomb site). The 'North Crew' Flight Engineer Sgt Les Morton is replaced by W/Cmdr Doubleday's F/E, Sgt J Slome. Also second Op for F/S GM Taylor, with Sgt GE Gaunt as F/Eng.**

**Detailed bombing height 11,000ft. Bombing load 8,538lbs. 21 Lancasters detailed. Met: clear, good visibility. Lancaster III, EE186, QR-D for Dog was the 5th a/c to take off, and the 15th a/c to return.**

Up---**22:42**---Down---**02:18**---Time out---**3hrs 36m**

**Debriefing report:-** P/O North considered this a poor show by the markers as they were very late, we were coned for about 5 minutes by more than 26 searchlights. Bombed cluster of red and green TI's at 00:39hrs from 11,000ft. PHOTO: Ground detail.

**Squ Ops report:-** 20 a/c were detailed for bombing Ops against PROUVILLE. 18 of the a/c bombed successfully, although the bombing was not very concentrated. Searchlights were in evidence more than was expected and were working in conjunction with the fighters. Five machines were seen to be shot down. Photos revealed ground detail. The two remaining a/c failed to return [F/Lt Forrest in LM518, QR-C and P/O Kramer in ND987, QR-B]

Bomber Command dispatched 739 a/c, 535 Lancasters, 165 Halifaxes and 39 Mosquitoes from all Groups which attacked 7 flying bomb sites including Prouville, Pommerval, Rimeaux and Ruisseauville. Heavy cratering was now occurring around the targets from the constant Allied Air attacks, making individual Squadron results difficult to determine. As explained by Bill and his comrades there was also heavy searchlight and NF activity which was aided by the clear moonlit night. 20 Lancasters and 2 Stirlings were lost from these targets mostly from NF attacks. Five Lancasters and two Stirlings were (7/7s) 49 crew, five (6/7s ) 30 crew, three (5/7s) 15 crew and two (6/8s) 12 crew. One 97 Squ a/c was lost NE124, OF-J and a further 11 crew died with the rest POW and evd, totalling 117 crew dead. It was a heavy night for Skellingthorpe Station with the loss of 4 of its a/c, 2 from 50 Squ and 2 from 61 Squ. There were two survivors from 61 Squ, Rear Gnr Sgt AN Avery (Kramer's crew), F/Eng Sgt K Chapman (Forrest's crew).

'Twilight taxi run'. NX611 Just Jane at East Kirkby. (photo, *Stephen Elsworth*)

Lancaster B Mk 1s from 50 Squ flying in a loose daytime formation, 'a gaggle'. The two a/c beyond the wing tip are JA899, VN-D and VN-J. VN-D was a FTR from Bill's Op to Prouville 24/25 June 1944 with P/O LG Peters (RCAF) (source, *TR1156, IWM*).

Some of the other 61 Squadron pilots who flew to Prouville that night with Bill were:- F/O HL Inniss in JB138, F/Lt BS Turner in ED860, P/O DE White (RCAF) in EE176, F/Lt JA Forrest, P/O JA Kramer (RCAF), 2nd Op for F/S GM Taylor (RCAF); Les Morton's future Skipper, with Sgt GE Gaunt as F/Eng, P/O RA Dear, F/L WE Jeavons, P/O DW Simmons, P/O HW Cooper, F/O ER Church (RCAF) and P/O D Street. It is interesting to note that F/S GM Taylor took off 2 mins before Bill but landed last at 03:15. 20 a/c took off in 61mins from 22:31 to 23:32 and all except Forrest and Kramer who failed to return, landed back at Skellingthorpe from 01:49 to 03:15. There was some confusion with markers and bombing. Church reports that the original markers were blown out and 9 a/c on seeing no markers bombed on Gee from 00:21 to 00:23 at ETA. Church, Turner and Sinclair bombed from 00:26 to 00:29 on remains of markers and Bill expresses disappointment at the markers going down late. North, Simmons, Dear and Martin bombed later on the remark from 00:38 to 00:39. Jeavons and Watkins failed to bomb due to technical problems. Therefore the bombing was not very concentrated and the delays seemed to have allowed NFs to be more successful. Church reports S/L and NFs very active in target area. 5 a/c were seen to be shot down, most likely two of these were Kramer and Forrest.

**W/O Norman Jarvis**

*'Bill was by this time one of the top skippers and we were considered to be one of the 'veteran' crews and we were going in on the first wave and often getting back first to Skellingthorpe. We were also very confident in our ability and thought, well the Jerries will be good if they get us, until the night the two senior men of the Squadron did not return from a very sticky job in the Pas de Calais area on 24/25 June, which was then the main source of the V1 Flying Bombs. We spent a long time over the target and were coned by searchlights for quite a while and saw the boys going down on all sides.'*

The two senior men from 61 Squadron that Norman Jarvis refers to are as detailed above, F/Lt JA Forest (RAAF) and P/O J Kramer (RCAF). Norman's comment is interesting and Max Hastings talks about over-confidence in crews. *'We were also very confident in our ability and thought, well the Jerries will be good if they get us.'* The statistics relating to tours of Operations were that the chance of being lost at the start of Ops was extremely high. Midway through the tour the chance reduced, but as crews became overconfident towards the end of tours the chance of being lost rose again. Bill and the boys were coned for 5 minutes during this Op by an astounding 26 plus searchlights. It was a clear moonlit night and as explained above 22 a/c were lost in the apocalyptic skies around Bill by Night Fighter activity aided by search lights. As Dennis Bartlett and Bill now explain some heavy evasive manoeuvres were made to escape from the S/Ls and NFs; they eventually ended up flying at sea level over the English Channel for the journey home.

Bill had a really cheeky grin on his face as he was recalling this event. I could see that he had got immense satisfaction from putting his Lancaster through some extreme flying to make their escape. Bill was doing what he did best, saving his crew from certain death, never ever letting them down. Yet again the 'North Crew' guided by Bill's firm, confident hands had tumbled and fallen in and out of death's ever-present shadow.

**F/Lt Bill North**

*'When we were coned that night I tried every trick in the book to get away from those searchlights, I threw that aircraft all over the sky and it took everything I gave it. I could make the Lancaster do whatever I wanted it to do! I really did things to that a/c that shouldn't have been done to it, but we*

*were in a desperate state and had to get out of the cone. The German AA was throwing everything it had at us and Night Fighters were tearing into the Main Force, in that situation our chance of surviving was extremely low. We ended up out over the English Channel almost at sea-level before we were finally clear.'*

**W/O Dennis Bartlett**

*'When we were coned on this mission it was by a large number of search lights and lasted for some time. From the Mid-Upper Turret you could see the searchlights streaking around the sky and Bill would weave this way and that to avoid them. A blue radar controlled master searchlight suddenly picked us up and then all the others which were coloured white swung in on us. When we were coned it was so bright that we virtually got blinded. Bill literally threw the Lancaster all over the sky while trying to get away, flak was blasting all around us and we saw other a/c going down. It was a hell of a ride, he dived steeply this way and that and we eventually ended up out over the sea before we finally got away at a very low altitude. The whole crew was relieved to have escaped and Bill's calmness in a near death situation had saved us all again. I'd never seen or been in a Lancaster that had been pushed to the limits like this.'*

'Crossing the Coast' by outstanding aviation artist Simon W. Atack. The full colour print of this painting is absolutely stunning (*www.simonatack.com*).

Again when Bill and I were originally discussing the losses for this Op, I handed him WR Chorley's 1944 Losses book and pointed to the two lost 61 Squ a/c on p302 that Norman Jarvis had mentioned. 'Bill there are two names here from 61 Squ, F/Lt Forrest and P/O Kramer, they are also mentioned in ORB alongside you. Do you remember them?' Bill sat looking at the pages in the book and after a short pause he looked up and said, *'It knocked the confidence of the Squadron when we found out that these two crews were missing. I don't remember P/O Kramer so well, but recall F/ Lt Forrest. He had a couple of close escapes that were talked about in the Squadron.'* One of these was when Forrest's Lancaster EE176, QR-M, was hit by lightning during an electrical storm on 30/31 March to Nuremburg. He was temporarily blinded and lost control of the a/c, eventually making it back safely after two crew baled out.

**W/O Percy Cannings**

*'There was always plenty of flak and searchlights which I particularly did not like having been coned by them on my first tour. I swear my skipper Flt/ Lt. Ken Harvey, a Canadian had the Lancaster upside down as the contents of the Elsan toilet had been strewn all over the inside of the plane and me. I bet the Ground Crew did not particularly like cleaning that lot up, but the main problem in being coned was both Gunners and Pilot lose all vestige of night vision, for at least 15 minutes, even if one catches you in passing, I did not like searchlights at all! It also allowed a fighter to see you more clearly. If on seeing a fighter, I would call out to our Skipper to corkscrew in the direction the fighter was coming in from. This would be either to port or to starboard and that is when the adrenalin rush really kicked in!!'*

**Operation No. 15 (Night Mission)**

**27/28 June 1944. Vitry, France, (Marshalling Yards) The 'North Crew' Flight Engineer Sgt Les Morton is replaced by F/Lt IM Pettigrew (DFM). Third Op for F/S GM Taylor with Sgt GE Gaunt as F/Eng.**

**Detailed bombing height 6,000ft. Bombing load 11,000lbs. 19 Lancasters detailed. Met: clear, good visibility.**

**Lancaster III, EE186, QR-D for Dog. was the 15th a/c to take off, and the 16th a/c to return.**

Up---**22:05**---Down---**05:42**---Time out---**7hrs 37m**

(Bill had flown on missions 19 times, 17 were recorded as Ops. At 7hrs 37m this was the longest mission Bill had flown on; the shortest was the daylight raid to Beauvoir at 3hrs 05m. Excluding St. Leu which was roughly 4hrs 30m and the 2 mission fails to Borg-Leopold and Watten, which totalled 3hrs 45m; the average time out for the other 16 missions was just over 5hrs.)

**Debriefing report:-** P/O North reported one very large explosion seen at 01:51, plenty of smoke rising from various small fires and explosions in target area. Bombed 1 RSF at 01:53hrs from 5,000ft. PHOTO: Failure—target conditions.

**Squ Ops report:-** 19 a/c carried out operations against VITRY as ordered. 16 a/c successfully bombed RSF's and TI's in the target area. Large explosions were observed with a great deal of smoke. Very little flak was encountered over the target though fighters were in evidence throughout the attack. The 3 remaining a/c returned early, two on instructions from the Controller and the other due to Port Inner engine failing. Part of the bomb load was jettisoned. [Bates and Church, with Passnant the early return at 23:29, engine fail]

Bomber Command's main targets this night were 6 flying bomb sites and railway yards in the Paris suburbs at Vaires and Vitry. 721 a/c were dispatched to the flying bomb sites and 214 Lancasters and 9 Mosquitoes from 1, 5 and 8 Groups attacked Paris. As usual there were also other minor Ops. The raids at Bill's target Vitry were only a partial success due to late marking causing disappointing bomb aiming and heavy smoke also obscuring the area causing many photo fails. There was a mixed account from the pilot's, some recording good bombing and others unsatisfactory. Some a/c did up to 3 orbits which broke up the concentration of the attack and the yards were only hit at the western end with two large explosions seen. 11 a/c were lost from the skies around Bill:- 6 Lancasters were (7/7s), 1 was from Vaires and two 106 Squ were (7/7s) at Vitry, (42 men, plus 3 more from Mosquitoes). 1 Lanc from 12 Squ was lost, but all survived. Also 1 Halifax and 3 Mosquitoes.

Some of the other 61 Squadron pilots who flew to Vitry that night with Bill were:- O/C F/Lt F Norton in JB138, F/Lt BS Turner in ED860, P/O DE White (RCAF) in EE176, 3st Op for F/S GM Taylor (RCAF); with Sgt GE Gaunt as F/Eng, P/O RA Dear who's bomb doors malfunctioned, P/O PG Bates, P/O DW Simmons, P/O HW Cooper, F/O ER Church (RCAF) and P/O D Street. It is interesting to note that Bill and F/S GM Taylor were up and down virtually at the same time. Again bombs from above are a danger, Bill bombed at 00:53 from 5,000ft and Taylor from above him at 6,000ft at 00:52. The Squadron again performed with great coordination as 19 a/c took off in 40mins from 21:29 to 22:09, bombing in 10mins from 01:46 to 01:56 and all except Passant landed back at Skellingthorpe from 05:03 to 05:45.

This night Lancaster ED860, QR-N was the 1st Lancaster to complete 100 Operations in Bomber Command. After the bombing run at 00:54, F/O BS Turner and crew had a close combat with a NF over Paris after detecting it on Monica Mk V. Both Gunners fired off 400 rounds between them as they were attacked from port beam and corkscrewed down to port. It was thought that 467 Squ's R5868, PO-S for Sugar had reached 100 Ops on 11/12 May to Bourg-Leopold, which would have made it the first. However, due to a mix up in the records this was only its 91st Op. It flew with 467 Squ on 9 of Bill's missions and finally reached 100 Ops on 7/8 July to St Leu, 2 days after Bill was shot down. This famous Lancaster reached 136 Ops and was preserved after the War. It is on display at the RAF Museum Hendon, which is where I took the photo of Bill next to it on 28 Feb 2010 (*Claims To Fame, The Lancaster*, Norman Franks).

ED860, QR-N, being bombed up at Skellingthorpe (source, *50/61 Squ Association*).

A point of interest from Steve Darlow, p99, *Sledgehammers for Tintacks*; 'On the 28/29 June the 2000th flying bomb was fired prompting a congratulatory signal from Hitler to Heineman' (Lt-General Erich

Heineman was the Commander of all secret weapons formations. Through mid to the end of June 1944, an average of 150 flying bombs per 24 hours were still being fired).

Bomber Command was now flying daylight missions to attack these sites and maintain tactical support to the Normandy Landings. Bill's next raid was a daylight Op to Beauvoir (located north of Amiens). It was the first time Bill and the crew had flown on an Operation during the day. It is interesting to note their observations and comparisons to flying on Ops at night.

**Operation No. 16 (Daylight Mission, written in green ink in Bill's Log Book)**

**29 June 1944. Beauvoir, Calais (Pilot-less Bomb Planes) The 'North Crew' Flight Engineer Sgt Les Morton is replaced by Sgt Slome. The third Op that Sgt Les Morton flew on alongside Bill and first Op as Flt/Eng to newly promoted RCAF Pilot P/O GM Taylor in F/Lt Jeff Gray's trusty ME725, QR-G. (This was Taylor's fourth Op as a Skipper)**

**Detailed bombing height 18,000ft. Bombing load 13,000lbs. 18 Lancasters detailed. Met: clear, good visibility.**

**Lancaster III, EE186, QR-D for Dog.**

Up---**12:10**---Down---**15:15**--- Time out---**3hrs 05m**

It is interesting to note that in daylight the Squadron all took off in the fastest time recorded during Bill's missions. 17 Lancasters took off virtually one after the other in 22 mins from 11:53 to 12:15. The sound of all those Merlin engines roaring on full throttle must have been phenomenal! The last one to take off apparently late was P/O DE White at 12:50. The landing times were slightly more spread out from 14:45 to 16:10. The target was confirmed visually and on Gee due to heavy smoke and drift cloud, most pilots mentioned no markers seen. The recorded bombing time was also tight from 13:45 to 13:50. The whole mission was very efficient and very fast at an hour and a half each way.

**Debriefing report:-** P/O North observed no markers and drift cloud prevented assessment of attack.

**Squadron Ops report:-** 18 a/c were detailed for daylight bombing attack on BEAUVOIR. All of which carried out their instructions successfully. Bombing was carried out both by visual means and by the use of Gee. The bombing was reported to be concentrated and many fires and smoke were seen. Heights were from 14-19,000ft.

The other 61 Squadron pilots who flew to Beauvoir that day with Bill were:- O/C F/Lt F Norton in JB138, F/Lt BS Turner in ED860, P/O DE White (RCAF) in EE176, 4th Op for F/S GM Taylor (RCAF) and first flight with Sgt Les Morton as F/Eng, P/O RA Dear, P/O RH Passant (RAAF), P/O DW Simmons, P/O HW Cooper, F/O ER Church (RCAF), P/O D Street, F/O S Parker, F/O HL Inniss, S/L J Woodroffe, F/L BM Acott, P/O PH Martin, P/O H Watkins, P/O WE Grantham and P/O EW Hallett.

Bomber Command despatched 286 Lancasters and 19 Mosquitoes from 1, 5 and 8 Groups to attack two flying bomb sites at Siracourt and Beauvoir. 7 a/c were lost this day. From Beauvoir, one 463 Squ Lanc was damaged by flak and written off on its return. One 467 Squ Lanc was hit by flak at 18,000ft and lost with 3 of its crew with 4 POWs. Two 627 Squ Mosquitoes were lost with one 2 man crew in DZ516, AZ-O dying in a premature V1 explosion. At Siracourt, 7 Squ lost its Master Bomber Lanc, (6/8) with F/Lt SEC Clark. One 12 Squ Lanc was a (3/7) and one 460 Squ Lanc was written off at home after flak damage. As we see with these daylight losses the ever present 'shadow of death' still claimed 14 crewmen, comparatively far fewer than Bill's previous missions; flak seeming to be the major culprit.

Norman, Dennis and Bill now offer their observations of their daylight bombing raid:-

**W/O Norman Jarvis**

*'The weather near the end of June was very poor and although we were kept standing by and were briefed every night for a week, we only got one trip in. It was during this period that the Lancaster's and Halifaxes started doing their first daylight raids. We set out one morning on our first daylight trip. It was a very clear day when we left and although the preparations were not as elaborate as the night jobs, we could see all our comrades take off and I was very impressed being up there. Above, below, ahead and behind us were Bombers and the first Fighter escort we ever had was wheeling and dodging about our formations. As we neared the South coast of England I could see the whole English Channel and the coast of France, lying there below us like a great topographical map. We crossed the French coast and were soon running up on our target; the Bombers all seemed to be closing in now. The ones in front were opening their bomb doors; we edged in and there was the target with sticks of 1000 pounders bending*

*across it to the right and left of the small woods which were concealing the V1 installations. The Gunners complained that there were bombs falling from above very close to us. I let ours go and watched them fall down, down and then bursting on the mass of smoke and flames that had been our target. The flak was quite heavy as we ran out of the area. It did not flash like orange stars, but in daylight left huge puffs of blue smoke.'*

Two of the Fighters used for escort duties were the North American, P-51 Mustang and the P-47 Thunderbolt. Left, P-51D, VF-B, 413317 at RAF Hendon, 28 Feb 2010 (CK) and right three P-47 Thunderbolts flying in formation; more than 15,700 P-47 units were produced in the United States. The long range disposable fuel tanks stored under the wings of these Fighter escorts enabled them to stay with the Bomber Streams deep into enemy territory. They were initially made of cardboard by a company called Hunt Industries. This was run by a dear friend of my father called Douglas Hunt. Douglas and his wife, Winnie, lived in Winchmore Hill, London, during the War and would watch the daytime Bomber Streams passing overhead from their back garden; 'It would sometimes take over an hour for them to pass by' (source, P-47 photo, *www.war-two-war-planes.com*).

## W/O Dennis Bartlett

*'I can remember our first daylight raid over France. In the distance we could see the formations of B-17 Flying Fortresses from the USAAF flying with us. I could see all the other Lancasters in our bomber stream stretched out around us. It was an impressive sight and thrilling to see. When we flew at night everything felt undercover, but here we were fully exposed. The flak was bursting around us and was a greyish-blue colour. When we did the bombing run we all realised how close the bombs from Lancasters above us were falling. It was quite unnerving and I called out to Bill that they were falling too close for comfort.'*

'Swirling vapour trails'. B17s on a daylight bombing mission (source, *US Air Force*).

## F/Lt Bill North

*'Our first daylight Operation was a completely different experience to Night Ops. I can remember feeling quite exposed. Although it was still full of danger with night flying we always felt comparatively safer, as if the darkness protected us. The a/c had special daylight markings on them. I seem to remember these being white stripes painted across the wing tips and tail sections.*The a/c would also fly in tighter formations or 'gaggles'. I could see all the other aircraft from the Squadron very close around us which as Dennis says was an impressive sight. We could also see how close the flak actually was when it was exploding around us and on the bombing run we watched the sticks of bombs falling away from the other Lancasters and exploding over the target. There was a large amount of smoke rising from the target which partly obscured the view of our bombing assessment, but Norman got a good view of our bombs hitting the target though. The other curious thing was watching the bombs from aircraft above us falling very close by, Eddy and Dennis were calling out 'Bombs from above coming very close Skipper!''*

*New tactics were required to form up and control large formations for daylight raids. 1 and 5 Group favoured combinations of coloured wing tips, fuselage and tail bands.

Before we come to Bill's final Operation we will mention the vital roles of the ground crews at Skellingthorpe which included Armourers, Bomb Loaders, Fitters, Electricians, WAAF drivers etc and some of the dangers they faced. All of whom were on 24/7 call to repair, service and arm 50 and 61 Squadron's fleet of 40 plus Lancasters. This task was thankless and carried out in all weathers often with little sleep and like the aircrews they became extremely attached to their aircraft. The repair of battle damaged a/c belonged to 58 (MU) Maintenance Unit who worked relentlessly in adverse conditions to repair Flak and NF damage.

# Chapter Fourteen

## Tragedy at Skellingthorpe

Three years ago when I attended the first 50/61 Squ Memorial Day I met a Veteran called Kenneth Green, he was one of the first people I spoke two alongside Arthur Smith. I had a long in depth conversation with Kenneth and he explained his role in the ground crew as a Leading Aircraft Man at Skellingthorpe. He was a mechanic whose speciality was Merlin engines and his memory is razor sharp. He revealed that he had been at Skellingthorpe the day that Bill and his crew witnessed a tragedy in which some ground crew were killed during the arming and bombing up of the Lancaster fleet. Kenneth can talk for hours recalling events from the War and I have had some fascinating conversations on the phone with him.

### LAC Kenneth S Green

*'I was a Fitter 2E with the 61 Squ ground crews at Skellingthorpe and Merlin engines were my speciality. I had been in the Fire Brigade and volunteered for RAF service. I was turned down for Pilot Training because I failed the eye test. Because I was technically minded I did my engine training at St Athans near Swansea and eventually ended up at Skellingthorpe after working at other bases like Syerston. At Syerston the Squadron was equipped with MK II Lancasters with had the Bristol Hercules engines fitted. These however were slowly replaced with the MK III Merlin 24 and 28's, these could fly at a higher altitude than the MK II's. Most of these Mk IIs were given to 115 Squ.*

*The ground crews at Skellingthorpe worked long hard hours on our Lancasters and I pretty much worked on all the A and B Flight engines which were mostly Packard Merlins by 1944. Our Flight Sergeant who was in charge of servicing was an ex Holton apprentice called Lofty Bennet. I was very friendly with one of the crews who flew in EE176, QR-M. It was P/O White's crew. His Flt/Eng was Sgt Ben Lyon who had done Radio Broadcasting. His WOP was Sgt 'Ginger' Harrow who actually was from Harrow! He was a cheeky sod always waving his hanky out of the a/c window. The Nav was W/O Blackwood who was very good looking with his slicked back hair. Anyway on their first Op in EE176 the Starboard Outer malfunctioned and they had to emergency land at Upwood. I then had to drive down there with a spare engine and replace it for them. It was from this point that Ben Lyon became good friends with me and he was always keen to see that the engines were serviced by me. We held the record for how many groundcrew could be carried on a David Brown Tractor. I think it was 22 or 23, you couldn't even see the driver! We were so busy in those days it really was relentless work and these funny moments were a way of letting off steam.'*

'Lofty' with his ground crew servicing Jeff Gray's Lancaster ME725, QR-G for George (source, original photos by *F/Lt Jeff Gray*).

On 19 May 1944 Bill and the crew were relaxing in the mess whilst the A and B Flights were being bombed up, fuelled, armed and serviced for the night Operation to Tours. The whole base was suddenly rocked by a huge explosion. Norman Jarvis, Bill North, Dennis Bartlett and Leading Aircraft Man Kenneth S Green now explain what happened. (F/Lt Jeff Gray was also relaxing in the mess when he too heard the explosion)

**W/O Norman Jarvis**

*'I did not realise what a devastating effect our bombs had until one day when we were lounging in the mess talking while the armourers and ground crew were bombing up and refuelling for a job we had on that night. There was a terrific explosion, the building shook, parts of the ceiling came in and the windows smashed. All the boys hit the floor together and we thought it was a German intruder that had sneaked through unnoticed. After rushing out we saw that a trolley load of bombs being towed around from the bomb dump had blown up; the unfortunate armourers were of course blown to atoms and so was most of the trailer and the tractor. An aircraft 200 yards away was peppered with holes. On the track was a huge crater and we were picking up red hot shrapnel down around the mess 400 yards away.'*

**F/Lt Bill North**

*'Oh yes, I remember this well. We were all relaxing in the mess when suddenly there was a huge explosion and we all dived onto the floor as glass and dust landed all over the place. We all rushed outside and saw a scene of devastation. A bomb had exploded on a trolley being towed by a tractor and there was a big crater on the field. A Lancaster next to it was severely damaged and there was no sign of the poor soul on the tractor. There was wreckage everywhere and we all piled in to help clear up the mess. It was quite shocking to see the amount of damage done and the fact that some of our ground crew had been killed in the explosion.'*

**W/O Dennis Bartlett**

*'We were in the mess chatting and joking with each other when an explosion suddenly rocked the building blowing all the windows in. We all dived to the floor as we thought we were being attacked by German Bombers. When it was clear there was going to be no more explosions, we rushed outside to see what had happened. There was a huge crater where a bomb trolley had once been and there was hot shrapnel all over the place.'*

**F/Lt Jeff Gray**

*'I remember this accident really well, 19 May 1944 was the last Op on my Tour. We were all lounging around at the base when a terrific explosion rocked the whole place. The poor chap driving the bomb trolley was blown to smithereens and we all helped clear up the mess to get the base ready for the nights Ops to Tours.'*

**LAC Kenneth S Green**

*'On the 19 May 1944 I was servicing the Starboard Outer engine on one of the Lancasters in 'B' Flight in preparation for that night's Ops. As usual the Station was a hive of activity with the a/c being bombed, armed, serviced and fuelled up. My mate LAC Roy Hodgkinson was working on the Port Outer engine of the same a/c. We were calling out to each other all the time, this 'blinking' thing this or this 'blinking' thing that as we worked away. I finished my engine first and Roy was having problems with his engine. We were waiting for Lofty to come down and run the engines up to give*

*them the all clear when Roy said to me, 'Don't worry, I'll finish up, you get going.' I said goodbye and waved to him, picked up my bike and rode off to get the train home to Nottingham where I lived. I was literally about 5 minutes away when there was an explosion and thought blimey I hope everyone's ok. When I got back to the base at midnight I was told that Roy had been killed in the explosion and I realised that I most definitely would have been killed as well. I was very grateful for being allowed to breathe for a little bit longer! I went to visit the church in Stoke on Trent after the War where Roy was buried and found his gravestone. I couldn't track down any of his family though. The thought of this has stayed with me all these years and I am 91 now. Apparently the bomb trolley was being towed by a 50 Squ member who had broken his collar bone. He was desperate to be doing something, so he was given the job of driving the bombing up tractor. One of the springs on the last trolley of about 15 broke and the 1000 pounder it was carrying fell off, fused and exploded. The poor chap didn't have a chance and the a/c I was working on with Roy was severely damaged.'*

The dangers of loading and carrying live bombs are self explanatory and I will just quickly mention a couple of other related accidents as comparisons. Even when they weren't flying in deaths shadow still moved close by to Bill, his crew and the many personnel that were part of Bomber Command.

On the 15 March 1943 at RAF Scampton a 'Cookie' was accidently released under a 57 Squ Lancaster W4834 causing a devastating explosion which destroyed 5 other Lancasters in the immediate vicinity. (2 from 57 Squ and 3 from 50 Squ) On the 3 July 1943 there was an explosion at RAF Binbrook underneath a 460 Squ Lancaster DV172 after an electrical fault jettisoned the bomb load. One other a/c was also completely destroyed and two others damaged.

Curiously 57 Squ was also involved in the following accident 2 years later. On 17 April 1945 just as the War was drawing to an end there was a horrific incident at East Kirkby, now the home of The Aviation Heritage Centre. It was a beautiful spring day and at 09:30 a call for a change in bomb load was made. 30 or so a/c from 57 and 630 Squ's had already been bombed up the previous day for the target at Cham in Germany and the order was to change the fusing from direct impact to long delays. Obviously this produced a complex and mammoth task for the ground crews, so the decision was made to do most of the work at the dispersal points.

Apocalyptic scene at East Kirkby. The wrecked incendiary hangar with unrecognisable remains of a Lancaster in the foreground (source, *TL Reading*, p148 *Lancaster at War 2*, Mike Garbett and Brian Goulding).

The work was nearly complete when at 05:40 the Station Armament Officer Lt John MacBean heard a dull explosion, a bit like a photo flash going off. There is some debate about what caused this initial explosion which occurred underneath 57 Squ Lanc PB360, DX-N; it was either petrol over spilling and igniting or a 1000lb bomb accidently releasing and landing on the ground. However, the result was this a/c's whole bomb load detonated causing a massive chain reaction of explosions and fires amongst 5 other nearby Lancasters. Bits of a/c, shrapnel, bombs and incendiaries were blown everywhere and Hangar 3 was completely wrecked, as was Hagnaby Grange Farm, with Fire engines from Coningsby and Spilsby attending the scene.

Utter devastation. The remains of two Lancasters, with one lucky escape for EE197, DX-Y tucked to the right behind the hangar (source, *TL Reading*, p148 *Lancaster at War 2*, Mike Garbett and Brian Goulding).

The whole area was eventually abandoned after being deemed unsafe and the last explosion occurred the next day as teams were defusing scattered bombs. This was from the delayed action fuses of three bombs left in a crater where a Lancaster used to be. It was a scene of utter devastation with some of the Lancasters unrecognisable; 4 airmen were killed, 16 injured and six 57 Squ Lancasters were written off. This was a tragic ending for these distinguished a/c and the brave men who attended them and so near the end of the War. Given the number of sorties flown by Bomber Command throughout the whole War it is surprising that there were not more large accidents with bombing up a/c. It is a testament to the skill, courage and efficiency of the ground crews and staff of all trades.

**Norman Jarvis now offers some more fascinating and thought provoking views of life at the time:**

**W/O Norman Jarvis**

*'I used to be amused at some of the superstitions of the aircrew; some refused to fly without their mascots, while others would not think of going on Ops in an aircraft of a certain letter. When we arrived on 61 Squadron, they said 'Well there's your Lancaster D—for Dog—we have lost the other two D's we have had*. Fortunately none of our crew was superstitious. Other crew hated flying with spare men; we also had our share of these. Then there were the boys who had premonitions about not returning from a certain trip—quite often too, they did not. Most of the crews were 'Happy-go-lucky'; they lived for the day and had about them, that intense gaze, that alertness and watchfulness that meant life itself to those Lords of the Air. There is talk of the Flak Happy Air Gunner, the Bomb HAPPY Bomb Aimer and Pilots with an Operational twitch. These are no figments of the imagination, they do exist and in some cases the sufferer has to be treated; some have even gone to mental homes. These are usually from crews who have been severely shot about or had terrific experiences in the air. Often a kite returns with a couple of its crew dead or badly wounded, but more often than not if they have been badly hit, they just don't come back and their story is never told.'*

*Bill had a Lincoln Imp, which was lost on the night they crashed in France. The two previous D for Dog Lancasters Norman referred to are:- R5703, lost when it crashed shortly after takeoff at Syerston on 1 Oct 1942, Ops to Wismar, pilot Squadron Leader GE Weston DFC. The Dinghy malfunctioned and opened fouling the tail plane causing the crash and loss of the

7 crew. (This a/c was an early Lancaster and was part of an original order of 200 Manchester's from A.V Roe, Manchester) The second ED332 was lost 16/17 Jan 1943, Ops to Berlin. The Skipper was the distinguished Squadron Leader EDJ Parker, George Cross and DFM, all 7 crew were lost over the target and lie in the 1939-1945 War Cemetery in Berlin. The new QR-D, PB436 that replaced Bill's EE186 was lost at Konigsburg 28/29 Aug 1944 with F/S BF Lonen (RAAF), who was on his 6th Op. All the crew survived (50 Squ had 4 FTRs at Konigsburg with only 1 survivor).

Night after night F/Lt Bill North and his faithful crew flew through the midst of hellish losses, riding right through death's shadow to return safely back to the peaceful Lincolnshire countryside. A poem by Paul Bewsher, himself an RAF Bomber pilot, captures some of what they must have felt:

## Searchlights, by Paul Bewsher

**'You who have seen across the star-decked skies**
**The long white arms of searchlights slowly sweep,**
**Have you imagined what it is to creep**
**High in the darkness, cold and terror wise,**
**Forever looked for by those cruel eyes**
**Which search with far-flung beams the shadowy deep,**
**And near the wings unending vigil keep**
**To haunt the lonely airman as he flies?**
**Have you imagined what it is to know**
**That if one finds you all their fierce desire**
**To see you fall will dog you as you go,**
**High in a sea of light and bursting fire,**
**Like some small bird, lit up and blinding white**
**Which slowly moves across the shell-torn night.'**

# Chapter Fifteen

## Disaster Strikes

For sixteen Operations (not including his two early return missions) thanks to Bill's nerve, skill and a large amount of luck, he and his crew had always returned safely. That was all about to change. The dry language of the official reports reveals the bare facts.

**Operation No. 17 (Night Mission)**

**4/5 July 1944. St Leu, France, (V1 site in caves) The 'North Crew' Flight Engineer Sgt Les Morton is replaced by Sgt Hatchett.**

**Detailed bombing heights 12,000-18,000ft. Bombing load unknown. (Not written in Bill's Log Book, his average bomb loads were from 8,000 to 13,000lbs) 20 Lancasters detailed. Met: clear, no cloud.**

**Lancaster III, EE186, QR—D for Dog.**

Up---**23:23**---Crash landed at 02:00 some 2km North of Harquency in the Department of Eure and about 6km ENE of les Andelys. German crash report number KE 9167 (This report only contains the salvage details of the crash, not which Night Fighter attacked it. See the appendix on this Chapter for more about the Night Fighter Squadrons that were operating on this night).

**Debriefing report:-** P/O North failed to return from this Operation.

**Squ Ops report:-** 20 a/c were detailed for bombing Ops against a Flying Bomb depot at ST LEU-*D'ESSERENT. Met: clear, no cloud. 19 a/c successfully bombed the target from heights between 12,000 and 18,000ft. Bombing was well concentrated and explosions and smoke seen. 1 a/c failed to return from this attack [EE186, QR—D], the other a/c returned early owing to misunderstanding Controllers remarks. [F/O S Parker in ME719]*

What happened next was this. On the night of 4/5 July 1944, P/O Bill North and his usual crew, with the exception of Sgt Les Morton who was replaced by Sgt Dennis Hatchett, left Skellingthorpe at 23:23. They flew off into the darkness in their Lancaster III, EE186, QR-D for Dog with 20 other Lancasters from 61 Squadron. In June 1944 Saint-Leu-d'Esserent and Nucourt were confirmed by British Intelligence to be V-1 storage depots. Bill's mission was to bomb the V1 storage depot located within the mushroom caves at Saint-Leu-d'Esserent and was a continuation of Operation Crossbow, the combined Allied Air Force offensive against Hitler's long range weapons.

They were part of the main force of 231 Lancasters and 15 Mosquitoes, mostly from 5 Group, with PFF marking the target. They attacked the underground flying-bomb store at St Leu with 1,000lb bombs, in order to cut communications to the site. The mushroom caves were one of three major underground V-1 storage depots in Normandy and the site at St Leu included blockhouses, bunkers, flak emplacements and railway links. (*Bomber Command War Diaries*, Martin Middlebrook and Chris Everitt and Steve Darlow, *Sledgehammers for Tintacks*)

In Bill's own words:

**F/Lt Bill North**

*'On the night of the 4/5 July 1944, I was the pilot of Lancaster EE186, QR-D for Dog 61 Squadron, Skellingthorpe, Lincolnshire. Earlier in the day my crew had taken the same aircraft on a 35 minute NFT—Night Flying Test—flight and found it to be satisfactory in all respects. Prior to take-off my crew and the other involved 61 Squadron Crews attended a 'briefing'. This briefing included the target details which were the V-1 site at St. Leu. The weather forecast during the flight, visibility, particularly in the vicinity of the target and our bomb load and bombing height. When we took-off to set course for the target the weather as I recall it posed no problems. The time for take-off was 23.23 hours and as the mission was during the night the entire flight would have been planned to take place in the dark.*
*Our flight to the target area was uneventful. On reaching the target zone I was able to see that our target had been suitably 'marked' by our Pathfinder Force and therefore set the pre-determined course and height for our bombing run. It was at this stage as was usual on our Operational trips, that my Bomb Aimer, F/Sgt Norman Jarvis took control. I maintained the bombing course and height, ensuring that the Lancaster was kept 'straight and level'. From time to time during the bombing run I altered course as necessary in line with F/Sgt Jarvis' instructions. We completed*

*our bombing run, dropped our bomb load and as soon as Norman said 'Bombs away, Skipper,' I turned very steeply away from the target area which of course was also the danger area and set course for home.'*

**Norman Jarvis remembers the events as follows:**

**WO Norman Jarvis**

*'On the night of 4 July 1944 we were detailed to attack a V1 site at St Leu, just north of Paris. It was a small pin point target believed by our Intelligence to be a former railway tunnel and very heavily defended, as were all the targets in Paris those days. At briefing we were given our instructions and our crew was to go in with the first wave and if possible bomb visually, if not we were to aim for the red target indicators dropped by the PFF. It was a full moon that night and therefore very dangerous for us as the Night Fighters of the Luftwaffe loved a full moon. All the way to the target was uneventful and as we ran in to bomb we could hardly see any flak at 13,000 ft. At zero × 1, I made a bombing run and saw my stick of 1,000 pounders burst across the target indicators, the first bombs for the night. As we closed the bomb doors and started home the tail gunner reported a terrific barrage coming up as the remainder of our force did their runs, so we thought that was good luck for us and settled down for the trip home.'*

**Left,** a vertical photographic-reconnaissance image of the underground V-1 storage depot at Saint-Leu-d'Esserent taken after the attacks by Bomber Command during July 1944 The original caption states that 'large areas can be seen which have subsided (C) and the entrances have been blocked by direct hits or near misses'. (HMP)

**Right**, another view of the tunnel entrances at St Leu. Note the bomb craters in the foreground. When the offensive against the V-1 sites finally ended after the capture of the Pas de Calais, it was noted that well over 3,000 sorties had been flown and a staggering 1,200,000 aerial reconnaissance images had been interpreted (Martin Mace and John Grehan, *Britain at War Magazine*).

We have some interesting evidence offered by Bill's comrade P/O Don Street which adds some more colour to the night's sequence of events.

P/O Don Street.

**<u>P/O Don Street in ME595, QR-Y, also explains the journey to the target.</u>**

*'The sortie commenced with a take-off time at 23:04 hours setting course over base at 23:46 hours to join the Lancaster force heading for the target. The first leg south, on a track of 163°, led to point 'A' east of London then onto a track of 150° to turning point 'B' on the mouth of the Somme, then onto the next leg, a track of 163° to a point 'C' just west of the target. The operational height was just under 10,000 feet which was unfortunate as the hazy atmosphere at this altitude reflected the light of a full moon creating very poor horizontal visibility.'* (61 Squ website Veteran's page and Steve Darlow, *Sledgehammers for Tintacks*)

It was a clear night and the moon was shining brightly, leaving the Main Force dangerously exposed to night fighters. This made everybody nervous. On board EE186 Bill's gunners Sgt Eddy O'Shea and Sgt Dennis Bartlett kept calling out to each other over the intercom 'You seen anything, Dennis?'

'Nothing Eddy, keep your eyes peeled everybody'.
Bill kept performing gentle banking manoeuvres with EE186, QR-D to increase their chances of spotting the dreaded attackers.

Eddy called out again 'I think I see something there is a black spot on the moon.'
They were being stalked by a night fighter.
Bill did another banking search and had just brought the aircraft level again when both gunners yelled 'Corkscrew, Port Go!'

'It's an ME 109!' shouted Dennis.
It was too late. The ME 109 had performed a port beam attack. Dennis Bartlett was looking right into the eyes of the German pilot as he fired into their Lancaster. As both gunners fired their guns, bullets and cannon shells raked across the port side of the Bomber. The Mid-Upper turret exploded in pieces around Sgt Dennis Bartlett, transfixed and unable to move he could only watch in horror as death stared him right in the face.

Even as bullets were ripping into the aircraft Bill confidently put EE186 into a steep dive to port.

**<u>WO Dennis Bartlett</u>**

*'I saw the ME109 fly right over us from the port side while he was firing. I was firing back and this was the one and only time I fired my guns at an enemy aircraft. Red hot bullets and tracers were flying all around me as the turret fell to pieces, passing my head and shoulders. I felt pain in my legs where miraculously bullets or cannon shells nicked my legs in four or five places.'*

BF 109 G-6, JG 2, France autumn 1943
(Source, *Bundesarchiv*, Bild 101I-487-3066-04 / Boyer / CC-BY-SA).

**F/Lt Bill North**

*'So far so good, the mission was proceeding according to plan. When suddenly my Gunners Sgt Dennis Bartlett and Sgt Eddy O'Shea called out the dreaded warning, 'Corkscrew Port, Go!' This was an evasive manoeuvre that was taught to Bomber pilots to escape from an attack by a Night Fighter, we had practised this many times during training. It was a violent dive to Port that put incredible stresses on the airframe and it wasn't for the faint hearted. We were being attacked by a German Night Fighter and machine gun bullets were ripping into my Lancaster. We lost our Port Inner Engine port fin and one of our petrol tanks. I was immediately wounded in the left elbow and thigh, my left arm just dropped down useless because the nerve had been severed.'*

**WO Norman Jarvis**

*'At 15 minutes after bombing Eddy said he saw something which might have been a fighter. We did a banking search which revealed nothing and had just resumed straight and level flying when there was a yell from both gunners: 'Corkscrew, Port—Go!' Down Bill went with a steep bank to the left. I heard the rattle of our machine guns and a couple of terrific smacks, then a piercing scream which I thought was one of the gunners mortally wounded. Actually it was Bill. Tracer bullets streamed through my compartment smashing all the perspex in front of me.'*

Ralph Cochrane, 5 Group's inspirational and experimentational Commander, famous for his command of the Dambusters raid, had put great emphasis on constant practise of tactics like the 'Corkscrew'. This manoeuvre was second nature to Bill; he could do things to a Lancaster that weren't supposed to be done. *'I had no nerves about throwing that aircraft around in the sky, I always got the Lanc to do what I wanted it to do'.* 5 Group were known to have their own customised version of the corkscrew and it required huge amounts of physical strength. *'Steep bank to port, full left rudder, fall sideways for a thousand feet, wrench the airleron controls to starboard, soar into climbing turn to the right, then opposite airleron and dive again.'* (Taken from Bomber Command, Max Hastings) Sgt E.A. McDonald, a Rear Gunner with 50 Squadron gave me his recollection of the corkscrew at the 12 June 2011 memorial day. 'Dive Port, Climb Port, Roll, Climb Starboard, Down Port....'

**WO Dennis Bartlett**

*'The first thing you did when you saw a German fighter was to fire some rounds at it, this was called a 'scare burst'. This would generally scare the fighter off to look for another crew that wasn't so alert. Although sometimes firing would give your position away if they hadn't seen you. As the fighter came in to attack, the gunners would shout the 'Corkscrew' instruction. Bill would dive to port 1,000ft, then he'd roll over and dive to starboard 1,000ft. Then he'd change direction and come up starboard for 1,000 feet and then port 1,000 feet, the whole manoeuvre was a diamond shape, which meant he hadn't veered off course. By the time the fighter had the chance to line you up again, you were over on the port side and it took them about another 1,000 feet to get you lined up again.'*

**F/Lt Bill North**

*'The aircraft was now not responding to the controls and in these circumstances I gave the order to 'Abandon Aircraft', it being my intention to attempt to bale out when the crew had left the aircraft. I didn't have to worry about clipping my parachute on because I had a pilot's chute and was sitting on it, it was ready to go. However at this stage Sgt Hackett (the replacement Flight Engineer for Sgt Les Morton) said his parachute harness had been shot off and he couldn't jump.'*

Flight Engineer Sgt Dennis Hatchett shouted to Bill, 'I can't jump - my parachute harness has been shot away!' Here was a dreadful dilemma. If Bill baled out, he would have a good chance of survival, but would leave Dennis Hatchett to certain death. But trying to crash-land the Lancaster in the state she was in after being hit meant almost-certain death for both of them.

Yet for Bill it wasn't a dilemma at all. He made up his mind instantly.

He took the decision to crash land the Lancaster because Sgt Hatchett couldn't jump. In his own words: *'I therefore immediately decided the only option was to crash land the aircraft, not something I wanted to do at night over unfamiliar terrain; there was no way I was going to leave him behind. I didn't know how, but just that I had no choice. When I took this decision I was not aware that two other crew members were still on board the Lancaster. In retrospect having this information would merely have confirmed my course of action.'*

EE186 was plunging earthwards at sickening speeds of between 90 to 200mph, the altimeter was spinning out of control and the instruments were showing crazy readings, dropping at up to 2,000ft per minute while the fuselage shook from the gunners rattling off their Brownings as the ME109 attacked again. The port inner engine had failed and the port flap and petrol tank was shot away, the cockpit had exploded around Bill and Sgt Hatchett, shattering the instrument panel.

Norman Jarvis heard a piercing scream over the intercom while the bomb aimer's compartment and front turret disintegrated around him. He thought one of the gunners had been hit but it was actually Bill. Bill had been shot twice through his left arm by the elbow severing the nerve and twice through the left thigh. There was blood everywhere and Bills left arm was useless.

The Flight Engineer sat frozen with fear while Bill battled with the controls. Bill shouted the abandon aircraft order over the intercom, 'I am hit bad and she's out of control, jump, jump!' The first to jump was Sgt Eddy O'Shea. He swung his rear turret back around unplugged his heated flying suit, oxygen and intercom lines then opened the turret doors behind him. He eased himself out of the cramped compartment grabbed his parachute, clipped it on his harness. He then turned the turret sideways so the rear doors were facing out into open space and threw himself backwards out into the darkness; as he fell away and watched the crippled craft thunder downwards he had no idea if he would see his beloved Skipper and comrades again (This was an extremely difficult manoeuvre to implement while the aircraft was out of control. James Flowers a Rear Gunner with 50 Squ told me he always wore a pilot's parachute to save time in an emergency like this, so he could just quickly turn the turret and fall out backwards. However, the extra padding under his behind made his head touch the top of the rear turret, a lesser sufferance rather than panicking to get his chute on).

Next to bale out was F/Sgt Norman Jarvis as the ME 109 came in for second helpings raking its deadly fire across the Lancaster again. The noise was deafening as bullets smashed in and the remaining Merlin's laboured under the huge stresses as it plunged downwards, with wind blasting down the fuselage from the broken cockpit and the smashed Bomb Aimer's compartment.

**WO Norman Jarvis**

*'Someone said the port fin is shot away and Bill said, 'I am hit bad and she's out of control, jump, jump.' I fitted my parachute and expected any moment to be hit; our guns seemed silent, but Jerry was still firing.*

*I jettisoned the front hatch and then something hit me and that is all I remember of the night's battle'.*

Lancaster front escape hatch, *Newark Air Museum*.

In fact Norman woke up the next morning with no memory of his descent, to find himself lying in a French field with no boots on, covered in condensation and unable to move because he thought he had broken his back. Standing over him were two pretty giggling French girls who both proceeded to bend down and kiss him. It is most likely that in the panic to get out that Norman Jarvis hit his head as he exited the front hatch, buffeted by the aircraft's slipstream. Given these facts it is amazing that Norman even managed to open his parachute!

The Navigator F/Sgt Dave Crowley followed Norman out through the front hatch apparently giving him a helpful push because, 'Norman was taking too long to get out'. This left Bill still fighting desperately to now regain control of the crippled Lancaster.

Bill had no idea that Dennis Bartlett was still on board and going through his own drama. Dennis had no idea what was going on only that they were in serious trouble, the intercom in the turret had smashed and he hadn't heard the order to bale out. After finally unclipping himself from his turret harness he crawled up the fuselage towards the cockpit hanging on for dear life as the g-forces kept wedging him against the sides of the aircraft. Coming back the other way over the main spa was the Wireless Operator Sgt Monty Monteith. 'Dennis, I can't jump my chutes been shot to ribbons! Get down on the floor we are going to crash land.' Monty then proceeded to hold Dennis down on the floor of the fuselage by standing on him. With the ME 109 now gone, back up front Bill had magically regained some control over the Lancaster.

**<u>F/Lt Bill North</u>**

*'If I had known Dennis and Monty were still on board (Monty's parachute was also shot to ribbons) this would have just reconfirmed my intention to crash land the plane. The altimeter was still working, but I could not rely on it fully as it was set at sea level and it would give incorrect information that close to the ground. With night time visibility less than 1,000 yards we knew the ground was close by. I did what I thought was best, initially judging my height by the altimeter and visually as we neared ground level. I managed to regain some control over the aircraft when suddenly tree tops appeared and as I levelled off we could feel them brushing against the underside of the Lancaster. I straightened up and I saw a gap in-between the trees on a hillside, this was our one and only chance to make it.*
*I decided our best chance of survival was to land the aircraft tail first from a height somewhat higher than that adopted during a normal landing. I was of course anxious to avoid creating too much friction on hitting the ground, thus having a situation where the petrol in the wings could ignite with disastrous results and taking us all with it. I brought the nose of the plane up and in we came, I then lowered the front as gently down as I could. We hit the ground and roughly travelled along for some distance before suddenly stopping with a terrific bang as the engines ripped out of their mountings. Sgt Dennis Hatchett was thrown forward into the cockpit and broke his arm and smashed his head open. I looked at my shattered left arm and felt grateful that it was only bullet wounds. If it had been cannon shells it would have been blown off. My uniform and pilots seat was soaking wet and I thought I had wet myself; when I looked down the wetness turned out to be my own blood everywhere. I remember thinking thank God it's blood and I haven't wet myself! Fortunately the crash landing was successful in that all three members of the crew on board plus me survived the impact. I certainly would not be here now if it had blown up.'*

**<u>WO Norman Jarvis</u>**

*'I later found out from Dennis that Bill put the Lancaster into its initial dive after the fighter attacked us and he was hit by bullets, two through his thigh and one through his arm. The kite was badly crippled too and he lost control temporarily. Dennis's Mid-Upper Turret was put out of*

*action and he was wounded. Eddy kept on firing until he got the order to jump, then he was out smartly. I was too from the front and Dave followed me. Bill then asked if they were all out and Monty came up and said he could not jump as his chute was shot up. Dennis was off the intercom and wounded and the Flight Engineer (Sgt Dennis Hatchet) had froze up so poor Bill did a great job of regaining control of the crippled kite and he crash landed in the moonlight. It was a marvellous piece of work, but the impact sent the Engineer through the front of the aircraft injuring him a bit. Monty and Dennis were suffering a great deal from shock and were in tears as they helped our injured skipper out and laid him on the grass some distance away. He gave Monty orders to destroy the aircraft and sent him for help. The Jerries found them and they were taken prisoner at dawn; the Engineer had wondered off though and I believe got back to our lines eventually, so also did Dave after baling out. Eddy was with some French people, but they betrayed him and handed him over to the Jerries. He had the unpleasant experience of viewing all the wrecks of crashed Lancasters with the Germans, all the time expecting to find us amongst the charred and mangled bodies of some of them. It seemed that the losses had been heavy and the other crews had not been as lucky as us to be alive.'*

## W/O Dennis Bartlett

*'After the attack by the Night Fighter I knew we were in trouble. Bill put the Lancaster into a 'corkscrew' and we were plunging out of control towards the ground. I didn't hear the bale out order because the intercom was smashed. With great difficulty I managed to unfasten my turret harness and dropped down onto the floor of the fuselage. It was difficult to move because of the G-forces wedging me against the interior surfaces. I started to crawl up towards the cockpit and suddenly Monty was coming back the other way over the main spar. He was shouting that he couldn't jump because his parachute was shot up and that we were going to crash land. He immediately stood on me to hold me down for the impact. This was a really brave thing to do and it still moves me. It all happened very quickly and all of a sudden Bill managed to level the plane up just before we hit the ground. It was a hell of a bump and Monty was thrown down. The aircraft was really still and quiet and we expected it to instantly explode, but it didn't. Monty and I made our way up to the cockpit where we found Bill who was seriously injured. The Flight Engineer had been thrown forwards as well and had cut his head open. Someone said, 'let's get the hell out of here.' We knew we had to get out fast as the Lancaster could still explode.*

*We all helped Bill out of the top of the cockpit and carried him as far away as we could. I stayed with Bill, it was really upsetting. I thought he was going to die. Monty went back to set fire to the aircraft with the flare gun, but came back a couple of minutes later to say he couldn't do it. Sgt Hatchett although injured decided to try and escape, but Monty and I couldn't leave Bill by himself. We all stayed together until the morning when some French civilians came. Bill was too badly injured to move and a Luftwaffe Officer came and took us POW. We all ended up at Beauvais Hospital together. We wouldn't have made it without Bill he was an outstanding pilot and friend; he saved us so many times. This was the third crash we had walked away from and there were countless other occasions where his calmness and quick thinking saved the day.'*

They all sat there in a dazed stunned silence. It took some minutes before someone shouted 'Let's get the hell out of here before she blows.' One by one they clambered out of the wreckage, all of them helping their injured Skipper out of the top of the cockpit and away from the smouldering plane which still hadn't caught fire. Monty and Dennis were suffering from shock and had tears in their eyes, Bill was in such a bad way that they thought he was going to die.

Monty went back to fire the aircraft (destroy the aircraft by setting fire to it so it would be of no use to the Germans). He came back to where Bill was stretchered out on the side of the hill and said he just couldn't do it. Fortunately for us now he didn't, because we now have a set of remarkable pictures of the final resting place of EE186, QR-D. Although injured, Sgt Hatchett decided to try and evade capture which he successfully did alongside F/S Dave Crowley, both of them linking up with our forces with help from a French farmer, and making it back to England.

**Sgt Dennis John Hatchett, 1834626, taken from M.I.9. Escape report.**

*'We took off from Skellingthorpe in a Lancaster aircraft at 23:30 hours on the 4 July 1944. I was a last-minute relief man and therefore did not know the exact target. On our return journey to base the a/c was attacked by a NF, a FW190. The pilot was wounded in both legs. One of our motors caught fire and we received orders to bale out. My parachute harness was damaged by a bullet which entered my shoulder and I remained in the a/c. We crash-landed near SUZAY (NW EUROPE 1:250,000, Sheet 7, R49) at about 02:15 hours on 5 July. All the remaining members of the crew got out of the a/c. With the help of Sgt Monteith, the Wireless Operator, I took the pilot and the Mid-Upper Gunner to the top of a hill about 50 or 60*

*yards away and gave them first aid. We then wrapped both of them up in a parachute because they could not be moved owing to the seriousness of their wounds. I was wounded myself in the right arm and left shoulder and had a fractured left arm. The Wireless Operator and I parted to evade separately.'*

**F/Sgt Dave Crowley, taken from M.I.9. Escape report.**

*'We took off from Skellingthorpe in a Lancaster aircraft at 23:30 hours on 4 July 1944 to bomb a target north of PARIS. We bombed the target and on the return journey were shot down by a Night Fighter. The order was given to bale out and I landed in the middle of a field near the village of CHAUMONT EN VEXIN. I buried my parachute harness and Mae West and then started walking in the direction of ROUEN.'*

Sgt Eddy O'Shea got given away by a French informer and taken POW. He then had the grim task of viewing all the crashed Bomber sites to see if any were his crew. Expecting any time to find Bill and the boys and hugely relieved not too, he later told Bill that the site of all the mangled bodies stayed with him for a long time. F/Sgt Norman Jarvis was taken POW and early that morning Bill, Monty and Dennis (who both would not leave Bill) after a visit from French civilians were taken POW by a Luftwaffe Officer. So battered, bruised and shot up the crew of EE186, QR-D were taken away to remain POWs for the rest of the war.

**F/Lt Bill North**

*'What is my overriding feeling about what happened to my crew and to me on the 4/5 July 1944? Firstly, one of immense relief and satisfaction that my entire crew survived. We had become the firmest of friends as well as comrades and had complete confidence in each other's abilities. It would have been a bitter blow if any one of my crew had failed to survive. In the event two evaded capture (Navigator F/Sgt Dave Crowley and Flight Engineer Sgt Hatchett, with me for the first time in place of my regular Engineer, Les Morton) and five became POWs. Secondly, it is a source of amazement that I managed to crash my Lancaster at night without serious injury to anyone on board. I was never scared of dying; the only fear I ever had was of letting my crew down. Whilst I hesitate to suggest we were unique—I have yet to meet any Lancaster pilot who has had a similar experience. Which leads me to ask, 'Was there a Guardian Angel looking after us?'*

Crash site of Bill's Lancaster EE186, QR-D, near Harquency northern France (source, *Laurent Viton and Jean Erisay*).

Bill attributes their saving that night to his Guardian Angel and perhaps there was some divine intervention (Eddy O'Shea firmly believed they were in God's hands), but what must be noted is Bill's outstanding skill as a Bomber pilot. The a/c was fatally damaged, it was dark and unfamiliar terrain and Bill was seriously injured. Staring death right in the face, he stayed cool and calm, miraculously managing to save that stricken Lancaster Bomber he had grown so fond of and his faithful crew. Bill had an exceptional quality akin to other great natural born flyers like Neil Armstrong, which was to stay cool and calm in adversity. I think he should have been awarded at least a DFC and most definitely a Victoria Cross for his outstanding courage, selflessness, skill and bravery, but sadly this was not to be. One thing is for sure though that as the drama unfolded in the dark moonlit skies over France and later on on that French hillside, is that those seven young men that night rode right through deaths shadow; stared death right in the face, eye to eye and emerged battered and bruised into the morning light with their lives intact and eternal memories burned into their very beings.

Somehow or other this outstanding act of valour from a truly extraordinary man was missed by the higher authorities and even after all this time I think he is still deserving of this award. 22 RAF personnel were awarded the Victoria Cross during WW2, 12 of those decorations being given posthumously. I am sure there are many other unrecorded acts of valour we will never know of from crews that were lost in similar circumstances.

**H.James Flowers 2011 (Rear Gunner 50 Squadron Skellingthorpe)**

*'Pilot Officer Bill North, though badly injured during an attack on their aircraft by an enemy fighter, made a conscious decision to remain at the controls of his aircraft when he found out two of his crew members could not bale out, he then performed a near miracle act by one-handedly crash landing his aircraft, thereby saving all their lives.*
*I find it difficult to believe that this act of unselfish bravery and skill has not received recognition of the highest order.'*

**Sgt Eddy O'Shea, 1945**

*'Wounded as he was, he worked a miracle of courage to bring his plane down safely in an unknown country in pitch darkness. He could have jumped as I and two others did, but the WOPs chute was in ribbons so he risked certain death to save them. The chance was a million to one—and if you think I am exaggerating ask any bomber pilot you meet whether he would like to risk a crash landing at night in the wooded area around Paris—or anywhere else for that matter.'*

**F/Lt Jeff Gray, April 2013**

*'Bill North was seriously injured, it was night time and unfamiliar terrain, his Lancaster was fatally damaged and out of control. I don't know how he crash landed without the aircraft exploding! It was an act of pure courage and I think they also experienced a certain amount of good luck too. It is unheard of!'*

**W/O Dennis Bartlett, 2011 (Bill's Mid Upper Gunner and last living witness)**

*'When Chris Keltie tracked me down and found me in March 2011 I could not believe that Bill was still alive and that we were going to meet each other again after all these years. When I walked into his room in Basingstoke on the 18 March 2011 and saw him again although physically different in appearance, it was like yesterday, he was the same true friend and man I knew in 1944. The memories of the night we crashed in France have been with me for 67 years and I and the crew owe our lives to Bill. Without a thought for himself and whilst gravely injured he stayed on board*

*our doomed Lancaster Bomber in order to save us. It still moves me to this day to think of this and it was quite an emotional day as we sat together and remembered our time together in Bomber Command.'*

**F/Lt Bill North**

*'No, I was not specially decorated. I simply received the normal medals. Of course one has to remember that no-one in authority would have learned of our crash landing and I for my part, was only too pleased that we survived the war – particularly as I have recently learned of the extent of the RAF losses on 4/5 July 1944. I was not afraid, there was so much to do and think about what would follow. Above all I was concerned about how strong my father would be when he received the telegram telling him I was missing.'*

**Kate and Harold Crowley (Dave's mum and dad) from letter 11 Jan 1945, quoting Dave's friend P/O Paul Slome, W/C Doubleday's F/Eng who also flew with Bill.**

*'Paul was saying how very fond of Bill he was and how cool headed and capable he was. We weren't a bit surprised to hear Bill landed his plane as by Dave's account of him he is the perfect pilot.'*

**John W Monteith (Monty's dad, May 1945)**

*'I seem to know the lad so well as Ivor was continually talking about him, they all seemed to be a happy crowd.'*

The 'North Crew' was now separated. Dave Crowley and Dennis Hatchet evaded capture with help from French civilians. Crews were supplied with escape kits which included, silk maps, foreign currency, chocolate bars and water purifying tablets. The MI9 escape reports record Crowley arriving back in the UK on 29 Aug 1944 and Hatchett on 9 Sept 1944. Both men resumed their duties, although not appearing in the 61 Squ ORB on any more Operations. (This was not unusual as evaders had knowledge of the escape lines. Also at this point Senior Officers should have become aware of Bill's courageous act from the escape reports) Bill and the remaining crew were taken POW and spent time in a French Hospital before being separated again. Bill went to Stalag Luft 1 for Officers at Barth on the Baltic Coast and Norman, Dennis, Monty and Eddy went to Stalag Luft 7 for Aircrew in Germany. Each would have their own perilous adventures.

Although miles apart from each other and later separated by time itself the bond between Bill's crew was and still is phenomenal.

After the war in a letter to Bill's parents on 10 June 1945, Sgt Eddy O'Shea said, *'As for me I will never fly again because of my responsibilities, much as I'd like to; but I'd fly to hell and back again with Bill North.'*

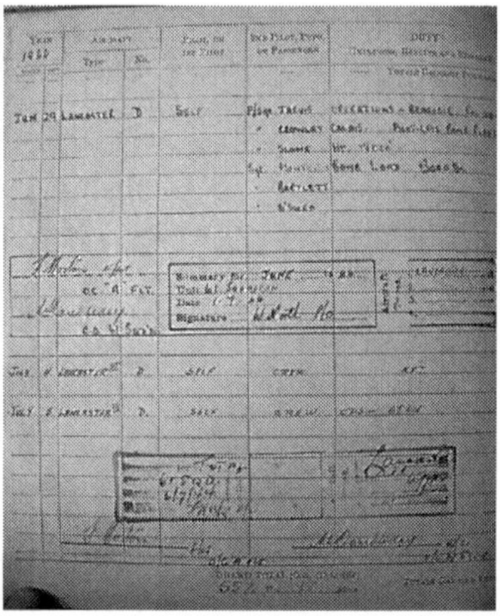

The entry in Bill's RAF Log Book for 5 July 1944, which has been left unfinished. The words 'missing' were typed in red on the adjoining page and the entry is signed by the Officer Commanding 'A' Flight F/Lt F Norton, who flew in JB138, 'Just Jane' on 5 July and Squadron OC, W/C AW Doubleday.

This set of photographs really do speak for themselves. A few points of interest must be noted though. The damage inflicted by the Night Fighter can be clearly seen. The cockpit, nose and mid-upper turret have all been shattered as described by the crew. When Dennis Bartlett saw the photos for the first time, he was astounded at the damage to his turret and still couldn't believe he got out of it alive. The aircraft itself is literally in pieces. The back section has broken away as can be seen in the above photo. The port inner engine has been completely ripped out of its mountings and is lying in front of the cockpit; the wing area behind it has been shredded. The remaining engines have all come out of their mountings and it is a miracle that the damage sustained on landing didn't ignite the fuel tanks.

# Chapter Sixteen

## St Leu, the appendix

This Chapter records some of the finer details to do with Bomber Command's Operations to take out the VI site at St Leu, including the horrific loss statistics and the Night Fighter Squadrons that were operating that night. Also shown are two examples of very similar crashes to Bill's that demonstrate how lucky he was to survive his experience that night.

Some of the other 61 Squadron pilots who flew to St Leu that night with Bill were:- OC 'A' Flight, F/Lt F Norton in JB138, F/Lt BS Turner in ED860, P/O DE White in EE176, 5th Op for F/S GM Taylor (RCAF), F/Lt BM Acott, P/O RA Dear, P/O JE Gibberd, P/O DW Simmons (RAAF), P/O PH Martin (RAAF), P/O DG Bates, P/O H Watkins, F/O ER Church (RCAF) and P/O Don Street who was attacked by a JU88 on the return journey. (See St Leu appendix) With the exception of Bill's Fail to Return and F/O S Parker's fail to bomb this Operation's timing and efficiency was excellent with great coordination with PFF (all pilots reported good marking and bombing). 20 a/c took from 22:25 to 23:35, bombed from 01:35 to 01:45 and all except Bill landed back at Skellingthorpe from 03:10 to 03:54.

The attack at St Leu on 4/5 July was made by two forces with the intention of caving in the tunnels and to heavily crater the area around the tunnel entrances causing major disruption to the road and rail links (communications). The first attack was made by 17 Lancasters from 617 Squ with W/Cmdr Leonard Cheshire marking the target in his Mustang. 617 were all carrying 12,000lb Tallboys. The Main Force with Bill and his crew in followed 617 Squ almost immediately carrying 1156.8 tons of high explosive and 5.2 tons of incendiary bombs, Zero hour was 01:45 hours. 463 Squ were given a specialist task of dropping fragmentation bombs on the numerous AA positions around the target.

The bombing at St Leu was accurate, but 13 Lancasters were lost when German fighters engaged the force; 8 Lancasters were complete losses 2, (8/8s) and 6, (7/7s), with all the 58 crew members dying, 3 more Lancasters were lost, 2 with (6/7s) crew and 1 with (6/8), (18 crew dead and 4 surviving).1 Lancaster from 106 Squadron that was lost went down with its Pilot F/O F Crosier giving his life, the rest of his crew baling out and surviving. 9 crewmen evaded capture including 2 of Bill's crew and 8 were taken POW including Bill and the remainder of his crew. 77 crew died at St. Leu and are buried at various French cemeteries in the surrounding areas, 7 crew members have no resting place and are commemorated at the RAF Runnymede Memorial (The names of 20,000 RAF crew who have no known resting place are on the ledgers here, when you walk around this peaceful place reflecting on these losses, it really does overwhelm the mind).

The other Ops this night were to attack Railway Yards at Orleans and Villeneuve, both targets were accurately bombed with 12 Lancasters and 4 Halifaxes lost. Of those lost was 1, 8/8. 3, (7/7s). 2, (6/7s), (41 men), with a further 18 crewmen dead and the rest POW, Evd. The only 2 crews to completely survive the Villeneuve Ops baleed out from two 419 Squ Lancasters. Out Of the 712 sorties flown by Bomber Command that night, 29 aircraft and 136 men were lost (3.9 per cent), a grave loss in men and machines for Bomber Command.

Bomber Command returned to St Leu 2 days later on the 7/8 July and Night Fighters again decimated the Force with even greater losses. 32 a/c were lost, 10 of them (7/7s). 50 Squ lost 3 a/c and 61 Squadron lost two familiar names; P/O RH Passant (RAAF) and his whole crew and F/L WE Grantham with 4 of his crew. It was a heavy night for 5 Group, 106 and 207 Squ's lost 5 a/c each. What is apparent and confirms Norman Jarvis's comment is that the Germans were prepared to fiercely defend the flying bomb storage depots and launch sites and this was at great loss to Bomber Command and its valiant aircrews. I have spent much time examining the Night Fighter activity that night (4/5 July) in an attempt to reveal which pilot attacked Bill's Lancaster. The time span we are looking at for the attack was from Zero hour-01:45, the bombing time, leaving the target and to 02:00 when Bill crash landed near Harquency.

The 20 Lancasters from 61 Squ took off at Skellingthorpe from 22:25 to 23:35 and formed up over England, leading to point 'A' east of London then point 'B' on the mouth of the Somme, then to point 'C' to attack from the west of St Leu. Their bombing heights ranged from 12,000 to 18,000ft and the bombing times were in a 10 minute time period, 01:35 to 01:45. Except Bill they all returned to base from 03:10 to 03:54 P/O Don Street being one of the first to land.

214 Squ were operating a Mandrel screen this night. This was an airborne radar jamming device working at 85-135 MHz to counter the Freya early warning system which was part of the Kammhuber-Line air defence system. Set up by Joseph Kammhuber, NF's would be vectored into a series of box grids according to where radar indicated Bomber Streams were entering enemy airspace.

So now we come to the German Night Fighter Squadrons/Groups that were operating on the 4/5 July 1944. *Nachtjagdgeschwader* 1/JG301, (Bf 109G and FW 190's, from Épinoy) 3/JG301, 2/NJG2, 3/NJG2, 2/NJG4, 8NJGF. There were also Me410's and Ju88's up in the air as well.

It is fascinating to follow the progress of the NF Squadrons against the Bomber Streams in and out of the target areas. As the Main Force is forming up over England from 23:29 to 00:29, 36 NFs from 2/NJG2 and 2/NJG4 are vectored towards Dieppe. At 00:20, 10 NF's of 1/NJG5 are vectored towards Paris. At 00:23, 13 Ju88's from Florennes are redirected from Arras-Cambrai to the Creil area. A Me 410 is shot down by a 141 Squ Mosquito, a 169 Squ Mosquito downs a Me 110 and a 239 Squ Mosquito downs a Me 110. At 00:35 the Villeneuve/Orleans Main Force is attacked. As the St Leu Main Force enters French airspace 1/NJG3 are vectored towards Abbeville at 01:00. From 01:01 to 01:15 the St Leu main force precedes SSE towards Paris. At 01:07 the German controller orders all NF's to Abbeville. From 01:16 to 01:30 the St Leu Force continues SSE, turns towards and arrives at the target. At this point aircrews start witnessing bombers falling from the sky. From 01:31 to 01:45 the St Leu Main Force attacks the target, flak is noted (Norman Jarvis) and many combats are seen with more bombers shot down. The Force breaks up into three waves for the journey home; this is when Bill is attacked as NF's follow the first wave North and West. At 01:32 a 617 Squ crew shoot down a Ju88 and at 01:39 a 207 Squ crew shoot down a ME 109. At 01:39 a 97 Squ PFF crew shoot down a Me410 and at 01:43 a 9 Squ crew claim an ME 110. At 01:44 a 630 Squ crew shoot down what they believe to be a Do 217. From 01:46 onwards Bill's Lancaster EE186 is attacked and shot down alongside 9, 57, 463 and 106 Squadron Lancasters.

At 01:50 P/O Don Street had a very close escape after being attacked by a Ju88 on his 23 Operation.

**<u>P/O Don Street explains leaving St Leu and the attack</u>**

*'It was with a feeling of satisfaction and relief that we turned out of the target area onto a northerly track of 026° towards turning point 'D'. In a short time turning point 'D' arrived, then onto a longer run to point 'E' on a course of 349°. The four Merlin engines were harmonized at 2,600 revs per minute, the pressures and temperatures were as they should be.'*

**<u>Don Street's Rear Gunner Sgt Geoff Gilbert explains coming eye to eye with the Ju 88 that had been stalking them after taking evasive action</u>:-**

*'We had gone into the violent corkscrew and he was underneath us. Then I saw the Ju 88. He was so close. I was looking right at him and I could see the Ju 88's crew looking right up at me. I just depressed my guns and fired. The next thing I knew he was going down in flames.'*

(A more detailed account of the St Leu raid and of P/O Don Streets story can be found on 50/61 Squ's website and in Steve Darlow's excellent book *Sledgehammers for Tintacks*).

One of the other 61 Squ crews that flew alongside Bill also had a close call with a NF. F/O H Watkins was the Skipper of Lanc R5856, QR-Q. Watkins Bomb Aimer F/S Edgar Ray explains what happened after the bombing run at 01:37:- *'Suddenly, Carson Jack Foy, our rear gunner, yelled out over the intercom 'Fighter, Fighter, corkscrew port. Go! Skipper Harry Watkins dived the a/c to port. At the same time we heard Jack's guns chattering away as the fighter dived past and disappeared underneath us.'* The crew were attacked a further three times with Jack's guns overheating from firing so many rounds off and leaving only one barrel working! After the fourth attack they managed to get away and the rear gunner was credited with a possible NF victory. This was an extremely stressful experience for this crew and they were all relieved to make it home.

The NF activity was intense on the 4/5 July and even more so on the return 7/8 July with over double the a/c lost. The Germans were prepared to and ferociously defended the V1 storage sites. After researching the list of which German pilot claimed individual Lancasters, I still have not tracked down the NF that shot down Bill. However, I have narrowed the search down to two names which fit the timing, 01:52 Jorg Sharing and 01:55 Heinz Horst, both claiming 4 engined bombers (There is not enough time or space to research this further at this point, some homework for the future perhaps).

Bill and his crew's survival circumstances on 4/5 July appear to be quite unique in that they were the only crew to all survive the St Leu Operation's losses that night and subsequent research of other Lancaster crashes seems to confirm this too. After an astounding recovery of the aircraft by Bill and an unbelievable crash landing, alongside the many other near death experiences they went through it makes the hairs on the back of your neck stand on end. If you examine the loss statistics from all Bill's Operations it really hammers home how lucky the crew were to be alive. They rode in the shadow of death right the way through their whole service and were blessed until the bitter end of WW2. Referring to his crash landing Bill's comment, *'I have yet to meet any Lancaster pilot who has had a similar experience,'* seems to stand on its own.

Two catastrophic examples of what happens when a heavy bomber attempted a crash landing at night and day are now shown. Back to 619

Squadron and the comrades of Bills friends P/O Davis, Peter Knox and George Moggridge. The crew of 619 Squ's Lancaster LM446 Captained by P/O JM Aitken (RNZAF) were an experienced crew, they had completed 15 operations, a similar number to Bill and on the 9 May 1944 they were about to fly on their 16th Op. Their Lancaster LM466, PG-H, its Merlin engines roaring in unison took off from Dunham Lodge at 22:15, this was the night before Bill flew his Op to Lille. One extra crewman was on board, P/O Goodwin, who was flying his first 'Second dickie' Op just like Bill had done on 8 May to Brest. The target was the Gnome engine manufacturing plant at Gennevilliers, just outside Paris.

Shortly after leaving the target at about 01:30 LM446 was attacked by a Night Fighter, possibly piloted by FT Neumann. The a/c was fatally damaged and the rear gunner W.O Officer Leslie Rhodes was wounded in the attack and with the port engine on fire P/O Aitken attempted to try and get back to England. Above the village of Aubergenville he like Bill, decided the only option was to crash-land his Lancaster and gave the order to abandon the doomed a/c. P/O Aitken circled the village for about 20 minutes trying to line up along the old bank of the Seine River where there was a flat area, so deliberately avoiding the village. Shortly before the crash PO Goodwin baled out, but the a/c was too low and his parachute failed to open. He died next to the railyards at Epone, about 5 km from Aubergenville. W.O Rhodes baled out at the same time, from the rear turret, and was captured wounded by the Germans the next morning. This was witnessed by the villagers who also were watching as LM446 lined up on the flat area and came in to crash-land. Although the crash was controlled at the end of the flat area LM446 hit a small raised bank and exploded, the noise was heard throughout the whole area. By the time the villagers arrived at the crash site it was too late for the remaining crew with exploding ammunition making any rescue attempts too dangerous.

In the morning schoolchildren on their way to classes told their teacher M. Depuissier what had happened. Conscious of the fact that they should mourn the dead M. Depuissier requested that the bodies be buried in the village cemetery with full Military Honours and male children between the ages of 5 and 15 were requested to witness the ceremony. The body of PO Goodwin was later retrieved from Epone and buried with his 6 comrades; this could quite easily have been Bill and his crew (This story came courtesy of New Zealander John Aitken, the nephew of pilot P/O JM Aitken whilst I was researching Lancaster crashes on the internet).

The second and most similar crash to Bill's that I have come across is recorded in the photographic section from page 52 of Steve Darlow's

*Sledgehammers for Tintacks* and WR Chorley's *1944 Losses* p369. Very similar to the above account this incident again demonstrates how easily aircraft explode when they crash land even in controlled circumstances, it also reinforces the fact that Bill should have been awarded a VC. This was a crash landing in daylight as opposed to Bill's night-time crash landing. On 4 August 1944 a 635 Squ Lanc ND811, F2-T captained by S/L IW Bazalgette VC, DFC, took off from Downham Market at 11:15 to attack the Flying Bomb storage depot at Trossy St Maximin. It was hit by flak which knocked out both starboard engines and the a/c was partially abandoned, four of the crew baleed out. S/L Bazalgette remained on board and attempted to crash land and save the remaining two crew members just like Bill did. As it touched down near Senantes (Eure-et- Loir) it exploded killing everyone left on board, for this gallant display of courage S/L Bazalgette was awarded a posthumous VC published on the 17 August 1945 (Les Morton and Percy Cannings also flew to Trossy the day before, 3 Aug). As Steve Darlow explains the Flying Bomb sites were the cause of heavy Bomber Command losses. As previously mentioned we know the authorities would have been aware of Bill's crash landing from Crowley and Hatchet's M19 escape reports, but somehow or other Bill was overlooked for a well deserved award.

The unrecognisable remains of S/L Bazalgette's Lancaster, ND811, FT-2 near Senantes. If Bill's Lancaster EE186, QR-D had exploded on touchdown, it would have looked very much like this (source, photographic section of *Sledgehammers for Tintacks*, Steve Darlow).

The loss rate in Bomber Command can be looked at another way. If a Squadron was able to put into the air an average of twenty bombers on operating nights, then over five operating nights it could expect to lose three aircraft. In just three months during Bill's Operational service at Skellingthorpe (May 1943 to July 1944) 50 Squadron lost 20 Lancasters, equal to its average fighting force. In the entire war 50 Squadron lost 1,002 aircrew. 61 Squadron lost 11 Lancasters during these 3 months faring slightly better during the Battle of Normandy, with a total of 981 aircrew lost during Operations (61 Squ returned to St Leu again on the 5 Aug 1944 with W/C AW Doubleday, there were no Fail to Returns this time).

The last 61 Squ loss was F/L AF Greenfield DFC (RAAF) in RF121, QR-J, (5/7) to Hamburg on 9 April 1945.

On the 27 January 1945 the Red Army liberated one of the largest German extermination and concentration camps freeing the remaining 7,500 inmates; it was called Auschwitz. In the spring of 1945 Russian reports started to filter through to the west of a network of camps in Poland where unimaginable horrors and mass industrialised extermination had taken place. These reports were played down in the Western press and thought to be exaggerated by the Allied Military and establishment.

On the 15 April 1945 Bergen-Belson was liberated by the British Army and on the 29 April 1945 Dachau was liberated by US Forces. The German war machine had finally been ground down by the strength, industrial might, eccentric scientific community and strong, stubborn political and military characters of America, Russia and Great Britain. The Allies now found out for themselves the full true evil horror of the war that Nazi-Germany had inflicted upon Europe. For those who had any doubts, never was it more apparent at this point what the Allies had been fighting for and that it was a just and noble cause; for one and all the consequences of not winning were unthinkable.

# Chapter Seventeen

## Les Morton finishes his Tour.

W/O Les Morton flew with some of the most senior men in 61 Squ. Squadron Commanding Officer, Wing Commander WD Pexton DFC, AFC, Squadron Leader HW Horsley AFC,(KIA) and Squadron Leader SJ Beard. Also some of 61 Squ's most outstanding pilots, P/O Bill North, F/O NT Collins (RAAF), F/O DW Boon, F/O NE Hoad, F/O NP Blaine, P/O D Street, and P/O Gerry Taylor,(KIA). He flew 9 daylight Ops and 4 nights Ops with GM Taylor. He also flew a further 5 daylight Ops with these other outstanding men.

The loss of Lancaster ME596 has a fascinating story behind it, both happy and sad. It involves Bill's Flt/Eng Sgt Les Morton who flew with P/O Gerry Taylor, 13 (lucky for some) times from 29 June 1944, Beauvoir to 11th Aug 1944 Bordeaux. It all starts back on Bill's first Op to Lille on 10/11 May 1944. As we know Lille was a horrific first Op for Bill and the crew and they saw many a/c explode around them in the sky. One a/c in particular exploded right in front of them on the bombing run and they amazingly flew right through the wreckage without any harm coming to them or their famous 'Ton-up' Lancaster EE176, QR-M, 'Mickey the Moocher'. Bill explained that Les Morton was never the same again after this Op and suffered terribly with his nerves. Australian W/C AW Doubleday spent a lot of time with Les and helped him to overcome his fears. Bill also gave Les huge amounts of support. While Doubleday was helping Les who flew on and off with Bill after this, he gave Bill his own Flt/Eng Sgt J Slome to fly with him.

Les was due to fly again on 4/5 July with Bill to St Leu, but was replaced by Sgt Hatchett. Bill was shot down on this Op and when Les walked into the Skellingthorpe mess everyone thought they had seen a ghost as they thought he had been lost with Bill at St Leu. Les who had already flown with P/O Gerry Taylor's Canadian crew was then permanently assigned to him and subsequently became really good friends with Gerry Taylor.

Now to the night where Lancaster ME596 was lost. Les told me that the pilots often flew in a Lancaster that they considered their own and would have great affection for it. With Bill it was EE186, QR-D for Dog, the a/c he was shot down in. With Gerry Taylor and his crew it was ME596, QR-H, 'Hell's A Poppin', Les had flown in this a/c 13 times with Gerry up to 11/12 Aug and was due to fly again with him on the 12/13 Aug to Russelheim (Remarkably ME596 was the same a/c that Tommy Farmiloe had his extraordinary lucky escape in on 24/25 March 1944 to Berlin, see Chapter 10).

**W/O Les Morton**

*'When Bill got shot down at St Leu on 4/5 July I walked into the mess the morning after and a few of the lads thought they had seen a ghost. I was supposed to go on that Operation, but had been ill so I missed it. I was really worried about Bill and the boys, I really missed him. A bit later in the year we eventually heard that he was a POW and it was a huge relief to me. I was then put with a Canadian crew Skippered by P/O Gerry Taylor. I had actually flown with this crew already and we settled down to do 12 or 13 Ops together. We were getting ready to go on the Russelheim mission when W/C Doubleday called Gerry and I in to see him at the last minute. He requested that I give up my place on this Operation for F/S JK Burnside, so this chap could complete the last mission of his 2nd Tour of Operations. Gerry wasn't too pleased and didn't want another Flt/Eng replacing me, but he was overruled by the W/C.* I was left behind again and in the morning Gerry Taylor's crew was posted in the Flight Room as a 'Fail to Return'. I really missed Gerry Taylor we had become really good friends and I didn't find out that the crew had died until much later on. There was only one survivor, the Bomb Aimer F/O J Meek. I felt awful and have done ever since; once again I had cheated death and felt lucky to be alive. Of course the other really sad thing about this whole story is that F/S JK Burnside was also killed on his last Op.'*

*It was in fact so last minute that although hard to see, Les Morton's name was left on the 61 Squ ORB for ME596 and its FTR.

Those cruel survival odds had finally caught up with F/S JK Burnside, who as Les says was sadly lost on the very last mission of his 2nd Tour. There is a beautiful Lancaster Memorial at Weiswampach, in Luxembourg which commemorates P/O Gerry Taylor's crew and also 7 crewmen from 75 Squ who were shot down in the same area that night.

In 2011 I placed a wreath at the 50/61 Squadron Memorial on Memorial Day in June on behalf of Les for Gerry Taylor and the crew of ME596. Les emigrated to Australia after the war after a long battle with Leukaemia, passed away on 4 April 2013, he has been a constant source of info to me. It really is quite miraculous how Les Morton survived his Tour, while those he flew with were lost on various Ops; he just kept on dodging his way through deaths shadow. Les managed to miss the St Leu Op that Bill went down on, missed the Russelheim Op with Gerry Taylor and one month after his Tour expired, S/L HW Horsley and his crew were killed at Skellingthorpe during take-off in the same a/c they had flown in together.

Bill North said, *'I think Les Morton was even luckier than I was, he managed to miss all the Ops that his crews went down on. Les was a courageous example of a crewman who overcame his nerves and went on to complete his tour of Ops.'*

Continuing on from the 29 June Daylight Op to Beauvoir that Les flew on with P/O Gerry Taylor:- After Bill was shot down at St Leu, Les had three weeks leave. He then resumed Ops with his new Skipper newly promoted F/O Gerry Taylor.

A quick point of interest: Eight days after Bill was shot down on the 5 July 1944, an extraordinary incident occurred at the same airfield that he had made an emergency landing on 7 June 1944. It had an immediate impact on Bomber Command's casualty statistics.

On Thursday 13 July 1944 a lost, almost out of fuel, Ju 88 G-1, code 4R+UR Night Fighter from 7 NJG/2 landed at Woodbridge airfield. The rookie German aircrew had misread their compass and flown in the opposite direction and believed Woodbridge to be their home base. The ground staff and the aircrew were as surprised as each other when they finally realised what had happened. The Ju 88 carried all the latest electronic technology the Germans were using to track and shoot down British Bombers. The Royal Aircraft Establishment (RAE) immediately started testing and flying the Ju88 and the results shocked everybody. The onboard radar tracking systems could pinpoint individual bombers in the night sky many miles ahead and explained the high losses experienced by Bomber Command. The counter measures implemented instantly started to save lives, with the average figure of 250 lost a/c per month dropping to as low as 50. It gave the Allies the upper hand in the constant technology battle that swung to and fro throughout the War.

Ju 88 G-1, 4R+UR at Woodbrige, July 1944 (source, Air Intelligence 2 (g), Inspection of Crashed or Captured Enemy Aircraft, Report Serial No. 242 dated 16th July 1944, Report No. 8 / 151: Junkers Ju 88 G-1 Night Fighter and BBC Radio 4, *Things We Forgot to Remember*, Michael Portillo, *The Junkers of Woodbridge Airfield*).

**25 July 1944**, ME596, QR-H, F/O G Taylor, Daylight Op to St Cyr, Paris (Aircraft Works) Hit by flak (1 Lanc lost on this raid).

**26/27 July 1944**, ME596, QR-H, F/O G Taylor, Night Op to Givors. Electrical storms (4 Lancs and 2 Mosquitoes lost).

**28/29 July 1944**, ME596, QR-H, F/O G Taylor, Night Op to Stuttgart (39 Lancasters were lost here including one 61 Squ Lanc LM452, QR-T, (6/7) with F/S WR MacPherson with 18 Halifaxes and 4 Lancs lost at Hamburg).

**30 July 1944**, ME596, QR-H, F/O G Taylor, Daylight Op to Cahagnes (Troop concentration, Villiers Bocage-Caumont) (4 Lancs lost, including one 97 Squ NE121, OF-E (6/8) with F/L HAB Baker and crew.)

**31 July 1944**, ME596, QR-H, F/O G Taylor, Daylight Op to Rilly-La-Montage (Railway yards and tunnel) 2 Lancs lost, including ex 61 Squ F/Lt Bill Reid VC who was flying with 617 Squ. His Lanc ME557, KC-S was hit by bombs from above just after releasing its Tallboy, as it broke up F/Lt Reid and F/O D Luker survived to become POWs.

**1 Aug 1944**, ME596, QR-H, F/O G Taylor, Daylight Op to Beach Head (No bombs dropped, cloud base to low) (No a/c lost) Percy Cannings flew on Daylight Op to mark Siracourt in ND961, OF-N, F/L WM Reid, mission also abandoned due to low cloud.

**2 Aug 1944**, ME596, QR-H, F/O G Taylor, Daylight Op, Bois de Cassan (Ammunition dump) (2 Lancs lost) Percy Cannings flew on Daylight Op to mark L'Isle Adam in PB156, OF-O, F/L WM Reid.

**3 Aug 1944**, ME596, QR-H, F/O G Taylor, Daylight Op, Trossy-St-Maximin or Maxim (Flying bomb storage site) (6 Lancs lost) Percy Cannings flew alongside Les to mark this target in ND961, OF-N, F/L WM Reid. (On 4 Aug 635 Squ's S/L IW Bazalgette VC DFC was posthumously awarded a VC for attempting to crash land his a/c to save his remaining crew; on touching down the a/c exploded.)

**5 Aug 1944**, ME596, QR-H, F/O G Taylor, Daylight Op, St-Leu-d'Esserent (Flying bomb storage site) (no a/c lost from this raid, but 2 Lancs from other Ops) Percy Cannings flew alongside Les to mark this target in ND961, OF-N, F/L WM Reid (Slight heavy/moderate flak, no sign of Fighters).

**7/8 Aug 1944**, ME596, QR-H, F/O G Taylor, Night Op to Secqueville-La-Campagne (German Army HQ) (10 Lancs lost, including two from 50 Squ).

**9/10 Aug 1944**, ME596, QR-H, F/O G Taylor, Night Op to Châtellerault, (Oil storage dump) Lost 2 engines. Percy Cannings flew alongside Les to mark this target in ND961, OF-N, F/L WM Reid. (2 Lancs lost in collision over target, 50 Squ and 619 Squ, one survivor).

**11 Aug 1944**, ME596, QR-H, F/O G Taylor, Daylight Op to Bordeaux (Submarine pen) (No a/c lost).This was Sgt Les Morton's 13th Op with F/O G Taylor, 9th Daylight Op and 23rd mission. On this day Percy Cannings was flown by Skipper F/Lt W Reid in ND961 to Horsham St Faith for his brother's wedding (Now Norwich City Airport).

On the **12/13 Aug 1944**, F/O Gerry Taylor and crew were a (6/7) FTR from Russelheim in the circumstances described above. 13 Lancs and 7 Halifaxes were lost here and 17 Lancs and 10 Halifaxes were lost from the Brunswick Op. A heavy losses night for Bomber Command and Les Morton was still courageously weaving his way through death's shadow. Les was now without a crew again and ended up flying 'Spare bod' for some of the more senior men in 61 Squ. Les had a weeks leave and then carried on with training missions and Ops.

The Lancaster Memorial in Weiswampach, Luxembourg commemorating ME596, QR-H and 75 Squ Lanc HK564, AA-P(photo by, *Michielverbeek*).

On the **15 Aug 1944**, Percy Cannings flew on his last mission to Deelan in ND961, OF-N with Skipper F/O WM Reid, thus completing his Tour of Ops with 97 Squ. It was nearly the end of his crew as 'bombs from above' passed within 5 feet of their tailplane to hit another a/c behind them. The a/c exploded damaging their rear Turret.

On the **26/27 Aug** Percy Cannings 97 Squ Lancaster ND807, OF-P Skippered by F/O TN McCurdy (RAAF) was shot down over Denmark to Konigsberg by a NF firing from below; Oberleutnant Arnold Brinkmann of 8 NJG3. The only survivor from the 8 crewmembers was Mid-Upper Gunner Sgt RA Swolf.

On the **28/29 Aug**, F/O BF Loneon (RAAF) was a FTR in PB436, QR-D for Dog to Konigsburg. All the crew survived, this was the replacement for EE186.

**23 Sept 1944**, ED860, QR-N, training with F/O NR Hoad (High level bombing) and ND865, QR-A, training with F/O NP Blaine (RCAF) (MUG and air-test).

On **23/24 Sept 1944**, Bomber Command visited Ladbergen, Munster and Neuss. It was a horrific night with 21 Lancasters and 3 Halifaxes lost. 61 Squ suffered its biggest loss for some time with 4 FTRs. Bill's comrade F/Lt DER Stone who had flown alongside him a number of times was a (6/8) loss in Lanc I, ME732, QR-P. Lost with them was 2nd Pilot F/O NF Alfred. Stones Mid-Upper Gunner Sgt WF Ravenhill, one of the two survivors had flown with Bill as his Rear Gunner on the 8 June 1944 to Rennes. S/L HW Horsley was a (2/7) FTR in Lanc III, LM718, QR-K for King. S/L Horsley, P/O CA Cawthorne DFM (on his 2nd Tour, 1st Tour was with 467 Squ) and Rear Gunner Sgt RT Hoskisson, all evaded capture and returned to 61 Squ. F/O IM Campbell (RNZAF) was a (6/7) FTR in Lanc III, ND988, QR-E (P/O DW Simmons regular Lanc) and F/O AK Hornibrook (RAAF) was a (6/7) FTR in Lanc III, ED470, QR-W. (The one survivor from each of these 2 a/c were both Rear Gunners.) 20 men from 61 Squ lost their life this night, 5 were POWs and 4 evaded capture. 50 Squ, 97 Squ and 463 Squ lost 2 a/c each. There were 2 (8/8s), 6 (7/7s) and 5 (6/7s), in total 124 men lost their lives.

**Left**, Lanc from 101 Squ, NG128, SR-B, releases 'window' over Duisburg and **right** releasing the 'cookie'.(source, CL1404/5 IWM)

F/Lt Stone's Mk I, Lanc, ME732, QR-P 'Ali Oop!' 'I go-I come back'. There are 42 missions marked on the nose. Bill flew in ME732 to Gelsenkirchen on the 21 June 1944 (source, *aircrewremebrancesociety.com*).

I spoke to Les Morton many times whilst the book was coming together and he sent me a copy of his Log Book in 2010. Again this proved to be an invaluable document to do research with and it threw up many questions. I had a long conversation on the phone with Les in early 2012 shortly after Bill's funeral and amongst a few questions, I asked him if he had any recollections of this sad night for 61 Squ:

**<u>W/O Les Morton</u>**

*'I had done a couple of training missions on the 23 Sept and I seem to remember it being a weekend. My name wasn't down for Ops and I think I had a few days leave. When I got back to the Squadron there were about 4 or 5 crews missing including S/L Horsley and F/Lt Stone who I knew quite well. There were a lot of men missing and everyone was feeling a bit down. However, we did get a lift when S/L Horsley returned to base after evading capture when he was shot down and we all got to hear about his lucky escape. I later flew with S/L Horsley as his Flt/Eng on 27 December to Rheydt in Germany.*

*I flew my last mission on New Years Day 1945 with F/O NT Collins to the Dortmund Ems Canal. The Daylight formations flew quite close together and there was a lot of flak on this target. We saw one a/c get some direct hits by flak, but it kept on going for the bombing run. I seem to remember it being quite a successful attack and we got some direct hits across the canal. I had finished my Tour now and it was a huge relief to have made it through in one piece. I was then transferred to Coastal Command which was much less stressful. I remember hearing about S/L Horsley's tragic accident while taking off from Skellingthopre, it was very sad he was an experienced pilot.'*

On **24 Sep** daylight raid to Calais another 61 Squ pilot that flew alongside Bill was a (5/7) FTR. P/O DC Freeman DFC was lost in Lanc III, NF914, QR-T, when it crashed into the sea of Calais after being hit by flak. P/O Freeman and 2 crew are commemorated on the Runnymede Memorial.

**3 Oct 1944**, ME725, QR-G, training with F/O DW Boon (RNZAF) (MUG, low level cross country).

**5 Oct 1944**, ND865, QR-A, F/O DW Boon (RNZAF), Daylight Op to Wilhemshaven (Naval Docks) (One 467 Squ Lanc lost).

On **14/15 Oct 1944**, 61 Squ's Lanc III, ME595, QR-Y was a (2/8) loss to Brunswick with F/O NE Hoad and crew. Hoad survived along with his 2nd Pilot F/O S Cadman to become POWs. ME595 was P/O Don Streets Lancaster; Les had flown in this same a/c with Don Street on 23/24 June to Limoge.

On the **28/29 Oct 1944**, 61 Squ's faithful 'Ton up' Lancaster ED860, QR-N for Nuts or Nan was written off after crashing on take- off at Skellingthorpe, Ops to Bergen with F/O LA Pearce (RAAF). It had flown an incredible 130 missions. Also 61 Squ Lanc III, ND902, QR-R with F/O SE Miller was written off after return to base from flak damage.

**1 Nov 1944**, JB138, QR-J, S/L HW Horsley AFC, Daylight Op to Homberg (Oil factory) (No bombs dropped) (1 Lanc lost).

On the **2/3 Nov** 61 Squ's PD199, QR-C was a (2/7) FTR to Dusseldorf with F/O W McGillivray and crew.

On the **6 Nov 1944**, EE176, QR-M, 'Mickey the Moocher' flew its last mission to Gravenhorst with F/O FA Mouritz and crew completing 119 missions, it was taken off Ops and at the end of Nov was transferred to 1653 HCU. Some sources record 128 Ops for EE176. Some of Mickey's regular Captains were S/L SJ Beard, F/Lt DE White and F/O HL Inniss (p98 Claims To Fame, The Lancaster, Norman Franks).

**11 Dec 1944**, LM274, QR-F, W/C WD Pexton DFC, AFC, Daylight Op to Heimbach Dam (Two 97 Squ Lancs lost).

On the **22/23 Nov 1944**, One 61 Squ Lanc I NG179, QR-C was a (7/7) FTR to Trondheim with F/O TC James and crew.

On the **6/7 Dec 1944**, two 61 Squ Lancs were FTRs. LL777, QR-S (1/7) with F/O IH Bryers (RNAZF) and ME725, QR-G (2/7) with F/O CA Donnelly (RAAF). F/Lt Jeff Gray had flown in both these Lancaster Is and ME725 was his regular a/c.

On **17/18 Dec 1944**, one 61 Squ Lanc III, LM729, QR-V was a (6/7) FTR to Munich with F/O ER Newland (RCAF) and crew (Two 50 Squ Lancs were also FTRs).

**27 Dec 1944**, NF912, QR-L, S/L HW Horsley AFC, Daylight Op to Rheydt (Front line, diversion to base) (1 Lanc and I Mosquito lost).

**1 Jan 1945**, LL911, QR-X, F/O NT Collins (RAAF), Daylight Op to Dortmund Ems Canal. In the debriefing report there is a chilling reference to 'bombs from above', if this had been a night mission it might have turned out slightly differently for the bomber spotted below F/O Collins Lancaster: 'On run up to bomb another a/c passed below and the release of bombs had to be held about 2 seconds to avoid hitting him.' (5 Lancs were lost, 4 from 9 Squ and 1 from 467 Squ). LL911 was a FTR on its 99th Op to Pölitz on 8/9 Feb 1945. Les Morton was now Tour Expired and he was signed off by W/C CW Scott AFC. Les was now transferred to Coastal Command where he saw the War out.

On the 14/15 Jan 1945, JB138, QR-J, 'Just Jane' flew its last mission to Merseberg with F/O EW Hutchins and crew completing 123 Ops. It was taken off Ops and transferred to 5 LFS on the2 nd Feb 1945. Some of 'Just Janes' regular Captains were F/Lt NF Turner, F/L F Norton and F/O AP Greenfield (RAAF).

As the above statistics show, since Bill was shot down on 4/5 July there are still further heavy losses sustained by 61 Squ. Although the end of the War was drawing closer it by no means meant that the danger had lessened. Even though the Lufwaffer's capability was seriously reduced, it alongside flak, mid-air collisions and accidents was still an ever present danger to Les and his comrades. The horrific drama continued and the shadow of death still kept on claiming more aircrews. Two more of the men Les flew with were also casualties, F/O Norman Hoad who became a POW and S/L HW Horsely who was killed in a crash at Skellingthorpe.

W/O Les Morton flew with S/L Horsley on 27 Dec 1944 to Rheydt in Lancaster NF911, QR-L which was later to be lost in the circumstances described below.

Horsley's 13th operation was to Seigen, 1 February 1945 in Lancaster NF 912. Take off was 1542hrs. Crew:- S/L H W Horsley (Capt), W/O H J Pyke (F/E), F/S S Fleet (Nav), F/S Merrow (A/B), F/S Chapman (WOP/ AIR), Sgt A A Sherriff (AG1), Sgt R T Hoskisson (AG2) The a/c crashed soon after takeoff due to port engine failure and all the crew were killed except the Rear Gunner.

**Frank Mouritz, an ex 61Squ Pilot:**

*'Take off time came and we were taxiing along the the taxiway in fading daylight. Aircraft L was two or three planes ahead of us. He took off and had engine failure just as he got airborne. All further take-offs were halted as he did a slow turn at a few hundred feet and lined up on the grass beside the runway, as his speed was too slow to lower his undercarriage. He landed on his belly, skidded about 200 yds and then hit a bitumen taxiway. The bomb load of 4,000 lb Cookie and 12,000 of 4 lb incendiaries instantly blew up. We were waiting on the other side of the aerodrome and the felt heavy blast and 4 lb incendiaries landed all around us. Horsley and 5 of his crew were killed in the explosion and the Rear Gunner, although badly injured, survived.'*

Another eye witness account of this crash was given by Sgt Alan Macdonald, a Rear Gunner on 50 Sqn, he had boarded his aircraft to join the same operation. His aircraft was still at its dispersal point, and he was in his rear turret, going through the pre-checks on his guns prior to take-off.

**Sgt Alan McDonald, Rear Gunner 50 Squ**

*'I saw that the fated aircraft, NF912 was in difficulties immediately after leaving the ground, and was vainly struggling to land back on the runway. Over the runway it plunged to the ground, to explode with great violence. The aircraft was completely destroyed, being blown to bits by its own exploding bomb load.'*

The runway was surprisingly not damaged and the area was quickly cleared up. The remaining a/c were inspected for damage as shrapnel had pierced some of them and after a 40 minute delay the Op continued. Sometime later an airman cycling across the dark airfield found the Rear Turret in a hedge with the gunner Sgt Reg Hoskisson still alive in it. The incident was all the more poignant for Frank Mouritz and his crew as their aircraft, QR-M, was unserviceable so they were allocated QR-L for the Siegen raid. However the take-off time was delayed by 2 hours, by which time his own QR-M became serviceable, so they were given back their own aircraft and Sqn Ldr Horsley took NF912, QR-L. Again EE176, QR-M had proved to be a 'lucky to the end' Lancaster (50/61 Squ website).

# Chapter Eighteen

## The Other 61 Squ Pilots

For those like Bill and I who are fascinated by his miraculous survival through the heavy losses suffered by his comrades, we have followed the statistics through to highlight this very fact. We have taken a 4 month period of time from the beginning of May 1944 to the end of August 1944. This equates to the average length of time a Tour was taking in Bomber Command at this point in the War. Bill's Tour sits within this time frame in which we examine the familiar 61 Squ's pilot's names who flew alongside him and the losses suffered by the two Squadrons based at Skellingthorpe. Percy Cannings and his crew continued to mark targets for 61 Squ during this time returning to the merciless targets of St Leu, 5 Aug and Châtellerault, 9/10 Aug; finally finishing his Tour on the 15/16 Aug to Deelan. He had flown an incredible 47 Ops, 22 with 100 Squadron during 1943 and 25 with 97 Squ PFF. 97 Squ lost 17 a/c during our time frame, 2 in the tragic training accident of 23 June.

61 Squadron were comparatively fairly lucky over the period Bill flew on Ops from May to July 1944, with fewer losses than their sister, 50 Squadron. 61 Squadron lost 12 Lancasters including Bill North and Jack Goodyer during this time period and 50 Squadron lost 32 Lancasters, 21 from May to July and 11 during August (This figure for 50 Squ equates to the loss of one and a half Squadrons in a 4 month Operational period). In the twelve 61 Squ losses from May to Aug were 9 of the pilots that had flown alongside Bill. They were **1**- P/O JH Eastwood, LM454, QR-Z, 11/12 May, Bourg-Leopold (6/7). **2**- P/O Jack Goodyer, ME783, QR-E, 15/16 June, Châtellerault (7/7). **3**- F/Lt JA Forrest, LM518, QR-C (6/7) and **4**- P/O J Kramer (RCAF), ND987, QR-B (6/7), both lost 24/25 June at Prouville. **5**- P/O RH Passant (RAAF), R5856, QR-U (7/7) and **6**- F/Lt WE Grantham, ND867, QR-V (5/6) were both lost on the 7/8 July revisit to St Leu. **7**- P/O HW Cooper with 2nd Pilot F/O JB Thompson, DV304, QR-V, 18/19 July at Revigny (8/8). **8**- P/O G Taylor (RCAF), ME596, QR-H, Russelheim (6/7). **9**- F/Lt ER Church (RCAF), PA998, QR-O, 25/26 Aug Darmstadt (4/7) and is on the Runnymede Memorial. Two more pilots who flew with Bill were lost in September:- **10**- F/Lt DER Stone with 2nd Pilot F/O NF Alfred, ME732, QR-P, 23/24 Sept Ladbergen (6/8). Bill flew in ME732 on 21/22 June to Gelsenkirchen. **11**- F/O DC Freeman DFC, 24 Sept 1944, Calais (5/7) and on the Runnymede Memorial (At St Leu 7/8 July 50 Squ lost 3 a/c with 1 survivor and Konigsburg 28/29 Aug was also heavy on 50 Sqn, 4 a/c lost with only 1 survivor.). It is not clear as to why 50 Squ lost nearly 3 times the a/c that 61 lost in this time frame; they were both flying to the same targets from the same base.

P/O HW Cooper's grave in Marcilly Communal Cemetery. All eight crewmen rest here.

The Runnymede Memorial, where 20,000 RAF crewmen who have no resting place are commemorated. It is a peaceful and extraordinary place that overwhelms the mind (17 April 2011, photos, CK).

In Sept, 61 Squ lost 5, 50 Squ lost 4 and 97 Squ lost 3 Lancasters. 83 and 97 Squ PFF lost some of their most senior men during these months including their Wing Commanders, many of these were (8/8) losses. Through October and November the Squadron losses reduced as Germany's NF capability was reduced and worn down by the Allied Offensive. Bomber Command losses overall were reduced too and 61 Squ lost 6 a/c. In Oct, Nov, 50 and 97 Squ lost 2 each and in Dec 61 Squ lost 3 more, 50 Squ also lost a further 2. Altogether during the whole of WW2, 61 Squadron lost 974 aircrew and ground staff and 50 Squadron 1,002. So by the end of the War the casualty figures between the two

Squadrons were nearly even with 28 men the difference (P/O Eastwood can be added to this figure making it 975 as we discovered due to the error in the ORB he is not mentioned in the *61 Squ Book of Remembrance*).

The other pilots Bill flew with who completed their Tours are mentioned in the movements of crew record in the ORB. This records where they were transferred to from Skellingthorpe (51 Base is Waddington). W/C Doubleday was appointed to the post of Chief Flying Instructor in Sept 44, and was posted to 27 OTU on 25th September. 3 of his crew, Gray-Buchanan, Sinnamen and Taylor, were posted to 11 PDRC in late July 44, for repatriation. (Alan Wells) ED860's F/L BS Turner was transferred to Bill's old 1661 HCU at RAF Winthorpe on 18.08.44. P/O EW Hallet went to Bill's no 5 LFS on 21.08.44. P/O Don Street went to 16 OTU on 20/08/44. P/O RJ Auckland went to 1660 HCU on 12/08/44. P/O RA Dear went to 84 OTU on 26.08.44. O/C 'A' Flight F/L F Norton went to 1660 HCU on 21.08. 44. P/O Vowe went to 17 OTU on 21.08.44. F/L GA Berry went to 22 OTU on 07.07.44 and S/L Woodroffe to 54 Base on 10.07.44. F/Eng IM Pettigrew also went to 1661 HCU on 31/7/44.

In his service to Bomber Command's 61 Squadron Bill North flew in Lancasters EE176, QR-M 4 times. ME719, QR-F x1. ME783, QR-E x1 (lost 15/16 June 1944). EE186, QR-D 16 times (lost 4/5 July 1944). JA872, QR-K x1 (This a/c came from 57 and 630 Squ's respectively and ended up at 46 MU, RAF Lossiemouth after its service with 61 Squ). LM718, QR-K x2 (lost 23/24 Sept 1944). JB138, QR-J x2. ME758, QR-P x1 (Lost 23/24 Sept 1944). ND865, QR-A, 8 times, (This a/c originally came from 83 Squ, OL-L and after service with 61 Squ was later transferred to No 5LFS Syerston). One of the familiar names that flew alongside Bill on Ops was Donald (Don) Street DFC who passed away in 2012, his ashes will be scattered at the former Skellingthorpe airfield at the 2013 50/61 Squadron reunion weekend.

## History of Lancasters EE186, QR-D and ND865, QR-A.

By trawling through the ORB, Chris Ward's 5 Group BC and WR Chorley I have managed to come up with the following facts. EE186 arrived at 61 Squ on the 17 Nov 1943 from 106 Squ and was originally delivered on 11 June 1943 to 49 Squ. The previous 61 Squ QR-A, JB 532 was transferred to 630 Squ at East Kirkby and became LE-X. This was a complete loss on 1/2 Jan 1944 to Berlin with S/L KF Vare AFC. In F/Lt Jeff Gray's Log Book he records EE186 as QR-A on 2/ 3 Jan 1944 Ops to Berlin (EE176 and ED860 are on the same page) and then again as QR-A on a training mission 14 March 1944. I have a copy of Jeff's Log Book and checked this with him and he assures me this is correct. So it might be safe to assume that when EE186 came to 61 Squ and JB532, QR-A left for 630 Squ, EE186 took the A coding.

Through Jan, Feb, March 1944 EE186 is flying on Ops to Berlin, Stettin, Brunswick, Leipzig, Stuttgart, Schweinfurt, Augsburg and Frankfurt mostly with the F/O GA Berry crew, also flying alongside 'Ton-up' Lancasters EE176, ED860 and JB138. Last Op was 24/25 March 1944 to Berlin with the Berry crew and then EE186 disappears until 14 May when recorded on 5 training flights in Bill's Log Book as QR-D and then back in the ORB on Bill's Op to Tours on 19/20 May 1944. Just another quick snippet regarding these two a/c. ND865 is also flying on the same Op as EE186, 19/20 May to Tours with F/Lt GA Berry's crew. It's the first entry on the ORB page for this Op, Bill is 3 down in EE186. Curiously the serial number ND865 is written again one above Bill with P/O Norton's crew. This I am sure is an error and should be ND867. I can only assume that EE186 was undergoing some sort of refit due to the length of time it was off for. Berry carries on with Ops flying in other Lancs until 18/19 April to Junisy and doesn't reappear until 10/11 May to Lille (Presumably on leave). So during EE186 and Berry's absence we see the first record of ND865 (a transfer from 83 Squ) in the ORB; which Bill has recorded as QR-A in his Log Book. ND865 first appears on the 24/25 April to Munich with F/S J Kramer who flies in it 7 times until F/O GA Berry returns and flies it to Lille on 10/11 May.

Again I can only assume unless there is a definite record of the change over that when transferred from 83 Squ ND865 took over QR-A code from EE186 while it was off Ops, EE186 then became the new QR-D for Dog when it returned to Ops. This coincides with what Bill North and his Bomb Aimer Norman Jarvis have said, that when they started Ops with 61 Squ from 7 May 1944 that they were given the new D for Dog to fly and told that the previous two D 's had been lost on Ops. (R5703 and ED332) They said they 'weren't superstitious and this information didn't bother them at all.' So EE186 became Bill's Lancaster until 4/5 July St Leu and 'lucky till the end' like the other famous veteran Lancs it had flown alongside during the Battle of Berlin and the Normandy Landings. EE176 and EE186 often have typing errors in the ORB, written as ME176 and ME186! Someone has marked a slanted line under the M when this occurs. Tony Bird also flew in EE186 when it was coded QR-A. EE186 was A Veteran of the Battle for Berlin and by the time it was lost at St Leu it had clocked up 40 missions with 61 Squ, it remains to be found out how many missions it flew with 49 and 106 Squ's. The new QR-D for Dog, PB436 that replaced EE186 was lost on 28/29 Aug 1944 to Konigsberg with F/S BF Loneon (RAAF), all the crew survived.

So as tactical support Ops were wound down towards the end of July 1944 Bomber Command visited the big German cities of Hamburg and Stuttgart again. As control of Bomber Command was given back to C in C Arthur Harris around the middle of September 1944 he continued the campaign against the German Industrial heartlands, with occasional tactical support given to the Army when it was requested.

An average tour of Ops was about 4 to 5 months at this time, more usually 4 months as crews were tearing through their Tours due to the heavy Tactical Support. (P/O Don Street's tour lasted from 27 April 1944 to 20 August 1944, just under 4 months. Bill was slightly behind him starting on 7 May 1944. Bill was just over halfway through his tour when he was shot down on the 4/5 July 1944, which was 2 months in. If he hadn't been shot down he would have continued his Operations and most likely have flown on the above mentioned missions to Germany probably mirroring the remainder of Don Street or Les Morton's Tour (Ladbergen and Konigsburg as shown are horrific examples of the continued heavy losses) So assuming he had completed it in this average time of 4 months, he would have then transferred to an OTU as a Pilot Instructor around the first half of September 1944. At OTU or HCU he would have spent the last 6 months of the War training the new pilots that were still filtering through the ranks of Bomber Command, this however as we know was not to be. Who knows, if Bill and his faithful crew had carried on flying on Ops, maybe they too might have become one of these fatal losses like the other mentioned 61 Squadron pilots who flew alongside him. One of the unique factors we see here is that Bill and his crew all survived every intense near death experience they encountered, whereas the majority was not so fortunate.

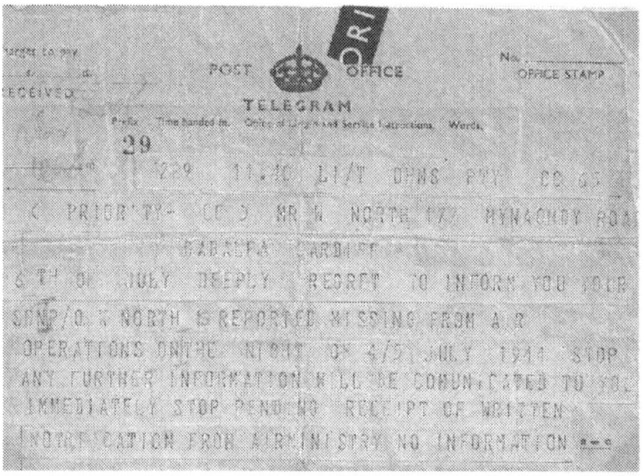
POST OFFICE
TELEGRAM
29
PRIORITY ... MR W NORTH ... MYNACHDY ROA[D]
... CARDIFF
6 TH OF JULY DEEPLY REGRET TO INFORM YOU YOUR
SON P/O W NORTH IS REPORTED MISSING FROM AIR
OPERATIONS ON THE NIGHT OF 4/5 JULY 1944 STOP
ANY FURTHER INFORMATION WILL BE COMMUNICATED TO YOU
IMMEDIATELY STOP PENDING RECEIPT OF WRITTEN
NOTIFICATION FROM AIR MINISTRY NO INFORMATION

Bill's missing from Operations telegram dated 6 July 1944.

# Chapter Nineteen

# Lancaster Take Off and Landings

Listing all the missions one after the other as I have done may make it sound as if, when it was time for a mission, the crew just jumped in the plane and took off. Nothing could be further from the truth. Taking a Lancaster Bomber on a mission was an immensely complicated procedure.

## F/Lt Bill North

*'From take off to landing there was a lot going on, there were so many procedures to follow. Each stage followed a correct sequence and any mistakes could result in the loss of the aircraft and its crew. This was where crew coordination was paramount.'*

## W/O Les Morton

*'On take-off and landings and all throughout Operations there was always a lot to deal with. As well as battling with nerves you had to concentrate on all the complex technical procedures and sequences that we had to follow.'*

The following extract is taken from the RAF Lancaster Pilot's note book, 'PILOT'S NOTES LANCASTER III, MERLIN 28 ENGINES.
This is available at the RAF Museum Hendon bookshop. It demonstrates just some of the many tasks a crew had to perform and Bill, Jeff and Les recount some of their experiences on take-off and in the air.

## SECTION 35. PRELIMINARIES

On entering the aircraft the pilot should:

1. Check oxygen main cock is on.

2 Check emergency air bottle pressure: Normal 1,200lb/sq.in
Minimum 800.

3. Turn master electrical switch to FLIGHT.

4. Check that fuel cross-feed cock is OFF.

5. Switch on fuel contents gauges and leave it on and check fuel contents.

6. Switch on the undercarriage indicator and flaps indicator switches and check the indicators. Check that the engine master cocks are OFF.

7. Check air supply pressure is more than 120lbs/sq.in and switch all our slow-running cut-outs to IDLE CUT-OFF. Then test fuel booster pumps by ammeter.

8. Test the performance of the fuel booster pumps with the fuel pressure warning lights.

9. Switch D.R. compass to SETTING and when it stops 'hunting' switch to normal.

10. Have a ground starter battery (24v) plugged in and then turn the master electrical switch to 'GROUND'.

**F/Lt Jeff Gray**

*'The battery truck would park next to the Lancaster and plug in the cables to electrically boost the start up systems. It was a no no to start the a/c on its own battery power. A member of the ground crew would stand on the wheel inside the undercarriage bays and operate by hand the Kygas Pump which would send fuel into the carburettors; he would do this until the engine was running. The engines were then revved up to check the magnetos were working efficiently and had power after idling. There were two magnetos and these controlled the sparking to ignite the fuel systems.'*

NX611 engine start at East Kirkby, 3 Nov 2012. Percy, Sandy and Bet Cannings (CK).

**Engine start up sequence at dispersal:- Bill North and Jeff Gray**

*No. 3. (Starboard Inner/right side) was started first; this controlled the pneumatic systems which in turn controlled the brakes.*

*No. 4. (Starboard Outer) was next then No. 2 (Port Inner/left side) and then No.1. (Port Outer)*

There were some differences between the Lancaster I, III, and X mostly to do with the power plants. The Lancaster I was fitted with Merlin XX, 22 or 24 engines which had SU carburettors. The Lancaster III and X were fitted with Packard Merlin 28 or 38 engines which had Bendix Stromberg pressure injection carburettors, Hydromatic propellers were fitted to all. The Lancaster X were Canadian built differed slightly in instrument and electrical systems, they were found to be perfect matches for spare parts made in England.

**The Hydraulic system**

Each turret was operated by an individual engine driven pump.

Starboard outer—Mid Upper Turret

Starboard inner—Front Turret

Port inner—Mid Under Turret, if fitted (Canadian Lancasters/Squadrons had these fitted).

Port outer—Rear Turret

Two pumps on each inboard engine, with hand-pump also, charge a small accumulator and operate, undercarriage, Flaps, Bomb Doors, Carburettor air intake shutters and fuel jettisoning. Hand pumps are not normally operable in an emergency.

**Pneumatic system**

A Heywood compressor on the starboard inner charges an air bottle to 300 lb/sq.in. and operates the Wheel brakes (8O lb/sq.in. operating pressure), Radiator shutters, Supercharger rams (III, X and later I) Idle cut-off rams (III and X only) Triple pressure gauge used to monitor these systems.

A vacuum pump is fitted on each inboard engine, one for operating the instruments on the instrument flying panel the other for the gyros on the MK 14 bombsight. An RAE compressor on the port inner engine also operates the MK 4 automatic controls and the computer on the MK 14 bombsight.

## Electrical system

Two 1,500 watt generators were located one on each inner engine, connected in parallel charging 24 volt batteries. These supply the lighting, instrument panel, prop feathering pumps, flap and undercarriage indicators, pressure head hunting, fuel booster pumps, radio equipment, landing lamps engine starting and booster coils, dinghy inflation, controls for radiator shutters rams, supercharger gear change rams, idle cut-off rams, bomb gear and bombsight, fire extinguishers, fuel gauges and fuel pressure warning lights, camera, heated clothing and DR compass.

When given the signal to go Bill would taxi out of dispersals and into the queue of bombers waiting to take off. When it was their turn to take off they would pause at the start of the runway, the brakes would be applied and the engines would then be revved up to see if they responded evenly. The throttles were then closed and the engines slowly revved up again, then the breaks would be released allowing the aircraft to move slowly down the runway to take off.

On Lancaster Bombers the props on the four Merlin engines all turned in a clockwise direction creating a huge amount of torque that could pull the plane to port;

'Open the throttles to about zero boost against the brakes, then release the brakes and open throttles (to the gate with boost cut out pulled if Mod. Merlin 1087 is fitted. Or through the gate if not fitted) with the port slightly ahead. There is a tendency to swing to port, but this can be checked initially on the throttles and as speed increases, by the rudders (Torque created by clockwise motion of four Merlins).'

The definitive book on British Aero engines is by Alec Lumsden and appropriately entitled, *British Piston Aero-Engines and Their Aircraft!* He refers to the Merlins as all having the following in common '..... spur-geared, reduction ratio varied, as in text, all having right-hand tractor drive.' (page 202). He explains on page 47 that '...Direction of rotation, as viewed from behind, .right-hand (R.H.) - clockwise, tractor or pusher.' What all this boils down to is that all Merlin engines turned clockwise when viewed from behind looking forward. Just for clarification, 'tractor' refers to a propeller at the front of the engine that pulls the plane forward whilst 'pusher' is a propeller at the rear of the engine which pushes the plane forward.

**F/Lt Jeff Gray**

*'So on taking off with a full bomb and fuel load there was a dangerous tendency for the aircraft to swing to port. The counteraction for this was to leave engine No. 4 lagging (not at full throttle). The Flight Engineer would assist with take-off by having his hands on the throttle controls, but be careful not to push the throttle for No. 4 all the way up until they were clear of the runway'.*

Jeff Gray also mentioned he had an inexperienced Flight Engineer push the No. 4 Throttle up to soon creating a drama on take-off early on in his career when he had to abort the take off due to a hard swing to port. *'I wasn't used to the slow acceleration of a fully loaded Lancaster and I opened up the engines too soon before I had full rudder control. Slowly but inexorably, we began to swing to port. It was decision time, I slammed the throttles shut and we ground to a halt.'*

One of 61 Squadrons famous 'Ton up' Lancs was lost in exactly this way on 28 October 1944. ED-860, QR-N for Nan had reached 130 missions, it was about to take off at 22:39 hours for Bergen piloted by a young Australian skipper F/O Laurence Pearce who had 211 hours flying time, with 20 on Lancasters. As it thundered down the Skellingthorpe runway it violently swung to port hitting a glim lamp, which burst a tyre collapsing the undercarriage. Part of the port wing was torn away spilling petrol everywhere from the ruptured tanks. The lower fuselage and bomb bay was crushed and the shaken crew all managed to escape; after 58 Maintenance Unit had dismantled and made the aircraft safe it was written off. A sad ending for such a distinguished aircraft, but the saying at the time was, 'Lucky till the end.'

**F/Lt Bill North**

*'Once up in the air the pilot would synchronise the engines and then set the trim control. Trimming was the fine or smaller control surfaces or tabs on the rudders and flaps that could be locked down to allow the pilot a degree of comfort (not fighting with the plane and a lighter touch on the stick) in allowing the plane to fly itself for the long journey ahead, making adjustments to settings*

*and course when necessary. The auto pilot 'George' was often used as well, although on some older aircraft this could prove to be unpredictable.'*

On the bombing run the pilot would fly on instruments alone to allow a steadier run for the Bomb Aimer who would be directing the aircraft's path.

What I find fascinating about Bill, Jeff and Les Morton's recollections is that it demonstrates the huge amount of information being processed by Bill and the crew at start up, take off time and during flight. As well as the technical side of flying there were also the many dangers that have been explained to deal with. It gives multi-tasking a new meaning!

# Chapter Twenty

## Stalag Luft 1. A Wartime Log

Towards the end of the War there were over 300,000 Allied POWs held by the Germans. Some had been in captivity for 5 years and approx 250,000 were held in camps on the eastern borders of Germany of which some parts are now modern-day Poland. The Germans also put some 80,000 of these POWs to work for the Reich working alongside other foreign slave labourers, although not allowed contact with them, especially Russian and Jewish workers.

The British YMCA sent blank log books to the POWs so they could record their thoughts and experiences; the British logs had a Lion stamped on them, the Canadian YMCA logs had a maple leaf stamped on theirs and the American YMCA logs had a set of wings and a bell on them. These log books became the touchstone of their war and for the generations to come their treasured musty yellow pages would reveal a unique insight into life as a POW. These log books contain memories, poems, autographs, drawings, cartoons and a record of day to day life. I have read Bill's log over and over again it really does give one a sense of life in Stalag Luft 1. The memories that have lasted a lifetime, the POWs and the friendships formed in adversity during their captive bonds and then their separation on liberation, most men never to meet each other again.

Food became a real focal point for the men and as a food lover Bill mentions that the dreams and fantasies about food were constant. The basic German rations were grim, thin gruel with unidentifiable lumps, ersatz coffee which was made from acorns, turnip jam, rotten potatoes and bread that was made partly from sawdust. Their saving grace was the Red Cross food parcels which contained an assortment of food. These parcels were pooled together in the barrack rooms and they would all share equally the contents, often with a designated cook taking on cooking duties. The tins and other packaging would be turned into cooking and eating utensils, nothing was wasted, everything was of value. British, Canadian and American Red Cross parcels varied in their contents, but were essentially pretty much the same. There was much discussion about weight and calorific content. Cigarettes were the main currency of the camp; prisoners could barter and swap with other POWS or bribe the German guards to varying degrees. A typical British Red Cross Parcel included:-

1 tin of Nestle's condensed milk, 1 packet of prunes, ½ lb of margarine, 1 tin of bacon, salmon or pilchards, 4 oz of cocoa (Terry's or Rowntree's), 12 oz tin of corned beef or gelatine, 1 cake of soap, 4 oz slab of chocolate, 1 slab of Tate and Lyle sugar, 1 tin of cheese, ½ lb of biscuits, 1 lb of

jam creamed rice or fruit pudding, 2 oz of tea, 1 tin of curried beef, 50 cigarettes or 2 oz of Tobacco, 1 tin of Tate and Lyle syrup.

In a conversation with Trevor Mullinder, in New Zealand in June 2010, who was a roommate with Bill and remembers him well, he told me that George Langford was the cook in the room. When the parcels came in they were put together and one of George's specialities was to make cakes out of crushed biscuits and other ingredients which were quite tasty according to Bill. Bill said that George who was a mate of his from before POW camp was a happy soul who was constantly singing Gilbert and Sullivan songs. (George Langford's name is signed on the back of Bill's EFTS picture taken in Canada.) I was put in touch with Trevor Mullinder by fellow New Zealander Chris Bretton who got in touch with me through the Stalag Luft 1 web site. Trevor was a Mosquito pilot with 487 Squadron.

As days turned into weeks and weeks turned into months, the morale in Stalag Luft 1 was generally good. Everybody found their own way of dealing with life and the long wait for their freedom. Morale was affected by different factors such as food, weather, home news and war progress. Letters from home rarely got to camp, but some men received letters from their families, wives or girlfriends giving them home news. Some wives or girlfriends told of finding new partners and this particular news could send them spiralling into the depths of depression. War news was updated daily from BBC news broadcasts from the crystal radio set that was hidden under the Altar in the Chapel. This could be compared to the German news and prisoners would get a fairly accurate impression of how the war was going. Some of the men had survivors guilt syndrome and found it hard to come to terms with the fact that they might be the only one of their crew to survive, fortunately Bill never had to go through that, but still was acutely aware of his own mortality then and right the way through his life.

I cannot do better than use Bill's own words to describe his experiences as a Prisoner of War. What follows are entries from the journal he kept at the time and which I was privileged to see over half a century later.

## **Introduction**

*'The object of my introduction is to let the reader know that this Log Book is merely a collection of articles etc, of particular interest to a 'Kriegie.'* It is to be hoped that these articles etc, will also be of interest to those who are always in a Kriegie's thoughts—namely the folks at home.*

*Within these pages will be found the names of men—all of whom have appeared in the British Lists of casualties—with whom I have lived intimately for some months.*

*Last but not least no introduction to a Kriegie Log Book would be complete without mention of the International Red Cross Society. This organisation is the one 'silver lining in the dark clouds shining' and so I shall end this introduction on this note of sincere thanks.'*

*Bill North*

*Kriegie was the POW slang for the German word *'Kriegsgefangener'*, war-prisoner.

**My capture in France**

*'On the morning of 5 July 1944 a group of Germans headed by a German Luftwaffe Officer found me stretched out on a hilly slope overlooking a pretty French valley. With two bullet wounds in my thigh and two in my left elbow—all of which were bleeding profusely –I was unable to walk and so had been forced to lay helpless awaiting capture by the Germans. Prior to the arrival of these Germans I had performed rude first aid upon myself and had also been visited by some French peasant women and children. These were all obviously in sympathy with me, but as was equally obvious, were very much afraid of the Germans who were in the district. To revert to the German Officer; he treated me quite courteously, offered me a cigarette and arranged for a French doctor to dress my wounds. After this painful duty was performed I was lifted onto a stretcher, placed into an ambulance and transferred over the bumpy countryside to German billets.*

**A Strange Incident**

*Here I was placed upon a bed and was offered food to eat. This, my first introduction to German food, was not very pleasant. Hungry as I was my stomach revolted against the abortion of German soup, German bread (atrocious to me at that time—but to become a delicacy in the very near future) and German Ersatz coffee. After having partaken very sparingly of this frugal meal I relaxed and managed to doze for a little while. I was awakened from this restless sleep by a strange incident. A French working girl, of about 21 years, on duty at this German billet had sneaked into my room kissed me on the cheek, motioned me to remain silent and with a smile, crept away as quietly as she had arrived. She was a very pretty girl and on thinking of this incident, I presumed it was her way of showing her friendship for the British. I'd hardly had time to think of this incident however, before a German entered my room and told me in halting English that I should be moving to a hospital in a short while.*

## The German Viewpoint

*Whilst waiting for the transport this German spoke with me in a manner in which I was to hear again and again. He pointed to my fair hair, remarked upon my youth and then said that we, the British and the Germans, should not be fighting together and that this war was 'all a mistake' (I myself said that it certainly was a mistake—a fatal one on Germany's part). This German pointed out to me that the German and British instead of fighting against each other, should rather band together to fight the common enemy—namely the Bolshevik terror in the east!! This I soon realised was the German's dream—to see the Western Powers at loggerheads with our Russian allies. This dream I believe has very little show of coming to aught.*

## I meet my friends/My journey to Beauvais/I lose two Comrades

*By the time we'd had this conversation a couple of stretcher bearers had entered the room and then followed the painful duty of being moved upon the stretcher and thence to a 'truck.' It was now dark and on being placed in the truck I was very much surprised to meet a number of my friends—namely Eddy, Dennis, Norman and Monty. Eddy and Monty were perfectly fit whilst Dennis had a few bullet nicks in his legs and Norman was badly injured from his decent by parachute. I now learned that I was to be transferred to a Luftwaffe Hospital at Beauvais—some fifty miles NE of Paris.*

*This motor ride to Beauvais was one of the most uncomfortable rides it's ever been my misfortune to go on. The springs of the vehicle were non-existent, whilst the roads over which we rode were certainly not the smoothest. With every bump of the road my whole body shook with pain, so that on completion of this night journey I heaved a sincere prayer of relief. It was a moonlit night and on reaching the town of Beauvais our first port of call was the local prison. The dark and ugly walls of this foreboding building stood out against the skyline and for the first time since my capture, I realised that my freedom was lost. This realisation as it came truly home to me caused a sickening feeling in the pit of my stomach. At this prison however I said good-bye to the able bodied of my comrades* [Eddy and Monty were sent on to Dulag Luft] *and the remaining three of us Dennis, Norman and myself continued to Beauvais Hospital.*

*We reached our destination at last, where upon we were transported to a ground floor of the hospital and were seen to by a German doctor. This German was to my mind a typical Hun and believe me he didn't treat us any too gently. As far as I was concerned the doctor simply ripped the bandage off my raw wounds and literally poured iodine into the bullet holes. As can well be imagined it took me all of my time to stop from calling out. Nevertheless this rude treatment probably helped my wounds considerably. After having my wounds dressed—incidentally it was here that I had my first introduction to paper bandages—I was transferred to a wing of the hospital and placed in a small room three floors up where I found an American Navigator who had strained himself on baling out.**

*This first night of mine at Beauvais was a most uncomfortable one. Instead of the bed I had to use the stretcher, so what with this and other things to contend with I got little or no sleep on this my first night in captivity.*

*Many Allied crewmen were injured during the baling out process, some injuries sustained when their bodies made contact with the aircraft often thrown onto it by the slipstream, others when they made contact with the ground in rough landings. Norman Jarvis' injury Bill thinks was probably due to him exiting the front hatch incorrectly in the heat of battle and bashing his head and back as he was thrown back against the fuselage by the slipstream. The correct procedure was to roll in a ball head first out of the hatch and drop into the slipstream. You can imagine how difficult it must have been to bale out of a bomber that was battle damaged and out of control.

## A German Breakfast

*The following day was one of many days which followed—each one more boring and more nerve wracking than the previous one. At eight of the morning the door was unlocked and breakfast was brought in. Breakfast as I was to find out never varied. It consisted of four slices of German bread—two with jam and two with margarine—and a bowl of coffee the like of which I'd never tasted before and please God, I'll never taste again. Following breakfast I was left alone until about twelve thirty where upon lunch was served. Once again a true princely repast was served up—*

*namely a bowl of soup which was certainly meant to be eaten at the same time as the coffee mentioned above.*

*Following this sumptuous repast I was left in peace until mid-afternoon when a German Officer entered and asked for my name, rank and number. This I gave, but on being asked for my SQU'D No. A/C TYPE, TARGET, NAMES OF CREW etc, I pointed out that I was a soldier of his Majesty the King and under the Geneva Convention I was required to give no information other than my name, rank and number. Nothing more was said and my next interruption came at five o'clock when my third and last meal of the day was brought in. This meal was just precisely the same as breakfast. Immediately after this 'meal' my American roommate was taken together with a British lad, from the hospital and transported, so I heard, to Beauvais Prison and from there to a German Stalag Luft. Following this removal I was taken from my room and carried downstairs where my arm and leg were X-rayed. After this I was returned upstairs only this time to a different room. In this room there were five beds, three of which were occupied by British aircrew. In one of the remaining two beds I was placed and in the fifth was Dennis.*

**Pride takes a fall**

*This room was about fifteen feet by twenty by twenty by twelve, with one window which of course, was barred. A German guard sat outside the door twenty four hours of the day in four hour shifts. Two of these guards—named Hans and Herman—were middle aged men who had seen service in the Great War and from what I gathered they were pretty well fed up with the present war. One of them had lost a son on the Russian front, whilst both of them were married and seemed only desirous of returning to the Fatherland.*

*This room into which I had just been put proved to be my prison until 20 August 1944. These days and weeks, turned out to be the most uncomfortable and painful it's ever been my lot to undergo. For the first three or four weeks I was confined to my bed with my leg in splints. During this period my pride suffered considerably as I was unable to do a thing for myself. Everything I wanted to do or have done necessitated the calling of a German guard. After this initial period my leg splints were removed which did enable me to stagger around the room somewhat. To describe these weeks at Beauvais would be dreary and uninteresting. Day followed day and the days grew into weeks—each one being more dreary than the previous.*

## Louise!

*The only bright spots in the days were the mornings from about nine o'clock to nine thirty. During these periods French girls cleaned up the hospital and every morning one of a trio of these girls used to enter 'the prisoners' room and clean up a little. These girls I got to know pretty well and with my limited amount of French I used to get as much 'gen' off them as possible. Of course this was utterly impossible on many an occasion as the German guard would be standing in the doorway. Still, I used to do fairly well and so was not entirely in the dark as to the progress of the war. The name of one of these girls was Louise and she in particular was a good friend to me and my comrades. From what I gathered she truly hated the Germans, whilst holding more than a liking for the British. Louise was not by any stretch of the imagination a pretty girl! In fact one might say she was the exact antithesis of this. On the other hand however, the nature of Louise was truly beautiful and her maternal instinct had certainly matured. When she first discovered that we British got no cigarettes from the Germans she began to smuggle in tobacco and cigarette papers. These she used to give to me when the guard was unaware and I in turn, gave the 'makings' to my roommates.*

## A German's Brutality

*One incident concerning Louise should, I think, be mentioned here. Firstly, however, I should mention that the guards, Hans and Herman, had been posted (possibly to the West Front) and in their place we had two fresh guards—both of whom were to my mind, brutal Germans. One of these was a middle aged man whom we used to call 'Toc H' (reason—we reckoned he was as dim as a Toc H lamp!), whilst the other was a young man in his early twenties. This type was a typical Hitler youth and it is concerning him that this 'Louise incident' came about.*
*One morning Louise was cleaning out the room as usual when this youngster entered and caught Louise about to talk to me. My word! I really thought this young German was going to beat the girls head in with a rifle butt!! Fortunately—note I say fortunately—he didn't do this, but 'merely'(?) kicked the girl into the passage way! Needless to say I remonstrated with the guard, but all to no avail. Perhaps, however, it was fortunate that I couldn't stand or else I'm sure I would have gone for the guard with but one idea in my mind. With such examples as this of German Brutality it amazed me that the French still had as much spirit left in them.**

*With the insight into our never changing meals and the character of our guards it merely remains for me to say that about once every four days our bandages were changed and slowly but surely our wounds began to heal. I was informed that there were a couple of bullets in my leg, but no attempt was made to remove them. Therefore I presume that I shall have to carry them around with me until I return home—wonderful thought!*

*The French girls did literally risk death on being found fraternizing with Allied POWs.

## Increased Air Activity

*As I say day followed day and one was the same as the previous—at least this was so until the 11 August 1944. From this date onwards Beauvais became a hive of activity. Air raids (they raised my morale again and again), became very frequent and the aerodrome at Beauvais was bombed and strafed daily. Whenever the sirens blew Germans scuttled to their shelters like scared rabbits whilst I would crawl to the window and give the lads a running commentary on the air raid. (Unfortunately Dennis was not with me to enjoy all this as he'd been transported off to Deutschland. In his place however was Norman who was now very much better).*

Dennis Bartlett had left Beauvais Hospital to be transferred to Dulag-Luft at Limburg arriving there on the 24 September 1944 and then onto Stalag Luft 7, Bankau on the 5 August. The details of his experience are recorded in the Chapter Stalag Luft 7. This was the last time they would see each other for many years. As Bill mentions in his log, German wounded were pouring into the hospital and there was a huge Allied air-offensive in progress which was part of the Battle for Normandy. Bill mentioned to me he found it extremely frustrating that the Allies were so close by and it was obvious to all that Germany was losing the war. Still, Bill had a front row seat from his hospital room window to the chaos and downfall of the battered and retreating German war machine.

Just a quick point of interest Bill has noted the 11 August 1944 as being a day when there was increased air raids and activity at Beauvais. The Allied Ground Forces were relentlessly pushing forward into occupied territory supported by the Combined Air Forces during the Battle of Normandy. They were coming very close to where Bill and the crew were being held. The US 3rd Army began crossing the Loire River SW of Paris near Tours and the German Army had began to buckle under the onslaught. Hitler refused to allow Field Marshal Kluge, commanding Army Group B in the west, to withdraw from the advanced positions at Mortain and the Germans then counterattacked US positions here. It soon led to a catastrophe as they were outflanked, which resulted in many German Divisions in Normandy being trapped in the Falaise Pocket. With the bad weather clearing the Allied air attacks increased and Bill's mate F/Lt Ron Grant a Typhoon pilot, was involved in these attacks which decimated the trapped German Armoured and Troop Divisions. Whole French villages had been obliterated, abandoned and destroyed with military equipment completely blocking many roads. Bodies of soldiers, civilians and hundreds of dead animals littered the whole area. With the warm August weather Allied pilots reported being able to smell the stench of the battlefield as they flew hundreds of feet above it. As the Germans now started to retreat they took the POWs including Bill and his crew with them.

Hawker Typhoon, serial no EK183 (RAF). Death and destruction in the Falaise Gap (source, *1st Polish Armoured Division, Press release*).

**Bill's wartime log continues:-**

**<u>The Retreat from France Begins</u>**

*In addition to this increased air activity German wounded began pouring into the hospital and this together with bits of 'gen' from Louise led me to believe the retreat from France was beginning. These wounded Germans looked to be in a very bad way—I could see them from my window—and seemed to come direct from the fighting line. These wounded men were arriving in all kinds of transport from the normal ambulance to the open lorry, to the humble horse and cart. From what I could gather as the days went by Beauvais Hospital had developed into a front line clearing station.*

*Men were coming in getting their wounds dressed and then being moved back again to presumably a different hospital. As can be well imagined the German doctors and nurses had their hands full with their own men and consequently I and my comrades were left severely alone and our ailments also.*
*At this time rumours were very prevalent as regards evacuation of the hospital patients and staff and as can be imagined we prisoners were hoping to be captured by our own forces. Discussion on these points increased daily until on the evening of 20 August 1944 our hopes were shattered when Germans entered our room, flung clothes at us and ordered us to get dressed quickly as we were 'moving'. On getting our clothing on those of us who were able to walk went downstairs into the hospital yard where an open lorry was waiting to convey us to Amiens*—as we later heard.*

**We Leave Beauvais**

*There were about eight of us prisoners and to guard us on this journey there were six armed guards. As we clambered aboard the lorry Louise and several other French girls came into the yard in order to see us off. As the lorry drew out of Beauvais Hospital these French girls completely ignored the Germans and waved to us British, wishing us good luck. In addition to this they gave us the good old 'V' sign, so it was with very mixed feelings that I saw the last of Beauvais.'*

*Amiens was the location of the Prison which was famously attacked in a low level raid by Mosquitoes from 464 Squ RAAF, 487 Squ RNZAF and 21 Squ on 18 Feb 1944 in Operation Jericho. The object was to free French prisoners due to be executed.

**Conditions at Amiens Hospital**

*My journey from Beauvais to Amiens was uneventful and after we had dropped two of our number at Amiens prison the remainder of us were taken to a hospital about two miles outside the town. The conditions existing at this hospital were the worst I have ever seen. On entering this hospital we men from Beauvais were put into a ward where there were some forty or so American and British wounded. This 'ward' as I have called it, was one of the roughest places it's ever been my lot to be in. To begin with there were approximately a dozen beds for all of us patients, so you can imagine the confusion that existed!! For the first night all the beds were bunched together and so we all slept together as tightly as sardines in a can.*

*During my stay at this hospital life became rougher and rougher. More and more Allied wounded arrived and as they were all placed in the same room as the rest of us, it can be imagined how crowded we were. Eventually the Germans threw straw into the room and we all slept on this. Our meals were very haphazard and if we got three half decent meals a day we considered ourselves very lucky indeed. The treatment of wounds here was almost non-existent and had it not been for the good nature of a couple of Dutch nurses I am sure we would all have been left entirely to ourselves. These Dutch girls were very good indeed to we prisoners and if there was anything to be done to lighten our burden then these girls did it.*

*Whilst at Amiens I met a Cardiff Wireless Operator—Sgt. Beal—living in Bannister Avenue, who'd had the misfortune to lose his leg just below the knee. The poor fellow I am sure was not quite 'all there' and I merely make note of this here as to remind me to look up his people when I get back home.*

*During my week's stay at Amiens I did nothing but dream and hope that our forces would over run us. In addition to this I seriously considered the escape angle. Escaping out of the hospital was a simple matter for a physically fit man. The main trouble was what to do on the outside. I had made up my mind to 'have a go' until I discovered that a wall some seven foot high would need to be climbed. As I was still limping and my left arm was almost useless I therefore gave up all idea of escape from Amiens. Incidentally two Air Force types did escape and I heard nothing more of them.*

## <u>We Leave Amiens</u>

*On the afternoon of the 27 August all my hopes of being overrun by the Allies were dashed away when the news of the evacuation of we prisoners was brought to us. We wounded were all transported to Amiens station where we were loaded into box cars—forty men to a car.* The floor of the box cars were strewn with straw and this box car proved to be my 'home' for six days. Conditions over this period were rougher than ever. Personal cleanliness was unheard of and at the close of the journey we certainly looked a bedraggled bunch. During the journey our attendance to the wants of nature were hardly even considered by the German guards and the only times we were 'relieved' were when the train providentially stopped in open country. The only food eaten on the journey was bread* *and margarine amounting to about two slices each. Our only drink was water—once a day! As can be imagined we suffered the pangs of both hunger and thirst.*

*Rail travel was a perilous affair as the Combined Air-forces were relentlessly attacking the road and rail networks, anything that moved was shot at! If you look at some of the film clips of trains being attacked it is quite shocking to see the locomotives exploding. Bill and his comrades were in constant danger from their own forces the whole time they were cooped up in these box cars.

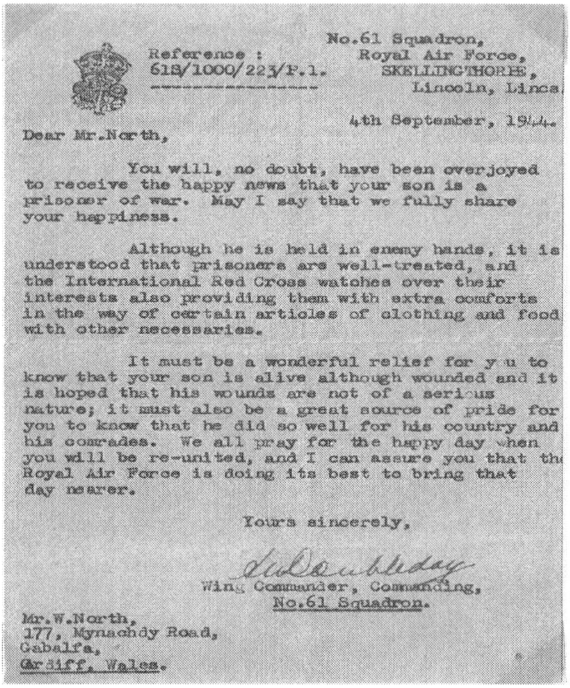

No.61 Squadron,
Royal Air Force,
SKELLINGTHORPE,
Lincoln, Lincs.

Reference :
61S/1000/223/P.1.

4th September, 1944.

Dear Mr.North,

You will, no doubt, have been overjoyed to receive the happy news that your son is a prisoner of war. May I say that we fully share your happiness.

Although he is held in enemy hands, it is understood that prisoners are well-treated, and the International Red Cross watches over their interests also providing them with extra comforts in the way of certain articles of clothing and food with other necessaries.

It must be a wonderful relief for you to know that your son is alive although wounded and it is hoped that his wounds are not of a serious nature; it must also be a great source of pride for you to know that he did so well for his country and his comrades. We all pray for the happy day when you will be re-united, and I can assure you that the Royal Air Force is doing its best to bring that day nearer.

Yours sincerely,

Wing Commander, Commanding,
No.61 Squadron.

Mr.W.North,
177, Mynachdy Road,
Gabalfa,
Cardiff, Wales.

4 Sept 1944, letter from W/C Doubleday to Bill's Dad.

## We Arrive At Limburg

*The whole journey was deadly monotonous and when on the 2 September we reached our destination—a transit camp in Limburg, Germany—sighs of relief were heaved by all. I and the wounded were taken by horse and cart to Limburg Prison camp and once again I realised that 'for me the war was over.' As I passed through the gates of the prison I observed the hated Nazi Swastika proudly flying at the head of the flag pole and heard the clang of the gates as they swung to, thus shutting me inside the barbed wire enclosure. England and home seemed a long way away at this hour.*

## My First Bath In Germany

*The first thing that happened at Limburg was a search of my person, but nothing was taken from me. Some fellows lost their watches, but as mine was without face or hands the Germans condescended to allow me to keep it. After the search the officers among us were taken apart and we were taken to have showers while our clothes were 'de-loused.' This incidentally was very necessary as we had all been living in sheer filth during our box car ride and many of our number required medical treatment in order to rid them of lice etc. The shower however was most acceptable to me as it was my first bath since my fated Fourth of July. Unfortunately though I had to use German soap which certainly wasn't of the best quality—or for that matter, quantity! After the shower there were no towels available and so we had to dry ourselves as best we could over a couple of radiators. What a life!*

## Living Quarters At Limburg

*After thus being introduced to German hospitality we were marched away to a building which turned out to be the Officer's barracks. The barracks consisted of one huge room which housed about two hundred officers. This room served for eating and sleeping so one can imagine the 'luxury' in which we dwelt!! The beds were arranged in three tier bunks which were filled with straw palliasses* [mattresses consisting of a thin pad filled with straw or sawdust]. *Food at Limburg was both scarce and of poor quality. The daily diet consisted of cabbage soup commonly called 'purple passion' by the prisoners. This 'purple passion' was very queer soup and while I was at Limburg it worked upon all the prisoners by giving them a dose of dysentery. However some of the prisoners didn't eat too badly as they were issued with Red Cross Parcels. Unfortunately I and those with me arrived a day after the issue of these parcels and so we were politely told that we were 'just unlucky.' Thus during my four days at Limburg I truly knew once again what it was like to feel hungry.*

## A Second Interrogation

*On my second day at Limburg I was called for by the Germans for interrogation. At this interrogation a form which was ostensibly a Red Cross form to be sent to Geneva, was pushed across at me by a German Officer. On glancing at this form I found that it required me to fill in various information. The form started off innocently enough with name, rank, number and a few other personal particulars. However, after this I found it required almost every conceivable piece of military information from my Squadron number, Group number and Command, to the target on which I was shot down and the date on which I was shot down! After reading this I filled in all the personal particulars on the form and then pushed it away from me. When the German Officer saw this action of mine he took me up and began to first plead and then ended up threatening me with the Gestapo. However I still wouldn't give him what he required and so eventually he let me go back to the officers' quarters.*

## I Meet A Friend

*After this I spent another two days at Limburg during which time I met Ron Grant,* a lad from Cardiff who's Mother knows mine. Quite a coincidence I thought.*

*Ron Grant as mentioned above was a Typhoon pilot and lived in Manor Street where Bill was born. Bill said Ron was flying with 609 Squ in Normandy from July to August 1944 and became a POW when he was forced to bale out after engine failure.

## I Leave Limburg for Wetzlar

*During the afternoon of this day I, together with quite a number of prisoners, departed from Limburg for yet another destination. I eventually found out that our next stop was to be yet another transit camp, namely Dulag Luft Wetzlar.* The journey to Wetzlar only took about twelve hours and so we spent only one night on the train. This time we were fortunate in our mode of travel in as much as we weren't confined to box cars. Instead we travelled in normal passenger cars built in the American style. The only difference was the windows were barred and the seats were wooden. Still as prisoners we couldn't really grumble.*

*On the following morning, 7 September, we disembarked from the train and were marched about a mile or so to 'Dulag Luft,' another German prison camp. This Wetzlar camp had much the same sinister air about it as had Limburg. However on gaining admittance we found that the place was almost exclusively run by British and American personnel as far as feeding and clothing were concerned. We had hardly arrived at Wetzlar when we were each issued with a Red Cross Suitcase containing almost everything a new Kriegie requires from a razor to a complete set of underclothes. In addition to this suitcase I also passed through a clothing store where my sleeveless battledress was exchanged for an airman's tunic. Having attired ourselves in our new uniforms we were marched over to the dining hall where I had my first decent meal since being shot down. This meal, breakfast, consisted almost exclusively of Red Cross foods. What a change! The tinned salmon and jams made the German bread quite eatable. During my six days at Wetzlar I ate reasonably well and so had no real grumble. Wetzlar had quite a presentable library and so most of my time was spent in reading—and waiting for the next meal!'*

*Dulag Luft was a holding camp where POWs were held before transfer to permanent Stalag Luft camps. This is also where further interrogation would occur in varying degrees of intensity.

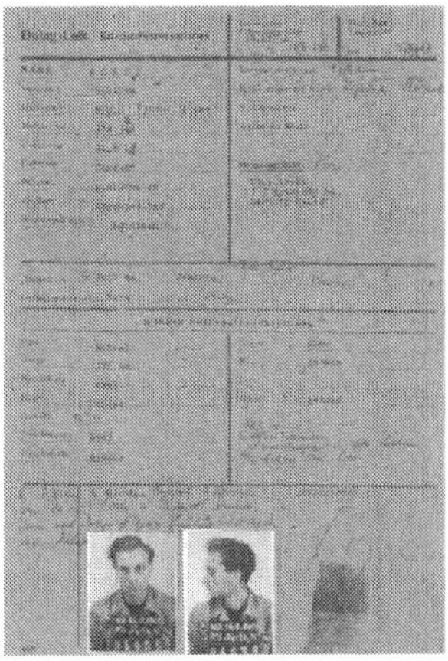

Bill's Dulag Luft 7A, Identity card.

**13 September 1944*, I Leave Wetzlar And The Journey To Barth.**

*On this day I found my name placed on a posting list for Stalag Luft 1 in Barth, Pomerania. As can well be imagined my feelings at leaving for a permanent camp were not exactly high. However as evening drew nigh I got all ready to leave Wetzlar. My person and belongings were searched by the Germans and I was issued with a Red Cross parcel of food for my journey. I travelled in the same type of train as before—eight to a compartment with wooden seats. During our three days on this train our greatest difficulty was sleeping. Eventually we had two sleeping on the luggage racks, two on the seats and the remaining four crowded together and slept on the floor. What fun! During the journey to Barth we had numerous air raids and on each occasion the train always stopped until the 'all clear' sounded. On several occasions we heard bombs dropping, whilst one in particular bombs dropped very close indeed and we actually heard strafing aircraft. When this happened all the German guards had gone to shelter, whilst we unfortunates were left locked up in the railway coaches. Apart from air raids however our journey was without incident. Our Red Cross rations were supplemented by German bread and a form of German meat sausage, so we certainly ate better than on the ride from France. More than this I can't say'.*

*13 Sept 1944 was two years to the day that Bill had set sail on the Queen Elizabeth from Gourock to New York. Bill's parents received the POW Telegram on the 1 September 1944 and on 2 September the Air Ministry Letter. On 20 Dec 1944 they received a Post Card from radio ham W. Cookson, recording that Bremen Radio had broadcast that Bill was a POW.

## 16 SEPTEMBER 1944. I ARRIVE AT STALAG LUFT 1.

This camp was located near the town of Barth on the Baltic coast about 30 miles west of Stettin. It was typical of many German prisons:- guards with dogs, searchlights, postern boxes manned with machine guns, barbed and electrified wire and barrack rooms/huts which were raised one to four feet above the ground. There were 52 escape tunnels built, but none of them were successful. There were constant roll calls and searches and the derogatory nickname for the Guards was 'Goons'. This was taken from a ridiculous looking Disney character and was disliked intensely by the Germans who eventually banned its use.

POWs arriving at Stalag Luft 1, September 1944. I have looked closely, but can't see Bill in this photo (source, p129, Derek Brammer, *Thundering Through The Clear Air*).

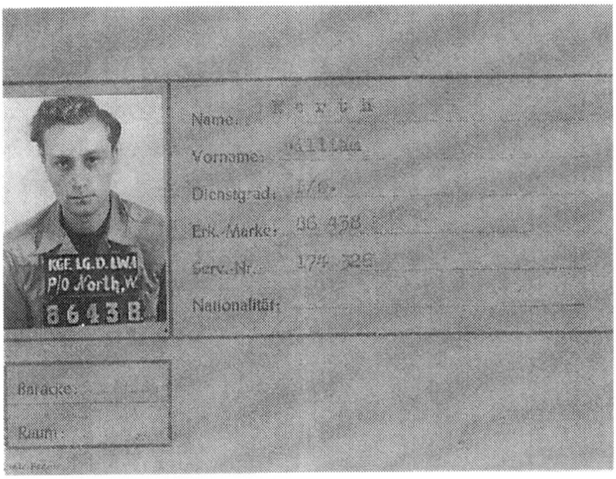


Bill's Stalag Luft 1 ID card.

This picture is taken from North 2 overlooking North 1 compound, between the warning wire and main fence is about 20ft of compacted barbed wire and a single strand of barbed wire about 18 inches from the ground. Anybody who touched or stepped over this low wire would be shot. The snow around the wire has been compacted by hundreds of prisoners walking around it (source, *Stalag Luft 1 Website*).

*'On this day I arrived at my permanent camp which was about a mile or so outside Barth Railway Station. This prison camp had the usual barbed wire fences complete with Postern Boxes filled with guards and machine guns. It struck me that the chances of escape from a place of this type were very remote indeed. Once I got inside the prison camp I was given a very welcome shower, after which I was overjoyed and surprised to see my old friend George Langford.* He immediately took care of me and led me off to a bed in the same room as himself. (Room 6, barrack 10) Here*

*we compared notes and made a lot of unique discoveries which cannot be recorded here.*

*George Langford was with Bill in ITW in Torquay and EFTS in Canada.

This picture is on the South compound inner border overlooking the shower block, parade ground and solitary confinement block, Barth Church can be seen in the background (source, *Stalag Luft 1 website*).

*After the first few weeks I managed to settle down, more or less to camp routine. The Kriegie's favourite cry then was 'Home for Xmas' and after what I'd seen in France, I really believed that my chances of seeing home and my folks for Xmas '44 were pretty good.* [The feeling amongst the Allies at this time was that the War would be over by Xmas 1944, unfortunately it dragged on until May 45.] *Well week followed week and so grew into months until Xmas was upon us and yet the war still hadn't ended. However, all things considered, thanks to the Red Cross especially, these months were a lot better than I expected. Red Cross food parcels were plentiful and so we didn't really suffer the pangs of hunger. One thing I did discover however was that a 'Kriegie's' morale fluctuates with three things. Namely mail,* Red Cross parcels and last but not by any means least, News. With the aid of these commodities a prisoner is helped to bear his lost freedom as a soldier should do. Unfortunately space does not permit me to write a full pen picture of a prisoner's life and troubles and so I shall carry on with this, my scanty story.*

*Some prisoners didn't like bad news from home especially anything adverse to do with wives or girlfriends; this would often tip them over the edge emotionally.

*Xmas and the New Year came and went with many a thought and wish for the folks back home. Then came the news of the Great Russian Offensive which we gradually perceived was sweeping across the plains of Poland towards the River Oder—and Berlin! Would this offensive end the war? Could the Russians keep it up? These were questions which every prisoner was asking.* Eventually good old'Joe' came to a stop along the River Oder and so once again we prisoners sat back and waited for the next big push. It was not long coming! At a given signal in February the Allies in the West struck. Before long the German Armies were in difficulties and the Allies had moved their front right up to the Rhine. Shortly following this we'd crossed the Rhine at Remagen and then on the 24 March 1945—' Monty' struck along the Lower Rhine and news of a great Offensive with airborne landings has come in! Once again the 'Kriegies' are waiting—and hoping! Again the same questions are being asked! The same hopes are being hoped! And everyone is saying 'it won't be long now!' God grant that it won't!'*

*It is worth noting that at no time did Bill or the others think we would lose the war and were counting down the days to the freedom that they knew they would taste again; the long wait however was unbearably frustrating. One of the greatest camp secrets were there crystal radio sets that kept POWs up to date with the progress of the war. Only a couple of POWs knew the secret location of these sets and they were never found in searches.

## A Transformation at Stalag Luft 1

*'In order that those who may read these few lines shall realise 'what it's all about' I intend writing a brief résumé showing—very roughly—what conditions were like at Stalag Luft 1 prior to the 'Transformation Era' which commenced on the 24th March 1945.*
*From the latter part of January until the 24 March 1945 conditions had gone from bad to worse. First and most important, our food situation had dropped to something bordering very closely on starvation limits. To illustrate this point I'll quote the camp medical authorities re our calorie consumption in the middle of March. A starvation diet gives a man 900 calories per day, whist our calorie consumption at Stalag Luft 1 was merely 1100 calories—normal calorie consumption is anywhere between 2000 and 4000 calories!! As can quite easily be seen the position was not exactly reassuring. This serious food situation was brought about primarily by the complete stoppage of Red Cross Food Parcels, but in addition to this, our*

*already meagre German Rations were cut and then again re-cut. Not only was our food ration cut, but also our coal and coke ration so that what with the wild March winds driving the dust and sand into our eyes, together with that gnawing feeling in the stomach, our thoughts were not of the happiest. To add to our feelings of misery, about the middle of March two of our members were shot by guards during an air raid. Subsequently one of these two LT Wyman of the USAAF died of his wounds. Yes at this period, we prisoners were going through a most trying ordeal!!*

*Then suddenly something happened which raised us from our apathy. On Saturday 24 March 1945 news was received that Field Marshall Montgomery had gone over to the offensive.*

*From this day on we began a most Golden week which completely transformed the inmates of 'Luft 1'. The following day, Sunday, was truly a gala day bringing with it great news of allied advances and treat of treats, a meat rissole per man! Having been off meat for months this horse meat rissole—the size of a billiard ball—was truly delicious. In addition to this undreamt of delicacy the camp orchestra played some popular music during the afternoon. All this combined with glorious sunbathing weather, succeeded in sky rocketing the camp's morale to unprecedented heights. Monday brought the news that a 'few' Red Cross Food parcels were in, so we all began 'sweating out' a ¼ issue each. Tuesday and Wednesday saw some more food parcels arriving until a full issue per man was assured. Also the war situation was improving daily, nay hourly, new crossings of the Rhine had been made and General Patton was sweeping across Germany at an unheard of speed. Thursday, Friday and Saturday brought the 'same old story'—more and more Red Cross parcels and better and better war news. 'Monty' had broken out in the north whilst Patton was still going like a 'house on fire' in the south. A gigantic move was on foot to cut off the whole of the Ruhr and well known large German towns such as Ludwigshafen, Frankfurt, Dortmund, Hagen and Gladbeck were being captured daily. Easter Sunday concluded this wonderful week of transformation when news was received that the Western Allies were now nearer Leipzig than were the Russians!! To celebrate all that this past week had meant to we 'Kriegies', large meals of Red Cross food were the order of the day and so for the first time in many months our hunger was appeased.*

*From the foregoing I hope readers will realise why Holy Week 1945 will live forever in the hearts of the inmates of Stalag Luft 1. For us prisoners of war the sun assuredly shone through and broke up the dark and dismal rain clouds. In addition to this we all realised that most precious of all, our liberation day, home and all a prisoner looks forward to was at last in sight...............'*

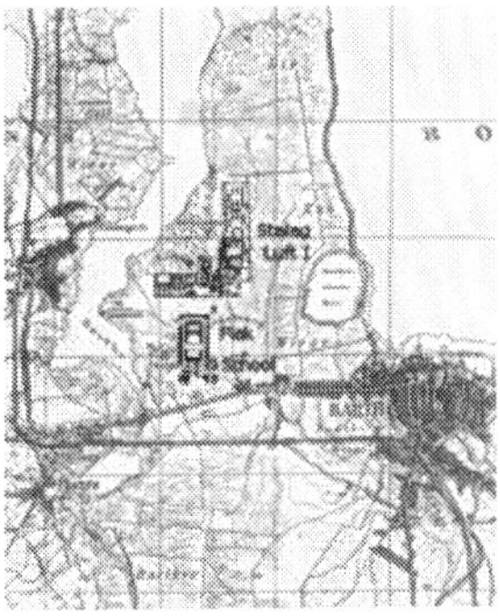

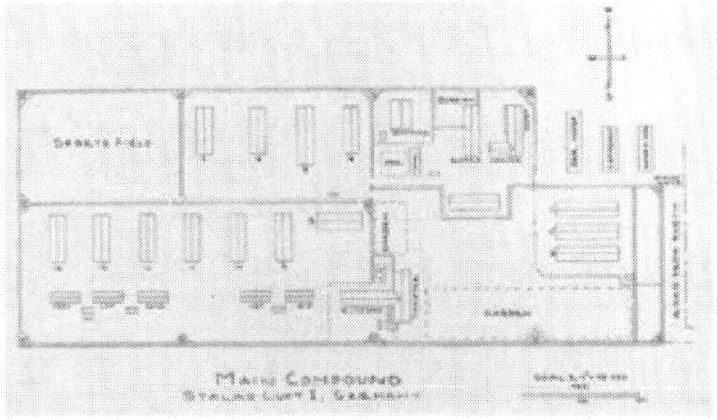

Barth map and drawing of Main Compound. The Luftwaffe was responsible for Air Force POWs and maintained a general degree of professional respect for fellow flyers. Approximately 8,939 Allied Airmen (7,588 USSAF and 1,351 RAF) were imprisoned at Stalag Luft 1 in Barth (*POW VETS.COM* and *Stalag Luft 1 website*).

Bill was in Barrack 10 room 6. The Barrack commander was W/Cmdr William David Gordon Watkins (DSO, DFC, DFM). While on his 2nd Tour on 16 Nov 1944, he was the only survivor in 15 Squ's Master Bomber Lancaster PB 137, LS-U as it exploded over Heinsburg ejecting him from the wreckage. While Bill was a POW the Senior Allied Compound Commander was Col. Einar Malmstom (The Malmstom Airforce base in Montana is named after him) The Senior British Officer was Grp. Capt. N.W.D. Marwood-Elton. The senior US Officer was Lt. Col. Wangeman. Rarely seen, the Camp Commandant was Oberst Williband Scherer, actually a very cultured man, a competent musician, and the best type of officer. He was in fact removed from Luft 1 and sent to Berlin to face charges of undue leniency towards the POWs. Luckily the end of the war saved him from any punishment. His Adjutant was Major Buchard and the Lager Officer's for South or West Compound was Hauptmann Luckt and Major Opperman. The German Intelligence Officer was Major von Muller who had lived in the States before the war owning a butchers shop in New York (he apparently recognised one US inmate asking how his mother was). He wasn't well liked and was said to be the man waving the white surrender flag for Barth to the Russians.

As the last days of the War were unfolding the Russians were fast approaching Stalg Luft 1 from the east and artillery fire could be constantly heard. It soon became clear that the Russians would reach the camp before the Americans. Shouts of 'Come on Joe' (Joseph Stalin) could be heard at night time from the POWs. The Camp Commandant Colonel Warnstedt and the guards realised they must move before the Russians came, so they approached the Senior Allied POW Officers of the camp, Col Hubert Zemke and Group Captain Weir* and advised them to evacuate all the POWs. Col Hubert Zemke, a US Eighth Air Force ace with 31 enemy aircraft to his credit, 19 in the air and 11 on the ground, promptly refused this request and said, 'the Gemans could do what they like, but they were going nowhere.' The Commandant then informed Col Zemke the Germans would leave the camp at midnight on the 30 April 1945. The responsibility for camp order and of the safe return of all the POWs now fell to Zemke and Weir.

When Bill awoke on 1 May 1945 and looked around he noticed that all the Germans had gone and there were POWs with armbands that said 'FF' manning the guard towers. Col Zemke explained that the POWs could not just start leaving the camp on their own, as there was a war going on all around them and they could be shot. He felt it best to keep the camp secure in an effort to protect the POWs. As frustrating as this was, Bill said he followed this advice as he didn't want to risk 'losing his skin' when freedom was so tantalisingly close.

Col Zemke sent a scouting party out to make contact with the approaching Russians and later in the day Lt Alec Nick Karmyzoff entered the camp. The Russian commander immediately ordered that the fences be torn down and many POWs left camp and went into Barth and the surrounding areas. The Russians arrived in full force on 2 May and on 4 May announced Berlin had fallen to the Russians and they had linked up with the Allies. There was also a flypast of two Thunderbolts from Zemke's 56th Fighter Group. American troops arrived on the 5 May after a camp parade for Russian Commander Marshal Rokatofski with details of the repatriation plan. On the 6 May the Russians rounded up pigs and cows for the hungry POWs to slaughter and eat. There was much celebration among the newly freed POWs and the Russian soldiers, with Cossack dancers and film clips. On the 7 May the inmates were informed that Germany had surrendered. Bill said his impressions of the Russians were that they were quite rough and imposing looking Cossack types. They were asking 'Why weren't the POWs leaving the camp to get drunk and rape the local women.' Bill's reply was 'That that was not the way Allied servicemen behaved.'

*G/C (Ginger) CT Weir had an extraordinary survival experience on 21/22 Nov 1944 on Ops to Gravenhorst (Mittelland Canal). He was in 49 Squ Lanc PB300, EA-K. It is believed that along with 49 Squ's F/O EC Maul PB354, EA-G these two aircraft exploded after being hit by bombs from above or light flak. GC Weir was ejected in the explosion and the only survivor out of the two crews, regaining consciousness lying on his back on the muddy bottom of the breached and drained canal. It was a double miracle for if 5 Group's crews hadn't being successful in hitting their target and draining over 30 miles of the canal he would have drowned!

## Operation Revival

Bill's journal does not cover this next period, but after discussing the evacuation with him he confirmed he felt impatient at having to wait these extra days after having already waited so long. He did however relate a fascinating story about how he was amongst the last people to leave the camp in a B-17 Flying Fortress.

Following the earlier celebrations tension had started to build up to boiling point between the Russians and Americans as to the exact fate of the POWs. This was the beginning of Cold War hostilities, with similar scenes witnessed by many across the wreckage of Europe. Considered to be our friends and Allies it was quickly becoming apparent the Russians had a different agenda. They wanted the Stalag Luft 1 POWs transported by land to Odessa, a port on the Black Sea, then finally home by ship. This idea was quickly rejected and further negotiations followed. The Russian hindrance was no accident, but intentional. Little did they know, but the POWs in Russian zones of occupation had become political pawns that Stalin was playing games with. The Russians stalled and delayed the POWs transfer while Stalin cemented his political control over Poland and demanded the return of Russian POWs and 'traitors' (p223-225, *The Last Escape*, John Nichol and Tony Rennell).

The delay at Stalag Luft 1 was a major cause for concern amongst Bill and the other British POWs. If the Russians got their way it would make his long-awaited journey home much longer and more uncertain, he must have followed news of these negotiations anxiously. It was a huge relief for Bill when he heard that on 11 May the Allies secured permission to use Barth Airport which was a short distance from the camp for the evacuation home. They only had a short time period from the 12, 13, 14 May 1945 to evacuate 9,000 liberated POWs.

The USAAF 91st Bombardment Group were assigned to the urgent mission to rescue the American and British POWs from Stalag Luft I at Barth, there still serious concerns that these men were going to be marched off to Russia. A fleet of B-17G Flying Fortresses were quickly modified to carry 25 to 30 POWs with a basic 5 man crew and strict orders not to carry more than 32 men. Over the weekend of the 12

May more than 200 USAAF Heavy Bombers under the command of Brig/Gen William M Gross were assigned to take part in the shuttle service. The POWs were gathered together with their few belongings and marched by barrack groups the short distance to Barth airport.

Cartoon caricatures from Bill's YMCA Log book depicting the daily POW grind.

Luckily for Bill and his comrades Stalag Luft 1 proved to be the only camp held by the Soviets to be evacuated by air. There was a reason for this. A US/Soviet deal had been struck to hand back captured Russian 'traitor' Andrei Vlasov, who had fought for Hitler. Vlasov was handed back to the Russians at 14:30 and the B-17s circling the sky above Barth were allowed to land at 15:30 (p226-227, *The Last Escape*, John Nichol and Tony Rennell).The first a/c to arrive on the 12 May was a B-17 with General William Gross on board, who was the Commander of the 1st Air Division of the Eighth Airforce. This was shortly followed by two more B-17s with communication equipment and personnel and later in the afternoon about 40 more B-17s arrived. Early on the morning of the 13 May the sick and wounded were evacuated in six C-46s, Bill was not one of these. Dozens of additional C-46s and C-47s joined the B-17s in the evacuation process, the aircraft crept slowly along as the men boarded. On the morning of the third day, the 14th, the remaining men were all flown out aboard B-17s. On 12, 13 and 14 May 1945 approximately 9,000 POWs were flown out of Barth and back into Allied control. The last prisoner aboard was Col.Zemke and according to Zemke's records 8,487 prisoners had been evacuated. Royal Air Force POWs were flown back to England to Bassingbourne and the American POWs were flown to Camp Lucky Strike in Le Havre, France, where they were processed and waited for ships to return to the US (*Stalag Luft 1 website*).

91st Bomb Group B-17s in line loading POWs and taking off at Barth airport (source, *Stalag Luft 1 website*).

Bill was in one of the last groups of POWs to be evacuated from Barth, bringing to an end a 6 month period of incarceration for him. This was because he had had a last minute operation in the camp hospital to rejoin the nerves in his shattered left arm. The op was performed by a Scottish surgeon called Mr J MacPherson from Kingspark in Glasgow. Bill was later told that under the rough circumstances the surgeon had done an extremely good job.

**F/Lt Bill North**

*'I was sent down to the infirmary where I was told to give myself an enema, 'I said a what?'and then somebody told me what it was, oh joy! I had to lie on a rough wooden table, there was no anaesthetic and I was knocked out with chloroform. When I woke up my arm was in plaster and there was a metal screw poking out which I had to turn a bit each day to stretch the arm. Ron Grant arrived back at home in Cardiff before me and when my parents who were extremely worried at my delay asked him what happened he had no idea, but could only tell them that I must have still been at the camp.'*

Bill was in fact on one of the last flights out of Barth because the operation on his arm had delayed him somewhat. He said, *'I don't remember much about the flight home it was a bit hazy, although it was in a B-17 Flying Fortress.'* It is possible that Bill was flown back to Basingbourne on Monday 14 May 1945, although the British POWs were flown back to various different bases first (Coincidentally, this is the base that Dennis Bartlett served at after the war).On landing they had a medical assessment, were deloused and showered, then given new uniforms to replace their battered, worn or battle damaged ones. Next came a debriefing session, before finally returning back to their hometowns and families for an extended period of leave.

Bill immediately sent a telegram home and was then transferred to Manchester Airport where his family was anxiously waiting for him.

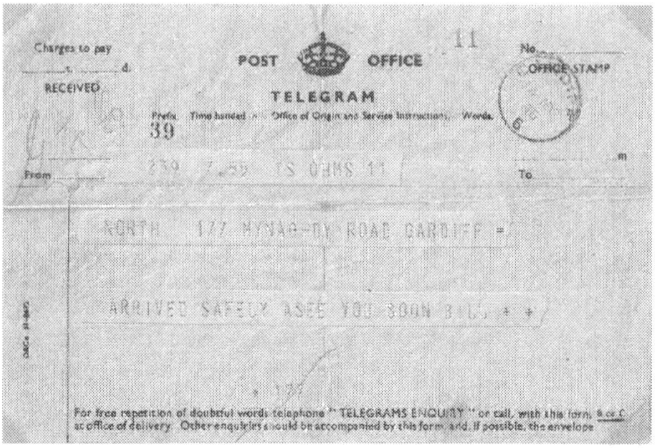

POST OFFICE TELEGRAM

Charges to pay

RECEIVED

39

NORTH 177 MYNACHDY ROAD CARDIFF =

ARRIVED SAFELY SEE YOU SOON BILL + +

For free repetition of doubtful words telephone "TELEGRAMS ENQUIRY" or call, with this form, at office of delivery. Other enquiries should be accompanied by this form and, if possible, the envelope

Bill's 'arrived home safely' telegram, 14 May 1945.

**<u>F/Lt Bill North</u>**

*'I do remember sending Mum and Dad a telegram saying that I had arrived safely. When I finally flew into Manchester Airport the next day my Mum, Dad and sister Iris were all waiting for me, what a surprise that was! My Dad then told me that my on-off WAAF girlfriend Sheila Randell was coming to see me that weekend. Looking back on it now it seems a bit off, but I said, 'What did you tell her to come down for?'*
*My Dad said, 'Well if you want to finish with her son, you will have to tell her yourself.'*

Bill and the POWs at Luft I had experienced the same frustration that the rest of the world was feeling as everybody anxiously waited for the news that the War was over. Impatience for the end of the War was overwhelming and that first week of May 1945 had seemed to drag on forever; especially for the POWs because they were stuck at Barth. Finally though after experiencing hardships that were beyond belief, Bill was back home with his family in Cardiff; all the waiting and frustration had finally come to an end. Although Bill had missed the VE day celebrations and the euphoric wave that swept across the country, he celebrated his freedom and the end of the war quietly with his family and friends at Mynachdy Road, Cardiff.

Bill told me, *'When Ron Grant got married shortly after our return he asked me to be his best man. I said, 'What, with my arm in a cast?'*

*He said, 'Don't be silly, they will all feel sorry for us.'*
*And so it was, there is a picture somewhere of me with my arm in a cast at his wedding.'*

Bill had looked for the above photo many times at Regal Way and couldn't find it anywhere. It was presumed to be lost. In May 2012 I had a meeting with Alun North and my editor Brandon Robshaw. Afterwards Alun gave me a box with some of Bill's books and WW2 stuff in. The box came back home with me and sat in our junk room downstairs for a few months until a small flood in the room forced me to clear out the room. I emptied out the box of books and as I picked up John Terrain's *Right Of The Line* something fell out of the book on the floor at my feet. I looked down and there was this 'lost' photo of Bill staring up at me. The hairs on my arms stood up on end as I bent down and picked it up!

After the eventual return home of the rest of his crew, Bill and his comrades now went on their own life journeys, never losing that incredible bond that was forged in death's dark shadow.

**List of 18 Roomates in Room 6, Barrack 10, South Compound**

K.J. Ayres, England
Bernard C. Baker, New Zealand
E.D. Cleary—TAF
F.J. Cleary, Australia
T.S. Coram, Australia
Robert W. Dunn, Canada
P.C. Gore, England
George A.H. Langford, England (Bill's mate from ITW in Torquay)
Oscar E. Libbey, Sydney, Cape Breton, Nova Scotia, Canada

H. Matthews, England

J.B. Morison, Canada

T.L.W. Mullinder, New Zealand (I spoke to Trevor Mullinder in New Zealand in July 2010 after making contact with Chris Brereton through Stalag Luft 1 website, he remembered Bill really well.)

William (Bill) North, England (Wales, Cardiff)

J.S. Prentice, New Zealand

T.A. Sheen—RAG

A.A. Thomas, New Zealand

I.R.M. Weir, New Zealand

A.J.R. Wilson, New Zealand

Bill's roommate Canadian, Oscar Libbey, drawn by a Stalag Luft 7 guard. This was sent to me by *Harold O'Connell*, Oscar's Libbey's nephew in Canada, after we made contact through Stalag Luft 1 website (Oscar passed away a while back, both his brothers were in service too).

# Chapter Twenty One

## Stalag Luft 7, Courage, Endurance and Friendship

While Bill eventually became an inmate at Stalag Luft 1, his crew became POWs many miles to the south of Germany in Stalag Luft 7, Bankau in Silesia. Theirs is a remarkable story of courage and endurance, and it's told here through the eye-witness accounts of Dennis Bartlett and Norman Jarvis. By early Jan 1945 Stalag Luft 7 held over 1,500 POWs, mostly RAF crews with a mixture of nationalities; British, US, Canadian, Polish and Russian. The site is now located at Baków near Kreuzburg in Poland.

Bill North's surviving crew members Norman Jarvis, Monty Monteith, Dennis Bartlett and Eddy O'Shea arrived at Slag Luft 7 at slightly different times to each other, due to their varying degrees of injury. This camp was not for RAF Officers, but for other Aircrew ranks, which included Gunners, Bomb Aimers, Navigators and Wireless Operators. RAF and USSAF Pilot Officers were separated from their crews and sent to different camps. The most famous of these being Stalag Luft 3 at Sagan, the camp that the Great Escape was from and subsequent film of the same name was based on.

Again the War Diary of Norman Jarvis gives us a detailed analysis and eyewitness account of what life was like for Bill's crew at Stalag Luft 7. Dennis Bartlett's injuries were superficial and he was separated from Bill in mid July 1944 and transferred to Dulag-Luft on 24 July 1944. His journey was eventful and he had more close encounters with death along the way, eventually arriving at Stalag Luft 7 on the 5 August 1944. (As told in a later Chapter Bill and Dennis had another life story of their own.)

From Bill's Wartime Log we know that Eddy and Monty weren't seriously injured and were transferred to Dulag Luft from Beauvais Prison soon after being taken there, this was the last time that Bill saw Monty in person. Norman was badly injured from his descent by parachute and stayed with Bill until their transfer to Amiens and then to Limburg.

### W/O Dennis Bartlett's eye witness account of leaving Beauvais to go to Stalag Luft 7.

*'The last time I saw Bill was in July 1944 in the Beauvais Hospital. My leg wounds were not serious and I was considered fit to be transferred onto permanent Stalag Luft. I stood at the door to Bill's room and called out to say goodbye, but the young guard with me shoved me forwards and that was the last time I saw him until 2011. I was put on a truck and with an old German guard. As we drove south out of Beauvais towards Paris the guard pointed out the Memorial to the R101 Airship which was at the side of the main road.* It's funny the things that you remember, this for some reason*

*made an impression on me. When I arrived in Paris we were left at some marshalling yards. I was still travelling on my own with the old German guard. There was a group of French railway workers going past us and they were cheering and waving at all the RAF boys, I will never forget that. Suddenly the air raid sirens went off and I saw a wave of Lancasters turning to come across the marshalling yards and then dropping their bombs. We all ran for cover as the bombs exploded around us all, how we were not killed I don't know. It was strange being on the other end of a bombing raid. Sadly however all the French workers who had been waving at us just moments before were killed at the other end of the marshalling yards.* [Dennis had tears in his eyes as he recounted this event to me]. *Eventually I was put on a train with my guard and this is where I met three RAF escapees. They called out to me and said, 'Come with us'. I said, 'What about the guard?' They said, 'We will take care of him' and one of them pulled his coat back to reveal a service revolver. I felt sorry for my guard because he was old and I didn't want them to kill him. I said, 'Don't worry I will make my own way' and that was that, they then disappeared.*

*I was transferred to Dalag Luft by train and then onto Stalag Luft 7 at Bankau in Poland. Norman, Monty and Eddy eventually came here too and I ended up sharing a room with Monty who really looked after me. Monty slept above me and life in the camp was pretty monotonous with roll calls twice a day. We had Red Cross parcels, but these eventually became scarce and food was always a topic of conversation. We were always hungry. There were regular bombing raids and we had to stay inside during them. During one raid a young Canadian wondered out of the billet before it was over and was shot dead by a guard. Everyone was up in arms about this, but there was nothing we could do. Apparently the guard's family had died in a bombing raid and he hated Air Force men.*

*Eventually at the start of 1945 the Russians were not far from the camp, we could hear the artillery fire very close by and we thought we would be liberated, but the Germans had different ideas. On the 19 Jan at very short notice we were told to take what we could carry and force marched out of the camp back towards Germany. It was during one of the coldest winters on record and this later became known as 'The Long March.' Years later I got a letter from a chap called Len Cooper who was at Luft 7 with us. He recalled all the events we went through there, but I lost touch with him as well.'*

*This was a 40 mile, 65km journey on the E46 or Route Nationale 1; the main trunk road between Paris, Amiens and Calais. The R101 British Airship crashed near here on 5 October 1930, killing 48 out of the 54 passengers; in comparison there were 35 fatalities on the Hindenburg on 6 May 1937.

The R101 Memorial (source, *Gleisgewurschtel*).

Norman Jarvis was also eventually transferred to Stalag Luft 7. It was common for aircrew to lose consciousness whilst baling out. Some did not remember their descent like Norman and he woke up disorientated to find himself lying in a field. Some landed in rivers or water to be drowned and never found, or others dying when they hit the ground. All aircrew whose lives were saved by parachuting out of a disabled a/c automatically became members of the *'Caterpillar Club'*.

The club was formed by Leslie Irvin in 1922 as an acknowledgement to the silk threads that parachutes were originally made from. A unique gold pin in the shape of a caterpillar was awarded to people whose lives were saved (It is estimated that some 10,000 RAF crew were saved by the Irvin parachute during the War).* Out of Bill's crew, Norman Jarvis, Dave Crowley and Eddy O'Shea would have been entitled to this wear this pin having parachuted to safety on the 5 July 1944 (Dave Crowley's daughter Janet Legg was wearing her father's pin when Peter Done met her whilst working in Kettering General Hospital).

*Aviation Heritage Centre.

Caterpillar Pin. 'Life depends on a silken thread' is the club's motto (photo by *Lou Sander*).

**Here is Norman Jarvis's account taken from his War Diary, starting form when he baled out of EE186, QR-D.**

**W/O Norman Jarvis**

*'I jettisoned the front escape hatch and then something hit me and that is all I remember of the night's battle. It was perhaps about eight o'clock when I regained consciousness the next day. I opened my eyes and thought where can I be? Am I dead? If not, why not? As I thought of the previous night, I could remember nothing after getting rid of the front escape hatch, but I must have fallen out. Some French girls were staring down at me and one bent over and kissed me on the cheek. Well I thought the natives are friendly, but I must have looked a wreck lying there half dead in my harness and blood soaked flying clothes. My fighting boots and two pairs of socks were missing, having evidently fallen off during my descent; my feet were cold and I was damp all over from the morning mist.* [This was a common occurrence with RAF flying boots on descent by parachute].

*The English lady arrived then; she seemed a tall, middle aged woman and she spoke very kindly to me and explained my position to me. There were Jerries all around and they must have known by now I was there and she said I looked to be badly wounded, and after a futile attempt to get me on my feet, they decided I would have to get medical aid straight away; that meant the Germans would have to know. By this time I was unconscious again and the next time I woke up I saw my first German soldiers. They were kneeling over me slapping my thighs and saying—'Pistola, pistola, haben ye pistola?' I realised they wanted to know if I had a pistol. It happened that this night none of our crew had worn the heavy .45 calibre revolvers we had issued to us. I was then put on a stretcher and taken to a magnificent French Château.*

*According to Eddy who had been rounded up by this time and saw them bringing me in, he said I was out all the time and the Jerries didn't think I had much chance of survival. Towards evening I remember waking up in the back of a truck with Bill and Dennis lying beside me. I asked them how they were and they both said they had been wounded, but were not too bad. They knew about five of the crew up to now; only Dave Crowley and the Flight Engineer Dennis Hatchet were unaccounted for.*

*Sometime on the night of the 6 July after a cruel journey over what seemed the roughest road in the world we arrived at a big German occupied French hospital at Beauvais.* [Bill also mentions in his Wartime Log that this was a really rough journey too] *I can remember sitting on a chair and a grim-looking doctor was putting some stitches in my chin where it had been torn open the night before. Later on I found myself in a room with an American Captain and a British Airman. They had broken legs or something, but seemed nice chaps. The pain of my back and arm was very considerable now, but I was not conscious very much in those first two days. When I was, I thought of everyone and everything I ever knew and wondered what my friends and family would think and silently prayed that my back was not broken and that I would not always be a cripple. From what I had seen of the Jerries up until now they were kind in a way. There was a nurse who constantly seemed to be watching over me in my little private room, now trying to give me some soft food and I know she gave me a lot of morphia injections. At the end of the first week the boys (Bill and Dennis) told me that it was to this kind German nurse that I owed my life and her maiden name was Maria: she did not treat me as an enemy, but she was a nurse for mankind and she did her duty nobly.*

*It was about the fifth day after I was shot down that Denny* [Dennis Bartlett] *came into my room and I was able to take in what he was saying. It was then that he told me the story of the rest of my crew after I left the plane. I felt better after that first week, but was still on my back and felt weak and tired and was out of danger. The hospital was heavily guarded, but when Bill got on his feet he came to see me for a few moments daily, so did some of the Americans who were able to move about. Our treatment was not too bad and I was later put in the ward with the other boys, but suffered a lot of pain from various contraptions they had on my arm to try and stretch it where it had been broken and could not move very much for a month.*

*It was then that the hospital started to get crowded with our own men and thousands of German wounded coming into the other wing of the place.*

*Our bombers were over constantly and bombs used to drop very close at times. We also learned from the French girls who swept up our ward that our Army was advancing rapidly and would soon be up to Paris.* [The German garrison in Paris surrendered to the Free French Forces and the Allies on 25 August 1944, so the boys were very close to being liberated.] *The girls risked a great deal to talk to us and we had to do it cleverly as the guards kept a good eye on them.*

*I had been up only one day and then only on my feet a few minutes when the doctor came in and pulled the pin out of my arm that was supposed to be stretching it; this caused me a great deal of pain. He then said we were being evacuated and on the night of 20 August we left Beauvais under heavy guard on the back of a truck, with the American Army only two days off Beauvais. We arrived at Amiens near day break and were put on the floor of a room in an old Asylum with many other Allied wounded. It was terrible to see those young soldiers and airmen with horrible burns and open wounds lying there, some near death on the hard floor and only with a swift inspection by one doctor daily. All around there were smashed limbs and the groans and cries at night was nerve racking, but two Dutch nurses tried their best to make them comfortable and the young Canadian medical orderly worked wonders. They gave morphia to the really bad cases sometimes, but the medical supplies and bandages were terribly scarce. It was here that I sat up with a dying British paratrooper and for the first time I saw a man die; he had been neglected and lain out for several days before they found him. The experience shook me, but later on I got hardened to all the suffering around me.*

*Then on 26 August the British crossed the Seine and we were moved out just a day ahead of the Liberation of Amiens. We were put in a box car,* [a closed railway carriage] *forty three wounded men to start what was the worst week of travelling possible to imagine. We could not all lay down together and there were no toilet or sanitary arrangements on the truck. We were allowed out for a few moments once a day and subjected to our Air Force's bombs and strafing. One night the 'Marquis' or Free French blew up the end of our train, killing only some German guards. The conditions were terrible and we had very little food. My broken arm set during this journey and after five days we were taken off at Limburg Prison camp (Stalag Luft 12A) and put in the hospital there, too sick and tired to care much. There was a British doctor here who tried to make us as comfortable in his crowded shack of a hospital as possible and we gradually recovered.*

*I received my first Red Cross parcel here; this was a great day indeed. We were like children on Xmas morning opening them and eating almost a two*

*week's supply those first few days. The Germans supplied a sort of turnip soup and a little bread which was black and hard, daily.*
*I met some firm friends here. Bill was sent away to another compound and I missed him, but my health improved and I made the best of things. After a fortnight at Limburg hospital the Jerries considered I was fit to move with the rest of the aircrew in this camp up to a place called Oberwertzel (Oberwesel or Dulag Luft Oberursel), where we would be interrogated at that dreaded place we had heard so much about from our intelligence back on the Squadron. We arrived about midnight on the 16 Sept and they took our shoes and placed us in cells. Mine was about 10 ft long and 5ft 6 inches wide. Next morning a guard called for me and placed me in front of an English speaking Nazi officer who pulled all the stunts we heard they would, but I remained sullen and said what I had been taught. 'Sorry Sir, I can tell you only my name, rank and number.' He stormed and he threatened, then tried to be nice, then finally said, 'Take this man away to the waiting guard.' I was marched back to the cell where I remained for two more days. All the food we got was a piece of bread and margarine, with a horrible mug of mint tea in the morning and the same at night, but the solitary confinement is the worst part of it; you see no one except the guard twice daily and cannot talk through the thick walls to your neighbour. I was perhaps a bit lucky having been shot down so long ago; they only kept me for three days and nights and let me go, but some men just down are made to sweat for up to a month if they think he has some good information. I was happy to know that I imparted nothing and did my duty though. I also met some of our boys on the train going to the transit camp at Dulag Luft Wetzlar.* [Klosterwald, Germany]
*At Wetzlar all Allied airmen were given capture parcels from the Red Cross, consisting of 'skirt underwear', soap, pullover etc, before they are sent to their various Stalag Lufts. It is rather a comfortable place and they have a good mess where prisoners prepare the food and they seem to have an unlimited supply of Red Cross parcels. The night I spent here was one of the happiest of my life, to be washed clean for the first time in weeks, to have clean clothes and to be able to talk to our own men, we sang and were entertained by the music of a piano accordion and almost forgot we were prisoners.*
*After two days we were put on another train and sent to what was to be our permanent camp right across near the Polish border at a place called Bankau. This time we travelled in 3rd class Italian carriages and I considered the three days of sleeping on the floor and comparatively light rations comfort after the last effort. We arrived at Bankau on the 25 Sept 1944. It was my first permanent Stalag Luft and I had been a prisoner for*

*twelve weeks. The camp was situated in Upper Silesia on the far eastern frontier of Germany and the former west boundary of Poland. Bankau was the nearest town, it was about 5kms away. Our new compound was on a great open plain with nothing to relieve the eye except an occasional young pine forest and a group of farm buildings on the east side.*
*We walked in through two great walls of barbed wire and came out at a building where they once more took our fingerprints and photograph, plus a personal description and the usual thorough search of our clothing and kit. Not having any hidden weapons or even a pair of pliers on me, they let me pass through to get my straw paliasse and hut number. It was then I saw all the occupants of the camp standing around watching anxiously to see if they knew any of us new 'Kriegies.' I heard my name called out and looked up to see Norman Page, an old friend and three members of my old crew. This encouraged me because they all looked well enough. Then I saw many more old pals who I hardly ever expected to see alive. We soon began swapping experiences and some of their escapes are absolutely fantastic. The Germans claim that on average only one member of a Lancaster crew escapes with his life and we have since proved it to be correct for all those shot down on raids.* I listened with sorrow to the reports of death in action of some of my old friends; the one that shook me the most was of Alan Duggleby, who died in Germany soon after receiving mortal wounds in a night raid.'*

*All the reader has to do is randomly flick through any of W.R. Chorley's *Bomber Command Losses* series to see this is true.

**<u>Excerpt from W.R. Chorley's B.C.L. 1944 pages 258 and 285:</u>**

16/17 June 1944, Sgt J F Tweed (Navigator, 102 Sqn): *'I do not know what happened to Jock (Sgt A J McD Barr the pilot) and the others, but according to the news I get here they were all killed. I am still confined to my bed. Actually I have broken some bones near my pelvis. I was the first to jump and Alan* (F/Sgt AM Duggleby, the Bomb Aimer) *should have followed me.'*

A Mk III Handley Page Halifax (source, *Charles E. Brown, www.raf.mod.uk*).

Sgt W Chapman (Mid-Upper Gunner) was the only other crew member to survive. 102 Sqn Halifax III MZ301, DY-M, Op: Sterkrade. T/o 23:12 Pocklington. Shot down by a night-fighter and crashed 02:00 at Luur (Gelderland) near Steenderen, 9km south of Zutphen. Those who died are buried in Steenderen General Cemetery. F/S Alan Duggleby's father was the Revd John Taylor Duggleby of North Essenden in Victoria.

Well, we now know from Norman's diary that his good friend Alan Duggleby did follow Sgt's Tweed and Chapman out of the aircraft, but died later from mortal wounds received in the attack. Four days after this Dennis Bartlett's good friend Sgt GH Moggridge died on 21/22 June over Belgium.

**W/O Norman Jarvis**

*'Down the years when we reflect on this odd pause in our lives we will remember some of these boys with deep affection. A record such as this was set out to be and would be incomplete without a tribute to the memory of some of these lads who were lost in the Royal Air Force of 1944. It is my sad privilege to share with their relatives the loss that is not easy to express in words. It is perhaps enough to record that on all occasions that I saw Alan he comforted himself in keeping with the true traditions of the RAAF in which he served. He was a gallant airman, a fine friend and I shall not forget him. There was his father who was a Minister, his mother and sister, what would they think of their only son being lost? Then there was that beautiful young blonde girl who clung to him at the station before we left home and said jokingly to me then, to look after him and bring him back*

*safely to her. Peter Knox* and Charlie Kruschel the other two members of the old foursome, were both shot down too, but they both got back; Charlie, after walking into neutral Switzerland, and Pete after many long months fighting with the Belgian underground movement. 'I have heard all this a year later of course."*

*Norman's best mate Peter Knox and Dennis Bartlett's best mate George Moggridge were both crew members on 619 Squ's Lancaster ME846, PG-C when it was a FTR on 21/22 June 1944. Skippered by P/O MAH Davis this crew also trained at Bill's 1661 HCU RAF Winthorpe. There is a fascinating web of coincidences that connect Bill's crew and the 'Davis crew' (See Chapter Lives Lived and Lives Lost).

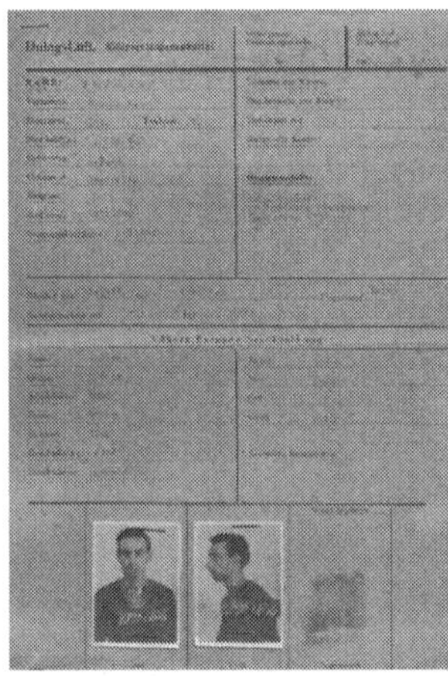

Dennis Bartlett's Dulag-Luft ID card.

**Norman now continues with his detailed account of life at Stalag Luft 7:**

**W/O Norman Jarvis**

*'At first life at Bankau was quite pleasant, the weather was good and we got half a Red Cross parcel per man per week and the German ration was not too bad. Living quarters were to the civilian or even the service man, very poor; eight men were living and sleeping in little wooden huts more like dog kennels than anything and all our cooking had to be done in the open, but a new compound was being built for winter, so we hoped it would be better. There was a big space where the fitter men were able to play games. We Australians in the cloudless years to come will remember with pride the 1944 cricket season in Germany. After being narrowly defeated in the first two tests, we beat the English team in the following two very easily; then the Silesian summer gave out and the deciding game was never played.*

*However all the players and spectators had had a very pleasant season of cricket and we look forward to next summer, but under the clearer, brighter skies back home.*

*We moved into the new winter quarters about the middle of October and it was not long after this that the first snow began to fall. Life though was moderately comfortable and I improved very much in health. The inactive confinement of an eight acre block surrounded by barbed wire was no place for fifteen hundred gay young lives and we all longed to be free. There were occasional attempts to escape by tunnelling, but as far as I know no one ever made a successful get-away from Bankau; besides the weather would kill anyone who was exposed without shelter for a few nights. As far as the eye could see from November till when we left there, there was a wild waste of snow and ice.*

*There was a heavy guard on all the time and at night we were all locked in our barracks and big Alsatian dogs were let loose in the compound. I lived in a room with fifteen other boys, mostly Aussies and we all pooled our resources and had a regular cook and quartermaster, with two men on duty to wash up and clean up the room; once weekly the turn came around, so the rest of the time apart from two roll calls daily was our own. All being Officers, Warrant Officers or NCO's we were not required to work for the Germans. There was a good library which was patronised very well and a school with plenty of willing young teachers. Towards Christmas we got our own British doctor and Padre, so twice on Sundays we went to church and later on they formed some really good bands from instruments sent from Geneva and a Dramatic Society put on a few really good plays.*

*The Germans made themselves awkward whenever possible, but did not interfere too much in our affairs so long as we did what they required of us. I might say here we did not always comply with their wishes and sometimes suffered the consequences. On one occasion during an air raid we were all supposed to stay inside the barracks. However, a young Canadian walked out thinking it was all over and a guard shot him in his tracks. He died soon afterwards; this incident aroused our anger and we resented it strongly, but could do nothing. Periodically they sprang searches on us, once finding some of our boys in a tunnel under the hut at midnight, other times finding us with unpunctured tins of Red Cross food. This was forbidden as they thought they would use it if we escaped. However we saved up quite a few luxuries for Xmas from our Red Cross parcels. Half the camp was sick as a result of having a full stomach for a change. We decorated the room as best we could and had a small Xmas tree in the centre of the room. Our thoughts though were far from here and we wished we could get mail from home. I had a letter from Australian HQ notifying me that they knew I was*

*a prisoner and my family had received word also; this made me feel better to know that the world outside knew of my existence at least.*
*At New Year we had another bit of a party and to an outside observer it would have looked very amusing. About twenty men in our position, singing and drinking hot cocoa in a room in our barracks, the morale was always high in those days.'*

Little did Norman, Monty, Dennis, Eddy and the rest of the boys from this camp know, but they were to suffer further hardships and extreme tests of endurance as the Germans decided to abandon Stalag Luft 7. Surprisingly they took all the POWs with them as they retreated westwards back into the heart of Germany, experiencing some of the worst weather conditions that century. The ever-present shadow of death relentlessly hovered over Bill's crew as they struggled physically, emotionally and mentally to stay alive on what became known as, 'The Long March.'

# Chapter Twenty Two

# The Long March

In the summer of 1944 Germany was clearly facing military defeat, but Hitler was unable to accept this fact. He was fanatical in his insistence that Germany must fight on and ordered the country to be put on a total war footing. Concentration camp prisoners were forced to work even harder on even lower rations. After the 20 July 1944 assassination attempt on Hitler, Allied POWs chillingly now came under the control of one of the most feared men in Germany; Reichsführer Heinrich Himmler.* The order went out for POWs to be moved far away from the front-line as the Nazis did not want their prisoners to be liberated by the encroaching Allies. The result was a series of gruelling forced marches, as weak, malnourished and often unwell prisoners were forced to march huge distances daily across Germany and Poland. Many thousands died. These various marches became known by the collective term, 'The Long March'. The eyewitness accounts of Norman Jarvis and Dennis Bartlett give us some insight into the dreadful conditions and suffering experienced by these men.

*p322, *The Last Escape*, John Nichol and Tony Rennell.

As the mighty Russian war machine now began closing in on Germany itself, W/O Norman Jarvis now continues the story of Bill's crew from his War Diary:

**Stalag Luft 7, Bankau, 17 January 1945.**

**W/O Norman Jarvis**

*'The Russians had started their big offensive and we hoped soon to be liberated by them; speculation was high as to whether the Germans would move us in that event. By the 17 January 1945 there was great excitement in the camp; we knew from our secret radios that they were heading our way and not far off; then came the German orders to be ready to leave camp in an hour's notice. You can possibly imagine how we felt. They said there may be a chance of rail transport, but we must be prepared to walk. This was a great shock as the weather was terribly cold and the snow was thick all about us. Then we began to feverishly pack food and clothing into whatever we could improvise as packs. I knew that I could carry very little as I was still unfit and walking was hard enough without a load on my back. We had to throw away a few souvenirs that we had collected and they got us all about 8.30pm that night and said we were starting and the threat given that for every man who tried to escape, five would be shot. We were*

*all ready to move out when a 'big shot' came driving into the camp and told the Commandant that he was not to move us out as the German Army wanted to use all the roads for their retreat. Our hopes rose and we thought they would leave us. The hospital cases only were sent on by transport. All night long we heard gun-fire and a stick of bombs landed just outside the camp and the next morning we wondered what would happen.*
*On 19 January at about 1 am we were roused by Tommy Guns and dogs and put on the road; the temperature was about 20 degrees below zero and the snow on the roads was as slippery as grass. We did not make a lot of progress because the roads were clogged with retreating German troops and thousands of civilian refugees with their possessions, some on horse drawn vehicles.'*
*What I saw of the German Army that day was perhaps a very sorry impression of it; mostly horse-drawn guns and equipment or decrepit old wagons and pack horses.* The horses were all in very poor condition except a few nice saddle hacks and they were sore shouldered and girth galled; there were others with infected withers and sore backs and all of them had great difficulty keeping on their feet. We saw dozens of dead along the track and they were continually falling over in their harnesses and adding to the chaos already existing. Although I was becoming very tired and in considerable pain I could not help feeling sorry for these whole families of fleeing refugees, consisting mostly of old men and women with young children. They like us did not know where they were going and the future looked grim. By mid-day I had to throw everything away except food and blankets as my back had gone altogether and my feet were blistered and sore. On and on through the snow and ice we all went all the afternoon; many times I thought I would have to give up and collapse on the side of the road as quite a few had done. Then I thought it can't go on forever, soon they will stop and rest. By night I was all in and finished the last mile between Bob and Clive, two of my pals. Then we stopped in a village called Winterfield and put up in several of the barns and haystacks.* [I could not find Winterfield on the map] *I collapsed in the straw and slept the sleep of the physically exhausted. We had done 28 kilometres that day.'*

*What is interesting to note here is that Bill witnessed the German retreat in the west and Norman witnessed the German retreat in the east. Their impressions were very similar in that the German Army was in a sorry state of affairs, lacking heavy machinery which had been lost in battle and were relying on horses to aid their withdrawals. Norman's experience with farm horses gives us an extremely accurate impression of the condition and type of horses being used by the Germans and that was basically anything they could get their hands on.

Amongst the chaos, human tragedy and his own physical discomfort and pain he has time to study these creatures that he is extremely fond of; his compassion and his observations of these animals are quite moving and poignant, especially as they would be the cause of tragedy later on in his life. The intensity of the situation that Norman, Monty, Dennis and Eddy experienced as they struggled to keep going in those extreme weather conditions, physical and mental hardship is hard to imagine, but their survival instincts and will to live kept them going. Quite simply put, hope was stronger than fear. It is amazing when pushed to the limits what the mind can accomplish over the body in life or death situations, as the POWs, civilians and the German Army all fell back together from the mighty Russian onslaught.

***Norman continues:-***

*'At 6.15 on 20 Jan we set off marching again—those who could—the others had to take a chance that seemed as hopeless as going on, but I felt a little better from the rest and decided to press on with my friends. After a few hours I was just plodding on in a stupor and the old guards looked as if they were done too and did not care how we straggled along. The chances of escaping for the fit men was pretty good now, but on the cold plains of Silesia a few hours out in the open and you would die if you lay down and some of the Germans thought nothing of shooting you if you looked like making a break.*

*By 11 that morning they could drive us no further so we stopped at a brick factory and rested up until 9pm. We only covered 12 km that morning, but set off again into the night with the information that we had to cross the Oder river, a distance of 30 km before morning, because they were going to blow it up then to try and stem the Russian advance.*

*Of all the trials of endurance the 1,600 men who were on the march will say it was the greatest. I fell on the roadside exhausted once and was picked up by our medical officer and his orderlies who had secured a horse and wagon for the very worst cases, but even they had to take turns at hanging on behind as there were too many of us all to ride at once and besides the temperature was so low that without moving, circulation stopped and you would die of the cold.*

*I saw several mirages of the Oder Bridge swimming before my eyes that night and thought often I must give in, but something made me press on and just at dawn we crossed the bridge which was mined and ready to be blown up. There was no shelter on the west side so they told us we would have to do another 10 km. This broke our hearts, but here I met up with the other members of my gang and struggled on, only half conscious most of the time.*

*We stopped at a big barn about 10am, having completed 41 km for the night and 53 km or about 32 miles in the past 24 hours. For aircrew who had nearly all been wounded or injured in some way when shot down and having had very little exercise in the past six months, that is a colossal distance and considering the appalling weather and no food, a feat of endurance seldom equalled.*

*In the barn they gave us a few dog biscuits and a small piece of bread, a little cold tinned meat and a cup of coffee. Rest was what I needed most so I lay down amongst the tired, aching bodies of my comrades and faded into sweet oblivion. From a friend's diary I find the place here was called Rosenfeld* [slightly NE of Dresden, today on the German/Polish border by Görlitz].

*At 5am we were all awakened by the yelling Jerries telling us that the Russians had crossed the river and would soon be closing in on us. Here I thought was where I will hide out in the straw and let the column move on and leave me. The chances of the place being shelled and also the risk of the retreating SS troops finding me had to be taken, but I thought that was better than moving on aimlessly in the snow. I did not count on about fifty other boys having the same idea; the Germans missed us and began a search with dogs and guns, finally routing us all out. We said that we were not going on; then they began to shout and threaten us and fired a few bursts from their automatic rifles and revolvers in the air and near our feet, so we decided that discretion was the greater part of valour and so joined the boys once more on the weary track. It's amazing what a few bullets will do towards making up your mind at a time like that. There had been about 30 men left in the village too sick to move; some had pneumonia and the others were mostly severe frost-bite cases and exhaustion.*

*I managed somehow to finish the 21 km to Schönfeld* [slightly North of Dresden], *where we were once more crowded into some barns to eat a little and sleep, but the next day we rolled on in the snow again and somehow I had acquired a strange new strength and was able to keep up better. We stopped about 2.30pm having travelled 19km.*

*On Jan 24 we rested all day, but were terribly hungry and weak. We tried to make hot drinks, which were forbidden, over the fires in our 'meat tin billy cans'.*

*Jan 25 we marched from 08:00 a distance of 19 kms to another barn at Hudersdorf. All these marches seemed to be getting us nowhere and we were continually losing men; some were in a bad way, but I think that they were taken to hospitals, then others acted on their own initiative and made their escape, but the lack of food and energy kept most of us together. The men grew haggard and weary-eyed and under the cover of their natural good humour, their nerves were stretched to breaking point from endurance, long hours of cold and danger. The strain of not knowing what the future held for them, made them ill tempered and on some occasions they reached a pretty low level of living. Day or night we were never out of our clothes and seldom had the chance to wash. I let my beard grow for the four weeks as did perhaps 90% of the prisoners. The bread ration was supposed to be 1/5th of a loaf, which is about 9 inches long, 3 ½' wide and 4' deep per day and 1/10th of a pound block of margarine. This we did not get. At rare intervals we received a small piece of tinned meat or dog biscuits; once a day we either got a cup of substitute for coffee or a sort of barley soup which was rationed to half a cup per man. We queued up for hours on some bitter nights for this and would have given anything to be behind barbed wire getting Red Cross parcels again and a little wooden bed to lie on.*

*We rested on Jan 26 and then moved out at 11:00am on Jan 27 and marched till 17:00 hrs, when we reached and stayed at Pffafendorf, 21 km away. Jan 28 we marched to Standorf, arriving at 12:15 hrs. Then we moved on again to Peterwity,* arriving at 04:30 on Jan 30.* [I think Norman's reference to Peterwity is actually Priestewitz, slightly NW of Dresden and west of Schönfeld, as I couldn't find another village along their route with this name.]

*Hay sheds were always the main sleeping quarter, but they were cold and airy; sometimes I managed to get into where there were cattle and horses; it was much warmer even if there was a likelihood of being trodden on by the animals. On one occasion I got a small tin of milk off a cow, but as a rule the guards watched the dairy and if they saw us trying to pinch milk they would shoot. On one occasion I did a crafty bit of cattle drafting, putting a pen of 20 yearlings in with another containing 30. Our gang slept warm that night and we got a bit more milk.*

*By this time all the exercise must have done my injured limbs and muscles a lot of good, because I had unusual strength and was not tortured when I walked any more. At the end of each day it pleased me more than anything not to be an encumbrance to my comrades. Clive, Harry and Monty* [Monteith] *had all got blood poisoning in their frost-bitten and skinned feet and were sent on by train to a camp further west with many more of our boys. I think what saved me though during those grim days on the march was the fact that we picked up an old pram left on the road by refugees. One of us used to pull it while another pushed it and it ran along those ice caked roads pretty well transporting our meagre kit and blankets that we could not carry on our backs. Several of the men also had improvised sledges which they pulled, they were very handy. The column of men was now strung out the distance of a couple of miles and you never saw such a rare, unhappy looking lot as we were.*

*The last night march was a killer; we trudged 23 km through a blizzard and at times the snow drifts were three feet high on the road and we saw the bodies of two people lying in the snow; they must have been refugees. On 1 February we marched 14 km to another place and stopped in the morning at a big barn in Pransnity, where we decided we could travel no further without better food. They also promised rail transport which actually arrived on 5 February; we then had to march another 5 km to get into some cattle trucks at a place called Am Goldberg.*
*There were 64 men in our truck and it was impossible for us all to lie down together. We had very little food between us and many of the lads were in the first stages of dysentery; still I considered it better than walking. We covered the ground a bit faster, but not much; it took three days for us to get to Stalag Luft 3A at Lukenwalde south of Berlin. We were really glad to have the compound gates close behind us and be packed into the rough buildings where we were to live, that was 8 February 1945 (a distance 255 km or 158.7 miles on foot).'*

Compared with some of the distances covered by POWs from other camps on 'The Long March', Bill's crew and the men from Stalag Luft 7 were fairly lucky, believe it or not, in that they had a shorter journey of 255 km (158 miles). However the hardships they experienced were similar to the stories told by the POWs who made it home from the many other camps located in the east. They left Bankau on the 19 January 1945 travelling directly west through 'Winterfield',* then crossing the Oder river on the 21 January 1945; moving on through Rosenfeld, Schönfeld, Hudersdorf, Pfaffendorf, Standorf, Peterwity (Priestewitz), 'Pransnity'*, Am Goldberg and finally Luckenwalde.

The Battle of The Bulge had signified the Germany Army's last gasp of organised resistance reaching its dramatic conclusion on the 25 January 1945. While the German war machine retreated in the west and the east, Bill's crew had marched in sub-zero temperatures passing through the countryside directly north of Dresden; it was three weeks before the devastating bombing raid on the fated city. With the Russian Army close behind them they finally reached Stalag Luft 3A Luckenwalde (25 miles south of Berlin), after a 3 week journey through an apocalyptic landscape. From 12 January to 2 February 1945 Soviet forces continued pushing forward from the Vistula River almost 300 miles (480 km) to the Oder River where they halted preparing to take the German capital; they were now only 43 miles (70 km) from Berlin. The Yalta Conference was also about to commence with the big three, President Franklin D Roosevelt, Prime Minister Winston Churchill, and General Secretary Joseph Stalin about to decide the fate of war torn Europe.

*These place names are taken as they are written in Norman's diary and I have tried to confirm to the best of my ability their exact location and that they are spelt correctly by following the 'March' route on various maps including Google Earth (Pransnity: after much searching I could not find this place).

Bill's crew had survived, marching alongside their comrades with the shadow of death hovering over them the whole way through their horrific journey, picking off many men along the route. They finally arrived at Stalag 3A at Luckenwalde on 8 February 1945 at the extreme end of the limits that any human beings could be pushed.

On the 11 November 2011, coincidentally Armistice Day, I took Dennis Bartlett down to see Bill at Basingstoke Hospital. Bill was asleep when we turned up so we sat down for a bit in the ward while we waited to see if he would be comfortable seeing us in a while. While we waited I asked Dennis about his time as a POW and his experiences on 'The Long March'.

**Dennis Bartlett, 11 November 2011, Basingstoke Hospital**

*'It was all such a long time ago, I can't believe it was me that went through those experiences. The forced march from Stalag Luft 7 to Luckenwalde was horrific. I was with Monty for the whole journey; we stuck together and helped each other. I can't really remember Norman and Eddy so much, but I know we were all in the same group of men.*

*It was so cold, the clothing we had on barely kept us warm and it hurt just to breath in and out. Our hands, feet and faces got frostbite and our feet became sore and infected, we couldn't even feel them most of the time. Many of the men just let their beards grow, but at one barn we sheltered at I had to break the thick ice on a water trough for the animals so I could shave with the freezing water. Travelling alongside us was the German Army and civilians who were all retreating from the Russians. We saw broken machines, abandoned military equipment, dead bodies and horses lying along the track and I tried not to look to at them for too long. Most of the German guards were a bit older, but could still be brutal if they wanted to. We saw a number of men who couldn't keep up or trying to escape shot right in front of us, it was all extremely upsetting. We were so hungry that the pain was unbearable, but we did sort of get used to that pain. We were covered in lice and fleas and were constantly scratching, if you lifted your collars there were creatures living in there. I don't know how we kept going, there were many times when I felt like I couldn't go on, but I did. In our group of friends we all kept encouraging and supporting each other. I think it was purely the will to survive that kept us all going, because we finally made it to Luckenwalde; it was such a relief just to rest properly.'*

# Chapter Twenty Three

## Stalag 3A, Lukenwalde

The camp that Bill's crew finally ended up at, Luckenwalde was notorious for its extremely poor conditions. It must have been a relief to be able to rest after the 'Long March', as Dennis said, but conditions were so bad that the hardship continued and many never left. It is estimated that there were some 30,000 POWs* in Luckenwalde when the camp was finally liberated by the Russians. Alongside the multi-national POWs, were inmates force marched from Stalag Luft 3 at Sagan and other camps in the east. Many of the prisoners lived solely off a limited supply of parcels delivered by the Red Cross, with drinking water for the entire camp accessible from just two taps. *Norman Jarvis.

Photo by *Flight Sergeant David Berrie, RAF,* who was a POW in Stalag 3A. Each tent held 400 men.

**W/O Dennis Bartlett**

*'The conditions inside Luckenwalde were horrific; it was really chaotic inside there with all the different nationalities. Dysentery was rife, the whole place was infested with fleas and lice and the rations were pretty poor, so we were still starving all the time. The mattresses were literally full of insects, so we just slept on the wooden floors of the huts. The Russian POWs were treated really badly and I felt very sorry for them, but there was nothing we could do to help as we weren't allowed to go near them.'*

**W/O Norman Jarvis**

*'The daily ration then according to my diary, which I will quote from for a while was:-- 1 loaf of bread between five men daily; 3 or 4 dirty potatoes cooked in their jackets: 1 cup of barley soup; 2 cups of mint tea or coffee daily; 1/20th of a block of margarine and 1 tablespoon of sugar. No Red Cross parcels as we all hoped there would be.*
*16 February 1945: There are two or three hundred cases of dysentery amongst the boys who survived the retreat from Bankau. We are warm, a bit hungry, but very weak and the M.O. is trying desperately to improve our situation.*
*20 Feb: We are still very weak but cheerful; there is talk of moving again, but I don't think they can move us this time; we are getting just enough to eat to enable us to walk out on parade for the count twice daily. There are no cooking facilities here but we have made blowers and 'smoky joes' which we boil the water on and try and make the little bit of food taste better. There is no fuel issued so I suppose that what we have will soon run out. In this camp there are 30,000 men of various nationalities, but we British are all together. I met Stan Sambell, an old pal who I joined up with, here today; he was shifted here from a camp in NE Germany. Each night about 7pm the lights go out and the sirens blow because of air raids in our vicinity. We are only 22 miles from Berlin so we see the Mosquitoes come over every night and raid the place. We could hear the rumbling of distant bombs and gunfire nearly all last night. Why don't these Jerries give up? I sleep a lot in the daytime so consequently at night I am awake a lot and listening to the racking coughs of some of the men and wondering how long it will be. There was a flock of wild geese flying north today. This is supposed to be a sign of spring; a few warm days would improve the morale a bit.*
*24 February: The place I now call home is a space on the floor of a barrack containing 250 men. I have approximately 2 feet of width and 6 feet in length to live and sleep. My bed is the floor and two blankets; my pillow is my boots and a card-board box containing my cooking and eating utensils (two black tins and a spoon), a change of underwear and a towel.*
*They secured 30 Red Cross parcels from somewhere and issued them to 1,500 men. It was like the feeding of the multitude and there was only a share of some item of food for each man. We made it a sort of lottery and I drew a cup of oatmeal, which I think was as good as anything; anyhow it will make a bowl or two of porridge.*
*28 February: So this is the end of another month, possibly one of the worst I shall ever know, but so far I am not feeling too bad. Of a morning when I*

*get up off the bed I feel faint and nearly fall sometimes; many others are so weak and thin they can't go on parade; they have nearly all had dysentery though.*

*The only topic of conversation now is food and I dream almost every night of some choice dish at home. It is quite a break though to be home even for a few moments in a dream and I know this can't be much longer. Last night four of our men were caught trying to get into the store containing the Serb's or French Red Cross parcels. Of course their action was prompted by hunger and the knowledge that these foreigners are getting American parcels while we British and Americans are going without. Two of the men were shot one seriously; that will give you an idea of what these 'hard hips' have driven our men to. Most of them have been well brought up in good families, but it is a shame to see some begging for a butt end of a cigarette from a Jerry. The majority of us are however coping with the situation very creditably.*

*2 March: The health of the camp seems to be improving with the better weather. Air raids continue day and night; we can usually hear the Mosquitoes on their nightly visits to Berlin; then the deep rumble of the heavy guns trying desperately to defend the city.*

*Articles of food and the proprietor of the stall receives a commission of one cigarette for each transaction. Cigarettes are the currency in all POW camps, so being a non-smoker I manage to do pretty well with the ones I get out of my parcel each week, but spend a lot of them on chocolate which costs from 40 to 50 cigs, for a ¼ block, 50 for an 8 oz tin of cheese and so on, but these days it is hard to get food at all for cigarettes. Bread is the most valuable of all food; the boys will pay the Jerry guards up to 100 cigs for a loaf of block bread. You see our present daily ration of bread is 1/8 per man per day. All this trading with guards or working parties from the French or Russian compounds is forbidden and great risks are taken by some of our men, but they seem to enjoy that. It is amazing to see the displays of clothing, toilet requirements and trinkets in some of the stalls; they have nearly all a POW requires if you have the cigs to buy it. Then there are the gambling games going on too, such as crown and anchor, two-up and so on, which attract a lot of attention. These things all go to make the camp more interesting or at least less monotonous.*

*23 March: The German ration has been cut again. We only get spuds every second day, so just as well we are getting parcels. Here I will give an idea of what one American food parcel contains. They are approximately 10 pounds in weight:--1 tin of powdered milk, 16 ozs; 1 tin of cheese, 8 ozs; 2, 4oz bars of chocolate; 1 box of sugar, 8 oz; 1 tin of coffee, 2 oz; 2 bars of soap; 100 cigarettes; 1 tin of spam, 8 oz; 1 tin of paste 4 oz; 1 box of prunes or raisons, 16 oz; 1 tin of margarine, 16 oz; 1 tin of bullybeef, 8 oz; 1 box of biscuits. The Germans puncture all tins before issue to prevent us saving up a food stock, but so far as I know they have never used any parcels themselves. One of these per week is the best ration I have had since I became a prisoner, but the German issue now is very low. I would hate to live on it alone like the Russians have to; many of them are dying and they look pretty terrible, but we are not supposed to help them.* [Three million Russians died in German captivity from starvation, disease and mistreatment].

*I have got all my clothes washed and we have more space now, but we are all 'lousy' and don't seem to be able to get rid of the lice with just cold water. 1 April 1945: I reckon I can see the end of this war pretty soon now. We are just waiting and hoping. Easter passed very quietly with Church services on Good Friday and today, Sunday. The Jerries are getting very fed up; they don't seem to care if we are all here on the counts or not, but the place is still heavily guarded. We now have only enough parcels for two week's supply, so I hope the war ends before then.*

*12 April: The Jerries tried to shift us by train today, but about half of us got down to the station and they found that such a venture would be impossible. So, here we wait for liberation; will it be the Yanks or the Russians.*

*Unfortunately some of our boys are getting too keen to get out; two RAF chaps were killed trying to escape last night during an air raid, they ran right into some guards and were riddled with bullets before they had a chance.*

*15 April: Last night I watched a full scale Bomber Command attack on Potsdam, 20 miles away.* It was a wonderful sight; the roar of aircraft and bombs was terrific and it must have been hell to be underneath a raid like that. We could see the TI's coming cascading down and the magnificent glow of the exploding bombs and the cones of searchlights. I wished somehow I was up there again flying home to England over the miles and miles of conquered territory since I last flew.*

*A quick point of interest here:-This spectacular raid that Norman witnessed was the first time that Bomber Command had sent four engined 'heavies' to the Berlin defence zone since March 1944. It was also the last major raid of the War on a German city. 2 a/c were lost. One (6/7) from 138 Squ, RF143, NF-O, F/O G Horsaman and crew, coned by searchlights and shot down by a NF (*Bomber Command War Diaries*, Middlebrook and Everitt and WR Chorley, *1945 Losses*).

*18 April: All day long the RAF and USSAF have been attacking the targets around us and at night the sirens never seem to stop.*
*19 April: We have received our last half parcel and the Jerry rations are just about all finished, but most of us have a small reserve I think.*
*21 April: This morning dawned grey and wet, but the constant rumble of guns told us that our liberators were close and this time they can't shift us. At 7am there were no Jerries rousing us up for parade, so I stayed in bed until 9am. Rumours have been rife all morning and the guns are pounding all around us. At 12 o'clock word was received that the Russians had surrounded our camp. We rounded up a few remaining guards and locked them up. Orders are to stop in camp as we have seen no sign of the Russians, but we are prepared for any emergency and wild with joy. I wonder what the rest of the day holds for us. The Wing Commander says he will do all he can to ensure our safety and get us out of barbed wire as soon as it is possible, so tonight we celebrate.*
*6pm, 21 April: We have control of the camp, but there are a lot of SS holding out in the woods behind the camp; he has given us a warning that if any of us attempt to arm his men will open fire on the camp.*
*22 April: Russian armoured vehicles entered our camp this morning after occupying the town of Luckenwalde. We are still strictly confined to the camp as there are still Germans in the woods who fired on some of our men this morning wounding them.*
*10am: I have just been out and watched a great spectacle, thousands of Russians passed through our camp on tanks, armoured vehicles and trucks. We lined the barbed wire and cheered them; some of the boys had tears in their eyes as they watched our liberators rolling on towards Berlin. Never have I seen such a tough, rugged looking lot of men: there were women too in the frontline spearhead. One heavy tank tore down the road and smashed down about a quarter of a mile of our outer compound fence as if it was matchwood. Now we were told we could not be sent home through Russian occupied territory, but would have to wait for the link up with the Yanks.*
*8.30pm: The Russians are still mopping up in the woods at the back of the camp. We hear constant bursts of machine gun fire. There has been a great deal of strafing here by both sides from the air and an artillery barrage or duel has been going on over our heads all evening, so we don't feel too safe. It is my first experience of shell fire and oh boy! Do they whistle over, the noise on the ears is terrific. I will be glad when it's all over; this front line is no joke, especially when we are part of the thing.*
*23 April: We are still wondering what they intend to do with us. We heard the BBC news for the first time officially since we were taken prisoner, but*

*here it would be safe to mention that through the ingenuity of our men we have been hearing it on improvised crystal sets right throughout the war. These were the best kept secrets in the camp; only two or three men knew where the sets were and the Germans could not find them, but the news was always taken down in shorthand and read daily.*
*25 April: Today all the Anzacs and Kiwis held an Anzac Day Service. We are still waiting though for news of getting home. The Russians have tried to make us more comfortable and we have taken over the former dwellings of our guards and officers. We are not yet supposed to leave camp, but many of us have been outside of the camp and some have been doing a bit of looting; some are already living in the town. The Allied troops are very popular there and the Germans encourage them to stay with them; this way the Russians leave them alone. The Russians have allocated us a village to feed from. We send our food parties daily and they return with a little meat, potatoes and such like, but the independent parties return with the strangest booty souvenirs; horses, carts, clothing and some have chickens under their arms; others drag home a fat calf or a pig.*
*26 April: I went out today to a village and returned with a replenished food supply, about 20 pounds of sugar, a bag of potatoes and a good idea of how the Germans will have to live for a few years after this war. The village was very quiet, with only the roar of a Russian motorcycle on patrol breaking the death like silence. The people were very subdued and we spoke to a few; they regret already their folly and have a deep hate now for Hitler. They also ask continually when the Americans are coming to take over their village. When we say they will not come here, they sometimes broke down and cried. I found I could not enter their houses and loot as many of our boys had done, but got my food stock from some stores out of town. Later on walking through a field at the back of some of the houses I met several kids playing with a gun. My pals and I thought it was a toy and advanced with our hands above our heads. Then I realised it was no toy and dashed forward knocking it from the boys hand. I picked it up and found it was cocked, loaded and contained three rounds. I stuffed it into my shirt and left hurriedly, thankful for my life and a good souvenir.*
*30 April, I was walking in the woods near camp today and found two Germans lying riddled with machine gun bullets. They were evidently a couple of die-hards that the Russians had just mopped up. There are still many in the woods, but they are a tired beaten lot.* [This was the day Adolf Hitler and Eva Braun committed suicide in the Fuhrer Bunker and Soviet Forces reach the Reichstag to raise the Russian flag over Berlin.]
*1 May, there was quite a battle in the area today; the last of the Germans*

*fought gallantly, but all is quiet tonight; indicating the end. We have heard on the wireless that 70,000 men had been mopped up in our area this week.*
*8 May, 1945: Today will probably go down as one of the greatest in history, as the end of the European war. We heard the Prime Minister's broadcast, but strangely we were not excited. Everyone thought, well what a dull end it was for us and how we longed to be home. We burned down a few huts and guard boxes and threw live rounds into the fires; the Russians fired guns and 'Very-cartridges'* [bright signal flares] *and of course we were all very happy. We were forcibly detained in the camp by the Russians who we were beginning to think were a lot of rough and ready gangsters. My first impression of the Russians was tremendous; they looked so fierce, hard and efficient in that tank spearhead that had gone through. Then came miles and miles of horse drawn equipment and cavalry; the horses were all beautiful animals especially the mounts of the Cossacks. Wagons, carts, guns, field kitchens and on nearly every cart was a girl. I have not yet been able to form an opinion of the part played by the women in the Russian Army; some are quite beautiful, but the majority are plump high breasted buxom type or thick waisted peasant variety and they all pack a gun or a knife in their belt. The men vary from the tall handsome white Russian to the Mongolian type from Siberia, for the most part uncivilised savages and any that can read or write are at least an Officer or NCO. The camp looks now like some frontier town of the Wild West and we are being crowded by the influx of refugees of all nationalities and sexes. There are Honkytonks, open air concerts, gambling dens and the two –gun men 'keeping the law' are Russians. Walking at night through this place, one sees signs of poverty, filth, love and a little glamour amongst these 35 different nationalities which I believe are here.*
*Fortunately we now have a separate home from all this. The aircrew of the British and Dominions now live in the former German barracks across the road, which is surrounded by nice gardens. Before the war ended hundreds of German girls were making their way westwards, posing as the wives of French workmen so they could avoid the Russians.*
*20 May, 1945: We left camp today on our way home. The Russians took us about 6 miles to the Elbe River, where we were met by the Americans.*

[As explained in the Chapter on Bill's camp Stalag Luft 1, the delays imposed by the Russians were intentional and the atmosphere soured very quickly. The POWs were due to be evacuated a couple of days earlier by a convoy of American trucks, but the Russians would not let the US convoy into the camp, so frustratingly delaying the POWs freedom even longer. After a nasty confrontation at the camp gate the convoy was sent back to the US lines at the River Elbe. There would be no release of POWs until Moscow said so. Bill's crew had also witnessed the start of many problems experienced at this stage of the War between East and West, leading eventually to the Cold War (p208-209 *The Last Escape*, John Nichol and Tony Rennell)].

*We travelled through recent battlefields and many times we had to cross streams where the bridges had been blown up on the main autobahns. These autobahns are the best roads I have ever seen, but some of the forests are still burning and there is destruction everywhere, but I never failed to appreciate the beautiful areas of central Germany. About 5 o'clock we reached the Elbe and saw where the beautiful bridge at Witenburg lay smashed across the river. We detoured about a mile upstream to where there was a pontoon bridge, the Americans met us and there was a short ceremony before we walked across and got on the American trucks. Now I felt secure and free at last and a great cheer went up for the Yanks. The flats on the west side of the River Elbe is lovely country and the crops of wheat, barley and rye looked prosperous.*

*Near the end of our journey we passed through the city of Halle which has been more than half wiped out by our bombers, but the people seemed much happier here than in the Russian occupied zones.* [This is where the negotiations had taken place to secure their release from Russian control]

*About 8pm we stopped at a big Luftwaffe station where the yanks gave us a good welcome, a first-class meal and a bath. Then we went to sleep in a barrack block that had formerly been the home of the proud German Luftwaffe. This was one of the biggest and most up to date aerodromes I have ever been on and we saw where the Germans had destroyed two hundred aircraft of various types before leaving the place. We had a very happy stay here for four days then we flew in a Douglass Dakota passenger plane to Brussels in Belgium where we were deloused again and given a grand welcome by the British Army and the people of Brussels. Were very impressed with the Belgian Capital and had an excellent night out there.*

*The following day, Sunday 27 May 1945, we flew back to England, the way I left it 10 ½ months ago, in the greatest bomber of them all, 'The Avro Lancaster.'**

*The flight back across the channel differed from any I had made before. This time we were all crowded in and there was no danger, but the excitement was as great, or greater than ever before. When we saw at last that coastline, that really meant home, even though it was 12,000 miles away from my real home. They gave us a great reception at the Aerodrome in England and pretty young WAAF's waited on us at decorated tables in one of the large hangars.*

*That night all the Aussies in the returning party got on a train and went to Brighton, where we proceeded to the Grand and the Metropole, which were to be our billets just as they had been two years ago. After a few days in Brighton getting re-kitted and put on a building up course of eggs, milk, etc we were sent on 28 days leave.*
*I visited my old haunts around Lincolnshire and Nottingham for a start, then proceeded to Edinburgh and Aberdeen where I had a wonderful time. A few more days in Brighton on the beach and all sorts of entertainment, then more leave; this time I stayed in Devon and saw all around this lovely old county and parts of Cornwall.'*

**W/O Dennis Bartlett**

*'When the camp was finally freed by the Russians we were really excited, but that excitement soon vanished; we had to stay put as fighting was still going on outside the camp. The Russian soldiers that followed the main force into the camp were really aggressive and they took my watch from me, also rings and other personal belongings from other POWs; that was a bit of a shock to us all as we had thought that they were our friends! We were supposed to be handed over to the Americans, but the Russians wouldn't let a convoy of American trucks through. We kept thinking that the Russians would never let us go! We then had to wait another few days before the Russians themselves transferred us in a convoy of trucks over to the American lines. It was a huge relief to be with our own soldiers again. We were finally flown back to England from Brussels in a Lancaster Bomber which was a wonderful feeling. We were finally home after enduring hardships that were unthinkable. I had bad dreams for many years afterwards and as you know I didn't speak about my experiences for a long time, even to my family.'*

*Both Dennis and Norman mention being flown home in a Lancaster Bomber, finally arriving back home on Sunday 27 May 1945. This was part of the RAF's Operation Exodus and was not without its perils either. Bomber Command's Lancasters started flying to Brussels and other airfields to bring home recently liberated British POWs. Transporting the thousands of Allied POWs back home from the wreckage of Europe was a logistical nightmare and fraught with danger. Lancasters were quickly modified so they could carry up to 25 POWs at a time. On the 9 May 1945 a 514 Squ Lancaster RF230, JI-B took off from Juvincourt airfield in northern France with 24 ex POWs and 6 crew on board for the journey home to freedom.

Experiencing control trouble the pilot F/L D Beaton DSO tried to re-land, but crashed killing all on board. This is believed to be the only accident involving loss of life to POWs in a Bomber Command a/c. This is such a heart wrenching tragedy, after surviving the War they were all lost a couple of hours of away from reaching home. The following day 10 May 1945 a 97 Squ Lanc ME623, OF-Z crashed on take-off at Brussels-Eve airfield (now Brussels Airport) with 24 POWs on board. Fortunately nobody was killed in this accident (WR Chorley, *RAF Bomber Command Losses 1945*).

Before Norman finally went home to Australia he stopped in Cardiff to see Bill. Bill recalls: *'I met up with Norman in Cardiff before he went back to Australia. This was the last time I ever saw him, although we did write to each other before his tragic accident in 1949. It was so nice to see him; we talked for hours about our times together and also went out for a drink in Cardiff.'*

**Norman Jarvis now completes his incredible journey and describes the trip home to Australia:**

**W/O Norman Jarvis**

*'On 8 August 1945 we went by train from Brighton to Liverpool and embarked on the SS Orion for our journey back to Australia.*
*This time we had a pleasant but uneventful voyage across the Atlantic, way down to the Caribbean Sea and entered that 8th Wonder of the World, the Panama Canal. This was an extremely interesting trip, taking all day, then we stopped at Balboa on the Pacific side on the night of 19 August. We went ashore to the accompaniment of an American Army band and ate our first good ice cream and bananas for a long, long while. American Red Cross women gave us cool drinks and doughnuts, then we saw a cinema show. On the next morning we went ashore for while, but sailed out into the Pacific about midday 20 August.*
*On 5 September 1945 we came ashore in New Zealand after a long trip across the Pacific, but the welcome those Kiwis gave us will always keep my opinion high of our nearest and friendliest neighbours. The Prime Minister and Mayor of Wellington came aboard our ship and welcomed their homecoming men, and then we were given leave there all day. Wellington is a very neat and modern city and has a fine big harbour. It was good to meet people who speak the same as we do and resemble Australia so much, but now the journey home is nearly finished and tomorrow we will be in Sydney.*

*It has been a long time and a hard one in many respects, but I have no regrets and feel that it was all worthwhile. The Australian air-crew shot down in Europe was some 9,000 and there are only 850 Ex POWs returning.**
*The Japanese war has ended since we have been at sea, so we shall return to a free country. That still seems a little beyond my comprehension and I hope to celebrate both VE and VJ days by gaining the greatest reward of all, the sight of the old home and loved ones.'*

*The Australian War Memorial indicates 19,235 battle related military deaths, with 13,754 RAAF casualties, 8,884 on Training and Operations and 3,000 wounded in action.

After Norman Jarvis returned to Australia he married his sweetheart Gwen Copeland and settled down to life running his family's farm at Cadugewa. Bill North and his crew all went back to civilian life after the War. After a short break we will follow their lives and find out that their bond and friendships stayed strong to the very end of their lives.

Gwen Copeland and Norman Jarvis, 1945. (Pam Livingstone)

# Chapter Twenty Four

## Lives Lived and Lives Lost

This Chapter details the contact between families, friends, the RAF, the Air Ministry and the International Red Cross after RAF crewmen were missing in action. We have included some letters which are extremely poignant. There is not enough room or time to include them all, as much as I would like too. I myself never fail to be moved by these letters every time I read them and I have read them many times over. I think the reader will gain a sense of the bonds between family, crews and friends and the heart wrenching sense of loss felt by loved ones, some having happy endings and some never ever finding out what happened to or where the bodies of their sons were. The Runnymede Memorial commemorates the names of 20,000 lost airmen who have no known resting place. They were lost at sea or in mid-air or ground explosions and the terrible sense of loss is touched on here with much detail attended to from the Commonwealth War Graves Commission which records the resting place of service men and women all over the world. *W.R. Chorley's Bomber Command Losses* series is again an invaluable source of information regarding lost crews and their resting places.

We shall start off with 619 Squadron Lancaster I, ME846, PG-C. On the night of 21/22 June 1944 the Squadron were part of a force of Lancasters from 5 group detailed to attack Wessling. The Mid-Upper Gunner was a 19 year lad old called Sgt. Moggridge. Sgt George Moggridge was Dennis Bartlett's best friend, they, as mentioned before, had trained together. The aircraft and crew were reported missing from Operations on 22 June 1944. Dennis Bartlett received a heartbreaking letter at the Sgts mess RAF Skellingthorpe that was a reply to his heartfelt letter at the news that George Moggridge was missing. The following letter was a reply to a letter sent from Dennis offering his sympathy on hearing George Moggridge was missing. It is from Sgt Moggridge's mum Clara and arrived on the 2 July 1944, two days before Dennis went missing on the St. Leu Ops. It is as she wrote it with many words capitalised, almost as if to emphasise the hope that her son was not lost.

Sgt D Bartlett, Sgts Mess, RAF Skellingthorpe, Lincoln
99 Lillechurch Road, Dagenham. 30 June 1944

Dear Dennis,

Forgive me for beginning like this, but my son often spoke of you. So I am sure you will understand. Well son it was very good of you to write to me, in this most terrible, trying and heartaching time. Yes I knew you trained together, you see my boy and I are great pals, he told me of you all. Thank you for your sympathy. God knows my heart is breaking.

But God will give me the strength to bear this heavy cross, so pray night and day with us here, that he is safe. May the chance be that as you say he took it and is safe. [This refers to the hope that he baled out]

Dennis I'm thinking too of the other brave lads like him (his crew) are missing too. Their mothers too have the heartache that I am suffering. May God in His mercy answer them as well. Yes my son as soon as I get any news I will tell you. I'm proud to know you and get your letters and any time if you go to your home, you can also come here for a night and you would be welcome, so thank you once again. + God Bless you always. + May He Keep you Safe now and forever.

Yours sincerely

Mrs Moggridge

Sgt George Moggridge, March 1944 at 1661 HCU Winthorpe.
(source, Jane Knox)

The news was not good and Dennis and the Moggridge family eventually suffered the heartbreaking moment that many families had to endure. George had died along with the Rear Gunner F/S JER Bowering (RCAF) and their Captain P/O M.A.H. Davis when ME846, PG-C was lost on Operations. As was so often the case the gunners seemed to be the first in line to become fatalities when attacked by night fighters. Dennis was never quite sure what had happened to George and where his final resting place was and had searched in vain for his name on the Runnymede Memorial. After meeting Dennis he asked me if I could find out more.

W.R. Chorley's *Bomber Command Losses 1944* proved yet again to be the conclusive documentation. After a long morning searching page by page and name by name I eventually located Sgt GH Moggridge and his crew on page 295. On my next meeting with Dennis which happened to be his reunion with Bill, I passed on a copy of the losses page. Even after all these years the pain which Dennis felt was quite visible and we left him at peace with his memories for a few minutes. The two gunners rest in Schoonselhof Cemetery, Antwerpen, the pilot has no resting place and is commemorated on panel 211 of the Runnymede Memorial; the rest of the crew survived.

Dennis Bartlett's sister Daphne Pearce now shares the heartbreaking moment when her family received the 'missing in action' telegram for Dennis that came to their home in Woodside, Camberley. *'I was four years younger than Dennis, so I would have been about fourteen at the time. We weren't really aware of the heavy losses suffered by the aircrews then, we just assumed that Dennis would come back. My mum and dad had one son in the Navy, one son in the Army, one son in the Air Force and two daughters working in the munitions factories. I don't know how my mum coped really thinking about it now. I was too young to serve and couldn't wait until I was sixteen to sign up, because it seemed to be very glamorous. When the 'missing' telegram arrived at home it was a real shock to the family as we were all very close. I took it really badly. I was terribly upset and didn't eat for a few days. We eventually found out he was a POW through the Red Cross. One of our friends found out Dennis was ok from a broadcast on the radio, where his name was announced as a POW. He cycled over from the next village to tell us that Den was ok, it was a huge relief for us all to find out that he was safe.'*

Again more 'coincidences' revealed another connection to the ME846 crew. Bill's Bomb Aimer Norman Jarvis's best friend was Peter Knox. They had come from Australia together and trained together in Wales. In Norman's War Diary he mentions Peter Knox being lost on Operations on 21/22 June 1944. I was familiar with this date from Bill's Ops and the George Moggridge connection. I ran through the losses for 21/22 June in WR Chorley's 1944 Losses book and was extremely surprised to find Peter Knox's name listed in a crew I had already highlighted. It was ME846, George Moggridge and Peter Knox were in the same crew. I then typed ME846 into the internet and got a hit straight away with a website run by the Knox family. This crew had also trained at 1661 HCU Winthorpe and just like Bill had a photo taken in March 1944 next to the very same Stirling

Bomber. I now had a photograph of George Moggridge which I later showed to Dennis Bartlett. Dennis looked at this photo for a long time. I could feel the years peeling away as he was taken back in time to March 1944. *'Yes, that is him Chris, that is exactly how I remember him.'* (Howard Heeley explained that there was a series of high quality photos taken during March 1944 of the crews standing next to this Stirling). I emailed Peter Knox's daughter Jane and had an amazing response. Jane knew Norman Jarvis's daughter Pam and Norman was Peter's best man when he got married after the War. I put them back in touch again and the charismatic Jane Knox and her wonderful family are now great friends of mine.

Jane Knox shared a harrowing experience that her father Peter had as he baled out of ME846. It leaves me with the heavy emotion that is felt at many points throughout the telling of this story. It is that of overwhelming sadness and how in the heat of battle, does one crewman survive and another not? As Peter Knox left their doomed Lancaster that night he shouted George Moggridge's name over and over again as he floated down through the dark skies and watched their Lancaster explode on the ground below him. *'I wondered if the others had got out and I shouted out the name of 'George', our Mid-Upper Gunner. I could recall his voice saying that he was preparing to jump and I thought he might have jumped about the same time as me. My voice seemed to be lost in the vast dark space around me and I realised there was no possibility of making any form of human contact'.* He carried this painful moment with him for the rest of his life. After Peter Knox was shot down he evaded capture and was sheltered by the Belgium Resistance until Brussels was liberated. He arrived back in England in early Sept 1944, to discover that ME846 had been one of six 619 Squ Lancs lost at Gelsenkirchen, along with 6 from 44 Squ who were also based at Dunholme Lodge. 8 of the other 9 Bomb Aimers he had trained with were eventually shot down. His story is incredible and can be obtained from the Knox family story online. There is a memorial to the ME846 crew and the Belgian resistance in Belgium (*courtesy of Jane Knox*) and also at Newark Air Museum (*courtesy of Howard Heeley*).

Next is Bill North and 61 Squadrons turn with the night of 4/5 July 1944. The dramatic sequence of events is told in the Operations Chapter in this book. The first event in the chain of correspondence is recorded in the ORB by Lancaster EE186 and is marked P/O North 'failed to return from this operation'. Next was the heart wrenching moment that all family's dreaded, this was the delivery of the 'missing in Action' telegram. The following chain of correspondence is the same for all missing Bomber Command crews. The families of each member of Bill's crew would have received the same telegram and correspondence. This process for informing families was repeated constantly from the beginning to the end of the War. One can imagine that the volume of information about missing RAF crews passing between families, friends, Squadrons, Air Ministry and Red Cross would have been overwhelming (and that was just for the RAF). This was the beginning of a painful wait for news of Bill's wellbeing and the family are kept well-informed by the various departments.

On the 6 July 1944 Bill's Dad William received another letter from Headquarters, 51 Base RAF Waddington. The RAF Police had the grim task of collecting Bill and his crew's belongings from their Nissen Huts.

The next letter home was from Wing Commander Doubleday dated 8 July 1944 expressing his deepest sympathy at the loss of the crew. It is worth noting that W/Cmdr Doubleday makes reference to Bill's exceptional skill as a pilot and outstanding Officer.

Next in the chain was a letter from the International Red Cross dated 14 July 1944 informing the family that nothing had been found out so far.

On the 12 July 1944 Bill's family received a very reassuring letter from the Air Ministry stating that the IRC would generally be the first in line to find out the fate of Bill and his crew.

On the 20 July 1944 the family received a very polite and sensitive letter from The Royal Air Force Benevolent Fund.

It was fairly quiet throughout August with the only record of correspondence being from Bill's WAAF girlfriend at the time, Sheila Randall, dated 7 August 1944. Sheila was another great letter writer and kept the families of the crew in touch. This letter is to Dennis Bartlett's mum and dad and Bill said the other crew's families would have received similar letters.

2106814 LAW Randall
SHQ Orderly Room
RAF Winthorpe, Newark, Notts.

Dear Mr and Mrs Bartlett,

I don't suppose this letter will be much consolation for you, but I thought I would like to write to you and express my deepest sympathy. You will probably wonder who I am. Well I go out with Dennis's Captain Bill and I have known the crew for many months. They are a grand lot of boys and from past experience I am sure they will be safe and perhaps very soon we shall be hearing from them.

I have recently heard from W/Cmdr Doubleday and also the Red Cross. Of course it is really too early to have any definite news through yet, but then W/Cmdr has great confidence in them and is sure that they will turn up. Also a few days ago an Officer from Skellingthorpe* was posted here and he informs me that he did two trips [actually four] with Bill and his crew and he also says there is nothing to worry about.

So let us keep smiling and hope to hear from them in the very near future. Should I hear anything further I will write to you immediately and I would be very much obliged if you would do the same.

Yours Sincerely

S. Randall.

*The Officer from Skellingthorpe mentioned by Sheila Randall is W/C Doubleday's Flight Engineer, F/Sgt Slome, who flew with Bill four times.

On the 1 September 1944 the most wonderful news that could be imagined came by telegram and for William, Rachel, Amy and Iris. The tenterhooks were released as they found out the fate of their beloved son and brother. It was also quickly confirmed in an Air Ministry letter dated 2nd September 1944.

On the 4 September 1944 another letter arrived from W/Cmdr Doubleday. Confirming Bill was a POW.

On 22 September the Red Cross wrote again.

29 Sept 1944 Bill's mum and dad received a letter from Eileen Hatchett, Dennis Hatchett's wife, letting them know that Hatchett had evaded capture.

Although the family now had news that Bill was safe there was some uncertainty as to where Bill was being held prisoner, the IRC were making enquiries on behalf of the family and radio broadcasts were constantly monitored. The news was that Bill was in Stalag Luft 1, but this had to be independently confirmed by Geneva. The family were desperate to receive a letter home from Bill and they had a frustrating wait ahead of them.

It is interesting to see that there are two confirmations on the 20 December 1944 from two different sources, in short notes to Bill's family from radio hams listening in to German broadcasts of lists of POWs. Their valuable hard work and dedication was much appreciated by families who had not heard the fate of their loved ones. W/233002 Pte EA Robbins (Owl) of ATS Signals Glamorgan and Mr W Cookson from Dudley.

There was much contact between the family members of the missing crew. The next letter is dated 11 Jan 1945 and from Dave Crowley's parents Kate and Harold who were the proprietors of The Prince of Wales pub Dowfais. Dave Crowley had also evaded capture.

The contact between departments and families then continues until it is found out that the crew have all survived and are POWs. For many families there was no news of their loved ones until the end of the War. It was only then that they discovered their fate and for many it was not good news. The 20,000 crewmen who were lost without trace and have no resting place are commemorated on the Runnymede Memorial. The Commonwealth War Graves Commission (CWGC) has a record of the location of the resting place of the RAF crewmen lost in WW2. There are seven men crew plots in many cemeteries where a crew were buried together, near to where they fell. Below is a picture of the resting place at Aubergenville Communal Cemetery in France of the crew from 619 Squadrons LM446, PG-H. It is not far from where Bill crash landed near Harquency.

P/O JM Aitken (RNZAF), F/S K Goodwin (2nd Pilot), Sgt FA Towse, F/S S Levy, Sgt RE Hickling, Sgt JR Presland and Sgt FF Dring (*CWGC* and *John Aitken,* the nephew of pilot P/O JM Aitken).

We now come to Jeff Gray's Wireless Operator Sgt Norman Jackson. After completing his Tour with 34 Ops on the 28 July 1944 to Stuttgart with F/Lt Jeavons. He was then transferred to a 16 OTU at Barford St John and 26 OTU at Little Horwood. Whilst on 48 hours leave on 2, May 1945 at midday Norman was knocked down by a lorry at the junction of the Strand and Trafalgar Square There were no witnesses to the accident, Norman had a fractured skull and contused brain. He hung on until 1 June 1945, but didn't regain conciseness. To have gone through so much and then die so tragically just before the War ended was heartbreaking. (Thank you to his Nephew Michael for supplying the background information)

**Left**, Norman Jarvis' friend, F/S AM Duggleby (RAAF), 17 June 1944, in Steenderen General Cemetery, Netherlands.

**Right**, Dennis Bartlett's friend Sgt George Moggridge, 22 June 1944, in Schoonselhof Cemetery, Antwerp, Belgium. The Rear Gunner from ME846, F/S JER Bowering, also rests beside Sgt George Moggridge. Their Skipper P/O MAH was lost with the a/c and is commemorated on panel 211 of the Runnymede Memorial (*CWGC*).

Norman Jackson, left before and right after 20 Ops, 22 April 1944 (source, *Jackson family*)

# Chapter Twenty Five

## Life After The War

Bill finished his service at RAF Hibaldstow on air traffic control. He received another promotion to Flight Lieutenant, but didn't enjoy his time there very much. *'It was pretty boring at Hibaldstow, not many aircraft came in and we drank a lot of tea and played a lot of card games.'* He was finally decommissioned on 21 November 1946.

Many pilots continued to serve in the RAF after the war, while others took jobs in the civil aviation industry, with airlines such as Don Bennet's BSAA and BOAC. Bill, however, despite his considerable gifts as a pilot, did not continue with his flying career. In discussing this with Bill it became clear he felt he had reached a turning point in his life and had to decide whether to carry on with flying as a career or go back to working for the NUR

In the end he opted to recommence his career with the NUR which amongst other things required him to enrol for night classes in Kenton. In choosing this option he turned out to have made possibly his best decision ever, since it was here that he met his future wife, Margaret Watkins. Bill finished his exams while he was courting Margaret and went back to work for the NUR at Unity House in Euston. On 7 May 1949 they married and initially lived at Margaret's parent's house in Churchill Avenue, Kenton where their first son David was born on 17 March 1950. Subsequently they moved to 105 Regal Way where Alun was born on 10 May 1952 and Rhys was born on 19 May 1963. Bill always talked with great affection of Margaret – it is clear their marriage was a happy one based on absolute trust and one in which they each enabled one another to grow. It also provided a loving and stable home life for the three boys. When Margaret died in 1998, a huge part of Bill's life was taken away.

Rhys, Alun and David North.

Bill's family are amongst the kindest and most gracious people you could meet. The immediate family comprised of Bill's two sisters, Nancy and Iris, and Margaret's brother and sister, Jim and Betty. All three sons married and as a result Bill and Margaret had eight grandchildren. Family gatherings were frequent and from talking to each of the sons it is clear that they had a wonderful relationship with their Mum and Dad. Whenever Bill spoke to his children about that fateful night, he never for a second depicted it as an act of great skill and bravery, but purely as a reflection of the outstanding training he had received from the RAF. Indeed, it is only in recent years that people who knew Bill for a lifetime learnt of his WW2 heroics.

Bill's children remember picnics on Stanmore Common and cooking sausages on the primus stove; family holidays by the beach; the rugby club; the NUR sports day; walking up the road to meet him from work and, above all, being encouraged in all they attempted. In later years they valued his wise words and the fact that, along with Margaret, he would always be there no matter the situation or circumstances. To his grandchildren he was fondly known as 'bushy eyebrows' granddad and would love to chat to them all, and was always interested in how they were getting on.

Although Bill lived most of his life in England, his roots remained in Wales and he was always proud of his heritage. A favourite quote was, 'British by birth, but Welsh by the grace of God'! This was perhaps most clearly evidenced by his love of following the Welsh rugby team – this involved trips to Murrayfield, Twickenham, Lansdowne Road and Parc de France, but most often to the Cardiff Arms Park and, latterly, The Millennium Stadium – trips which always carried special memories for Bill.

This love of rugby resulted in him becoming a member of the local Pinner and Grammarians Rugby Club where he served as a player, captain, fixture secretary, ran the Colts team, Chairman and eventually became a life-long President. Throughout his life he showed an amazing ability to communicate at all levels with all types of people regardless of their background or age. This evidenced itself in all parts of his life and at Pinner, he was renowned for his ability of roping people in to do all sorts of things including playing, serving behind the bar, organising Boxing Day matches, Committees and the teas, which of course meant Margaret being involved. He made lasting friendships through rugby and his good friends at Pinner and Grammarians visited and looked out for him in his later years, particularly when his mobility meant he was unable to get out and about.

At heart, Bill was a committed, but not unquestioning socialist and Union man. His career rose from clerk to the position of Office Manager. As manager of the Movements Department, he would accompany Sid

Green and later on Sid Weighell to negotiations with British Rail. During one crisis he was called to a meeting at Downing Street and was even on the TV outside Number 10! (as mentioned in the introduction)

Bill was an active member of his local community and never seemed to be able to turn down a job that needed to be done. As a result he volunteered and served for many years on organisations as diverse as the Kenton and Kingsbury Scout Committee, the local Abbeyfield Home and Harrow Sports Council. He was also a Justice of the Peace, serving for 13 years on the Harrow Bench.

## BILL'S CREW

After the war Bill's crew went their separate ways and there are some fascinating stories to tell; some are happy and some sad. Sadly the North Crew never met again as a complete unit all together in one room. When the War finished people wanted to return to normal as quickly as possible. Lives had been changed forever for some and disrupted for others, many families and loved ones were finally reunited again. Everybody got straight back to living their lives and in some cases veterans never saw their comrades ever again; some met up years later and some religiously kept in regular contact through associations and clubs.

Before Norman Jarvis went back to Australia he went to visit Bill in Cardiff. This was the last time they ever saw each other. Norman wrote a couple of times to Bill, followed later by his wife Gwen and then other members of the Jarvis family.

When Norman Jarvis finally got back to Sydney, Australia on 12 November 1945 he was euphoric and all set for the rest of his life. He was reunited with his sweetheart Gwen Copeland of Sydney, who was also a WAAF. They lived in a cottage called 'Fairyvale' in Cudgewa, Upper Murray, Victoria, where they worked on farmland owned by Norman's family. They got married on 25 May 1946 and soon had a baby girl called Pamela. He was also due to be given a soldier settlement block by the Australian Government at Tallangatta in August 1949.

In October 1949 Bill and Margaret received a letter from Norman's wife Gwen Jarvis passing on some devastating news. Bearing in mind what they both went through in the war, Bill has never got over this and whenever he talks about Norman his eyes always fill with tears. Whenever I was with Bill and this happened I found it hard not to be moved by this sadness and the incredible bond that the two men had. I think it is why I felt such an affinity with Norman Jarvis and was fascinated by his War Diary. Bill also kept in touch with Norman's brother Ken Jarvis by letter. This is a copy of the heart wrenching letter that was sent from Gwen to Bill.

'Fairyvale'
Cudgewa, Victoria.NSW.
Australia.

Sunday 9 October, 1949.

Dear Bill,

It is very hard for me to have to write and tell you of the tragic passing of Norm on the 24 of August last. He was bringing in a cartload of wood when the horse bolted and he was thrown under the wheel which passed over his back. He was only conscious for a few minutes and when his brother Ken ran to him all he said was 'Ken I think my back is broken—get Gwen.' The accident happened about ½ a mile from our place and by the time I was told it was too late to help in any way for my darling was then in God's hands.

I don't know how I have lived through these last weeks, the heartache and yearning has been almost too much to bear. Everyone has been most kind and done everything possible to help, but there is just nothing in this world to ever atone for the loss of my beloved one. Our little girl Pamela of course can't understand and keeps asking where her Daddy is, the two of them were such grand mates, but it makes everything just so much harder to bear.

Norm counted you as one of his very special friends, having shared so much during the war and I feel as if I know you through him. He was so pleased when he received the piece of your wedding cake with card enclosed and he had this Air Letter in readiness to write to you. Little did he know of the tragedy which was to crush forever all our hopes and plans for the future. Having spent so much time with him in the RAF you would get to know his sterling qualities and fine character and these attributes made him a very wonderful husband and Daddy. He only deserved the very best from life; he was always so good and kind and loving and this sudden ending of his young eager life will always remain a mystery and heartbreak to me.

Only the previous week he had won a block of 14 acres under the soldier settlement scheme at Tallangatta about 40 miles from here and he was so excited at getting a start on his own and we were planning to build our own home, in fact we just lived for each other; now there is nothing and everything seems so empty and hopeless. Our married life together couldn't have been happier, our love for each other a very tender and wonderful thing. I am staying with Norm's parents with little Pam for a while until I can try and think of some way of adjusting my life.

On behalf of Norm and myself, as I know he would want it that way, may I offer congratulations to you and Margaret and may your married life together be all that you could wish.

With best wishes to you both,

I remain,

Your Sincere Friend,

Gwen.

No words can really describe the complete and utter sense of loss experienced here; it is almost more tragic than being lost in the War itself. Gwen never really got over Norman's untimely death, but found some happiness again when she married Bill Honeycombe in 1952. She and Bill were very happy living at Katoomba, NSW until Bill became an invalid. Gwen moved to Tweed Heads NSW in 1975 where she enjoyed playing bowls in her retirement. Pam and the family had to move her closer to Grenfell in 1997, so they could look after her until her death in 2006. Pam was Norman and Gwen's only child. Pam and Rob Livingstone's two sons are Mitchell and David.

In August 2009 Pam Livingstone, Norman's daughter came to visit Bill at Regal Way and gave Bill a copy of Norman's War Diary. Her son, David Norman Livingstone, spent a few days with Bill and his family in 1998. Pam's cousin, Norman Webster (named after his uncle Norman, her father) and his son, Andrew Webster visited Bill on a number of occasions, between 2000 and 2009.

I have kept in close contact with Pam Livingstone and the Jarvis family throughout the writing of this book and count on her as a wonderful friend.

The next in line is Ivor (Monty) Monteith. Bill didn't see him again after the war, but they kept in close contact by letter and phone. Monty emigrated to Australia shortly after the war and Norman Jarvis gave him a lot of help settling down and finding a house close to Cudgewa. Monty was present at Norman's funeral in August 1949 and was also devastated by the tragedy. Monty didn't talk much about his wartime experiences with his family, but was frequently in touch with Norman's brother, Ken.

Monty had a daughter called Katrina who is married to Will Allen. I also have been in close contact with her throughout the story. Her family met up with Pam Livingstone and the Jarvis family at the Australian War Memorial in recent years. Bill and Monty spoke on the phone every year on 5 July to commemorate their crash landing and their lucky escape. The last time Bill spoke to Monty was on 5 July 2007. Monty had trouble remembering their time in the RAF together and Bill was quite saddened by this. Monty passed away in Oct 2007.

Next is Patrick (Eddy) O'Shea, who went back to his life in Dublin and then at Cork Road in Limerick, Ireland with his wife Maureen O'Shea. Bill and Eddy kept in touch and he got a job with Aer Lingus, although not flying as he was 'done with that.' Bill went to see Eddy in Ireland in the mid 1950's with his family. Bill's son Alun North can remember travelling over on the ferry when he was about 4 or 5 years old and seeing Eddy O'Shea in Ireland. Bill saw Eddy again in 1979 when he came to visit his friends in London, one of whom worked at the school at the end of Regal Way, St. Gregory's.

In later years Eddy suffered from ill health and in August 1984 Bill and Margaret received this sad letter from Maureen O'Shea. Even though they were leading different lives, this heart breaking letter demonstrates the eternal bond that existed between Bill and his crew; they were always in each other's thoughts.

c/o 6 Lord Edward Street, Dublin 2
3 October 1984

My dear Bill and Margaret,

This is my 3rd or 4th attempt at writing to you and this time it is my intention that I will post this effort.

I need to tell you that my Patrick (Eddy) died on August 9 of a massive coronary. You have always been such an integral part of the fabric of his life and you would be very surprised indeed if you had travelled with us when Pat would refer to his time in the RAF and the marvellous Welshman who at a mere 21/22 was his Skipper, who not only expertly took care of him while flying, but also ensured that he got home after, 'after-flight relaxing periods'. You were one of the people whom he always treasured and most importantly respected all of his life and as such I feel you should be notified on his death.

I am glad to say that he was mercifully spared suffering at the end as it was all over within about half an hour and I am deeply grateful to God for that. Also, from my point of view he was prepared to meet his God as he had (as was his wont), he had been to Mass that day and that has given me great solace. He was deeply religious all of his life although he would have killed me while alive if I ever revealed that very private and personal part of his life, yet it was so much a part of him that I wish to share it with you as an esteemed and very special friend.

Well Bill and Margaret, I am desolate to be without him and constantly want to share this and that with him and cannot quite believe that I will never see him again. We would have been married for 34 years on August 23! I am still working for the Association (which is incidentally now in jeopardy, but that is a long story which I need not get into at the moment). I had so hoped that it would stay together and build on the hard work and base, which he had built which was one of the reasons for me remaining here, but like a tent which has the main pin knocked the Association is now on the point of collapse – I will know for sure next Monday.

I have been blessed to be back in Ireland so that I am surrounded by my own and Pat's relatives who have cushioned me so marvellously ever since. I have been staying with a first cousin and his wife and will shortly move into a house – brand new – and hope very much that I will manage to survive there on my own. I have not been back to the flat save for a couple of times to pack as I must confess that my weakness is that I am oppressed there. If it had been our own home things would have been different I imagine. Ironically Pat was on the point of entering into business on his own account in conjunction with this when he died which is so sad. However, that is life and as I have said before I hold no bitterness for I am so grateful to God to have taken him without suffering too much, for I loved him with all of my heart and can only hope that from here on I will honour his name and memory by behaving with dignity and that I will be able to do something worthwhile with my life in the future. I don't always feel strong yet I do try to avoid passing gloom and doom around, for nothing can bring him back to me and I feel that each person whom I meet or contact has to live their own lives and need optimism rather than pessimism.

I hope that this letter doesn't ramble too much – that is one thing of which I am well aware of these days, the tendency to meander far too much. Forgive me if I have done too much to you.

Yours very sincerely

Maureen O'Shea

**Bill's reply to Maureen is equally as moving.**

105 Regal Way
9 February, 1985.

My Dear Maureen,

At long last I have settled to replying to your letter dated 3 October which conveyed the shattering news concerning Eddy (Pat). Since receiving your letter I have read and re-read it on numerous occasions with the avowed intent of writing to you. The effect your letter had on me is difficult to explain. Pat was one with whom I had a 'special relationship'. My memory of Pat goes back to October 1943 when we 'crewed-up' at No.17 O.T.U (Operational Training Unit) at the RAF station called Turweston. Pat acted the part of the rebellious, scruffy, couldn't care less, uneducated and uncaring Irishman. 'Acted the part' is the significant phrase of that last sentence. The remainder can be ignored. I very quickly became aware of the sharpness of Pat's intellect. He was no ordinary Irishman and he and I struck up a friendship which really did stand the test of time. I knew him as a caring, kindly man who would stand loyally by his friends. I grew to regard him with affection and respect and count myself lucky to have served in the RAF with someone such as Pat.

I hope that what I have written will – even if only partly - explain how I felt when I received your letter, the void your news created and my unforgivable delay in writing to you.

I know that Eddy (Pat) would undoubtedly say that life must go on, so I will continue this letter by asking you a few questions and then give you news about my family.

The questions simply relate to the 'Association' for which Pat and you were working. What is this Association and are you still working for it? The latter part of this question is asked as, in your letter, you stated that the Association is in Jeopardy and that your position might not be too secure. I do hope that things have worked out favourably for you.

Turning to the North family: David, the eldest of the three sons, will be 35 on the 17 of March (St Patricks Day!!). Married with two children – another David aged 12 and Lisa aged 10. David senior worked for quite some time as a secondary school mathematics teacher in England and Botswana. At present, however, he is a full-time pastor at a Pentecostal (Evangelical) Church in Basingstoke. He is very happy in what he is doing and is part of a small, but very caring community in Basingstoke.

Son No. 2 (Alun) will be 33 next May. An outdoor type who loves the countryside and is very capable in a practical way. He also started his working life as a teacher but, in his case, he taught in a London primary school. All this, however changed in August 1982 when Alun decided to see if he could settle in France and for the last two and a half years has been living in Aix. He made a living initially by teaching English on an ad-hoc freelance basis. He then obtained a post as an Animateur – a job which I can only describe as a sort of cross between a social worker and a probationary officer. He was reasonably qualified for this type of work as he had been employed part-time on social work whilst teaching in the London area. Last September/October he resigned this job and is now self-employed with a friend on a building/decoration project (which seems to be giving a good return) and is also trying to import French herbs into Britain. This latter project seems to be progressing reasonably. Margaret and I consider ourselves lucky as we see quite a bit of Alun by holidaying in France, two or three weeks in Aix in the summer and perhaps a visit to Paris where Alun joins us in the spring. Additionally he usually visits England about twice a year.

The youngest, Rhys, is 21 (he'll be 22 in May) and is in his final year at Loughborough University. Hopefully he will gain his BSC in Management Sciences – a widely based course which embraces such subjects as mathematics, statistics, economics, business law, computer studies, etc. In a nutshell the course is designed to prepare graduates for a career in industry/commerce. He is a reasonably bright lad who is also proficient in most sports. He broke the news to us on New Year's Eve that he hoped to get married next August or September. His girl friend Stephanie (they have been going out together for about three and a half years) is a trainee nurse at Barts Hospital, London, and hopes to qualify in May/June which is about the same time Rhys will be taking his finals. The future so far as Rhys is concerned clearly depends on what happens in May/June and on the steps he is already taking to obtain a job. From a purely selfish point of view we hope they do not move too far away so that we can continue to see them from time to time. All three boys have given us a good deal of pleasure and no real problems. They have all been keen on sports, Rugby in particular which is a pastime where Margaret reckons I've brainwashed them!!

Talking of Margaret, she keeps very well, puts up with all my shortcomings –and still helps to prepare the after match tea and refreshments at the local rugby club!! She has a part-time job as a general assistant in the Home Economics Department of St. Gregorys, a nearby Catholic school where Pat's friend also teaches. I've been trying for some time to remember this lady's name without success so perhaps you can give me the information if you find time to write. I met the woman and her husband when I saw Pat at her home about 4/5 years ago.

Incidentally Margaret has a close friend who has recently moved to Crosshaven, Co. Cork and it is quite likely we will visit her in the not too distant future. If we do it would be marvellous if we could also fit in a visit to you and talk of old times. Perhaps, therefore, you will be sure to let me have your present address. Although I shall address this letter to Lord Edward Street, Dublin, I am aware from your letter that you will be now have moved into a brand new house. We both hope that you have settled in and that living alone has not posed too many problems.

You may be interested to know that my mother is still alive and for her age (84) very fit indeed. Mentally she is extremely alert and ever ready to discuss current problems. No difficulty with either her hearing or sight and when I visit her in Cardiff it is great to see her so happy. She is fortunate in that she lives next door to my sister which means that whilst my mother has her independence my sister (Iris) is able to ensure that she eats well and regularly and keeps warm, etc. etc.

I feel that I cannot conclude this letter without referring again to Pat. Like you I am pleased to know that when his time came it was quick and he did not suffer. This knowledge was clearly of great consolation to you. For my part I cannot help but feel the loss of someone with whom I shared so many experiences, and who I respected enormously and was more than pleased to call my friend.

How nice it would be to meet again. Margaret and I do hope that this will prove possible. Meanwhile – take care, look after yourself and, when you have the opportunity, perhaps you will write and let me know how you are progressing.

Yours very sincerely

Bill North.

During the course of this book coming together one of the things I tried to do for Bill was to track down the O'Shea family in Ireland to re-establish contact and let them know about it. I sent letters to the addresses Bill had in Dublin and Limerick explaining what we were doing, but both letters came back 'unknown' and 'sorry we couldn't help you.' I searched on the internet as well, but time was pressing and we had to move on with the book. (If anybody can help here, please contact me)

Next is Bill's fellow Welshman, Dave Crowley. Bill met Dave in London shortly after the war with his wife and said they had a great meeting. There was an attempt to get Dave, Eddy, Dennis and Bill together by Bill and Dennis in the early 1950's, but the meeting didn't happen and they again moved on with their lives.

In the 1980's Bill was contacted by Peter Done a friend of Reg Payne who was Sir Michael Beetham's W/Op on 50 Squadron. Peter Done worked in Kettering Hospital and working on one of the wards there was a lady called Janet Legg. She was wearing a Caterpillar brooch that was unique to RAF servicemen that had parachuted out of doomed aircraft and lived to tell the tale (as explained earlier in the book). Peter Done asked her about the broach and she mentioned that her father was a Navigator in the RAF during WW2. Peter offered to do some research for her and find out more about her father. During his research he tracked down Bill at Regal Way and found out that Janet Legg's father was in fact Bill's Navigator Dave Crowley. Peter passed on everything he had found out to Janet Legg and put her in touch with Bill. During this correspondence Bill found out that Dave had died, but not much more detail than that.

Unfortunately the contact was lost between Bill and Janet Legg and that is how it was left for a while. Bill asked me if I could possibly track down Janet Legg for him and I contacted Peter Done who was extremely helpful. We managed to find an address in Kettering which we wrote to, but sadly nobody replied. Bill didn't get to find out any more news about Dave Crowley's later life and felt saddened by that. I did some research into Dave Crowley's mum and dad, Kate and Harold Crowley who were from Merthyr Tydfil, but didn't make much progress. They lived in and ran a pub called 'The Prince of Wales' Hotel in Dowlais, Glamorgan, which is no longer there now, so anybody who can find out more it would be much appreciated.

Bill's Flight Engineer, Les Morton, moved to Australia after the war with his wife Peggy (also Margaret), and they had two children, Phillip and Glenda. Les returned to his career in carpet manufacturing and was offered a position with United Carpet Mills in Melbourne, establishing a broad loom carpet section. He later started his own carpet retail company and then retired and moved to Queensland, where he took out an Owner Builder License and built his own home. He also spoke to Monty a couple of times on the phone over the years. Les managed to contact Bill again after nearly 48 years and was reunited with him at Regal Way in 1993. They both attended the 50/61 Squadron reunion at Skellingthorpe in 1993 and 1994. They also went to see the Battle of Britain Memorial Flight Lancaster Bomber based at RAF Coningsby.

Les Morton and Bill North with Peg (Margaret) and Margaret, 5 June 1993.

I spoke with Les in Australia on the phone many times and we also wrote to each other. He provided some fascinating insights and memories of life with Bill's crew. I have also kept in close contact with his daughter Glenda as well and they like everybody else have become good friends. Les was not well and after a long battle with leukaemia and having regular blood transfusions passed away peacefully on 4 April 2013. Les had become a great friend whilst writing the book and I felt honoured to have parts of it read out at his funeral on 9 April 2013.

When Bill first asked me to write the book I had no idea of the scale of the project and the workload that I was about to take on. I was prepared to go anywhere and do whatever it took even though I had a very limited amount of time each day to contribute to the book. The first thing Bill asked me to do was to track down his Mid-Upper Gunner (A.G.1) Sgt. Dennis Bartlett. We knew pretty much what had happened to and the whereabouts of the other crew members, but Dennis Bartlett had seemingly disappeared. After extensive searches at the Public Records Office and many RAF Associations including Bomber Command I kept drawing a blank. Each time I went to visit Bill he asked me if I had found Dennis and I my constant reply was 'Not yet Bill, but I will do.' One day Bill and I were looking through some of his documents when he found a letter dated 3 February 1954 to Dennis Bartlett; on it was an address in Camberley. This was the last written contact with Dennis that Bill had. I said to Bill, 'This is a shot in the dark, but I am going to drive down to Camberley and knock on doors and see if anybody knows of Dennis.'

So on Friday 11 February 2011, I drove down to Camberley, it was a beautiful day and I had high hopes. I started knocking on doors and posting a letter through each door I came to explaining what I was doing. Suddenly a lady called Maria Gunston from no. 22 came running down Woodside after me and told me to go back to number 20. She explained that the Bartlett family still lived there. When I got back to number 20 and knocked on the door a man called Ian Jarret came out from no. 18 and said he may be able to help me. My heart was pounding with excitement. He was Dennis Bartlett's nephew and informed me that Dennis was still alive. In fact he rang Dennis there and then and asked him if he would like to meet up with Bill again. The answer was yes! On Friday 18 Feb 2011 I met Dennis in Camberley with Ian Jarret and showed him the pictures of the Lancaster crash site in France. He could not believe he was looking at his crashed Lancaster after all that time. In particular what fascinated him was how wrecked the Mid-Upper Turret was, he couldn't believe he had survived being shot at by the NF.

I had got to finally meet a face from that picture of Bill's which had fascinated me since I was 7 years old. I had often wondered over the years as I had with the other crewmen what had happened to him and what he had done with his life. It was an amazing feeling to find him. Dennis Bartlett was just like Bill, an absolutely lovely and unassuming man; it felt like I'd known him forever. It took me 18 months to track him down during which time I never gave up hope and always had a strange feeling that he was out there somewhere.

In early February 2011 Bill fell over at home (Regal Way) and was transferred into Willesden General Hospital. I turned up at Regal Way to see him for our usual meeting and there was no answer. After a huge panic and fearing the worst I spoke to Alun whose number I had lost and found out Bill was OK. I visited Bill there on Mon 21 Feb 2011 where I informed him that I had tracked down Dennis Bartlett. The look on his face was a moment I will never forget. I rang Dennis on my mobile and they spoke to each other again for the first time since the end of the War. Again to witness this event felt like a real privilege. When Bill came out of Willesden General Hospital he was moved into Basingfield Court Care Home in Basingstoke. His son David lived nearby and it was agreed that he would be much safer here than living by himself at Regal Way.

The next step in the story was now to reunite Bill and Dennis; they hadn't seen each other for 67 years! The last time they had seen each other was in Beauvais prison hospital in France in 1944 after they had survived being shot down. I went down to Basingstoke on Fri 18 March 2011 with my brother John and daughter Izzy and we met Bill's son David at the care home. We all sat excitedly waiting for Dennis to turn up with his nephew Ian Jarret. When Dennis came in and gave Bill a hug it was like they had never been apart, their eyes were shining with happiness. It was a truly emotional day and everybody had tears in their eyes. The two men strangely only lived 20 minutes away from each other. I felt honoured to witness this event and to watch and listen to the two War Veterans talking to each other like the past was only yesterday.

In late 2011 I contacted Richard Smith at the Daily Mirror after reading a story in which two D-Day Veterans were re-united after 60 years. I explained that I had a similar story that might interest him and he immediately agreed to run it. So on Thursday 1 Dec 2011 the story of Bill and Dennis reuniting appeared in the paper under the title, 'Hero Bomber Pilot's amazing untold story.'

On Sunday 17 April 2011 I visited Dennis and his sister Daphne Pearce with my daughter Izzy. Daphne said this was first time she had heard the full story of what had happened on the night they were shot down, Dennis would never talk about it and had nightmares for a long time. On the way home Izzy and I stopped at the RAF Memorial at Runnymede. It is an extraordinary place; the peaceful atmosphere and sadness are overwhelming. Dennis also came up to Bill's suprise 89th birthday party at Basingfield Care Home on the 2 May 2011; again I quietly observed the incredible bond that was still present between the two extraordinary men.

Bill and Dennis re-united 18 March 2011. Dennis, Bill and Chris 22 May 2011 (Bill's 89th birthday).

After the war Dennis Bartlett finished his RAF service working as a VIP steward on flights all over the world. When he was decommissioned in 1946 he got a job as a personal assistant to Winston Churchill's son Randolph Churchill in Victoria in London. Dennis said this was quite challenging as Randolph Churchill had quite a temper and used to throw things around if things weren't done as he liked them. In 1950 Dennis started worked in the menswear department of Allders in Camberley for the next 31 years. After the department closed Dennis transferred to linens where he was ADM until he semi-retired in September 1989, working two days a week to give him more time to continue his passion for gardening.

WO Dennis Bartlett by an Avro York (a long-range transport aircraft based on the Lancaster); on the way to the UK Trade Mission in Hong Kong, 12 December 1946 (*Dennis Bartlett*).

Sgt Dennis John Hatchett was Bill's replacement Flt/Eng on the night of the crash on 4/5July 1944. On the 26 May 2013, just as the book was going to print I was contacted by his Nephew Ian Hatchett, who supplied the following information: 'Dennis never spoke about what he did during the War, apart from the fact that he served in the RAF and flew in Lancasters. I was stunned when I stumbled across the story of P/O North and my uncle's involvement. What Bravery by P/O North to have stayed with the stricken aircraft, which in the end saved my uncle's life. After the War he returned to his wife in Worcester and had two children. He ran a successful Cabinet making business until his retirement and died at the age of 73 in December 1986.'

There now follows an extraordinary account with more 'coincidences', that eventually led Bill and his family back to the site of his crash landing in France.

# Chapter Twenty Six

## The Return to France

On the 11 June 1999 Bill received an unusual letter in the post from a Frenchman by the name of Laurent Viton. Laurent is a French researcher who was researching all RAF and USAAF crews lost over Normandy during WW2 for a book he was working on. He was looking to get testimonies from the survivors of these crashes and find out whether they were evadees or POWs. Laurent was researching a crashed Lancaster site near Les Andelys and Bill's name and address had been passed onto him by the ex POW Association as a survivor of the crash.

Bill thought it was a hoax and regarded the letter with a great deal of suspicion and in the meantime went off on a holiday to Canada. The letter was niggling Bill however, and he sent a postcard to Laurent requesting the name of the person who had given him his address. (Rex Chuter). When he returned to London on 22 August 1999, after being satisfied this was not a wind up Bill replied to Laurent Viton's letter supplying the information he had requested. This was to be the start of an incredible journey and an amazing series of friendships.

On 22 August 1999 Bill received another letter from Laurent Viton thanking him for supplying his crew picture and testimony and with this letter came a huge surprise. One week after Laurent had received Bill's testimony in the post he met another WW2 researcher from Les Andelys to look at WW2 crash photos. Amongst the various photos of crash sites were three pictures of Bill's Lancaster EE186, QR-D! Laurent said to Bill, *'It was chance, purely chance, to find these photos only one week after you sent me your testimony.'*

Laurent had sent three photo copies of the crash site of EE186, QR-D for Dog. They were quite poor quality, but Bill instantly recognised his beloved a/c and the memories came flooding back again. He could not believe that after 55 years he was looking at his crashed Lancaster. There was another surprise on the way.

In Bill's next reply to Laurent dated 25 October 1999 he answers a question that Laurent asked and everybody has asked out loud through the years. Did Bill receive any special decoration for his actions on the night of 4/5 July 1944? Bill's answer to Laurent was: *'No, I was not specially decorated. I simply received the normal medals. Of course one has to remember that no-one in authority would have learned of our crash landing and I for my part, was only too pleased that we survived the war – particularly as I have recently learned of the extent of the RAF losses on 4 July.'* (Bill had obtained a copy of W.R. Chorley's *Bomber Command Losses 1944*).

The surprise came in Laurent's next letter dated 9 November 1999. There were actually six pictures of QR-D and they had been put on display in a collection at the WW2 Museum in Tosny. It is run and owned by a man called Jean Erisay who had actually sat in Bill's blood covered pilot's seat as a little boy. The Museum and Jean Erisay had agreed to let Bill have proper copies of the six pictures. There was also a detailed copy of a map showing the St. Leu target and the crash site near Harquency. Bill had always though he had crashed at Beauvais and now had found out exactly where he did crash. Bill said: *'In a strange sort of way I found the photograph showing many children clambering over my crashed Lancaster particularly moving.'* The German crash/salvage report number was KE 9167.

On 17 January Bill informed Laurent that in view of the positive way their correspondence was going that he and his three sons David, Alun and Rhys would like to visit Tosny on Saturday 8 April 2000. On 18 Jan 2000 Bill wrote to Ivor Monteith in Australia sending him copies of the correspondence and the pictures. Bill and Ivor 'Monty' had kept in close contact though the years and would ring each other every year on the 5 July, the anniversary of the crash day. This incidentally was also Dennis Bartlett's birthday, so Dennis was also reminded every year even though he had lost touch with Bill. Shortly before Monty died in October 2007 Bill rang him on the 5 July to reminisce. As previously mentioned Bill was shocked to find that Monty had trouble remembering what had happened and sharing the memories with Bill, due to his ill health. This was quite a shock for Bill and he gets quite emotional when he recalls this experience of his crew mate's failure to remember.

The correspondence continued up to April and as the excitement of the return to France grew, everybody could hardly wait. The trip itself was truly eventful and was made very special for Bill. It was attended by the Mayor and other dignitaries and many other veterans and their families who turned up to make the day so memorable. It was reported in the newspapers *'l' Impartial'* and *'Paris Normandie'*. The Museum at Tosny is very impressive and Bill and his sons recommend that everybody should visit it if they are in France.

Bill said to Jean Erisay on 29 May 2000:*'The welcome you and your wife and the many others whose names I do not know gave to me and my sons, made the day one which we will remember in years to come. We all regard you as a friend and I feel very indebted for all you have done. For my part, visiting the site of my crashed Lancaster and hearing you talk about sitting in the pilot's seat, brought back many memories of what happened so many years ago and has made me realise, yet again, how fortunate we were that the entire crew survived; something which for many years has given me much cause for satisfaction.'*

The following is a translation from the two newspapers that covered Bill's return to France.

**<u>'L'Impartial' LES ANDELYS THURSDAY 13 APRIL 2000</u>**

Welcomed by the Mayor of Harquency and the Tosny Museum.

**<u>BILL NORTH RETURNS TO THE PLACE WHERE HIS BOMBER CRASHED IN 1944.</u>**

It was a very emotional time on Saturday afternoon at the Museum on the Second World War at Tosny, where Jean Erisay received the veteran RAF Pilot Bill North (78), whose bomber had crash landed at Harquency in July 1944, having been shot down by the Germans. Immediately he was taken prisoner and sent to Germany. Now he has come back for the first time.

Passionately interested in history, the young Laurent Viton had decided a few years ago to write a book tracing aerial battles of the war. This undertaking led him one day to think about the Lancaster EE186, QR-D from the 61st Squadron of the RAF, which was on a mission to destroy the V1 German flying bomb site at St-Leu d'Esserent. An objective that was never achieved.

Piloted by Bill North, a smart, young Englishman aged 22, the bomber was shot down on the night of 4/5 July 1944 at 1am over Andelys by a German Night Fighter. There were seven people on board, 6 English and 1 Australian, they decided to parachute down from the plane when one of them noticed that the straps of his harness had been damaged in the attack on the plane.

**<u>HE SAVED HIS SIX COMRADES BY LANDING THE PLANE.</u>**

Without panicking for a single moment he then asked each one of them to hold on tightly and decided to crash land, in order to try to save the entire crew. Avoiding the village he succeeded in landing in a field at Harquency, but not without injury. Five men, including the pilot were wounded. Two others were able to escape before the Germans arrived. They were taken in

by an inhabitant of Leomesnil, Georges Patard, who sheltered them until them until August 1945.
*'I was wounded in my legs and arms. The Germans came quickly. They sent me to a hospital at Beauvais where I had some primary care before they sent me to Germany.'* This is what the heroic pilot of the Lancaster remembers. Surrounded by his three sons, who had urged him to visit France after a phone call from the young enthusiastic historian who was researching evidence of this time. A tear ran down his cheeks when he discovered the photographs of his plane on show at Tosny Museum. *'In the end my comrades and I were very fortunate,'* he explains to his sons.
The founder of the Museum, Jean Erisay explains that at the time he was an adolescent and he would go to see the plane everyday and even climbed into the cockpit. He had moreover salvaged several pieces of the bomber including a manometer (pressure gauge). A navigation aid that Bill North was seeing it again 56 years after he had last seen it!
*'I am truly moved'*, he stressed, his voice low and almost inaudible because of a lump in his throat. *'This morning the Mayor M. Blanchard, took me to the place where we crashed. Everything is coming back to me as if it were yesterday. Indeed it was extraordinary that we all survived. I have, moreover, been in contact with my comrades for many years, all except one, the Australian, who died after the war in a farming accident.'*

## 'IT IS A VERY IMPORTANT MOMENT IN MY LIFE.'

The brother-in-law of Jean Erisay, was also there. He was one of the first to arrive at the scene of the crash. The plane was still smouldering. The Germans had gone with their prisoners. *'In the following fortnight they entirely dismantled the aircraft: but had left in one corner a copper radiator weighing 23 kilos, which I collected and took home. Later I sold it and was able to buy my first bike. I was 12'*, he remembers.
*'Then you owe me some interest,'* joked the pilot, who did not want to return without leaving a further memento. He therefore donated to the Tosny Museum his pilot's tunic that he wore at that time, but not before having one last look at it.
A small souvenir in the hand, but a souvenir much in the heart. *'I will never forget this day, it is indeed a very important occasion in my life'*, he stressed before leaving for Beauvais with his three sons, on the last stage of his trip before returning to his usual routine.

## 22/23 APRIL 2000 PARIS/NORMANDIE LES ANDELYS

## THE PILOT OF THE ENGLISH AIRCRAFT THAT CRASHED IN 1944 RETURNS

The Museum of the Second World War has paid homage to the pilot of the English plane that crashed at Harquency in 1944.

On 5 July 1944 the Lancaster EE186, QR-D, piloted by Bill North, was on a mission to attack the V1 flying bomb site at St Leu-d'Esserent and was making its way back towards Vexin.

At 1am it was attacked by a German Night Fighter. The aircraft suffered damage. Two solutions were open to the pilot: leave the plane and parachute down, or attempt a forced landing of the machine. But the straps of the parachute of one crew member had been torn. Bill North went all out and decided to land his Lancaster in a field.

The pilot and 4 of his men were taken prisoner. The Navigator and Flight Engineer were saved by a local inhabitant Georges Patard and sheltered in his home at Leomesnil until the liberation.

In July 1999 Bill North received a strange letter. A young man, Laurent Viton, from Normandy, who was interested in the allied planes that had crashed in his area was aiming to write a book about these matters and asked for details of his crash. The thought that it could be a bit of a hoax soon left the pilot's mind, when he saw the photographs taken at that time that were enclosed with the letter.

April 2000. The pilot's three sons, who had grown up with sad memories they had been told by their father urged him to accept Laurent Viton's invitation to return to the scene of the crash.

A ceremony was arranged in the museum of The Second World War in the presence of selected local dignitaries and inhabitants of Harquency who had returned with him for this chapter in their history. Emotion filled the occasion.

## 'I NEVER THOUGHT I WOULD RETURN.'

His memory is quite clear: *'It is truly moving to return to this place. I was 22 at the time. I realise how fortunate I was. I was not afraid, there was so much to do and think about what would follow. Above all I was concerned about how strong my father would be when he received the telegram telling him I was missing. I was wounded, with one of my comrades we were conveyed to a hospital at Beauvais. I returned to England in April 1945. Since then I have kept in contact with certain ex-crew members. I never ever thought I would come back here.'*

In the museum several parts of the Lancaster with the report of the disaster are on display. Jean Erisay greeted Bill North and his three sons very cordially. Memories were also rekindled for the inhabitants of Harquency which they will never forget.

*'I was eleven years old and I wanted to be a pilot,'* Louis Picache relates, *'I climbed into the cockpit of the aircraft. I even collected the copper from the radiator, sold it and bought myself a bicycle.'*

## THE PILOT'S TUNIC IS ADDED TO THE COLLECTION.

From his childhood Jean Erisay accumulated unceasingly objects relating to The Second World War. 'I salvaged whatever I could find when I was a boy during the war. Later I found all these articles again in my parent's loft. Then I began to make a collection of these things.'

And in 1994 this collection of material was sufficiently large enough for Jean Eisay to open his own museum at Tosny.

At the time of the tribute paid to Bill North, the pilot gave him (Erisay) his pilot's tunic and also a medal which will be added to the collection.

On 7 May 2000 Bill finally received his six good copies of the crash site photographs and on 21 June 2000 thanked Laurent Viton. *'We did have a truly memorable day – one which from time to time I found very emotional. One of the advantages of meeting you personally is that I (and my three sons) now have the utmost regard for you both as a researcher and as a true friend.'*

Laurent Viton has worked on a BBC documentary with Dan Snow on a Spitfire crash site in France which was dug up on camera (This was Canadian Flying Officer Fred Heninger's Spitfire Mk XII which crashed in Normandy on 6 Jan 1944, it was one of only 100 Spitfires of this model that had the Roll Royce Griffin engine fitted).

The close relationship between Bill and his family, Laurent Viton, Jean Erisay and Jeans daughter Cathie continues to this day. On 6 April 2006 Alan's wife Thea North helped make arrangements for Bill to return to France again. On the weekend of 21/22 April 2006 Bill, David, Alun, Rhys, his two grandchildren David and Lisa, (also Peter and Harry Brown) visited Tosny again. On the Saturday afternoon they all visited Jean Erisay's museum again and then had a wonderful meal together in the evening with Jean and his family at the Auberge Au Pechens Martinal, La Roque. It was only a short stay, but again the warm welcome and friendship extended is ever-present in Bill and his family's lives.

These are events alongside many others generated by the everlasting ripples from the pebble thrown in Bill's life pond. All these emanating from the period in his life that was his RAF service and he and his crew's close call as they fell through the French skies on the 4/5 July 1944, passing right through death's shadow, to return home safely to their loved ones and their families to be.

Bill mentions his Guardian Angel in reference to that night, *'I thank my Guardian Angel that I am here and can share this with you.'* His Rear Gunner Eddy O'Shea mentions divine intervention in a letter to Bill's parents dated 10 June 1945.

**<u>Sgt Eddy O'Shea</u>**

*'What I want to impress on you most of all is that you should be very thankful to God for the extraordinary luck Bill had that night—for no man on earth, no matter how collected, could have done it without his guidance.'*

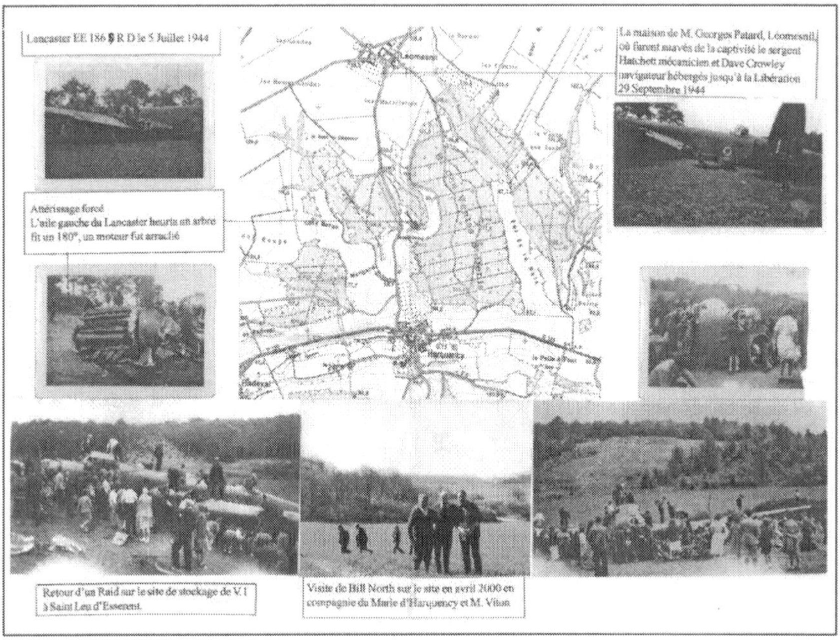


Bill North revisits the crash site near Harquency in France, with Jean Erisay and Laurent Viton.

# Chapter Twenty Seven

## A Strange Experience.

After Bill's birthday in May 2011 I continued to visit him throughout the summer and autumn months, often bringing my daughter Izzy with me. We continued to run through Chapters in the book and everytime I saw him he would add more fascinating eyewitness accounts to his story. On one occasion I left to go home and realised that I had left my camera in his room. I went back and as I opened the door I found Bill lying on the floor. Needless to say I was panicking like crazy. To my immediate relief Bill looked up and said, 'Get me up off the floor as quick as you can!' I hooked my hands under his armpits and hoisted him up and back onto his walker. He was fine he had just lost his balance. I called for help and then after making sure he was ok left for the journey home. The next time I went to see him we were both in trouble for not calling for help straight away when he fell. Bill with a cheeky glint in his eye said, 'Never mind that Chris, you only did what I told you to do.' During November 2011 Bill became ill and went into Basingstoke Hospital, he slowly started to fade away. I visited Bill here a number of times and took Dennis Bartlett with me to see him as well. Daphne Pearce also took Dennis to see him as well.

On the 1 December the article in the Daily Mirror came out and I took the paper up to Basingstoke Hospital for Bill to read. When I got up to the ward I gave it to Bill and said, 'this is it', he then asked me to read it to him. As I was reading the article I suddenly became aware that the whole ward had become silent and everyone was listening to me reading. It caught my breath and I had to hold on tight to the waterworks until I had finished reading. I showed him some old photos of his Bomb Aimer F/Sgt Norman Jarvis which Pam Livingstone had recently sent me. He was very happy with the story and got a bit emotional as he reminisced. I spent about 3 hours with him and every time I got up to go he asked me not to leave him. Just before I finally left we had a hug and said goodbye to each other. I said we all loved him and he said, 'Thank you for coming'. I felt happy and sad to have spent this time with him. It really felt like we had said our final goodbye and I felt honoured to have known him for the last 40 years. As I walked away from his bed I looked around one final time and saw that he was lying peacefully with his eyes closed. I knew in my heart that I wouldn't see him again.

.I had had a funny feeling all day on Wednesday 14 December and I felt the end was near for Bill. In the evening I had a bit of a strange experience, which I am not quite sure how to explain. At about 9pm I suddenly became quite calm and peaceful inside, I felt like I didn't have a care in the world. I immediately started to think of Bill and knew that he was not far from leaving us. This feeling stayed with me while I was working, intensifying and overwhelming me shortly after midnight. I instantly knew that Bill had died, but it didn't scare me, I still felt calm inside. I got home at about 3am and the feeling was slowly subsiding. I have never felt anything like this in my whole life. I spoke to my Mum about this experience and she said she had felt exactly the same as me at the same time. Her explanation for this was that we were experiencing exactly what Bill was feeling, in that he was ready to pass on and had no worries. It was a bit spooky, but not spooky in a bad way, more just happy and sad. Alun North rang me on Thursday morning 15 December 2011 at 9:20am and confirmed what I already knew, Bill had passed peacefully away at about 12:30am.

One of the hardest things I have I ever had to do in my whole life was to ring Dennis Bartlett and tell him that Bill had died; I rang him shortly after I got the news. I spoke to Daphne first and shared what had happened, she then asked me if she should tell Dennis or if I wanted to, I could. I immediately said I would speak to him. As I was passing on the events and describing my last visit with Bill we both got very upset and agreed to speak later when we had calmed down a bit. It was at this point that it really hit me hard. It felt really strange for Bill not to be here after all this time. He always seemed to be timeless and indestructible to his family and friends, but time was the very thing that took him in the end. One of the beautiful things for Bill's family and friends was that they each had time to spend with Bill and all shared a similar experience with him where he said good-bye.

When Dennis and I had visited Bill at Basingstoke Hospital on 11 November 2011 Bill was very tired and only spoke to us for a couple of minutes. The first thing he said when I woke him was, 'Hello Dennis, you really were the lucky one, thank you for coming'. We then left him alone to sleep. Although we were all expecting it, it still came as a shock. I had a long chat with Dennis later on Thursday and we both felt much better, he took it quite hard as well as he only just met Bill again after all these years.

Bill was many things to many people during his life. He was a loving and caring husband, father, and grandfather. He was our kind and caring good friend and next-door neighbour. He was an RAF hero and War Veteran. He was a true Union man in the original sense of the word, coming from a long line of Union men and an inspirational rugby coach. He touched many people's lives from start to finish and was a great letter writer keeping in touch with people from all over the world. He lived his life to the full and like so many of his generation, Bill always came across as a modest and gentle man. We all have a lot to learn from him.

Bill's funeral was in January 2012 and the Church in Harrow was packed with about 200 people. It was a beautiful service and when Bill's son David read the eulogy everybody had tears in their eyes. I remember speaking to David Hines at Pinner and Grammarians Rugby Club for the get together afterwards and he said something quite striking about Bill. 'A few years back our Rugby Club went to France to play a match against Les Andelys. We later found out that this was near where Bill crashed in 1944. The whole time we were in France he didn't say a word about his crash landing there all those years ago. I guess that is Bill though!'

Bill's passing and funeral added more content to constantly evolving book. The interest and support that I have had along the way has been inspiring and it seems to touch people's emotional centres in the same way that it does with me. The last part of the journey to get the book finished has felt like it has taken forever and I've really missed him.

# Chapter Twenty Eight

## What Has Changed

What has changed in society since Bill came home in April 1945 with his eternal memories and I met him in 1970 and got to know him through my childhood and adult years? The Nazi regime was stamped on by the Allied forces and Germany began again from its year zero, bleached of extremism. It was replaced for the next 50 years by the Cold War and the nuclear age. During my childhood and teenage years living at Regal Way, the overriding fear was of nuclear war. The country we went to war over, Poland, remained sadly enslaved by the communist regime as did all of Eastern Europe. Eastern Europe and Russia are now free from communism and its people integrated in to European culture.

Bill's wife Margaret also had her part to play in the fight for freedom. Bill particularly asked me to ensure that her contribution was recorded in this book.

During the War the Germans used what they thought was an unbreakable code for sending messages to their armed forces. It was generated by an encrypting device, the Enigma machine. Unknown to the Germans, Polish Intelligence had managed to obtain a copy of an early version of the machine which they successfully smuggled through to London at the start of the War. The Enigma device became more sophisticated throughout the war as the Germans added extra wheels to make its messages even harder to decrypt. But fifty miles North West of London was a country house called Bletchley Park; this became the centre for decoding the German messages and was code-named Station X. The official name for Bletchley was GCHQ (Government Cipher Headquarters) and at its height 10,000 people worked there. One of them was Bill's future wife, Margaret Watkins.

The main challenge now for the code breaking teams was how to break the German Military Code and read these messages. The first task before deciphering could take place was to break the daily key and wheel orders. Bletchley had a brilliant team of decoders made up of the finest translators and mathematicians in the country.

Alan Turing was an inspirational personality and outstanding mathematician from Cambridge who in 1936 had worked out the theory for a modern computer; he would focus on breaking the daily key changes. His real love was machines and ideas that involved contradictions. Turing helped to design and build the cryptanalytic machines (primitive computers) known as Bronze Goddesses or 'Bombes'.

The 'Bombe' was an electromechanical machine set in a bronze cabinet, with up to thirty rotating drums equating to the rotors of ten Enigma machines, it checked intercepted messages at high speed against different possible encipherments and helped break messages from 1940 onwards.

Group Captain Fred Winterbotham of Air intelligence was in charge of recruitment and the distribution of Ultra at Bletchley. He recalled that all new members of staff had to swear an oath in front of him that they would never divulge the greatest secret of the war; or and as he said this an Officer present would step forward withdraw a pistol, point it at them and say 'and if you don't I will shoot you'. Whether or not Margaret suffered this initiation we are not sure.

Margaret Lucy Watkins was born on 17 February 1923 and during WW2 served in the WRNS (Women's Royal Naval Service), more affectionately known as the 'Wrens', this was the women's branch of the Royal Navy. Some 300 WRENS were also drafted into service at Bletchley Park, Margret Watkins being one of them. The work at Bletchley Park, unknown to the general public at the time, was one of the most vital and successful parts of the war effort.

Margaret North (WREN).

At the time Margaret Watkins was going out with a fighter pilot called Sgt. H C Grove who was killed in the Battle of Britain. Harry Cyril Grove, of Herne Hill, London, joined the RAF in May 1936 as a direct-entry Airman u/t pilot. He joined 3 Squadron at Wick in August 1940 and moved to 501 at Kenley on 29 September. In an action near Sevenoaks on 8 November 1940, Sgt. HC Grove was shot down and killed in Hurricane V6805, which crashed and burned out at Pound Farm, Blackham Grove. He was 29 and is buried in St Luke's churchyard, Whyteleafe, Surrey.

Sgt HC Grove

Operators like Margaret who worked on the 'Bombe' would set the machines to test Alan Turing's menu of different combinations. The 'Bombe' was like a great big metal bookcase set in individual bays. The operators were given a wheel order from Turing and would fasten the drums in the given order, then go around to the back and set them in place to run their infinite permutations. It was the first electro-mechanical computer and used valve power to help it work. The work done at Bletchley Park was the biggest secret of WW2. It gave Churchill and a select few virtually real time viewing of the German Army, Navy, Air Force and Hitler's High Command's messages on a day to day basis. (Curiously the CinC of Bomber Command, Sir Arthur Harris was not privy to this critical intelligence source. Please read the excellent book, *Kept in the Dark,* John Stubbington ) Ultra allowed the Allies to make major tactical decisions that affected the outcome of WW2, effectively shortening it by as much as two years. All the equipment at Bletchley was destroyed after the War on Churchill's orders. Bill told me he that he pestered Margaret for years and years after the War to try and get her to reveal what she had done at Bletchley. She held fast to her vow of secrecy and didn't tell Bill until the 1980's. They both went to visit Bletchley where she explained her secret life and put his curiosity to rest.

Margaret North served from 7 October 1942 to 12 July 1946 and was a Leading Wren based at HMS Pembroke III. Her service included 'Special duties X'( 7 Oct 1942 to 31 May 1944), 'Special duties P5'(1 June 1944 to 18 Sept 1945), and 'Writer' (Royal Marines, Plymouth. 19 Sept 1945 to 12 July 1946) . Station X was the codename for Bletchley Park. Her service ran through the critical turning point of the War and while Bill was flying on Ops.

The technology we use today like Satellite Navigation Systems and Drones enable bombs to literally be put through letterboxes without the need for large Squadrons to area bomb. We still live in a great free country where democracy reigns. We probably take this for granted as we go about our day to day lives, but we still have water, food, gas electricity, and infrastructure that includes public transport, roads, railways, an education system, health service and jobs. Some aspects of these things might not be perfect and we all moan at some stage or other, but we still lucky to have them.

I, for one, value the sacrifices that Bill and his crew and their lost comrades made. The ultimate sacrifice still continues today as we see our lost armed forces returning home to Wootton Bassett and now Brize Norton. There we see the overwhelming support and respect the people of this country show for our War Heroes.

There is still darkness and fear of atrocities out there and all around us, but we are naturally optimistic as human beings. As we evolve and technology gets slicker and quicker we should always keep looking into the light and follow the just and noble cause that separates right from wrong and keeps securing the fate of freedom.

If I could have the ability to slow down or stretch out time, I would find this a most welcome attribute, but unfortunately we only have what we are given. Whilst writing this book I could literally watch the hands on the clock spin around during the days and nights as my time seemed to come and go faster than I can ever remember. The sadness that Bill's family and I personally felt when he passed in December 2011 was overwhelming, especially as we were so close to completing the book. He never got to see it finished, but did follow many of the stages it went through.

Bill sadly is no longer with us, but will always be in our hearts and minds. He showed the same constant life determination at 89 as he did at 19, just to take the slow walk down the long hallway from his room at his care home to the dining hall; making any life stress I was experiencing seem insignificant. I sometimes still reach for the phone to ring him and suddenly realise he is not with us anymore. My questions go unanswered, but I just ask him out loud like he always asked me to do. I really miss him as do his family, friends and acquaintances; there is a big hole where he used to be, his presence was phenomenal.

My good friend historian Dr Helen Fry expressed some very kind words to me after Bill died:

*'You have had an extraordinary relationship with him. You have immortalised him through the book and no one can take that away. He died in peace knowing what you have done to preserve his heroic story (although he probably didn't see himself as heroic! None of them do!!) He has allowed you to share in his life and death, which is a huge privilege.'*

# Afterword

When Bill and I first started to put his story together over four years ago, there was no permanent Memorial to the 55,573 lost Bomber Command Crewmen. There was also no official medal for them either. For many years after the War the Bomber Command Veteran's had felt forgotten and ignored for their hard contribution and their comrade's ultimate sacrifice against Hitler's tyranny. I had many discussions with Bill about this injustice and finally there was a glimmer of hope as the pace picked up and a memorial site was chosen in Green Park thanks to HM Queen. After many years of campaigning and raising funds and awareness, the Bomber Command Association, Sir Michael Beetham and celebrities like Robin Gibb had raised enough money to build it. As this book evolved so did the Bomber Command Memorial and it was finally built and ready to be unveiled on the 28 June 2012. Very sadly Bill just missed out on attending this historic event when he passed away in December

2011.

HRH Prince Charles talking to Dennis Bartlett and Chris Keltie on the 28 June 2012. Photo by Elisabeth Cox and CK.

I arranged for Bill's Mid-Upper Gunner Dennis Bartlett to attend the Unveiling Ceremony along with renowned aviation artist Simon Atack. I had also arranged to meet the son and daughter of Peter Knox, Louisa and Paul Knox there as well as we know. Bill's Bomb Aimer Norman Jarvis was best friends with Peter Knox. The three men were all in our hearts and minds as were 'the many'. It was a beautiful day with 6,000 veterans and family members meeting in Green Park. The whole event was wonderfully hosted by Carol Vorderman. I had been in touch with Peter's other daughter Jane Knox through the 'coincidences' explained in the Chapter Lives Lived and Lives Lost. Jane gave me Louisa's mobile number and said we should try and meet on the day at the Memorial Service. Well, we all had a spooky experience.

Chris and Dennis. (CK)

Simon W Atack, Dennis and Chris. (CK)

When I arrived at Constitution Hill with Dennis and Simon, I rang Louisa to see where she was. I said, 'Hi its Chris, where are you?' and she said 'I'm wearing a red polka-dot top' and as I turned to look for her there she was standing right in front of me in the queue. We both looked at each other and turned our mobile phones off. Bearing in mind we had never ever met each other it was strange. Jane said it was Norman, Peter and Bill all having a joke with us. It really did feel like they were all there with us. It was good to have family and friends of both crews at the service which was very emotional. The look on the Veteran's faces said it all and many were lost in thought with their memories. The highlight of the day was the Flypast by the BBMF Lancaster dropping thousands of poppies from its bomb bay (My mother-in-law Carole said that afterwards she found poppies in her back garden, in Belsize Park, 3 miles north). The other highlight was meeting and talking to Prince Charles with Dennis Bartlett. Dennis was thrilled to bits and Prince Charles showed the kindest and upmost respect as he talked to these extraordinary men. With Dennis Bartlett's encouragement I even managed to slip a flyer about the book to Prince Charles. When the day was over we all returned home tired and emotional, to dwell on the day's unforgettable events.

**Left:** The Bomber Command Memorial. (CK)

**Right:** BBMF Lancaster PA474, 'Poppy Drop' (CK).

So the circle is complete and the aircrews of Bomber Command have finally been honoured nearly 70 years after the end of the War. Just before we end I would just like to leave you all with one final thought provoking surprise.

I discovered the following poem when I was going through Bill's papers. I found it extraordinarily moving, and asked Bill if he had written it. 'No, I wish I had!' he replied. Bill could not remember how it came into his possession. All we know is that it's the work of an unknown British airman who was a prisoner in Stalag Luft 1 in 1944; we can't even be sure if he ever made it home.

RAF BOMBER COMMAND ASSOCIATION

THE BOMBER COMMAND MEMORIAL
DEDICATION & UNVEILING CEREMONY

GREEN PARK, LONDON, SW1
12 NOON - THURSDAY 28TH JUNE 2012

IN THE PRESENCE OF
HER MAJESTY QUEEN ELIZABETH II

SALUTE AREA

ACCESS TO WHEEL
CHAIR SPACE

ALL GUESTS MUST BE SEATED BY 11.30AM
(IMPORTANT - PLEASE READ THE INFORMATION SHEET THAT COMES WITH THIS TICKET)
ADMISSION ONLY PERMISSIBLE BETWEEN 09.00 AND 11.00

ROYAL AIR FORCE

## I'LL COME BACK TO YOU

I'LL COME BACK TO YOU
I'LL COME BACK TO YOU MY DARLING
I SAID THAT LONG AGO
NOT KNOWING WHAT THE FUTURE BRINGS
THAT BOTH OF US KNOW NOW
I SAID GOODBYE TO YOU THAT NIGHT
UNTIL THE DAWN NEXT DAY
A TEAR RAN DOWN YOUR CHEEK SO BRIGHT
TO HELP ME ON MY WAY
INTO THE NIGHT MY COURSE WAS SET
TOWARDS A DISTANT LAND
A BIRD OF DEATH WITH GUNS TO BOOT
THAT WOULD RESPOND TO TOUCH OF HAND
MY MISSION OVER I TURNED AROUND
AND HEADED WEST TO YOU
AND THROUGH THE NIGHT FLEW HOMEWARD BOUND
TO KEEP OUR RENDEZVOUS
BEFORE I LEFT THE GERMAN LAND
FATE BROKE THE VOW I MADE
PLUCKED FROM THE SKY BY GIANT HANDS
I SAW MY PROMISE FADE
ON SILKEN CHORDS I FLOATED DOWN
MY LAST FLIGHT ENDED THERE
ON DISTANT SHORES YOU WAIT FOR ME
I HAVE LET YOU DOWN I FEAR
NOW I CAN SEE THE SKIES ABOVE
NO LONGER THERE FOR ME
A THOUSAND MILES FROM YOU MY LOVE
O'ER DISTANT LAND AND SEA
BUT I'LL COME BACK TO YOU MY DEAR
THOUGH FATE HAS CLIPPED MY WINGS
I AM COMING BACK TO YOU MY DEAR
WHAT JOY THAT SWEET THOUGHT BRINGS
I BROKE MY WORD
BUT TO IT I'LL BE TRUE
WITH A MEMORY OF THAT GOODBYE KISS,
'TILL I RETURN TO YOU.

**Unknown, Stalag Luft 1, 1944**

# Thank you's

Firstly thank you to Bill and Margaret North for their true kindness throughout our family's not so good times. Alun North for being my main contact along the way, David, Rhys, Lisa and David North Jnr. The whole North family have been amazing in that they have trusted me and left me pretty much alone to record Bill's life.

Wendy, what can I say, sorry for all my blank moments and thank you for putting up with me, we got there in the end, love you more than chocolate.

Thank you to the industrious and boldly informative Max Hastings without whom we would live in a much less enlightened world. Derek Brammer for his fascinating record of 61 Squadron. W R Chorley for his dedication in recording Bomber Command's losses in such accurate detail, without him I would have been lost. Thank you to Martin Middlebrook and Chris Everitt for the superb *Bomber Command War Diaries*. This was an invaluable reference source; the 1944 pages are virtually worn away in my copy. Chris Ward for his meticulous record of 5 Group, Bomber Command, this was also invaluable.

A big thank you to Sir Michael Beetham for his contribution to the Foreword and his endless campaigning over the years for the Bomber Command Memorial.

A special thank you to PM David Cameron for the work the Government has done to ensure due recognition for the heroes of Bomber Command. The waiving of the debt for the Bomber Command Memorial, and also awarding the Gold Clasp to Bomber Command Veterans and the Arctic Star to the Arctic Convoy Veterans past and present.

Ian Jarret, Dennis Bartlett, Daphne Pearce, Iris North, Jeff Gray, Percy Cannings, Sandy Cannings, Sharon Cannings, Stephen and Sue Elsworth, Melinda Coxhall, Simon Atack, Di Ablewhite all have been wise and true friends and also everybody else from our aviation gang on Twitter.

In Australia:-Les Morton and his daughter Glenda Vere. Katrina and Will Allen (Monty Monteith's daughter and family. Pam Livingstone (Norman Jarvis' daughter and their huge family in Australia. Pam you have become a true friend and such an important support to me through this whole journey, I will love you forever. Jack Goodyer's cousin Noeline Arnott for her true support and friendship.

Thank you to all at the Aviation Heritage Centre, East Kirkby, especially Louise Bush and Sean Taylor for their kind and generous support.

Thank you to Howard Heeley at Newark Air Museum, your support is selfless and our 'coincidences' are unbelievable. Mike Smith, the curator at Newark for his knowledge on Stirling crashes. Jane Knox, Peter Knox's daughter whom I met through more George Moggridge and Peter Knox 'coincidences'. Her tireless work and dedication to immortalise 619 Squadron's Lancaster ME846 and crew is outstanding. Love you Jane.

Thank you to my editor Brandon Robshaw for his expert guidance and firm hand, I couldn't have done it without you.

A big thank you to Rob Harris from Copy Write printers in Finchley Road. Rob you are a true friend and your technical advice and professional touch are really appreciated.

Thank you to Historian Dr Helen Fry for your kind support, encouragement, advice throughout the years since our children were babies. Peter Kay at the de Havilland Mosquito Museum in Hertfordshire.

Thank you to Jeremy Isaacs and Thames Television for *The World at War* series which alongside Bill ignited my fascination with history and WW2. Also all the other aforementioned film/documentary makers.

Everybody at 50/61 Squadron Association who took me under their wings and have been so wonderfully helpful and kind. Gerry Collins adopted me and I feel like he is the extra unexpected Grandfather in our family. (James) H J Flowers for his dedication in recording Bill's story and the other veteran's stories on the Squadron website, also his insights into the life of a Rear Gunner. Sir Michael Beetham, AVM Nigel Baldwin and W/C Peter Jacobs especially for their fantastic encouragement. Arthur Smith, Kenneth S Green and all the other 50/61 Veterans who shared memories with me. Mike Connock, S/L Richard Jones, Gerry Collins from 50/61 Squ Association.

A big thanks to Alan Wells at the 50/61 Squadron Forum, for the whole1944, 61 Squadron ORB and vital help with research.

Henry Velleman for much kind encouragement and technical advice on Word documents. Thank you for the last minute proof read and fine tuning.

Peter Elliot at the RAF Museum Hendon for essential help and advice.

Martin Simpson at the A26 Invader web site for his kind assistance in posting Bill's story.

Peter Done, Reg Payne, Roger Morley, Ruth Pullis (Grosvenor House Publishing).

Bill and I wanted to contact Eddy O'Shea's and Dave Crowley's families during the writing of the book and although much effort and time was spent trying to find and contact them we kept hitting dead ends. Anybody who knows them it would really mean a lot to Bill to say thank you to them. (Janet Legg is Dave Crowley's daughter and the last point of contact was in Kettering, Northamptonshire, but Bill lost touch a few years ago and we couldn't find her)

Mark Rodwell has been a good friend and constant source of useful advice and encouragement, thank you. Also a big thank you for the time and effort spent for proof reading and corrections for the second edition.

A big thank you to Rob Harris from Copy Write printers in Finchley Road. Rob you are a true friend and your technical advice and professional touch are really appreciated.

Thank you to Historian Dr Helen Fry for your kind support, encouragement, advice throughout the years since our children were babies. Peter Kay at the de Havilland Mosquito Museum in Hertfordshire

Thank you to Jeremy Isaacs and Thames Television for The World at War series which alongside Bill ignited my fascination with history and WW2. Also all the other mentioned film/documentary makers.

A big thanks to Alan Wells at the 50/61 Squadron Forum, for the whole 1944, 61 Squadron ORB and vital help with research.

Henry Velleman for much kind encouragement and technical advice on Word documents. Thank you for the last minute proof read and fine tuning.

Peter Elliot at the RAF Museum Hendon for essential help and advice.

Martin Simpson at the A26 Invader web site for his kind assistance in posting Bill's story.

Peter Done, Reg Payne, Roger Morley, Ruth Pullis (Grosvenor House Publishing).

Bill and I wanted to contact Eddy O'Shea's and Dave Crowley's families during the writing of the book and although much effort and time was spent trying to find and contact them we kept hitting dead ends. Anybody who knows them it would really mean a lot to Bill to say thank you to them. (Janet Legg is Dave Crowley's daughter and the last point of contact was in Kettering, Northamptonshire, but Bill lost touch a few years ago and we couldn't find her)

Mark Rodwell has been a good friend and constant source of useful advice and encouragement, thank you. Mark, kind thanks for the extra time and effort spent on proof reading and making corrections for the second edition.

The Society of Authors for their much needed advice, seminars and encouragement which helped me to eventually self publish. Neilsons what an amazing organisation. Amazon just for being there.

Louise Dalrymple and Melinda Coxhall for their spiritual guidance, love you. Miriam White, Elaine Bentley, Roger Eustace, Matt and Alex Woolfe. Big thanks to Mark Thornhill for setting up the website, Face Book and Twitter accounts. Our Uncle Kelvin Blyth (Kelvin Blyth Studios, Cambridge) for the stunning book cover which captures the whole adventure beautifully. Kevin McKellar the inspirational head of Hendon School.

Big thanks to John Luckhurst, Michael Demidecki and Peter Grey at the LTDA's legal department; this would have fallen by the wayside without you.

Thank you to Elisabeth Cox for her lovely photo of HRH Prince Charles talking to us at the Bomber Command Memorial Day on the 28 June 2011. It was a pleasure to meet Elisabeth and her husband John, who was the second Veteran after Sir Michael Beetham to receive the Gold Clasp from PM David Cameron. (John sadly passed away in Sept 2013)

Richard Smith at the Daily Mirror for having a true understanding of what we were doing and his thoughtful help in ensuring Bill's story is immortalised. Also the kind messages of support I got from members of the public that I met along the way.

A huge thank you to my family who have given me mountains worth of emotional support. My mum Anne Keltie, my dad David Keltie and all the staff and partners at his Patent and Trademark firm *Keltie*. My brother Richard for spending hours and hours repairing the whole document on *Word*. My brother John Keltie for all the technical support and also his wife Agnes for all the French translations. I hope I haven't missed anybody out.

# Acknowledgements

**The list below includes the principle sources, references, books and documentary films used in the writing and research of Riding in the Shadow of Death.**

The personal reference material relating to Bill North and his crew members is archived at Chris Keltie Publishing. This includes many photographs taken by Chris Keltie and also many that have been supplied by Bill North, Dennis Bartlett, Les Morton, Percy Cannings, Jeff Gray and Pam Livingstone (Norman Jarvis' daughter). Many documents including letters, war diaries, maps, RAF Flight Log Books etc are the property of Bill North and his family. Jeff Grey, Dennis Bartlett, Les Morton and Norman Jarvis' family are the owners of similar documents too. Their eyewitness accounts have been recorded personally by Chris Keltie on video and also hand written. Norman Jarvis' War Diary has been a major contribution in its entire form.

The public material is available at the Public Records Office in Kew, in local libraries, on film/TV, online and at bookshops. Reg Payne is the copyright holder of the photo of the two D for Dog Lancaster Bombers. Barney Case is the owner of the copyright to the A26 crash at Biggin Hill. Jeff Gray is the owner of the original photo of Lancaster EE176 'Mickey the Moocher'. The Air Ministry map of RAF Skellingthorpe was supplied by Roger Morley, Skellingthorpe Village. Peter Done supplied the original copies of the M19 POW escape reports from Public Records. Other photos are from Das Bundesarchiv, (The German Federal Archive) and the Imperial War Museum (IWM). As far as the Author is aware he has taken as much care as possible to name the source and check that other photographs used are in the Public Domain. Information and eye witness accounts have also been collected from interviews with other 50/61 Squadron Veterans, including Sir Michael Beetham, Arthur Smith, H.J. Flowers, Kenneth Green, Jeff Gray; also Bill North's sister, Iris North and Dennis Bartlett's sister Daphne Pearce. Laurent Viton and Jean Erisay supplied the original photographs of the crash site of Lancaster EE 186, QR-D near Harquency in France and these are also on display at The Museum of WW2 of Tosny, Louviers Road, D135 Tosny, 27700. The RAF Museum Hendon Archives contained the original copy of the Lancaster Bomber Pilot's and Flight Enginneer's Notes.

The 50/61 Squadron Bomber Command Roll Of Honour 1939-1940 book is available from 50/61 Squadron Association. Association members Gerry Collins, HJ Flowers, Richard Smith and Mike Connock have also supplied additional information. Alan Wells from the 50/61 Squadron Forum who has supplied hard copies of the 61 Squ ORB and much additional info regarding research requests and queries. (Alan what would I do without you!)

The letter to the Daily Telegraph dated 27 October 2008 by Sir Michael Beetham, is reproduced with kind permission by Marshal of The Royal Air Force, Sir Michael Beetham.

Wikipedia was used as a file sharing source and also used to cross reference material.

**Books:-**


The 50 and 61 Squadron Roll Of Honour, *5 Group Bomber Command* RAF, 1939 TO 1945

Brammer, Derek (1997) *Thundering Through The Clear Air*, No. 61 (Lincoln Imp) Squadron at War, Toucan Books, ISBN 1 873257 57 0

Bird, Tony DFC (2000) *A Bird Over Berlin*, Woodfield Publishing, ISBN 1-873203-74-8

Cawthorne, Nigel (2010) Lancaster *WWII Night Bomber and Dambuster*, Abbeydale Press, Annes Publishing Ltd, no ISBN

Chorley, W R (1996) *Bomber Command Losses of the Second World War 1943*, Midland Publishing, ISBN 978 0 904597 90 5

Chorley, W R (1997) *Bomber Command Losses of the Second World War 1944*, Midland Publishing, ISBN 978 0 904597 91 2

Chorley, W R (2008) *Bomber Command Losses of the Second World War 1945*, Midland Publishing, ISBN 978 0 904597 92 9

Darlow, Steve (2002) *Sledgehammers for Tin Tacks*, Grub Street, ISBN 1 902304 96 9

Falconer, Jonathan (2010) *RAF Bomber Crewman*, Shire Library, ISBN 13: 978 0 74780 796 4

Franks, Norman (1995) *Claims to Fame The Lancaster*, Arms and Armour Press, Cassel Group, ISBN 1 85409 311 8

Fry, Helen (2009) *From Dachau to D-Day*, The History Press, ISBN 978 0 7509 5111 1

Garbett, Mike and Goulding, Brian (1988) *Lancaster at War 2*, Ian Allan Ltd, ISBN 0 7110 0966 X

Hastings, Max (1999) *Bomber Command*, Pan Books, ISBN 0 330 39204 2

Hastings, Max (1984) *Overlord: D-Day and the Battle for Normandy*, Simon & Schuster, ISBN 0-671-46029-3

Hastings, Max (2004) *Armageddon: The Battle for Germany 1944-45* Macmillan, ISBN 0-333-90836-8

Hill, Roy E, (2000) *Survivor Published* by Roy E. Hill, no ISBN

Hinchliffe, Peter (1996) *Other Battle: Luftwaffe Night Aces vs. Bomber Command*. Minneapolis, MN: Zenith Press, ISBN 978-0760302651.

Jacobs, Peter (2011) *Stay The Distance The Life And Times Of Marshal Of The Royal Air Force Sir Michael Beteham*, Frontline Books, ISBN 978 1 84832 552 4

Lumsden, Alec (1994) *British Piston Aero-Engines and Their Aircraft*, The Crowood Press Ltd, Alec Lumsden, ISBN 9781853102943

Middlebrook, Martin and Everitt, Chris, (2011) *The Bomber Command War Diaries, An operational reference book 1939-1945*, Midland Publishing, ISBN 978 1 85780 335 8

Nichol, John and Rennell, Tony (2003) *The Last Escape*, Penguin Books, ISBN-13: 978-0-14-100388-7

Stubbington, John, (2010) *Kept in the Dark,* Pen and Sword Books, ISBN 978-1-84884-183-3

Ward, Chris (2007) *5 Group Bomber Command, An Operational History*, Pen and Sword Aviation, ISBN 978 1 84415 579 8

Williams, Andrew (2004). *D-Day to Berlin*. Hodder, ISBN 0-340-83397-1

*RAF Records in the PRO*, (Simon Fowler, Peter Elliot, Roy Conyers Nesbit, Christina Goulter), PRO Publications, Crown Copyright, ISBN 1 873162 14 6 (1994)

*Lancaster Pilot's and Flight Enginneer's Notes,* Crown Copyright, Her Majesty's Stationary Office, Crécy Publishing Ltd. (Original 1942, present- day 2011)

**Magazines:-**

*The Lancaster Bomber*, Hatchette Partworks Ltd, ISSN 1758-0226 (2011)

**Websites:-**

*www.bombercommandmuseum.ca/* (Canadian Bomber Command website)

*www.merki.com/the_roomates.htm* (Stalag Luft 1 website)

*www.rafbombercommand.com/master_the_association.html* (RAF Bomber Command Association)

*www.onwar.com/* (chronology of WW2 web site)

*Google Earth*

**Film/TV Documentaries:-**

*Bomber Boys*, documentary, Harvey Lilley, BBC Television, 2012. *Downfall*,

Film/DVD, directed by Oliver Hirschbiegel, distributed by Constantin Film, 2004.

*Hitler's Bodyguard*, documentary series, Nugus/Martin Productions Ltd, 2008.

*Lancaster Bombers*, DVD, Delta Music PLC, 2005.

*The Long March to Freedom*, documentary series, UKTV, 2011.

*The Nazis: A Warning From History*, documentary series, Laurence Rees, BBC Television, 1997.

*The War,* documentary, TV series, Ken Burns and Lynn Novick, written by Geoffrey C. Ward, 2007.

*The World at War*, documentary series, Jeremy Isaacs, Thames Television, 1973-1974.

*Wings of the Storm,* documentary film, Australian Broadcasting Corporation, 1986.

**<u>Museums and Heritage Centres</u>:-**

*RAF Museum, Hendon & RAF Conningsby Museum.*
*Imperial War Museum*, Lambeth.
*Aviation Heritage Centre*, East Kirkby.

*50/61 Squadron Museum*, Skellingthorpe, Lincolnshire.

*The de Havilland Aircraft Heritage Centre*, Hertfordshire, (The Mosquito Aircraft Museum).

*Nanton Lancaster Society Air Museum*:
(renamed Bomber Command Museum of Canada 2010) Nanton, Alberta.

To my Uncle Kaye Slack who served with the RCAF, completing his Tour of Ops in Burma flying in Liberators.

Warrant Officer Dennis Bartlett's Gold Clasp award, received in August 2013 (CK)

# Author's note:-

The highest casualties during WW2 belonged to Russia; an estimated 25 million soldiers and civilians dead and their homeland devastated by Hitler's Holy War in the East. Six million of Europe's nine million Jews had been wiped out in death camps and by Einsatzgruppen killing squads, countless other races and creeds had suffered the same fate. Many cities, towns and villages across the European continent had been laid to waste, including many in Germany itself. In comparison to WW1 the civilian populations on all sides had suffered heavily alongside the Armed Forces. For the second time in 30 years Europe was in ruins. All in all some 55 million people perished in WW2, a human tragedy that is unprecedented.

During WW2 many courageous men and women from across the world took part in the many campaigns to bring this tragedy to an end. Many did not like or enjoy what they had to do, but they still with courage and endurance carried out their duties; some have never been truly acknowledged or thanked by the establishment for their contributions.

This was the account of seven of those young men and their comrades in whose skilled and capable hands lay the fate of freedom; they alongside the many others around them played their part in helping to shorten and put an end to one of the most indescribable horrors that has been inflicted upon the face of this planet. They have finally got the recognition that they truly deserve.

## Bomber Command Veterans meet PM David Cameron

On Wednesday 9 October 2013 our group of Bomber Command Veterans travelled from all over the country to meet British Prime Minister the Rt Hon David Cameron. The purpose of the visit was to thank him in person for his hard work to gain recognition for WW2 Veterans. This included wiping the debt for the Bomber Command Memorial in London, the award of the Gold Clasp to Bomber Command Veterans past and present, and the Arctic Star Medal for the Veterans of the Arctic Convoys.

Our group included four of the Veterans featured in this book: Jeff Gray (61 Squ) and his granddaughter Charlotte Gray. Bill North's Mid-Upper Gunner, Dennis Bartlett (61 Squ). James Flowers (50 Squ, Rear Gunner and representing the 50/61 Squadron Association) with his two sons Phil and Robert Flowers. Representing their father, Bill North were his three sons David, Alun and Rhys North. Percy Cannings (97 Squ PFF) was due to come, but was unable to as he was unwell. Representing Percy was his daughter Sandy Cannings.

The idea to contact David Cameron came from F/Lt Jeff Gray. He suggested we both write to Downing Street and offer to present David Cameron a copy of the book as a thank you on behalf of the Veterans. After a challenging task to organise and arrange the travel arrangements and timing of the event, we all made it to the Central Lobby on time. Although Sandy Cannings and I had a serious moment of panic at the front gate when we couldn't find our Veterans anywhere, they had already gone in without us.

We were then met in the Central Lobby (which is stunning) by the PM's assistants Julia and Lawrence. With two of our Veterans in wheelchairs we then had to take quite a long detour around the Commons network of long corridors to the PM's office. James Flowers kept us entertained on the way with his distinctive Yorkshire accent. 'That was Lord so and so, oh look there's this MP or that MP!' I don't know how he recognised them all! At various points along the way we could see David Cameron on the in-house TV screens getting a 'grilling' on Prime Minister's Question Time. We finally made it up to the reception area outside the PM's office where we all paused for breath and gathered our thoughts.

David Cameron suddenly appeared, greeted us all, shook everybody's hands and led us into his office where we sat down on armchairs and sofas. The meeting was very relaxed and everybody had a chance to chat and talk. The Veterans thanked him for his work gaining recognition for them and he explained the complex and difficult process he had gone through to push through the Gold Clasp award and the Arctic Star Medal. I presented him with a copy of the book and he joked that 'it was his birthday and this was the first present of the day!' Then to our surprise James Flowers then piped up that it was also his birthday as well and he was 89, there's a great official picture of them shaking hands.

James then took the opportunity to mention that Bill North had received no medal for his courage and bravery when he crash landed his Lancaster on 5 July 1944. I also highlighted the extraordinary circumstances surrounding Bill's crash and the whole crew's survival that night. Sandy Cannings then read out her father Percy Cannings' speech explaining how Percy also thought that Bill had been overlooked for a medal for his outstanding skill and courage as well. The PM took Percy's speech and was very sympathetic explaining that it was very difficult to get medals after such a long period of time, but he would look into it and to leave it with him.

As David Cameron sat amongst us we found that he was very down to earth and easy to talk to. He was extremely knowledgeable about Bomber Command and its critical contribution to shortening WW2. He also suggested reading a book by Andrew Roberts, called *The Storm Of War*; 'It has an excellent chapter on Bomber Command.' We were told it would be a very short meeting, but to everybody's surprise we actually got over 20 minutes of the PM's time. As it came to a natural end David Cameron then got up and shook everybody's hand again and said goodbye.

Our convoy then made its way back downstairs to the front entrance. We then got a fleet of London Taxis to take us from Parliament Square to the RAF Club at Piccadilly, where Bill's sons had booked a fantastic lunch for us all. We also met up with the book's editor Brandon Robshaw who joined us at the RAF Club. On behalf of the whole group I would like to thank David Cameron for meeting with us. It was a special day for our Bomber Command Veterans and they were extremely appreciative of their Gold Clasp award and the recognition they truly deserve. The look on their faces said it all. A big thank you to our chaperone's Julia and Lawrence. The PM's secretary Jennifer Snell for helping me to organise the meeting and all the staff in the Central Lobby who were so kind and assisted with the wheelchairs. A big thanks to David, Alun and Rhys North for a wonderful lunch and also all the London Taxi drivers who ferried us around London that day. Much missed was 97 Squadron's Percy Cannings who couldn't be with us because he was not well.

**Left to right:-** Charlotte Gray, Chris Keltie, Rhys North, Alun North, Sandy Cannings, Dennis Bartlett, Phil Flowers, James Flowers, David North, Robert Flowers and Jeff Gray. (photo, *James Flowers*)

**Talking to the Prime Minister. Left to right:-** Alun North, Jeff Gray, Sandy Cannings, Charlotte Gray, PM Rt Hon David Cameron, Chris Keltie, Rhys North, David North, Dennis Bartlett and James Flowers.